AN ANTHOLOGY OF

NEW ZEALAND POETRY

IN ENGLISH

Edited by

Jenny Bornholdt
Gregory O'Brien
Mark Williams

Auckland

OXFORD UNIVERSITY PRESS

Oxford   Melbourne   New York

OXFORD UNIVERSITY PRESS NEW ZEALAND

Oxford New York
Athens Auckland Bangkok Bogota
Bombay Buenos Aires Calcutta
Cape Town Dar es Salaam Delhi
Florence Hong Kong Istanbul Karachi
Kuala Lumpur Madras Madrid Melbourne
Mexico City Nairobi Paris Port Moresby
Singapore Taipei Tokyo Toronto Warsaw

and associated companies in
Berlin Ibadan

OXFORD is a trade mark of Oxford University Press

ISBN 0 19 558355 8

Edited by Simon Cauchi
Cover design by Heather Jones
Typeset by Kimberly Williams, Blue Orange
Printed through Bookpac Production Services, Singapore
Published by Oxford University Press,
540 Great South Road, Greenlane, PO Box 11-149, Auckland, New Zealand

CONTENTS

INTRODUCTION

you get hints and shadows of the pattern but never
a complete and steady sighting.
Keri Hulme, 'Fishing the Olearia Tree'

I

This anthology begins with poetry written in the last few years and works backwards to some of the earliest poetry written in English in this country. By moving backwards in time we sought to reflect the energies, the tremors, that recent poets send back into the past. While the anthology contains a narrative, it is not one of the triumphant evolution of consciousness from colonial dependence towards postcolonial national maturity, but rather the story of struggle and interaction between different versions of where we are and how we perceive ourselves. The poems, however, are not simply the record of their historical occasions, part of the tale of the nation's unfolding history. They talk to each other as well as addressing the world, its history and its particulars.

In the poem that opens the anthology, Chris Orsman's 'Ornamental Gorse', a history of Pakeha responsiveness to New Zealand is invoked:

It's ornamental where it's been
self-sown across the hogback,

obsequious and buttery,
cocking a snook at scars,

yellowing our quaint history
of occupation and reprise.

Behind this poem lies a whole history of poetry reflecting on the nature and usefulness of the cultural baggage brought with settlement. Orsman, in 1994, is reflecting on the history not only of settlement and adjustment but also on the terms in which poetry has sought to register and be part of that process. What Orsman calls 'our quaint history' is composed of many voices, reflecting on the landscape and the contradictory messages it contains.

Nearly a century before Orsman, William Pember Reeves in 'The Passing of the Forest' mourned the effects of colonisation and settlement (although in another poem, 'A Colonist in His Garden', he observes complacently how bush-clearance can enhance the view). In 1941 Charles Brasch finds behind the Pakeha's 'shallow occupation of the easier / Landscape' the 'unprotesting memory' of its earlier inhabitants. For James K. Baxter in 'Poem in the Matukituki Valley' (1949), the land is 'matrix and destroyer, / Resentful, darkly known'. Since the sixties, environmental issues have been synonymous with depictions of landscape, with poets such as Cilla McQueen, Brian Turner and, most notably, Ian Wedde transforming the lyrical, pastoral tradition into something strident and politically engaged. In McQueen's 1993 poem, 'The Mess We Made at Port Chalmers', the landscape has been reduced to a 'Tongue-stump of headland bandaged with concrete, / Obliterated beaches stacked with chopsticks'.

Land and settlement is just one of the narratives to be found in this anthology. In 'Fishing the Olearia Tree' Keri Hulme says that one may get 'hints and shadows of the pattern but never / a complete and steady sighting'. There is no single pattern here, merely a body of work into which we may read various patterns, discover threads, if only in the way Bracken's 'Hymn to New Zealand' (the national anthem) is revisited parodically in David Eggleton's 'God Defend New Zealand' or Dinah Hawken's 'Writing Home' (a series of letters from New York to New Zealand) invokes the earlier poetry of Ursula Bethell and, beyond that, revises the notion of England as home which dominated the colonial era.

II

Over the last decade there has been an increasing interest in New Zealand's colonial period. Novels, plays and films — most notably *The Piano* — have looked to the past to find pertinent or viable meanings for the present. New Zealand's colonial past has been demythologised (and perhaps remythologised) in an effort to reconfigure our collective understandings of the cultures that make up New Zealand.

Our approach to the nineteenth century has been to summarise the poetry of that era rather than attempt to represent a comprehensive range of contemporary poets, a job that has been done convincingly by Harvey McQueen in *The New Land*. Generally, we found the poetry exhibited all the obvious difficulties of grafting an English consciousness on to an antipodean landscape. Part of the problem arose from the transposition of a set of linguistic signs from a familiar to a new and strange world. As MacDonald Jackson puts it, 'simple words such as "spring", "farm", and "bush" had changed their denotations, while their connotations "remained stubbornly rooted in centuries of English rural life"'.[1] Not surprisingly, many nineteenth-century versifiers simply failed to notice that there was a problem. Hence their predilection for romantic diction, Wordsworthian tonalities and metrics derived from Longfellow.

Myths — in the sense of inherited structures of meaning — had to be transported as well, and the dislocations involved here were to prove still more troubling and more persistent for the Pakeha. While the landscape had been mythologised by the Maori, it proved unreceptive to the influx of gods and myths from the northern hemisphere. The attempts of colonial poets like Blanche Baughan and Jessie Mackay to build a New Zealand poetry by marrying Maori

---

[1]MacDonald P. Jackson, 'Poetry: Beginnings to 1945', *The Oxford History of New Zealand Literature in English*, edited by Terry Sturm (Auckland: Oxford University Press, 1991), p. 351.

mythology and nineteenth-century English poetic form read awkwardly now.

Yet there are achievements, anticipations and links worth keeping sight of, and some contemporary poets have found much to value in nineteenth-century verse. Michele Leggott places Jessie Mackay at the beginning of a long line of committed, accomplished women writers.[2] Mackay's poetry, according to Alan Riach, can also be seen as part of an early vernacular and socially engaged line that was driven underground by colonial verse.[3] Baxter's social criticism and democratic voice can be seen to be anticipated in the verse of Mackay and of John Barr of Craigilee. There are many such ways in which poems engage with each other, suggesting linkages and ruptures. Despite our reservations about the quality of much of the early colonial poetry — or poetries — we nevertheless see it as the halting beginnings of a national literature and a visible shift on the part of Pakeha out from under the cultural blanket of the British Empire.

We have sought to show the several cultural strands in colonial society. Culturally, this period comes before nationalism. In nineteenth-century New Zealand the various immigrant groups — Scots, Irish (Protestant and Catholic), English — maintained the distinctiveness that still marked those separate cultures in Britain. Donald Akenson has noted the reluctance of New Zealand social historians to acknowledge that the British Isles 'was not a land of one people, but of several'. Paradoxically, he observes, they thus extended

> a form of British cultural imperialism now quite dead in the British Isles. That is, although the peoples of the British Isles of the last century did not share a common land system, were far from being economically integrated, and spoke four separate languages and a myriad of regional dialects, many of which were virtually incomprehensible to outsiders, one still finds New Zealand historians studying English society and then suggesting that this was the way things were in the British Isles. It was not.[4]

This homogeneous picture no more describes nineteenth-century New Zealand than it does Britain at that time.

By 1900, it is true, David McKee Wright in 'Our Cities Face the Sea' celebrates outback democracy as the basis of a nation in the making:

> Jack came from Cornwall, and Pat from Donegal
> 'Arry came from London, the first place of all,
> Sandy came from Aberdeen, and Tom's native-born,
> But they're all mates together in the lands of the morn.

---

[2] Michele Leggott, 'Opening the Archive: Robin Hyde, Eileen Duggan and the Persistence of Record', in *Opening the Book: New Essays on New Zealand Writing* (Auckland: Auckland University Press, 1995), pp. 266–94.

[3] Alan Riach, 'James K. Baxter and the Dialect of the Tribe', *Opening the Book*, p. 113.

[4] Donald Harman Akenson, *Half the World from Home: Perspectives on the Irish in New Zealand, 1860–1950* (Wellington: Victoria University Press, 1990), p. 6.

> Pulling, pulling on the one rope together,
> Bringing up the future with a golden tether,
> Cousin Jack and Cockney, Irishman and Scot,
> And the native is a brother to the whole blooming lot.

Yet in the colonial period we find vigorous expressions of Scots, Irish and Anglo cultures with little evidence of a unified Pakeha culture. Settler society was no homogeneous manifestation of Anglophilia, and in recent years, under the pressure of post-colonialism's multiplicity of inheritances, there has been a reawakening of the variety of the distinct cultures it contained. For example, both Keri Hulme and Robert Sullivan acknowledge a Celtic inheritance, and find this sits more comfortably with a Maori heritage than the 'British' model.

III

The between-the-wars period has traditionally been seen as falling into two nearly even sections. The twenties was a period supposedly dominated by genteel female poets producing pale imitative verse, which differed from colonial versifying chiefly by the addition of decorative local flora — 'kowhai gold'. The anthology of that title, edited by Quentin Pope and published in 1930, consolidates the poetry of the twenties and distinguishes it from the more vigorously nationalist, realist and socially engaged poetry of the next decade.

Yet the twenties was also a period in which New Zealand poets — notably Ursula Bethell and R. A. K. Mason — began paying serious attention to the local world, both social and geographical, and seeking new ways of reflecting that world. In some cases this was manifest simply as the ticks and mannerisms of 'kowhai gold'. In other cases, notably Ursula Bethell's, it produced serious efforts to come to terms with what was here. Bethell's 'Response' shows the process of noticing and adaptation at work. Although the words she uses are in the main 'English' rather than New Zealand English, and certainly not colloquial, Bethell allows for their new associations in a world where the things they denote pull against their ancient connections.[5] The epistolary form of address employed in the poem may be seen as a means of dramatising an internalised dialogue between colonial and local loyalties.

> When you wrote your letter it was April,
> And you were glad that it was spring weather,
> And that the sun shone out in turn with showers of rain.
>
> I write in waning May and it is autumn,
> And I am glad that my chrysanthemums
> Are tied up fast to strong posts,
> So that the south winds cannot beat them down.

---

[5]In another poem, 'Primavera', Bethell displays her strong nostalgia for the traditional English associations of names that had not made the voyage to Canterbury: 'Coomb, coppice, spinney, aye, and primrose-wood, / Not understood, dale and meadow, not understood'.

No poem by Bethell appears in *Kowhai Gold*, and only two by Mason. Bethell did not begin writing poetry seriously until the mid 1920s, when she was in her fifties, and 'Response' appeared in her 1929 volume, *From a Garden in the Antipodes*. Her absence from Pope's anthology is perhaps, therefore, more excusable than the slim selection from Mason's work. The real problem with Pope's anthology lies in his misplaced generosity, not his occasional surprising meannesses. *Kowhai Gold*'s long service as whipping boy for the poetic vices sternly noted by Allen Curnow has drawn some protest, but is largely deserved.[6] Curnow was generally well disposed to Bethell's verse, acknowledging her 'rare invention and rhythmic skill', but he was scathing in his criticism of Pope's anthology.[7] His analysis of the limitations of the verse Pope selected is, for the most part, just and accurate: *Kowhai Gold* contains far too much 'magazine verse'; the selections are frequently sentimental, slight and laden with cliché. Nevertheless, several of the poets in Pope's collection still merit consideration, and work by Eileen Duggan, Katherine Mansfield, A. R. D. Fairburn, Robin Hyde, Mason and Arnold Wall is included in this anthology. *Kowhai Gold* represents a broad, often populist range of work. It is a part of the literary landscape, not as decisive or authoritative as Curnow's anthologies, but it has achieved a curiously negative force without being much read.

Rather than dismiss Eileen Duggan's Georgian mode, we feel that at least some of her work calls for more complex readings than she has received. Duggan's work was sidelined as a result of the nationalistic bias of the Caxton poets with their secular prejudice and male mythologising. Her active Catholicism told against her in the climate of the thirties and forties. Sympathetically viewed, her best work shows less the marks of pious conviction (though her belief is present in everything she wrote) than the ability to register tensions within an established faith that at its most accomplished recalls metaphysical verse:

> The tides run up the Wairau
> That fights against their flow.
> My heart and it together
> Are running salt and snow.
> 'The Tides Run Up the Wairau'

In the thirties, poets were urged to direct their attention to realities immediately to hand. This was a period dominated by the desire to bring into being a national consciousness; literature and the arts were seen as the means of representing that consciousness struggling to be born. The crucial expression of this effort to formulate such a consciousness was carried through in the thirties and forties in the work of a group of writers and painters — Allen Curnow, Denis Glover,

---

[6] See Trixie Te Arama Menzies, 'Kowhai Gold: Skeleton or Scapegoat?' *Landfall* 165 (vol. 42, no. 1, March 1988), pp. 19–26.

[7] Allen Curnow, *Look Back Harder: Critical Writings 1935–1984*, edited by Peter Simpson (Auckland: Auckland University Press, 1987), p. 35.

Charles Brasch, Leo Bensemann, all associated with the Caxton Press established by Glover in Christchurch in 1936 — who set about overcoming the colonial sense of distance, isolation and inferiority by establishing a distinctive local literary tradition.

In order to achieve a specifically New Zealand tradition the Caxton poets felt that it was necessary to distinguish between their *serious* efforts to fasten a poetic to New Zealand conditions and the ephemeral and colonial poetic outpourings of their predominantly female predecessors. The characteristic styles of existing schools of New Zealand poetry were held to be marred by colonial deference, the decorative use of native flora, sentimentality, Georgian diction and outmoded verse forms.

Certainly, the effect of Curnow's sternly administered corrective of bad habits is immediately and trenchantly felt in his own poetry, once he had found his voice. Curnow brings a new level of attention to the local actualities of language, society and landscape, registered in tough, intelligently wrought verse.

> The sensitive nor'west afternoon
> Collapsed, and the rain came;
> The dog crept into his barrel
> Looking lost and lame.
> But you can't attribute to either
> Awareness of what great gloom
> Stands in a land of settlers
> With never a soul at home.
> 'House and Land'

This sense of realities sharply apprehended signals the force of an effort to close the gap between connotation and denotation that MacDonald Jackson observes in colonial verse. After so much time in which, as Curnow puts it, settler imaginations had recoiled from what lay to hand, an imagination sure of what it wanted to achieve and possessed of the means — intellectual and verbal — to achieve it, had announced itself.[8] The need to address those present actualities, however, was prompted not only by the problem of fitting words to place but also by the recognition of economic and social conditions. It was not simply a physical landscape that preoccupied the poet — and contemporaries like Glover and Fairburn — it was a human landscape composed in part of small farms loaded with debt and worked by desperate families.

In all New Zealand anthologies since 1960 the thirties and forties have figured very prominently. This is a crucial period in New Zealand's self-definition as a nation, and the confidence and vitality of the best of this verse needs to be acknowledged. However, without denying the achievement of the mid-century poets, we have not empha-

---

[8]Curnow, Introduction to *The Penguin Book of New Zealand Verse*, in *Look Back Harder*, p. 136.

sised this period at the expense of the whole range of New Zealand poetry in English.

IV

'Love is not valued much in Pig Island / Though we admire its walking parody', wrote James K. Baxter in 'Pig Island Letters'. The fifties and sixties were dominated by this dour figure who resisted Curnow's instructions to attend exclusively to the 'reality that was local and special where we pick up the traces'.[9] Baxter chose to wrestle with his own ambiguous soul — part sensualist, part mystic — as well as with the soul of the nation locked in its inarticulate landscapes and baffled citizens. Rather than emulate the dense precision of Curnow's concentrated and sometimes forbidding verse — the baroque splendours of its syntax and diction — Baxter preferred more and more to address New Zealanders in the guise of mate and outcast. As mate he chose a verse of democratic forms — ballads, lampoons, obscene lays — as outcast he chose the voice of the Old Testament prophet, railing against the false gods of a materialistic and puritanical culture. Often he combined both roles in sharply satirical popular verse.

> ... Hush!
> It is the living make us blush
> Because the young have wicked hearts
> And blood to swell their private parts.
> To think of corpses pleases me;
> They keep such perfect chastity.
> 'A Small Ode on Mixed Flatting'

Baxter was associated with 'the Wellington Group', less a clique than an amicable circle of poets including Louis Johnson, Alistair Campbell and W. H. Oliver. The Wellington Group, which produced a succession of small magazines during the late forties and early fifties, favoured a more universal, less hieratic poetry than the Caxton poets. This was the period of the Auckland/Wellington split. Curnow had by this time moved to Auckland and become associated with a group of younger 'academic' poets, chiefly Kendrick Smithyman, C. K. Stead and Keith Sinclair. The Auckland poets were even less a clique than the Wellington group. Smithyman in particular resisted the nationalism of Curnow's poetic as vigorously as Baxter did. What connected these poets was a characteristic voice of cool intelligence and formal rigour.

But something of the mood of Auckland itself also permeated their verse. If Wellington, as the bureaucratic centre of New Zealand, is associated with a tone of high-minded social concern, Auckland has been the city where a generous physical environment has encouraged the sensual life. In Keith Sinclair's poem, 'Te Kaminara', the lovers, 'lying all day together in the grass', make 'the land more lovingly [their] own'.

---

[9]Curnow, p. 133.

This accommodation to clime is not, however, simply a matter of adopting a careless hedonism. It represents a hesitant move away from the Pakeha struggle with imported ghosts and gods towards an acceptance that the place itself is indifferent to such angst. It might be related to the sensual exuberance of Pat Hanly's paintings of the sixties, so at odds with the dark brooding landscapes of the Canterbury painters a generation earlier. Significantly, it lacks the strained anti-puritanism of Baxter, who never wholly abandoned his ambivalent relationship with Calvin's God. Curnow's rather stern religious scepticism has also dissipated. Curiously, these Pakeha poets thus prepared the way for the Polynesian cultural renaissance in that city since the seventies, reflected here in the very different poetry of Albert Wendt.

By the seventies the Auckland/Wellington split was less important than a fierce dispute about formal procedures, which blurred the lines of the old allegiances. Stead's controversial 1979 essay, 'From Wystan to Carlos: Modern and Modernism in New Zealand Poetry', argued that the mainstream of poetry in the twentieth century had moved away from the closed forms identified with Georgian poetry towards an American-influenced formal openness to experience.[10] Both Baxter and the later Curnow were enlisted in this argument about literary-historical direction and poetic procedure, along with selected younger poets, notably Ian Wedde.

Compiling this anthology we found the categories fitted at best imperfectly. Modernism of the T. S. Eliot/Ezra Pound variety is not strongly in evidence before Stead's poems of the late fifties and sixties. In the thirties and forties modernism is filtered through contemporary English poets, especially W. H. Auden. The American line that runs from Pound and Williams to Olson and Creeley appears in force in the late sixties with *FREED*, but was rarely doctrinaire in practice. The local manifestations of postmodernism are mixed and, for the purposes of categorisers, impure. Ian Wedde, claimed by Stead for 'open form' and consigned by Wystan Curnow to a 'laid back modernis[m]', is uninterested in pigeon holes, and frequently adopts the traditional forms of ballad and sonnet.[11]

Such mixing of styles and formal procedures is inevitable and positive in postcolonial societies. To insist that poetry is proceeding in some specific formal direction — whether that of modernism, postmodernism or LANGUAGE poetry — is merely to update the colonial cringe. Where does one stand to make such judgements? Poetry affords few empyrean views and literary history does not proceed in straight lines. What is striking is the continual adaptation to local conditions of an enormous variety of influences from all sorts of sources

---

[10]Stead, 'From Wystan to Carlos: Modern and Modernism in Recent New Zealand Poetry', in *In the Glass Case: Essays on New Zealand Literature* (Auckland: Auckland University Press/Oxford University Press, 1981), pp. 139–59.

[11]Wystan Curnow, 'Speech Balloons & Conversation Bubbles', *AND/4* (October 1985), p. 126.

— high culture and low culture, salon and street, literary and oral.

Often the most radically new fashion turns out to be a revisiting of some now forgotten fad. Len Lye's work in the thirties is as avant-garde as any written in the eighties. LANGUAGE poetry, which has occasioned strong animosities and fierce defences in the nineties, is anticipated in the sixties poetry of Janet Frame, although she would no doubt have found the term odd. Bruce Andrews, co-editor with Charles Bernstein of the anthology, L=A=N=G=U=A=G=E, defines the term as 'a spectrum of writing that places attention primarily on language and ways of making meaning, that takes for granted neither vocabulary, grammar, process, shape, syntax, program, or subject matter'.[12] This would seem to apply neatly enough to Janet Frame's 'Impard a Willow-Cell in Sordure':

> Impard a willow-cell in sordure
> chance or chead in fascendure
> the sweetable clightly photation
> frambling in the quintolution.

Andrews further observes that 'that refusal to take things for granted [in L=A=N=G=U=A=G=E poetry] can in turn pose a direct challenge to *social norms* about vocabulary, grammar, process, shape, syntax, program & subject matter'.[13] This corresponds still more closely to Frame's poems which use seemingly nonsense vocabulary to deal with atrocities committed during the Vietnam War.

By the late seventies, when Stead's essay appeared, the informing energies of a new poetry and a new poetic had already moved on from such disputes, away from academia altogether. Ian Wedde didn't want to be a professor. Along with the young and not-so-young of his generation — those born just after the Second World War — he had gone out to encounter experience in the variety and intensity of its immediate forms. His 'Earthly: Sonnets for Carlos' is a major poetic sequence of the period, along with Curnow's 'Trees, Effigies, Moving Objects' and Baxter's 'Jerusalem Sonnets'.

> Diesel trucks past the Scrovegni chapel
> Catherine Deneuve farting onion fritters
> The world's greedy anarchy, I love it!
> Hearts that break, garlic fervent in hot oil
> Jittery exultation of the soul
> Minds that are tough & have good appetites
> Everything in love with its opposite
> I love it! O how I love it!
>   'Earthly: Sonnets for Carlos'

A further major poetic sequence of the period, Vincent O'Sullivan's Butcher poems, took yet another formal direction, extending a feature of Baxter's poetry with vigorous colloquial satires. In O'Sullivan's

---

[12]Bruce Andrews, 'Poetry as Explanation, Poetry as Praxis', in *Postmodern American Poetry: A Norton Anthology*, edited by Paul Hoover (New York: Norton, 1994), p. 670.
[13]Andrews, p. 670.

Butcher persona, the rustic archetypal New Zealand character of Glover's 'Arawata Bill' is reinvented, made more complex and relevant to a country in which town as well as wilderness was becoming a site for the formation of culture.

> Don't get him wrong.
> The Butcher when time permits
> folds his arms, can lean
> lovely as any man in the throes of thought,
> shouldering the doorway in summer,
> bum on winter's block.
>   'Fish for All That Rise as Rise Wet Stars'

V

Perhaps no voice has been as important in establishing the distinctive stance and tone of the last few years as Bill Manhire, because — more than any previous New Zealand poet — Manhire teaches us to relax about the old settler anxieties of where we are, where we were and where we might be. As late as 1960 C. K. Stead observed that 'as New Zealanders we suffer a certain isolation from experience', and this is not simply a function of geographical remoteness but a 'combination of remoteness and *insignificance*'.[14] For Manhire, New Zealanders are no more isolated, and certainly no less significant, than anyone else in the late twentieth century. His 'Milky Way Bar' rebuts Stead's case by invoking R. A. K. Mason's 1924 'Sonnet of Brotherhood' in which humans find themselves 'here in this far-pitched perilous hostile place / this solitary hard-assaulted spot / fixed at the friendless outer edge of space'. In Manhire's poem the speaker is more unassuming, less metaphysically worried — at ease with his situation:

> I live at the edge of the universe,
> like everybody else. Sometimes I think
> congratulations are in order: . . .

For Thomas Bracken in 'The New Zealand Hymn', where we are is a sign of our collective destiny as inhabitants of a uniquely favoured Edenic land, isolated and special. For Charles Brasch in 'The Islands', ours is a condition of peculiar exile; we are victims of distance and geography. For Manhire, our position in the world, like that of everyone else, is both central *and* peripheral, depending on how we choose to construe it.

Some younger contemporary poets see our situation as more radically informed by international influences than Manhire, for whom the local forms of adaptation are always a source of pleasure and curiosity. In the early eighties a young poet, Leigh Davis, produced a sequence of sonnets, *Willy's Gazette*, and co-founded a little magazine, *AND*. For Davis, who became a merchant banker after completing his MA,

---

[14]C. K. Stead, 'For the Hulk of the World Between', in *In The Glass Case*, p. 246.

the financial markets were a prime source of contemporary cultural meanings. At a time when the economy was being opened up to international forces, Davis observed how much New Zealand was already integrated into the larger world of information flows, the traffic of goods, styles, ideas, capital and technologies. The eponymous hero of *Willy's Gazette* is interested in poetry, but not conspicuously more than he is in magazine fashions, corporate architecture, rock music.

Willy is not given to soulful reflection or lyrical self-advertising. He is aware of earlier New Zealand poets but their looming presences, the weighty topics they addressed, do not bother him. For Baxter the preoccupying subject had been the lapse of meanings once the old icons — God, Mary, home, sex, poetry — had fallen down. For Willy, Baxter himself is an iconic figure, part of the storehouse of familiar images that make up New Zealand literature and New Zealand culture, rather than the suffering or sublime man revealed through the poetry.

> You're a big ghost, Jim St. John,
> nice sheen on your forehead and noseridge's catchy,
> spread over the billboard, nine years later . . .
> Leigh Davis, *Willy's Gazette*

A distinguishing mark of the present is indicated in this playful relaxation about inheritance. Poetry in New Zealand since the thirties has at times exhibited the marks of masculine struggles for succession — fathers seeking suitable sons and sons resisting the burden of filial loyalty. Since the seventies such struggles have been less prominent. Manhire's slyly irreverent nods to the past and to the commanding figures it contains have been exemplary in this respect. Younger poets no longer seem to feel that the presence of their precursors calls for either deference or strenuous rebellion (although there have been some vigorous feminist revisions of the masculinist canon).

As editors, we wished to avoid canonical lines of poetic influence. The accumulated repository of New Zealand material is by now so extensive that it can be drawn on without self-consciousness, indeed it is probably impossible to avoid. So it is possible to talk about a 'New Zealand tradition', not as a single line of established greatness but as a field of multifarious influence, where the imagery and meanings of the past are continually being revised, revalued and recycled. This involves both exotic and indigenous influences. Just as Hone Tuwhare can assimilate Biblical sources into a poem like 'Thine Own Hands Have Fashioned', so Robert Sullivan can evoke and draw upon James K. Baxter in one of his 'Tai Tokerau Poems':

> I found an old copy of Pig Island Letters on the shelves
> of Kawakawa Library. I can still taste its seasoning: kina,
> puha, pork and kumara: the Maori own the land.
> 'Opua'

In the last three decades, local poets have turned more and more to American models, enriching and complicating the notion of tradition. Robert Lowell is at work in James K. Baxter, Wallace Stevens in Allen Curnow, Adrienne Rich and John Ashbery in Dinah Hawken. With the progressive disintegration since the sixties of residual loyalties to Britain, possible sources of influence have broadened so that the whole decentred world can be a rejuvenating force. Thus we sense the presence of the Yugoslav-born American poet, Charles Simic, in the work of Andrew Johnston, of the French poet, René Char, in the prose poetry of Richard von Sturmer, and of the Russian, Osip Mandelstam, in Brian Turner's poetry.

Contemporary New Zealand literature includes poets who come from or reside elsewhere, and in whose work more than New Zealand influences of culture and geography are present — for instance, the Scot, Alan Riach, and the Samoan, Albert Wendt. In a sense to ask whether Fleur Adcock is a New Zealand or an English poet is to miss the point. To adapt Robert Muldoon's wicked remark about New Zealanders who emigrate to Australia, her dual citizenship (in the poetic sense) enriches both countries. Her work has grown by what she has encountered, and New Zealand poetry has been enlarged by what she has continued to bring to it.

VI

We have not included poetry in the Maori language but have sought to recognise the strength of Maori poetry written in English and to capture the different ways it deals with and addresses its world:

> Gissa smile Sun, giss yr best
> good mawnin' one, fresh 'n cool like
>
> yore still comin' — still
> half in an' half outa the lan'scape?
> Hone Tuwhare, 'Sun o (2)'

For a broader picture of contemporary Maori poetry the series of anthologies edited by Witi Ihimaera, *Te Ao Marama*, is recommended, as well as his earlier *Into the World of Light*.[15]

Looking at contemporary work, we have tried to paint as broad a canvas as possible, including a rich diversity of poetry from different sources. We have included strong representations from the work of Dinah Hawken, Bernadette Hall and Michele Leggott, among others, to represent a mature, persuasive revisionist poetry. We have also sought to highlight some of the central bodies of work of recent decades, hence the generous selections from mid-career writers such as Ian Wedde, Bill Manhire and Elizabeth Smither.

It seems extraordinary now to think of the neglect Iain Lonie met with during his lifetime. Accordingly, a rich selection of his work is included here. We have also included four poems by John Male writ-

---

[15] *Te Ao Marama*, edited by Witi Ihimaera (Auckland: Reed, 1992–94), 4 vols.; *Into the World of Light: An Anthology of Maori Writing*, edited by Witi Ihimaera and D. S. Long (Auckland: Reed, 1982).

ten during the Second World War. Independently of local influence and subject matter, Male's poems were written during the Italian Campaign. His unadorned narrative combining personal perspectives and historical immediacy contrasts with the lyrical self-advertising and rhetorical excess of contemporary male poets like Fairburn and D'Arcy Cresswell.

We have included a short selection from the multi-media artist Len Lye, who was writing his Gertrude Stein-like prose poems at the same time as R. A. K. Mason published his first volumes. It's useful to think of him as a precursor of later poets such as Wystan Curnow, Richard von Sturmer and Michele Leggott.

We have included work by the short-story writer Maurice Duggan, who, while publishing no collection during his life, had a cache of work appear in *Islands* in the early seventies. These poems bring to mind Samuel Beckett (a comparison the prose could also stand) in their knotted music. Curiously, they also look forward to the peremptory voices, staccato measures and deliberate anti-lyricism of Damien Wilkins.

Hilaire Kirkland was another poet who never published a book during her lifetime. We have included work here from *Blood Clear and Apple Red*, published posthumously by the Wai-te-ata Press. These poems call to mind R. A. K. Mason, while heralding the reinvention of feminist mythologies by poets like Dinah Hawken and Roma Potiki.

Albert Wendt, who was educated in New Zealand before returning to his native Samoa and then finally settling in New Zealand nearly a decade ago, is included in this survey, his work opening up the Pacific as a field of reference for New Zealand writers. His recent anthology, *Nuanua*, eloquently broadens the scope of Pacific writing both within and beyond New Zealand. Paul Sharrad has suggested that we abandon the notion of the Pacific Basin as an emptiness surrounded by a fullness from which important things come.[16] It is the scene of journeys, encounter, traffic and exchange. Extraordinarily, in 1995 the French, justifying continued nuclear testing, reiterated the colonial belief that the Pacific was a void, 'a desert'. The sense of New Zealand as part of the Pacific, drawing into itself many cultures and experiences, is to be found in the poetry of Ian Wedde, Alan Riach and Alistair Campbell as well as that of Albert Wendt.

In respect of poetry by women our strongly held view was that no counting of representations in order to ensure strict parity with men was called for. The poetry stood its own ground and needed no special advocacy. We also wished to avoid giving the impression that 'women's poetry' (a term we disliked as it suggested a spurious homogeneity of purpose or method) in this country began round about 1975 with the rapid publication of collections by Lauris Edmond, Elizabeth Smither and Rachel McAlpine. Eileen Duggan, Mary Stanley, Ursula

---

[16]The [Pacific] Basin is full, and it is defined not by its rim but by its contents', 'Imagining the Pacific', *Meanjin* 49, no. 4 (Summer 1990), p. 605.

Bethell and Robin Hyde were producing strong work much earlier than this date and accordingly are also well represented here.

We remarked at the outset that we did not see the history of New Zealand poetry in English involving a narrative of triumphant evolution towards a national consciousness. Nevertheless, there has been a process of accommodation between what was brought and what was encountered from the moment settler foot touched settled ground, and the achievement of that acclimatisation is indicated in the sense of ease in contemporary poetry, particularly poetry by women — ease with the body, with language and with the physical world:

> she goes down into the sexual garden, under its dark spread
> and into its detail: ecstatically branching magnolia, tuberous
> roots thrusting up huge leaves. Fuck the tulips in their damned
> obedient rows. Stop. They're finally opening their throats!
> They have dark purple stars! They have stigma! They have style!
>   Dinah Hawken, 'Small Stories of Devotion'

VII

In constructing the anthology we proceeded by way of engaged reading and passionate discussion. Most of the poetry was read aloud in order that we should *hear* the material. Where problems or disagreements arose we addressed them not by recourse to abstract principle but by working through the poetry itself until the difficulty was resolved. In other words, the key terms behind the organisation of the anthology — culture, poetry, tradition, canon — have been adopted in an open, exploratory manner rather than a closed, authoritative one.

Our aim was to represent, selectively, the diversity of poetry in this country rather than privilege any particular style. While including much verse concerned with defining the nation and national character, we have looked closely at the personal lyric. We have also included some light verse (occasional or humorous) and some from the bardic tradition, spanning the performance poetry of Kim Eggleston, Sam Hunt and David Eggleton and moving back to early rustic balladry:

> The birds gang to rest when tir'd wi' their warblin',
>   But rest I get nane frae the mornin' sae early;
> For either I'm mawin', or thrashin', or sawin',
>   Or grubbin' the hills wi' the ferns covered fairly.
>   Grub away, tug away, toil till you're weary,
>   Haul oot the toot roots and everything near ye;
>   Grub away, tug away, toil till you're weary,
>   Then take a bit dram, it will help for to cheer ye.
>   John Barr of Craigilee, 'Grub Away, Tug Away'

Our intention has not been to include poetry merely because it is of historical or sociological interest, nor to provide a series of poetic exemplars of social attitudes. An alert poetic tradition will inevitably reflect shifts and crises in a culture. We have based our inclusions ultimately on principles of literary value. That is to say, poems have not been included unless they hold some interest to us *as poetry*. However, we believe it is important that such an approach be applied without dogmatism, arrogance or unexamined confidence. We are aware that one's value judgements are inevitably influenced by matters of personal taste and by what is called these days one's 'subject position'. Nevertheless, we believe they are unavoidable and necessary in the compiling of any anthology and are better made honestly than disguised.

Above all, we started out with no fixed idea — individually or collectively — as to what exactly New Zealandness is or how it might be represented in poetry. In past anthologies what has been excluded or given prominence has often had to do with the progressive efforts to construct a satisfactory identity or contest existing formulations. We took the view that the question of identity calls for no assertive, anxious or prescriptive statements. This is not to say that identity has taken some final and immutable shape. It is in a process of constant change and revision, a process of which this anthology is a part.

*

A note on the ordering of the poems. The selections have been arranged backwards, starting from the present. The year 1994 was our cut-off date for poems, published in journals or books. In a few cases a poem published in a journal before 1994 appeared in a book after that date. In order to give a more accurate historical sense of the material we arranged the individual poets according to the date of their first publication of a volume of poems rather than by age. Thus Lauris Edmond appears in the mid seventies along with Rachel McAlpine and Murray Edmond rather than among her generational peers, Louis Johnson and Alistair Campbell. We have departed from a strict application of the method where it seemed appropriate. For example, we did not count obviously minor publications but tried to settle on the work that signalled the arrival of the particular poet. John Male, who published no volume, is situated with his peers. J. C. Sturm appears according to the publication date of her collection of stories, *The House of the Talking Cat* (1983).

Within the individual selections the poems are organised chronologically, from the earliest to the most recent. We have made small departures from this method where it seemed appropriate to do so.

The date given at the foot of each poem is the date of publication of the book from which the poem is reprinted. In the cases where publication in a journal is indicated, the date is placed in parentheses.

Jenny Bornholdt
Gregory O'Brien
Mark Williams
1996

CHRIS ORSMAN

Born in Lower Hutt in 1955, Chris Orsman studied architecture at the University of Auckland, teaching there briefly and working in architectural practices before training as an ambulance officer. He now lives in Wellington and writes full-time.

Ornamental Gorse

It's ornamental where it's been
self-sown across the hogback,

obsequious and buttery,
cocking a snook at scars,

yellowing our quaint history
of occupation and reprise.

The spiny tangential crotch,
gullied and decorative,

I love from a distance,
a panorama over water

from lakeside to peninsula
where it's delicate in hollows,

or a topiary under heavens
cropped by the south wind.

I offer this crown of thorns
for the pity of my countrymen

unconvinced of the beauty
of their reluctant emblem: this

burnt, hacked, blitzed
exotic.

1994

Ancestral

Some were Irish pirated from obscure editions
of the *Book of Life* — townsmen, potato-farmers,

ambitious peasantry of County Cork; they washed up
on any strange shore as the Irish do.

My great-grandfather, a stocky man with a red beard,
not tall, planted in stony Omaka

barley and corn and grew in turn
melancholy, retiring each night with Dickens

and a pint of gin. An unsuccessful prophylactic.
His daughters loved their letters: nurses, nuns,

schoolmarms in the provinces; my grandmother
taught at fifteen and prayed each night

on her knees, remembering a mixed-marriage
sometime back in the twenties; broad-boned

women all of them, foil to the English reticence
bred in Devon or who knows where.

My grandfather last wept in 1918:
offloaded on the quay he watched

the troopship sail with his horse. Influenza
decimated the boat by Gravesend and the Armistice.

He married and became a grocer. My mother's father
was as handsome as a film star; he drowned

one night in Havelock harbour and is buried there
under an octagonal headstone, a farmer

who married a schoolteacher. His wife
lies there too, dead of a stroke at forty-seven,

Scot and Irish blurring the old prejudice,
and the Church triumphant in the end. The irony

would have been appreciated whatever the lapidary
nature and function of this present silence —

ancestral, yes, and fragmentary, a kind of truth,
the detritus gathered on the sea floor

seen from above as the tide changes.

1994

Death by Drowning

It was once called *The New Zealand Death:*
apt enough in the days before bridges

when torrents broke down the riverbanks,
the horse and laden cart midstream;

and the legerdemain of waves over unseen
holes and rips near the shore;

and the innocuous whitening line
concealing a bar, a chronic ship-breaker

whose clumsy ministrations conferred
a citizenship at break of day. And I recall

a ferry-boat foundering at the harbour mouth
one morning in 1968,

as macrocarpas flailed the trolley-bus lines
over Karori Road, and the gravel flew

into our faces as we walked to school
bent into the same wind battering

Seatoun and the eastern beaches.
The New Zealand Death again — a fifty soul

harvest of paired and threshing storms.
My brother and my grandfather both drowned,

twenty-four years apart or seventy miles
as these things are reckoned.

A fine balance of tides weighs the debt
owed by that thundering cogency

which swung its casual strength against
muscle and membrane and their frailty.

Whatever is empirical is commensurate
with the excrescence of a salted lung.

The froth of treacherous shores carries us
nearer sea's anatomy, cartilage and bone.

1994

ANDREW JOHNSTON

Andrew Johnston grew up in the Hutt Valley, where he was born in 1963. He completed degrees in English at the Universities of Otago and Auckland. He presently lives in Wellington, where he edits The Evening Post *books page.*

How to Talk

It was on the ferris wheel
I was introduced to

the art of conversation.
She was thirteen,

I was fourteen;
many times we passed the point where we'd climbed on.

How high it is, up here, she said
when we were near the top.

I could see my name
on the tip of her tongue.

1993

The Picture

This is the poem of the big questions.
This is the film of the poem. People wander

in and out of the picture
theatre. Every so often

a flash of light from the screen
or someone laughs, or someone screams

or someone falls asleep and dreams
of Christmas in Lapland, of being

pursued along a pale unspoilt beach
by a family of curious whales.

1993

Fool Heart

1. *The evergreens*

Rich scents, guess — yes, the evergreens,
there is something in the wind,

it is blowing from the Dwarf Conifer Collection,
whistling *I wish*

IwishIwish
and never completes the sentence ...

Shapes, shades, the Garden of Remembrance,
something out of stone — a hard look

at your fool heart, printed
with warnings.

2. *Sensible shoes*

Gravel, an avenue, a gate thrown open —
we've been down this path before.

Here you are, and
here: note this footprint's

toehold on the real, the whole
an accurate absence: it's yours

and so are these, where you went
in your sensible shoes, each neat outline

getting you ready
for the next step.

3. *The shallows*

A shag shakes, dives — for its other name
and comes up with *cormorant*, a bottle

rolls in the shallows — it's empty
for a moment — it's clear

you can't stay serious here.
The bay breaks into laughter, its surface

nervous as Mercury — god of scholars,
travellers, thieves,

is he after
your heart, the fool.

4. *True north*

North, true north, magnetic north —
don't ask the heart for directions,

lost in the forest. New leaves
put themselves out for you,

for your trouble, for your
fool heart, filling itself

with meaning.
Tell it to stay

an obedient tree
whose roots yet crack the path.

5. Stern bird

Stern bird sings — at the top of its twig
'I've come to see the done thing done'

Stern bird in the undergrowth,
listening ...

A man goes by with a noisy heart —
I wish   IwishIwish —

he might need a new frame of mind,
something to fit the facts:

stern bird in its tree,
fool heart in its cage of ribs.

6. New view

Sea like a lake today,
strait like a door, water

leaving of its own accord.
Here's a new view,

a hill of shale for a lover to look over,
a slope, a slight rise, a house over-

looking the harbour, its
points of departure, a port.

Here's a boatload of hope held up by customs,
a courtship caught before the boat could sail.

7. Old magnolias

A mind made free in the Main Garden goes
slowly over the sense of what you've said.

Old magnolias burst into Latin —
white flowers flare, fall silent, leaves all

point to their divinity, a pink tree
thinks nothing of such perfection. The eye

leads naturally to where the sky is clearing
above the Sundial of Human Involvement

which can be located next
to the Observatory.

1993

The Sounds

Rain, a restful place: a plain
negotiation led to this, one small
lit room, in lieu of a camera, and the
drowned valleys, windless, listening
to the rain, on leaf, on water
in winter. Disentangled thus, we touch

as if deciphering a prophecy, we touch
as ocean, held by the land, made plain
a difficult map, whose cove-smooth water
uncoils with travel, surrounds a small
arrival, a larger departure. Listening
to the sounds as we pronounce them, the

waves, the bright particulars, we hear the
way we've been so far, we touch
speech, our bodies fearless listening
devices. And days unravel as on a plain
a road will travel straight with small
perceptible corrections. But water

under the hand of the wind, and water
in darkness: things we see and cannot tell, the
sounds are full of these too, as small
fish, late, in a bell of light, touch
the surface once and disappear. It's plain
each morning, talking and not listening

how plain things aren't, how whether we're listening
or not, the sounds go on around us, and water
will erase all previous arrangements. It's plain
how prophecies succumb before the
evidence, words in sand that crumble at a touch,
that need to be unwritten or forgotten, and small

reliable ambitions fashioned, parts for a small
cast — two, who move from stage to stage, listening
to the places where their different futures touch.
Rain-fast, a stream falls, to clear salt water
where just such a lean crew rows, the
dinghy iffing and butting, a plain

afternoon. The small boat drums the mingling water;
the rowers, listening, will remember the
sounds, when they touch, that these days made plain.

(1993)

DAMIEN WILKINS

Born in Lower Hutt, 1963, Damien Wilkins studied at Victoria University before completing an MFA in Creative Writing under Stanley Elkin, at Washington University, St Louis, Missouri. Primarily a fiction writer, Wilkins has published two novels, a story collection and a book of poems.

My Father's Stutter

Struck at certain times as when his mother
interrupted him or at the quick demands
his older brothers made. We kids, too, knew
how to force it, though that was a terror
of its own as if someone had him by his great
singer's throat. Otherwise he lectured quite
happily, growing lucid the further into molecular
structure he got.

There was also his part-time opera
career and the endless afternoons of
rehearsals we were taken to. His big smooth
chorus bass shaking our best seats in
the house. The same Italian phrases
sounding over and over on
over our heads.

And now just recently I have noticed odd
impediments in my own words. Nothing
to snap my head back but false starts, beginnings
of wild alliterations. A programming
thing, though I tell myself I am growing into it, slowly
and from dislike, as I work at his music:
the crowd scene — his favourite — in *La Bohème* when all the
bohemians, I guess they are, rush about, sing
at once and from the talky noise emerges — there!
Tune.

1993

The Prodigals

Don't let your parents sell
the house. They weren't children
there.

Threaten to marry and bring
the brood around adoring and

brilliant. That place they're considering
in town it's too small with no room for the
pyjama parties, the overnighters and
emergencies. Summon some

accident. Disaster is nicely
expansive. Find an outdoorsy

woman to go visiting with and coach
her in compliments. My, but this is

freedom! Call on the land agent and
while he's asleep pour out your
poison.
Failing this, one night creep around
the side by the glossy-leafed
bushes and the old washing machine
your cousin never collected because

he went mad and slip through your
window. Now stand in the hallway
your bare feet in the light from the
white keys of the piano your sisters

gave up on and listen. People are being
murdered in their beds. The children
are making love to themselves with
furious fists, pillows. It's unforgivable
how things have slipped in the time
you've been in jail.

1993

ROMA POTIKI

*Born in 1958, Roma Potiki lives in Paekakariki. A multi-media artist as well as a poet
and short fiction writer, she freelances as a writer and consultant.*

Palazzi

sitting out on the palazzi
with my back to the open lounge
my lowered lids let the shine in.

a white porcelain bowl, used each morning,
the only religious ceremony left today — break fast,
an old one from the testaments.
it came from a rubbish dump at Kohukohu.

saw an Italian sun and thought about fast cars on the slopes.
red cars 'n long scarf wommin, a trip on the grey gravel of Europe.

i'd wear me blue dancing shoes and take me
fishes eyes.
daydreams on a cracked concrete slab in Rotorua.

(1987)

The Flax

The flax is tender/hard
wet growth
the colours fluid white, fluid yellow, then rust
then green blade

bending up, up, up and out
strong centered soft-tipped plant.

the smell is someone weeping
fresh life.

the coarse roots hold
round earth

intend to stay.

(1992)

Compulsory Class Visits

they come in classes now
many pakeha ones too
and even the maori start to call themselves
new zealanders.
and even the maori stand on the marae saying 'this is the only place
you can be maori on.'
it is not enough for me.
the young are in constant challenge with the middle-aged,
the men who take their teeth out.

at the powhiri they are directed to sing
there is no kaea there is no ihi.
holding their papers, they look at the words —
Ao-te-a-roa.

1992

For a Father in Hiding

take me away
i used to travel.

i hear the breath of the people
in each corner
and scraping at the glass.

someone must have sent the dreams
of meeting houses
low and dark,

earth floors
and slits for windows,
each old face watching silently.

and i am searching, searching,
for the smallest entrance.

blind horses
scent the air
that blows through you.

1992

And My Heart Goes Swimming

and my heart goes swimming

wet and lipid it hangs between waves of salt.
a warm heart in cold green waters
deep
to the bottom.

wave after wave washing the little skin
saline.

and my heart goes swimming

a fisherman scoops the sea,
finds a heart in his hand.

no cold fish warm red blood black hair
blonde.

a night of swimming,
open eyes laugh
see us
love
the man and my heart celebrate

and in the morning warm water from a tap.

but now the fisherman has fish to catch
see, he has a net, and sinkers.

back

to the sea
my heart goes swimming
wave after wave

no cold fish could swim like my heart goes swimming.

1992

Bound To

bound together in the darkness
our faces push out of the night
man and woman struggle with each other
sigh and breathe as one wrist locks another
and hip-bones press
flat against the boards.

catching and getting caught.
Maui's net is thrown
and scoops us both in its rough binding.

lashed by old seas
the new fish gasp and twist onto the shore.

one thigh rolls
the other slumps
a summer crescent hitches itself into the sky.

no one is crying,
we both smile.

1992

ROB ALLAN

Born in 1957, Rob Allan lives in Port Chalmers and works as a teacher of deaf children in Otago schools.

from Karitane Postcards

2.

If I catch myself staring at an object
I must decide what I will tell you.
Gertrude Stein struggled to get rid of nouns
— the nouns had to go
I want history to go and politics and art
and images and symbols. I am looking at a plate
of shells named after Captain Cook
and I hear my boy sleeping in the bedroom
next door. I want description to go
I want the hoons revving up over the road to go
Captain Hook that's what Richard calls him
and his breath is a small surf through the wall.
Karitane it breathes all around my body
and the stars of the visible universe
I want the past and future to go
and my single-mindedness.

52.

Tune your ears to get rid of ideas
is that rain?
those barely tangible attentions.
I wanted to talk to the old people in the valley
but I had no time
landscape rushing out of me
seems to say it all
they are all indoors as Autumn deepens
along the ridges sub-tropical rainforest
bush with sycamore and boxthorn
all kinds of talk
and evasion at a local level   Mihiwaka
the mountain itself named after the first shopkeeper
Mrs. Walker   a quiescent volcano misrepresented
people who cannot step back far enough
to get a decent look.

58.

Clearing the mind knots and branches
under the pull of the moon
Rona made her way   she flew after the moon
turned into shadow
invulnerable up there   her husband and children
returned home to the glow of oven stones.
Rona come back   where are you
we are pulled   through your absence and again
some early morning you are turning the hills
in your gaze.

80.

Songs of passion   wouldn't want to rush
though the heart hammers
the hill's slope   Taiaroa on the peninsula   Muaupoki
and out of view where the sun rises   Pukekura
sacred place   the words you don't want to use
lie fallow in the ground
what fertility of lip tongue heart
touch the face of a new mythology
a collection of human errors.
Who can balance on the earth heart and head
ineffable chance reading the thin line of feeling
pathways of right and the good.
Picasso encompassing   lovers as one
catching the arcadian in sunlight
pinks of flesh roses opening
tender shoots such warmth parting   uniting
you up there Rona   distraught sweeper of ashes
the left over cooking pots all that is left of daylight.

1991

ROBERT SULLIVAN

Robert Sullivan was born in 1967. He is of Nga Puhi and Galway Irish descent and works as a librarian at the University of Auckland.

from Tai Tokerau Poems

1. *I walked over the hill*

Pockets of totara forest reclaim what few remains there are
of the Karetu pa. Young black ferns protect crumbling earth,

punga roots exposed where punga walls once rose, but no more
room for sentiment. It's a chief's eye view of the valley too —

the river at hills' feet glides, in repose, by the old metal
that brought you here, took us home so often. September

the second, a softer season, brings teatree blossoms, scatters
wasps, bees loud as fire engines, sends adrenalin through me

as if I were a fireman. Over the hill Nanna Bella shows me
orchids, warms goat milk in a microwave oven, lets me feed

the bleaters. 'Wash your hands when you leave the pa.'
I observe the ritual of bread too. It is no man's hill.

1990

Sitting in Front of the Karetu Marae

Ngati Manu's flag hugs the staff.
Ping pong in the dining hall.

The sun spills light over the hills across
the creek. A horse flicks its tail.

The door to Grandad's house is shut.
Ten goats nuzzle on a higher hill.

A dog rolls in front belly up.
This day fills us: slow breeze in a cloth.

1993

Doing It

We stand at the back of Grandad's house
in the regenerating bush with Drew and Trace.

We stand at the top of a rock which
we climb by wedging ourselves upon flax

and roots of pohutukawa. We crouch
inside that rock in the sea cave where

penguin tracks trail the deeps
and our voices fill the hollow left

by the tide. We glide and stroke in
rock jacuzzis where the tide just reaches

and our shoulders sink into bright saltwater.
I sleep and am woken with a sunburn warning.

1993

Christmas Day

The separate families of the Harawene whanau
gather in front of the tree for their photos.

The long tables set with napkins, bottles of bubbly
and fizzy drinks from my childhood, have come back

to visit this place. I remember the weekend
when the marae reopened, and the dance on Saturday

when the air was filled with smoke and the floor
was covered with booze and sweat. Already

some of our elders have left from that time.
The kitchen at the back replaces the old open

fire with electric stoves and a furnace with
a gleaming flue. And the ablution block has

showers and new flush toilets. It's all very
swept up, and it takes a lot of cleaning.

When it comes my turn for the photo I'm in
the back row beside James next to the tree.

1993

On Display

In the Travel Display we showed *Headhunters*
of Borneo and the journal of Joseph Banks.

Best bits of that display were the Africa cabinets
with Speke Stanley Livingstone hamming it up: 'the sound

of trumpets, and the Totties were off!' (Speke).
Grey's explorations through Western Australia

were also of interest, though he seldom wrote
an original thing here. Autograph Letters features

a strongman known as the 'Patagonian Sampson'
of Sadlers Wells — Giovanni Belzoni, and William

Colenso who printed the first book in New Zealand,
Ko te Rongo Pai, but the first press was that of William

Yate, who printed New Zealand's first booklet.
There's also a letter from von Tempsky outlining a massacre.

Recently, a man came in with a Sotheby's sale price
on our scrappy 1813 edition, inscribed by Grey,

of a book on Australian birds, a previously unknown copy.
It's worth 250,000 pounds! So I put it in the safe.

1993

Southerly
(*for Alexa*)

Waves crack like glass at Makara —
we watch behind perspex at the cafe.
Temuera swings from a fisherman's knot,
later he tackles the crawl and two-step.

Our tipuna walked here too. They passed over
unmarked stones, managed the shelled paua,
leap out in shapes. White noise is the breaker —
mumbling, and listening to it, our inheritance.

Kaikoura's chill breath and its Wellington
presence: principles, peninsulas, pamphlets,
the narrator steams to the capital. What blowing!
The Historic Story of Visitors (an abstract):

Deaths of whales, trees and people. Pigs
ashore. Gold petitions pans. Subdivision.
Guilt ends this (late, and too). Archives bear
the pall of those who knew 'the ancient ways'.

Few autographed their names. Settlers
wrote alpine tunes, Canterbury plainsongs,
bought bagpipes, noseflutes, and a Fomison.
Ah, South Island, your music remembers me.

1994

VIRGINIA WERE

Born in Australia in 1960, Virginia Were grew up in Auckland, where she completed a degree in Fine Arts at Elam School of Fine Arts, University of Auckland. Subsequently a member of the cult band Marie and the Atom, she now writes prose and poetry in Auckland.

We Listen for You on the Radio

We know that there is
a yacht out there
struck into our map,
a star disabled north of Cape Reinga.
The cyclone blows it backwards
so that the land is
two hundred miles away; more than that.

You are out there
and the sea
will find its way into your ears
and mouth, it
fills your eyes with salt.
And *land* is somewhere.
You hold it in front of your eyes

in the small place that is safety
and walking down the street,
slow walking soft *light*,
your lover curled into the
small of your back,
a child clinging to the tips
of your fingers,

and the apples falling from the tree,
rotting in the yellow grass.
You can't see the horizon and
your life passes in the
time it takes to fall from
the top of a wave
and rise to the next,

and you fall fall fall
an eternity of apples
falling,
and the breaking of
branches.
The face of the next wave
is the face of your lover.

You have never seen
anything like it (these waves).
The sea will swallow you
if you don't get it right,
straight up the face, tremble
on the eyelash of the wave —
down the nose and into the hungry

mouth where it is hollowed,
still.

(Your child)
The branch snapped
and she fell
cried and you were there
with comfort and you

bound and soothed, held her
in your arms.
(The ribs are sprung,
the water finds its way in)
and we hear your voice crackle
out of phase down the radio,
the child and I.

(If you had two arms you would
hold us both.)
We cling to each other
even as you cling to the back
of your life,
cling to the few words that tell us
you are somewhere out there alive,

with three broken ribs,
running hills and valleys
our photograph safe inside your oilskin.
That you are alive,
eking out a can of spaghetti
some biscuits,
plumbing the wet chart

the face of land, the face
of each new wave mountain.
Time stops, three more days
of gale force winds
crawl on their bellies towards
you.
We don't know if you can

hear us, we can hear you.
We watch the tiny star which gives
your position make its way
down the TV screen on the
six o'clock news.
Your face is a little square
on the front page of *The Sun.*

The ends of bone crunch each other.
The radio threads you in
to us, then there is silence.
We would have the land moved
for you,
peeling back contours, licking
them and sticking an entire island

down,
its outline for you to step off
onto *land.*

1989

BERNADETTE HALL

Born in Central Otago in 1945, Bernadette Hall has an MA in Latin from the University of Otago. She now lives in Christchurch, dividing her time between teaching and writing plays and poetry.

Amica

for Joanna

The house is a reliquary
of insects, flowers & fingernails
& this is rare, Amica, that you assume
with your Etruscan air its essence;
lying on the hill arch of your arm;
on a sarcophagus. Someone is whistling
in the kitchen, laying down new territory
with aluminium brightness. All the windows
are open. Ivory tides wash out, wash in
& you sing the mysteries: that love
is a gift; that nothing is ever lost;
that death is the centre of a long life.

1989

Bowl

for Viv

i

You carry the bowl around
in your head till one day
the block jolts.
    You press
the grain against the lathe,
fiercely, gently. The bowl
is well aware of its own
shape,
   a hemisphere of honey
light, flawed to perfection.
You go back & back to the same
leaping off place.

ii

Falling in love
is a 'genetically instinctual

component of mating behaviour.'
Falling in love is shapelessness,
a collapse of boundaries.
                              The bowl
takes a bite out of the white
window frame.
                    It has shed the grand
& shaggy gestures of a tree. Compact
now, it pulls itself together,
alert, passionate, reticent.

iii

        Miracles are a matter
of timing, grace is routine.
Run your fingers on the lip
of the bowl round & round
without end.
                Gradually
you will come to the place
where you know what you are doing.
                              1990

Miriama

i.

On crossing the border, I always
change my name. A simple precaution
& you to guard my back.
                        Maheno, Monte
Cristo, Waianakarua, Mt. Misery & all
the wildflowers.
                    I am heavy with loot
& disappointment, heading south again down
the soft underbelly of the island, shedding
skins like coke cans on the Kilmog
& already the rain.

ii.

You are waiting, with or without
my blessing, in a blue room of pictures
torn from magazines:
                        Mother Teresa, Athena's
sandalled Victory, a sequoia forest, an avocado

pear, gazelles, two babies in a bath with a chimp,
Ayer's Rock by sunset, Hare Krishnas in their
old gold, mud pools, a street kid.
                                    You have
a bruise on your cheek.

iii.

'Sit down & I'll tell you a story.

At Moeraki in the old days lived a prophet,
Kiri Mahi Nahina who taught all the people that
Tiki had made them, not Io.
                              Te Wera, the warrior,
struck him down with his taiaha. Plugged his eyes,
ears, nose, mouth, anus with moss to contain
the heresy. Then he & his warriors ate him.'

iv.

Nothing is high, nothing is low, nothing
is hidden.
            This is the song, Miriama, you sing,
doublestopping on my heart strings.

                                              1994

Drawing a Conclusion on a Paper Dart

such is the language   you wash & cut
of exigency   & core yellow pears

                                            you could do
                                            with a pig

white & cool   the lawn is
as ointment   littered with them

                                            1994

Anorexia

these are the acts of power
to give birth   to kill

you have a new notion

    *

in a monochrome of beige sheep & paddocks
you try to say your unclear thing

you curl up like a wild rabbit

*

living out now in the open
you are the original food

1994

Cancer Ward

in memory of Juliet Robinson

This time is as a hinge
& I've been gone too long

cutting a swathe through the tinny
supermarché, amazed to have made it

back today of all days to the radiance
of your changing face. You are feeding

yourself through a tube in your navel.

*

The old woman opposite falls out of bed,
whimpers, 'Lady, lady, lady.' You cover

her up with a thin green blanket, push
the rubber bell for a nurse. Lady, lady,

lady. Her grandchildren bring in a greasy
lamb with black cleft feet. It bleats through

the red striped curtains of your cubicle.

*

The cleaner has left you someone else's
flowers. You wander with them through

the labyrinthine wards. 'There is no one
of that name here!' But there is, of course,

& you find her. It is much harder going
back. You are too thin to hug

more than gently under your straw hat.

*

Your voice is apt, enticing in the dark
& Odysseus stands there stark, dripping,

his heart seething like a blood pudding.
The Phaeacian girls giggle, turning their

heads sideways. You chortle, exuberant &
quaint in a world that is so transparent.

You say that everyone can be taught something.

*

The surgeon doubles over with exhaustion
in the lift. Like Socrates he says

that he just doesn't know. Your breathing
changes as you leave the ground, like Tristan

Vasilav three years old in a new red
dressing-gown, leaping out of a cupboard.

'What is the most beautiful thing in the world?'
'That which you love.'

1994

JENNY BORNHOLDT

Born in 1960 in Lower Hutt, Jenny Bornholdt now lives in Wellington. She has published four collections of poetry and has co-edited an anthology of New Zealand love poems.

Reading the Body

I

Back lit
clipped
on the board
light goes
through you
shows you up in
black and white for
what you are — a
gather of bones
a curled frond
of a spine
lightly embraced by
that scooped-out
smoothness of hip
cavity whose bones
like open palms
seem to
offer themselves out
in a kind of
blessing.

II

Here are some pictures
of the body.

These are the bones
of my beginning.
They have stayed
with me like
true friends. They
have given
very fine
support.

See the way the
spine tails down
to a fine twitch

the way the ribs
are arms curved
in welcome

the way the hip bones
lie like an open book.

And finally

There would be
a series of paintings:

The Body as Ant

The Body as Incident

The Body as Intention

The Body as Masterpiece

The Body as Desire

The Body as Ant

The body
is small
and crawls
fast.
The body has
lots of
legs.
The body
lives underground
in a nest
and collects food.

The Body as Incident

The body
happens to itself
by itself.

The Body as Intention

The body
means well.
It means so well
that it falls
backwards
over itself.
The body
is full
of good
intent.

The Body as Masterpiece

The body
is a big body
is a work
of Art.
The body
is still
life.

The Body as Desire

The body
desires
a body
any body
just not its
own body.

1988

Make Sure

Make sure you fall in love with a man who you know will survive
in the bush.
This way, when he is three nights overdue from his trip and the
search and rescue team is out looking for him and the helicopter
has been called back because the weather is closing in and they're
interviewing you on television in a close-up camera shot, asking
you what you think his chances are — hoping you will cry and
your lip will tremble — you can look them straight in the eye
and say you *know* he will be all right, he has had plenty of
experience and he knows what to do, he was carrying plenty of
food and warm clothing and he is strong.
Even if he is hurt, you know he will be all right.

He's a fighter, you'll say. He won't give in.
But the weather is closing in, you must be worried, they'll ask.
You keep your resolve. He will be all right, you say.
I know he will.

1989

The Boyfriends

The boyfriends all love you but they don't really know how.

They say it is tragic that you will not be together for the rest of
your lives. You will not be together for the rest of your lives
because they are lone spirits and you are a nice girl.

Because your father is a lawyer and because they like to think they
come from the wrong side of town, they say you will marry a
young lawyer. Someone nice, someone stable, someone able to
provide you with all the things you need and are accustomed to,
not a rogue, not an adventurous spirit like themselves. Not
someone who is destined to the lone life.

They say it will be all right for you. You will be very happy, they
can tell. It will all work out for you. You will find a young lawyer,
or a young lawyer will find you and you will get married and be
very happy.
This is what you want, of course.
They say you are made for happiness, anyone can see that.
You will be very happy, you'll see.

They imagine their own sorrow when the day finally comes.
They tell you about this. They imagine seeing you in town with
your new young lawyer. He will have his arm around your
shoulders. You will be looking happy. He will be looking happy.
You will both be looking very happy. They will look on and feel
tragic about it not working out, about the impossibility of the
great love. Because yours *is* the great love. The true love. Oh yes.
But it cannot work. The great love never works. The true love is
doomed to fail.

You suspect they have seen too many westerns with too many
cowboys riding off into too many sunsets.

In the end of course, you leave him. There isn't really much choice.
He is unhappy. Very unhappy. It is not all that romantic.

When you see him in the street you often cannot speak. You just
look at each other. You both cry a lot in public places. Other

people find this embarrassing and so do you.

He says   please come back.
He says this is the worst thing that has ever happened. And it is.
Please he says. Please.

But you can't. Because it would be going back to leaving him.
You prepared yourself to leave him for years. It took such a
long time.

It took years of listening to him leaving you, knowing that
he wouldn't.
All that leaving.
All that is left is the leaving.

1989

Instructions for How to Get Ahead of Yourself While the Light Still Shines

If you have a bike, get on it at night
and go to the top of the Brooklyn Hill.

When you reach the top
start smiling — this is Happy Valley Road.

Pedal at first, then let the road take you down
into the dark as black as underground
broken by circles of yellow lowered by the street lights.

As you come to each light
you will notice a figure
racing up behind.
Don't be scared
this is you creeping up on yourself.
As you pass under the light
you will sail past yourself into the night.

1989

The Bathers

Les Grandes Baigneuses — Cézanne
(begun about 1898 or 1899 and finished 1905)

Left for eight years amidst
the intense green and blue

of trees   pleased Cézanne
abandoned them in such a
pleasurable landscape.
Bodies slanted towards trees,
water, a dog asleep on the
ground. They sighed, over those
eight years, talked amongst
themselves quietly, each morning
a small *ah* of pleasure
at the day, wondering if
today . . . for eight years
until the trees grew thick
with colour, the lake
darkened and their bodies'
cool formation fixed
beside the admiring water.

1991

The Man Dean Went to Photograph

The man Dean went to photograph
has the Easter Island statues on
either side of his back, the
pyramids in between, across the
top the Pyrenees and above them
the sky. In between is a gap
he is worried about. He plans the
Niagara Falls down one
side, the pink and white terraces
down the other. He likes things
big so you can see them. Like
when he climbs the Pyrenees and
sees the country displayed
before him like the sea
inviting pleasure craft to play
upon its surface — he finds enormous
satisfaction in this. Likewise, when
he gazes down on the plain and
sees his wife, the great wings
of the eagle spread across her back
impatient to rise.

(1992)

from Estonian Songs

Waking the birds

Wake birds,
the sky loses its dark
because of you, light
slowly coming around
the corner to surprise
you.

A lion worries a bone
into morning
and berries come out
from behind their green
shields.

Boats in the harbour
planes in the sky
the wings and wheels of the
modern world are
moving.

Instructing the newly-weds

Listen bride
listen groom
don't be afraid.
At night, the dark trees at the end
of the street — how frightening
they seem, then
morning comes and uncovers
nothing but leaves.

Praising the cook

They say the sexual impulse
is like a fiery horse.

When you break an egg
        one-handed
into the frying pan
it sounds like distant hooves
crossing a dusty plain.

A weeping maiden

The world's in a
spin. Yellow continents turn
and turn until the
little caravan of feeling topples
forward and runs wildly
down the road.

(1994)

MICHELE LEGGOTT

Michele Leggott is a graduate of the University of British Columbia, Vancouver, where she completed a doctorate on the poetry of Louis Zukofsky, subsequently published as Reading Zukofsky's 80 Flowers *(Johns Hopkins University Press, 1989). She grew up in New Plymouth, and now teaches at the University of Auckland.*

from Tigers

wavejumping
down the coast   a
eight months a year call up   step
the weather office every morning   into
second-guess the winds at the cape   heaven
at Kina Rd   deliberate
the swell   more coffee a look around the windows
west sou'west getting up now   more avocado on toast
good thing that long season on Hass
why settle for less   the best avo the best coast
another balanced judgement   the best driver in the world
from those who should know (best)   load up Bluey and go
nose into the slipstream that may or may not be worth it
he learned in the summer of cold southerlies we   all   remember
he was out   fierce concentration   it was strange
in the waves   pulling in the new as the old   weather
when she died   stripped heart and sail from him   then
late on a windy afternoon in January   she just stopped
one of those days around the bed   breathing
he said to us   back there in the house on the hill
I'm going   after scares vigils the descent
to blow glass   hyaline   and its stations
oh   WAVE, DURABLE FIRE   she'd gone
yes   A SEA AZURE A CLEAR SKY
and   went   off   to   measure   up
the workshop

a pot of tea
at six o'clock   vantage
a quiet smoke looking at   points
the day beginning   dear Phoeb it's
black as the proverbial or   almost sunrise
you could reach out and touch the mountain
bare maybe   funny and unpredictable
or snow down to the ranges   any time of year   some
I'll be very low key he said   horsetrading
at least   JACKIE V. THE BANDITS   a bloody performance
for starters   workbooks on the stairs   Jack at his shirtiest
read   guns smoking in the manager's office   best
about it   the rushes show them all shaking hands afterwards
at Lucy's Gully the redwoods wave about   but he's gone
in powerful upper airs   she was the only one saw him go
in the grove itself   break apart in her arms
shelter   she didn't MISS a thing   the tears
he might have courted her there POLYVALENCE   came
a Taranaki girl from way back   into her heart
good at connections   a survivor   then she called us
you aren't going to hear   these shapes (snarl)
but here you are   reading them
right onto it   touch and turn   around
half a world away he's there don't
take it too hard   cry now
Phoebe dear

```
                    dear bird
          there it is      stormy locus
      MATER CARA       of your conception
    she who is beloved        chick you are care
    staying up late             and it will keep you
  again        the sailors        take care      nestling
    Mother Carey        call you         your stars prove gentle
  a lineal sign          out in the waves         singing NOW
   to kick away     WELCOM SOMER WITH THY SONNE SOFTE
  suckling     from        this time he's gone to learn        (huh)
 they knead the soft belly         from Master Lino        one's
 fierce          they tear              (the best)       good two
tiger eyes      then spring off     swinging        better get them
lock          away        planetary   December babies        all
that perfect    distance from     rings        three a            pride
down curve when        her      off the punty        of tigers
 The Child sets in          turn around and        full eyes
   drives deeps and skies        planetary    it's done            like
   winds howling around the tank            reading painting
      Mercator's world isn't everything there is        pictures
       aerodynamically the        old lingua letters
        edge        a set of reef breaks            singing
          where        four metre faces      HO the tiger
            someone is        attempting      the
               always        nemesis
                    cutting loose
```

from Blue Irises

1

I wanted to mouth you all over

spring clouds spring rain spring

tenderness of afternoons spent

blazing trails to this

place where breath roars through

the famous architecture of a poet's ear

Rose and peony buds and tongue

ichthyous tumble honey and pearl —

the runner's foot has touched and adored

wistaria sprang after you, figs tipped

green air astounded by your passage

to the audient quays of the city

Now it begins, another voyage after nemesis

blue-eyed with the distance of it all

2

I didn't know about this passion

for oh she is also mine

delirium tympanis from the Portuguese

wind in her hair alongside us here

on the deck unhidden she slows your reading down

Fine ground darkness pours into the vessel

beans and flowers adorn the fall —

ichor! ichor! drink to the eyes locked on yours

the mouth that smiles and will speak for itself

I have always done the talking and she

put the words in my mouth saying do melisma

like sunlight be melisma like no sunlight pressed

redness before dark print an iris on her

& do melisma like sunlight astir oh & os etc

3

from the corner of this mouth take

kisses that begin in moonlight

and pitch slow fire over a history of you

reeling in the universe   Rhapsode

you and I have some walking to do, some

stitching together of the story so far, its feat

of silence, of sleeping lightly and listening

for the touch that outstrips all sense

in the hour before dawn   Look we have come

to the walled garden   See how the roses burn!

The lovers in the fountain spoon each other up

their drenched talk stretches the library resources

and when pubis and jawbone snick into place

you face my delight an uncontrollable smile

4

Honeyed learning!   I traced her once

to an island in spring, pointilliste mouse-ear

drifting down the margins   Then she was

phlyctena in the eye of the sea-ear reworking

a disturbance in my name   I found wild choral

allusions and scents that drew a white bee

to not-madness in the folds of her blue gown

This morning the whole world is wet wistaria

battered gutters running and everything drowning drunk

extends a big hand for the reprise

Which comes   Up the road on small trees

is a honey blue inflorescence I can't name

When the gardeners say cyanotis trust your ears

though rain fall into an open mouth

5

She made him a porpoise *gills a-snort*

because it was so hard to configure that body

The words weren't there or they rolled over

and supplied mermaids and mariners   For him

the language is a woman's body and she

will stand out in the rain a hundred years

running it back at him   Hast 'ou seen the rose

in the steeldust (or swansdown ever?)   Have

you seen a falcon stoop?   Hast thou found a nest

softer than cunnus?   Can yee see it brusle

like a Swan?   O so white! O so soft! O so sweet

is she   The sonneteer coughs sneaks

another look at her dolphin scores out

the ellipse after *his vibrant tail*

Richard von Sturmer

Born in Auckland in 1957, Richard von Sturmer was lead singer with the punk band The Plague in the late 1970s. He has worked as an actor, film-maker and writer, publishing two books of prose poetry to date. He divides his time between Auckland's North Shore and a Zen Centre in upstate New York.

from Expresso Love Letters

Monday 25 September

A walking-stick stands in the corner,
placed against the wall.

The day is a pale green Volkswagen,
heading towards a pale green sea.

Arms at the surrounding tables
are moving in slow-motion.
Each movement has a specific weight
(the weight of a coffee cup,
    of a piece of cake),
as if the people exist
in the middle of a long sea voyage,
and not at the end of a day
in early spring.

The tap-tap-tap of the walking stick
now passes through the doorway.

I could cry out: 'man overboard'.
But it's simply 'man returning'.

Into the outside world.
Into the late afternoon.

                              1991

from Dreams

As the sun slips below the horizon, a swan closes its eyes

At a Chinese restaurant, a Chinese waiter eats his evening meal
   with a knife and fork

A woman drops her child on the carpet, and instead of crying it laughs

In the car-wrecker's yard, fragments of window glass sparkle in the
   sunlight

A strip of red balloon hangs from the beak of a seagull

*

A man holds a bicycle wheel and walks into a cathedral

In the middle of summer, a band-aid has melted on the asphalt

A wooden swan sits in a bakery, its back hollowed out and filled
   with loaves of bread

A wasp picks up a single grain of rice, disappears, then returns
   to pick up another grain

The dark clouds are darker through the skylight of a limousine

*

Outside a tropical hotel, a hotel worker is struck by a large
   leaf

A young mother drives around the block until her babies are fast
   asleep

A chandelier of icicles hangs from the underside of a rusted fire-
   escape

Light shines through a blowfly as it settles on a television
screen

Lotuses are opening beneath high-tension wires

*

An ice-cream van breaks down right beside a waterfall

A dog barks, and snow falls from a tree

(1993)

JAMES NORCLIFFE

*Born in 1946, James Norcliffe has worked as a teacher in New Zealand, China
and Brunei Darussalam. As well as writing novels for children, Norcliffe has
published a collection of short fiction,* The Chinese Interpreter, *which appeared
in 1993, and two collections of poems.*

The True Story of Soap

1

the number of bubbles
in any given cake of soap
is not something that can
be computed with any confidence

yet it is through such
global imponderables
a cake of soap can spin
and briefly fly

2

you can clean most parts
of the body with soap
but you are advised to avoid
the mouth and the eyes

sight and vision
speech and song
you cannot hope to lather
such things with soap

soap is happiest among
feet armpits and genitals

3

a cake of soap
will not function in air
a cake of soap
will only function in water

in the water
that destroys it

we function in time
and soap ourselves
from time to time

4

to soap they add
attar of roses
secretions from
the sweat glands
of certain mustelines

this to disguise
the fact that
soap once had
four legs hair
and adipose layers

5

the paradox of soap:

the harder it is
the softer it makes the water
the softer the water
the more brutally it cleans

6

the hardest soap
comes from Castile

the hardest steel
comes from Toledo

the Spanish must be
a soft good-tempered people

7

soap lingers

it hangs about
like a pleasant smell
it waits patiently
until you lift
your fingers
to your nose

and then it leaps
up at your nostrils

8

the economics of soap
are confusing

is it for cleanliness
we pay soap the price
of dirt

or is it for dirt
we pay soap the price
of cleanliness

9

humans and cats
are each
fastidious creatures

but as we cannot
easily reach
our backsides

soap is a convenient
extension of the tongue

10

soap is relentlessly
literal
            neither
Pilate nor Lady Macbeth
would have found it
especially handy

11

soap shines
soap softens
soap suds

in the grammar of soap
these are transitive verbs

12

if there were not
{for example}
justice and humanity
we would be able to say
there is no
justice and humanity

but if there were no soap
we could not say
there is no soap

13

it is the tragedy of soap
to be soap right through

soap remains soap
until the very act
of evanescence

when soap
becomes nothing

1993

ANNE FRENCH

Born in 1956, Anne French has published four collections of poetry. For some years managing editor of Oxford University Press, Auckland, she is now Publisher at the Museum of New Zealand Te Papa Tongarewa in Wellington.

Eucalypts Greenlane

And now they're cutting down the trees behind the back fence
for their dangerous habit of falling on ratepayers' houses

sixty feet of trunk to the first fork & they shed blossom or limbs
    as
lightly 'as a girl' two men in peajackets with no particular
    grievance

fell them the white limbs chains bite into sever trunk
branch bough cast a red dust & then burn sap sparks red into
    black

miscarried & scraped out one red baby who'd not stick
in this fallible nest whose grey-faced father goes into the park

alone to weep where lately we walked 'I imagine the womb'
as a clenched fist opened as a blank patch of blue

sky where lately leaves shone as an emptiness I must hold carefully
lest it spill over leak out as a rented room

after an eviction this death which is a silence unlike that other you
'il migliore fabbro' at Karekare contemplate the black descent into

1987

All Cretans Are Liars

Consider the lie as self-reflexive, leading
to an infinite regress. 'Do you do this often?'
sincerely asked is easy to deny
ease being all or most of it, and I
compliant and complicit most easily. One lie
laid to rest then facts resemble bait
and thus were readily taken — picture it,
they say, the Backs, those green lawns, rowing
for your college, the sonorous echo of boys' voices —
i.e. a fly or finger to land a small fish
out of a backwater. That lapse or fault
was simply a failure of imagination. After all
a little water clears us of this act
and the truth is just a small and wrinkled thing.

1987

Simultaneous Equations

All day I try out simple sums
such as *in 1967* a year I can almost
remember as a shareholder with voting
rights *you were only four years older*
than I now am

or complicated ones, a kind of higher
mathematics of the heart *since you can offer*
her a house with an extra room and a Dishmaster
will she fulfil her half
of the bargain?

But my new differential calculus
cannot solve pairs of simultaneous

$$x = \begin{cases} \text{she will come} \\ \hline \text{if she came you would want her} \end{cases}$$

equations

$$y = \begin{cases} \text{my love can make no claims} \\ \hline \text{she will reclaim you} \end{cases}$$

which it renders as $x + y =$ $\begin{cases} \text{I love you} \\ \hline \text{she is your wife} \end{cases}$

It is midnight, the storm that blustered all day
has blown itself into stillness, the fire has died
to embers, and I am no closer to the answers
than when I began *when did I begin to love you?*
and *is it too late now to pull out?*

1987

A Summer Storm

Last winter I tore up poems full of animals —
possums, eyes glazed, blood congealed on claws,
dead faces grinning, entrails spread for yards.
Today in Cornwall Park it was business as usual —
nature doing everything it does
without fuss. Only a deep litter of leaves,
drifts of pine-needles, a few branches down,
to show for Saturday's storm. In the garden
yesterday we collected fallen wood
from the jacaranda. 'This will make good kindling,'
I tell my son, 'when autumn comes.' 'Autumn,'
he repeats, not knowing what I mean, the seasons
of his two years confused by travel. Today
there are no furry bodies thrown clear into
the gutter. Just the pale khaki shape
of a hedgehog, flattened out, desiccated, brittle,
lifting and curling like a sheet of paper.

1987

All You May Depend On

At heart it is not without
complications, which is why
there are several houses and children
and any number of marriages
and the red queen does not lie
neatly next to the black king but falls
crooked on a jack
of the wrong suit

as though they had been blown into dis-
arrangement by a strong wind
such as a sigh escaping
from the builder: edificer, that is to say, walls,
bones. At night you hear small
sounds there, as though they breathed; the bones
being a kind of tree, where the flesh perches, singing
and the heart a ticking egg in a nest of ribs.

That part at least you know to be illusory, and succumb
to an awareness of the fine distinctions. And you
are polite, restrained in this by a need to cry
out. It's an impulse which concerns old-fashioned things
such as possessions, intentions and the passing of time.

Take what you need. A white stone, the branches the moon
shines through, and a memory of how it would
have been, otherwise. They are talismans for a journey

against the cold winter nights, when a thin
man waits at the edge of the light. What
you have left is the conventional wisdom. Eat
well, beware small birds in the house and the song
of the riroriro which means loss. All this sun
which hangs down golden with dust
between the houses will go, and the rain,
a hypocrite imitation, will ease the heart nonetheless.

1987

The Lady Fishermen

Imagine Jane Austen in thigh waders perfecting
her rolling cast, or Miss Elizabeth Barrett
dashing off to the bush for a weekend's
pig-shooting. Mrs Melville perhaps, at the helm
for the two a.m. watch while Herman snatched
some sleep? Ludicrous. There's no tradition.
We'll just have to improvise (with improvements).

Take yesterday, for instance, drift fishing
in the dinghy off Rakino, five snapper in an hour.
Hauled up from thirty feet they screeched
as their swim bladders burst. Dead on arrival
in the bucket. And tonight I performed the graceful
act in my civilized kitchen: a sharp knife turning
one fish into two fillets and a pile of odds and ends.

Almost taken in by it, the poetry of catching
dinner, the magic of flesh turning white in the pan,
golden in its jacket of crumbs, decorated with a salad
of tomatoes and red onions as lurid as a paperback.
You might prescribe it as a known antidote to *branlement
littéraire* (that common affliction). Emily, pulling
steadily on the oars; Janet, slicing up the mullet bait.

1990

Cabin Fever

Three weeks of cyclone weather, and we're all starting
to get a bit scratchy. From Vancouver my brother writes
that he's practising for global warming. Rain every day for
weeks. On CBC Stereo they're predicting a green Christmas;
further east the live Xmas tree companies will be going belly

up. Can you blame them? Here at least I can still get out
and run, even in rain, I tell myself, even in a thirty-knot
easterly. Have you noticed the sound of rain on a Moreton
Bay fig, for instance, Captain Fyans? Dry and pellety. Or
the way the black ones grunt and snort as the wind lashes

them, as though they're alive? See, now that we're out here,
how it is the tracks in the park fill up first with water,
down there on the edge of the paddock, or up here, on the lawns.
Not that I run this way much, not since the car backed up, and I
took off in the dusk like a rabbit, running towards the light.

Six of them. I'd have had no show. Today I stay clear of the
    road,
take note of parked cars and moving ones, and plan my route
towards the houses in case of trouble. From a distance the mutter
of the city rises towards me. *Time were simpler, once: given
a length of four by two and some fencing wire a bloke could
    invent*

*anything really, art unions, smoko, ladies a plate, all your major
social institutions, race relations included.* Sheilas didn't run,
either — away or for any other reason. So you could say they,
i.e. the jokers in the car, were only trying to reclaim
the recent past using what was near, and served. It all depends

on where you're looking from. The country viewed from an Air New
Zealand F27 on a misty winter morning might just resemble a J
boat, very broad in the beam, sailing bravely south away from
Europe and towards the ice, or a waka, small as a room,
    unstable
in a big swell, blown off course and heading nowhere in particular.

                                                                    1990

DINAH HAWKEN

Born in Hawera in 1943, Dinah Hawken works as a counsellor in Wellington. The first of her three collections, It Has No Sound and Is Blue, *won the 1987 Commonwealth Poetry Prize for Best First Book.*

from Writing Home

1.

Bev, it's easy in this crudely driven
city to betray what is delicate

and what is deep. I'm writing 'delicate' and 'deep'
to you because they're exhausted

words and to avoid them now I know
would be a greater betrayal. Recently I've wanted to breach,

like the female whale I saw in 'Natural History',
right out of this pack (this pod!) of sparring males,

twist my massive body in the air
and land on the ocean with an almighty crash.

Behind me, behind her, at the precise moment
of suspension in the photograph

are the volcanos of western Maui, halfway
between here and home, halfway between you and me.

2.

It's October and the deciduous trees
and the homeless people I know are wrenching

me into their exposed tenacious lives.
Across the river, which still endlessly

saves my soul by running off with it
towards the harbour, a crane is dangling its steel claw.

Winter swings down so fast on Martha, Steve and George.
Already they're in their thick coats. Already

they need to dream of spring while I'm dreaming of them
trying to bring them directly and deeply inside.

The trees though go on as usual accepting everything
like the holy creatures we'd love but fear to be.

Let's excel ourselves, they say, let's set the world alight
before the long clenched collective withdrawal.

3.

Judith is on the cold street talking to herself and I'm
in the park talking to trees. That's how lonely we are.

All along the New England coast oaks and maples
have been lashed and fractured by the hurricane and their leaves

have gone in shock from green to grey.
It's indifference in trees I've been resenting. And often

envying. But now I wonder why we think they have no senses:
how much rationality, on its own,

can possibly know. Coming off the phone to you
this morning I called out your name again and again.

Presence gathers weight by repetition. How we count on
repetition of our own first names. These oaks, on the verge

of celebration are intensely seductive in a contained,
oh Bev, in a crucially responsive way.

4.

I wonder if the journey from cob and thatch
in Devon, to rimu and totara in Taranaki — where

every tree was evergreen — is the longest my family ever made?
What we dread, at least as much as being snagged

away from home, is being confined inside it.
Madness easily happens either way. Igor has flickered off

like a tree with no roots into a world
where politics and espionage have a cogency

all their own. Martha has found some dough to knead and knead
in a trash can in mid-town, and now like a child

— or the best kind of clown — she is lifting out a carnation
bud with its stem broken at the neck.

If there's a knack to juggling attachment and
detachment, I'm writing to you trying to find it.

5.

You have to laugh and you have to cry steeply
— without friction, fluently — in this climate to stay alive.

Coming here, into the firing line, into the shrieking
shifting centre of things, coming here nine thousand miles

from that slow green complacent place called home
where — at last — I'd gathered balance, I lost

my lightness, Bev: I fell down my own hollow
leafless trunk. Now you see me nosing my way out.

The trees across the river are still holding onto their gold
and today, as I began to drift down without a qualm

in the first snow, between the light flakes came Martha
with her precise, grimy, ungloved hands and Margaret

outside the liquor store door, stubborn — with a stick!
All I've wanted is to sing the seasons in — in peace.

10.

Since you left the trees have been standing against the snow
making those small inexplicable gestures

children make in their sleep. Today they were strictly
still. They gave nothing away, as if

they themselves were the dead
of winter. The sirens, the long echoing boom in the sky,

the angry traffic, made no impression on them, and I stood there,
as still as they were, acutely aware of my human breathing,

watching the birds move in them, moving them, making them
    move,
and I knew that too many people had given up, that

too little had been simply given and I decided, tossed back
onto my own faith with absolutely nothing

to go on, that their outstretched branches were not,
as they seemed, an empty gesture, but a sign of life.

12.

While new leaves, like flowers,
are pressing out into the air

the paired outer husks are letting each other go,
settling back and disappearing into the branch's story.

What a colossal job they have done.
Lying down, on the steel tracks of politics and history,

part of the desperation is draining
out of my limbs into the past and into the future.

Sun is releasing the smell of things, blossom and dogshit,
and a mockingbird is singing for the first time — and warmth,

at last, is jostling in under our skins.
Homeless people are coming out — with unavoidably

mixed feelings — into the open.
How spring is here — with its double-edge!

13.

Some women will tolerate anything to become
profoundly self-possessed. Yesterday, Anne, leaning with her bags

against a stone wall in Central Park said, 'I don't want to talk to you
because I have been waiting all my life for this time

to myself. I want to be alone.' The U.S. has gone obsessively
ahead with another nuclear test. Crudely, profanely

they gave it a name. 'Mighty Oak.' Do they truly believe
they are doing something beautiful? Are they longing

then to bring their brilliance up out of the ground?
Perhaps Igor — since he works for the K.G.B. *and* the F.B.I.

and since he was born 'as a matter of fact' in both
the Soviet Union and the United States — is far ahead of our time.

'This,' he says, pointing to his soft toy, Santa Claus, taped
to the back of the park bench, 'is Yuri Andropov in disguise.'

                                                        1987

from The Harbour Poems

The harbour is hallucinating. It is rising
above itself, halfway up the great
blue hills. Every leaf of the kohuhu
is shining. Cicadas, this must be the day
of all days, the one around which
all the others are bound to gather.

The blue agapanthus, the yellow fennel, the white
butterfly, the blue harbour, the golden grass,

the white verandah post, the blue hills, the yellow
leaves, the white clouds, the blue
book, the yellow envelope, the white paper.
Here is the green verb, releasing everything.

Imagine behind these lines dozens and dozens
of tiny seed-heads whispering. They are a field
of mauve flowers. What they say is inexplicable
to us because they speak another language, not this one
written from left to right across them, made up of
distinct and very subtle, ready-to-burgeon sounds.

We need words to take us towards what words
reveal. But if words are ripped from their roots,
lose truth or become unloveable, how can we take their lift toward
what they could gracefully offer. Take fuck,
for example. Take intercourse. Take Him,
the all-powerful, single-minded, single-sexed god.

Having broken the argument down and down
we come to a place in the text — a clearing —
where a man and a woman have unexpectedly met.
We have been led to believe, remember, that one
will take advantage of the other, as we have been led
to believe that there is only one God.

How odd that there is no name for the place
above the poet's lovely upper lip
where fine stubble grows. He is wondering,
as his fingertips flicker across it, and as he
deftly clenches his broad brow, what else he can
say to his kind father and his kind uncles.

The plumbers have come. They're ripping iron off the roof.
They're tramping over her head with hammers.
Another hammer is sounding out in the valley,
striking a different material, a different note.
Inside she is living the oldest side of love, wiping soft
shit from the soft cracks of his little bum.

To examine her right breast with radiation
they are clamping it under pressure in a vice.
She wonders how on earth she let this happen.
And she let a stranger pierce her breast with a needle.
It's time to let herself sound out the longing,
and the knowledge in her soul of another way.

The path she's on is deserted. So is yours.
So are all the others which is wonderful.
To meet you'll have to wander off into the dense
bush where vines hang and soft ferns and mosses

cover the uneven ground. You won't know whose territory
you're in — if the wild-life's at home, or at large, there.

She's the fissure, the source where no one has been,
the secret to be discovered. She may be too generous
for you, and too ruthless. Too fruitful, too fierce,
too gentle, too precise, too sensual, too naive. Of course
she hasn't let you in. She can't. There's a collage of passwords
to be found and learned and loved and spoken.

She is in an empty room. A curved bay window
fills a whole wall and each blind is drawn.
She has no clothes on her body. You are naked too.
Being sensual and strong and straightforward, you can
kiss her left breast, and then the rest
of her body while she — irrepressible — is exploring yours.

Turned away from the lecture on sexual economics
she goes down into the sexual garden, under its dark spread
and into its detail: ecstatically branching magnolia, tuberous
roots thrusting up huge leaves. Fuck the tulips in their damned
obedient rows. Stop. They're finally opening their throats!
They have dark purple stars! They have stigma! They have style!

1991

A New Word

I have a new presence inside me.
You. It is a pale still day.

The tuis are really here,
I have seen them, three of them.

Thrush, tui — which is the more mellifluous?
A word I learned from Phyllis Webb.

'Drunken and amatory, illogical, stoned, mellifluous
journey of the ten lines.' If I could sing

like you, like her, tui, like spring water and
far off a rock falling.

1995

Quiet Hills

all her attention
has left her body

the most unlikely event
she has ever imagined
is actually happening

leaving her free
to speak your language

which I too want to learn
since I need to know
what to hold in my hands
and what to put harshly
or gently down

because billions of hands
are calming and triggering
these charged times

and in the city, Sarajevo,
she can hear the hard hearts
softening into song

1995

GREGORY O'BRIEN

Born in Matamata in 1961, Gregory O'Brien has published fiction, poetry and non-fiction, including a book of interviews with New Zealand writers, Moments of Invention *(1988), and another with painters,* Lands and Deeds *(1996).*

A Visiting Card

How lightly we
carry ourselves

that stirring in
the long grass yes

five minutes ago
that was us.

1987

Carnival

Sesquicentennial, Wellington, February 1990

Morning, ballerinas retire into clown suits
moved to music, a grey-nose shark is lowered
by a crane just over your head as you paint
puddles on the asphalt. Earthquake Survival
Day at the carnival, among truckloads of

golden sand — once a beach near Gisborne.
Rain on the pavement yesterday, the freshly
painted stars running oceanwards past the
well-intentioned lighthouses, a singing police dog.
Voices installed in walls — bear, rat, laughter

a tape of birds so the parrots don't need
to sing. The sun also ran. Never done a day's
work in your life like this, the Sacred Heart
Synchronized Skippers a backdrop to a career
that might have been yours. You too might have been

lost among these nowhere trains, your life
painted a blue even the sky could see through.
All those lives to be led but only one of them
yours. Where a peacock shelters from a
green paint-gun, a child asks 'if I was once

swimming inside someone, then were there
sharks?' Giggle palace or enchanted garden
the Wellington foreshore with lengths of
East Cape blowing among the stagehands.
A national event, a flying display, something

to enrich the soil before it's washed out
to sea. And if arriving is only another way
of describing where you have left and one hundred
and fifty years of getting here is just a job
someone did once, then this is what belonging is:

being lost in a low cloud of Gisborne sand over
Port Nicholson where a runabout is towing a
plaster shark into waters even shallower than these
while, on a distant shore, someone is shouting
for a forklift to move the string quartet.

1991

Verandah on Kauri Point Road

If the suit fits, why aren't you wearing it?
The broken parkbench has as much to say.
Already the Pacific Shelf is sinking

which means we're all living on a
volcano that's about to erupt, or so the
newspapers say. And there are people

out there who hold you personally responsible.
The world, after all, isn't all that's at risk —
there's Art and Knowledge, an end to it.

But don't hold your breath. You look
beautiful standing there in the midst of such
information — your floral skirt, just

the right amount of air, the flowers beyond
the skirt. Roy Orbison on the verandah and out
over the avocado ocean. There are laws

that govern what we're told, what we listen to.
Yesterday I overheard two lovers in the park —
I thought she said, *I would like to*

undress you
            with a toothpick. Around the
circumference of the park at a certain hour
the light reaches for its lamps, drawings

cover my floor — boats without wakes, wakes
without boats. My thoughts of you moving off
in the direction of themselves. At Laingholm

Maria has become, she says, *a grass widow*
her husband gone to Chicago to visit an elderly
woman who refused to pay her telephone taxes

during the Vietnam War because that was how
they paid for the bombs. The *grass* part of
widow infers, perhaps, an illicit wavering in

the breeze in the absence of a husband, Maria
laughs and, if you ask, after the barbecue she
will show you a slide of her kissing Ernesto

Cardenal in 1985. Imagine that on the living
room wall: the face of the Nicaraguan Minister
of Culture! The lips of a Jesuit priest!

And our friend Maria, *the grass widow*! Romance
always upstages politics, you might say. History
has always said there's prestige in keeping

your hands clean or, failing that, a smile
on your ankle. Remember the last time
we were in Rawene — the shops on stilts walking

out into the harbour. Graham said that last
century the governor of Hokianga tried to put
a tax on the ownership of dogs and nearly started

another Maori War. Out of his depth at
dead low tide, he might as well have tried to
drain the harbour. There was prestige, for

the Maori, in the number of dogs they kept.
The governor had to paddle backwards, waive
the new laws and let dogs roam free around the

harbour's rim. 'A parable in there somewhere,'
you said. 'Taken to kindly, such a lord should
know how to treat the penniless on his lawn.

Some people are so sure they're the high and
mightiest thing on two legs they never ask
themselves why they still need a ladder to clear

ground level.' Makes you despair that the globe
will ever find its way home. Which is about
as likely as you or I making it beyond here —

especially if that never-before orange sky
has been keeping something from us. Come a little
closer and I'll whisper something in your ear:

It is evening and everything whispers. The
problem is to find a way of avoiding taxes, of
drawing the whole lousy business up in one breath

and seeing what's left. Maggie, the other day
was talking about making bricks out of mud
the new Hokianga industry, mixing in flax and

leaves (moths, if you like) telephone bills
and traffic offences. Then assembling these
beautiful textures into the splendid mud huts

that will take us into the next century
if we are prepared to wait around that long.
Even the most changeable winds will still

be there and you'll recognise the dunes
even though they will have shifted across the
harbour. A motorboat will take us to them.

1991

from Sea Wall and Egg

Wellington Harbour

Such reflections as
flow from her

a day beside water
a shed feeding red and black

balloons into the sky above
the harbour, waves crossing

the sea-wall. These times
of day she retreats to.

Too late for you to
join her there

you might have lost
an afternoon, but gained

a towel, warm
across her shoulders.

1991

The Camera Is a Small Room

The camera is a small room
large enough for you or me
but one of us
    will have to
stay outside. A small room
with a red hedge
bamboo grove
    and mirrored sun.
The camera is a

home for old people. A small country
where the inhabitants

live simply
their long lives
pass swiftly. Trees grow

instantly to any size that suits.
The camera is a chatterbox
    of the eyes
a barge on the faintly etched
surface of the harbour.

An article of hope
    of fine weather
a brave new whirl
    its cool ripe visions
slowly digesting the snake-earth.

1991

The Ten Most Beautiful Women in the World

Flying junk, clouds thrown from the tops
of buildings, where we find ourselves

lost between uncomfortable bars, the moon clearing
a patch beneath our skin, a longing

or long arcade where we search our pockets
to find a coin small enough for a rusted slot-

machine, a converted pinball or one
armed bandit. We have not seen our mother

in eleven months, but have lately found
The Ten Most Beautiful Women In The World

in 3D. A shutter twitches, and night outside
becomes night inside their hotel or

emporium. A coin drops into the upholstered
darkness. The machine's two eyes

staring into our two eyes. Then, faded
into her background, (1) a woman

in a vast bikini, c.1950, only the pink material
remaining, brighter than ever,

hovering, almost, in space. (2) following: a lime-
green outfit, the colour touched

by hand. A fizzing bulb has faded (4), (5) and (7)
completely. (6) has melted down. Only the

artificial colours remain, these costumes like
flags of modesty. (10) dissolves into milk,

then a shutter snaps. And it is night again
inside The Ten Most Beautiful Women In The World.

1993

FIONA FARRELL

Born in Oamaru in 1947, Fiona Farrell now lives at Otanerito, Banks Peninsula, where she writes short stories and plays and has recently completed her second novel. She is best known for her 1993 novel, The Skinny Louie Book.

Reading About the Kendalls, Cambridge 1983

Poor Tom. Poor Jane.
Life was tough in the
Pater Noster valley.
People were odd a
toe was not a toe
a tree not a tree
love not love.
Only death a
prohibited certainty.

You coped. Wrote letters
words skittery as
bugs on a clean sheet
hit the kids ate pig
read your bible
skimmed the pit on
bottle or bed.

Your place was here
not in a country which
pitched under your fingers
that slippery bastard
of a fish flicking out
there on a tight line.

Here it was brick-certain
mortar-sure the eels
thousands of them in the
black Fen mud long gone.
Here the exhibits were numbered
words formed columns
God knew his place
didn't trick fuck
or grow in a tree.

Poor Tom. Poor Jane.
Tipped from this box into
a doubtful morning and a
country dragged
clean from the sea.
But it's tough anywhere to
twitch between life and death.

And what luck to learn
the difference.

1987

Charlotte O'Neil's Song

You rang your bell and I answered.
I polished your parquet floor.
I scraped out your grate
and I washed your plate
and I scrubbed till my hands were raw.

You lay on a silken pillow.
I lay on an attic cot.
That's the way it should be, you said.
That's the poor girl's lot.
You dined at eight
and slept till late.
I emptied your chamber pot.
The rich man earns his castle, you said.
The poor deserve the gate.

But I'll never say 'sir'
or 'thank you ma'am'
and I'll not curtsey any more.
You can bake your bread
and make your bed
and answer your own front door.

I've cleaned your plate
and I've cleaned your house
and I've cleaned the clothes you wore.
But now you're on your own, my dear.
I won't be there any more.
And I'll eat when I please
and I'll sleep where I please

and you can open your own front door.
1987

WYSTAN CURNOW

Born in 1939, Wystan Curnow is a widely published art critic as well as poet. Alongside Roger Horrocks, with whom he teaches at the University of Auckland, he has been instrumental in introducing American poetic practice and theory to New Zealand. He coedited Splash *magazine in the late 1980s. The date after each poem indicates the date of composition.*

from Cancer Daybook

Now that
I
have it
                (death)
        in my
        sentence

I'm the
more
composed.
     27.7.82

                    now to
            face
                            known
            facts
                  not yet
                            known
                                 27.7.82

leap
          (for Sue)
yes, let's
                    leap
into a
     leaf
              heap   7.9.82

Chemotherapy is
Not taking
life lightly
       5.11.82

                get   me
                for   not   7.11.82

JANET CHARMAN

Born in Auckland in 1954, Janet Charman trained as a nurse at Taranaki Base Hospital. She has worked as a nurse, a telephone operator and a teacher at the University of Auckland.

two deaths in one night

in each side room
a body
dropped in the sheets
after long pain
and a look of tense
hectic
between breath
fright

      we were going to a rugby party
      after work
      that night

      how we washed their bodies

i took down the cotside
and cut away
the drip
old dressings
and the oxygen mask

Jean said
i'll wash
you hold
      i held
      the dull blank weight
         against warm   me

    his unknown soldier chin
    propped up finally
    and we found a bit of carnation
    to stick between
    his tied together hands

    this was just
    the first one
across the hall
we started on   the other

    how we washed his body

    had to laugh
    in the low light of
    sister's
    office

sipping tea
waiting for the orderlies
to load their long white parcels away
on cold trolleys
    All that shit

I don't know how you girls can
Do it
     says the lock forward
brushing his finger into what he hopes is my breast
     Come down the beach with us —
     we went
     two deaths in one night

1987

the smell of her hair

i thought it an elusive citrus
but he said
'that's the scent from the yellow knob
on a wild duck's bum'

wild duck
and picked her up
'why aren't you a boy?' he said
and breathed her hair

1992

not so fast

my child's a limpet
stuck asleep

this eye's lid
excludes colour

close out the sun
look through the skin

to see a darkness
tinted red

i would pull down
your horse's head

and in your mouth
a kiss i'd plant

a solemn plum

1992

ELIZABETH NANNESTAD

Born in 1956, Elizabeth Nannestad studied medicine at Otago University and has worked as a forensic psychiatrist.

Black Dress

I like it, second hand, dirty and soft
I like the swing and the openings
Black dress given to me.

Who wore it? Whose waist's the same as mine?
And what say she wants it back again?

High time
she wore it.
The black's a
perfect fit.

I'd go up to anyone
dressed like this
snap my fingers and say:
Bring me sweet black tea.
I'm cold, so cold
the beds of my fingernails
and my lips are blue.
Make it hot
put rum in it
and spill it on me.

I will if you like pick up my skirts and get out
but first, speak to me. Say at least, That suits you well.
Can't you tell that I'm wearing
a material of hell.

                              1986

Queen of the River

Here the boat set me down, and I wait. The oarsman swung
      on the pole
and we came to the bank, lifted my belongings, and I got out.
Four days and five nights, the canoe does not return.
I waited at the river bank. Oh, the river. How I wept, and now
how dry I am.
                    This is only a tributary, and a thousand miles to the sea,
a lifetime to the other side. The river bends, or is it that my eye
bends what I see with distance and time.
                                        The military walk in the town.
The old giantess behind her stand in the market refuses to bargain
selling fallen fruit smelling of diarrhoea, golden and black.
She looks down. The tiny captured monkeys
tethered to her, they also look down.

In the evening I walk to the river, at the end of town
and I watch the sun set in equatorial calm.
I see the circles on the slow-swift stream
and I hear the monkeys scream. It is all one.
I walk back to my hammock and lie down.

Opposite in the street is the tailor's shop, a carbox with an open side
where the tailor works through the night. In the evening
his family comes and sits with him, a laugh breaks, and one sings out.

Outside my room the night has turned to flowers. The tailor's daughter
lines up her back with the side of the shop, looks down the street.
The military drift, looking in at bars.
                              I am the queen of the River

and I go as I please. The river is as wide as this arm of mine,
I reach out and measure the river with my arm and touch on the
     far side.
I will leave now. Why should I not go down?
A mosquito steps on my arm and clings.
My arms are bitten by the dark bougainvillea
and ignored by the spines.
                              I am the Queen of the River,
and I know by now the one song they play, over and again,
down in my throat I know them, all the songs to this hour in time
and I will drive the oarsman mad.

The tailor's little daughter kicks a foot at midnight.
It is cool now, and I who have flown in my dreams and died
stop sweating, pull the sheet up onto a shoulder, and sleep.

                                                    1986

The Kiss

There we were — two people
and a lot of scenery.

I don't know what business
you had to kiss me — now

everyone is interested:
the low boughs of pohutukawa

the shoulders of sand and the marram,
our radiant moon.

Don't stop now — think
how we'd disappoint them.

                    (1994)

La Strada

Let us call it love: your absences, your violence.
Take this in reply, a poem less flattering than the rest
I seal with my sort of love and send
towards a little man on a long road.

The people you meet, in their tents and their towns
are actors, people whose faces light up
before they turn around, forget you, and go home.
What you go looking for I daresay you will find.

I know what you'll say — what does she know? She exaggerates.
And so I do. Your everlasting meanness rules our lives,
your freedom by now nothing but a bare covering.
What do you want from me? Remember — I don't lend. I give.

Sunshine on a plain wall. I know it's there.
My skin knows it, and knows when it is gone.
That is what I like: the sun. And when
it is gone, I mind. But not for long.

Eventually God will dispose of us. He will
give us a number. We forget almost everything
and later, too, will forget what it is like to be side by side,
to lie and listen to your fist of a heart opening.

(1994)

Ramose

This was my station: wealthy enough to portray you,
not too important to sit beside you.

The wildfowl rise together from the reeds. The hippos
lie undisturbed in the shallows.

Our two youngest slaves
throw out a welcome beside the door
and winds from the desert arrive upon stone.

My hands hold you as the calyx holds the flower.
My household, my lands, I hold in balance
and together they weigh not more.

In all these rooms I most admire
your expression where I see my thoughts of you

and here I sit where I would choose to.
The living, tell me now, are they so happy.

(1994)

Immediately After —

Immediately after my grandmother died
we saw nothing had ever held her house together —
where we had visited her
for years and years,
the cunning old thing, time's unresisting
favoured daughter,
the path beside the house
was cracked, not even a path,
the boysenberry vines in the old chookhouse
not a garden,
and what we thought was a house
is only broken pieces of board, making no effort
to lean together.

Along the windowsill in the kitchen, all
those small things
are no longer there for a reason.

My grandmother is obviously not here.
She might be down on the beach then,
wiggling her long fingers down holes in the sand
after pipis.

(1994)

Rooster

A good man
is easy to find
as the sun
first thing in the morning.

That's my song.
One verse.
No rhyme.

(1994)

DAVID EGGLETON

David Eggleton is renowned for his rapid-fire delivery and spirited performances in schools, pubs and venues around New Zealand and abroad. Born in 1952, Eggleton now lives in Dunedin.

Painting Mount Taranaki

Mainly I was led to them, the casinos of aluminium,
by the gift of eyebright, whose hollow core contained
a vision of the coast and on it the cone shape,
like a pile of drenched wheat, of Mount Taranaki.
In a world covered in silica and
chucked-up alkathene, fibrolite, aluminium,
it is just a peak surrounded on three sides by water.
For the Soviets, holding down a floor
of the Los Angeles Hilton is a forbidden
progression of the open society.
So, to the French, whose own symbol is an ageing Brigitte Bardot,
the mountain, just the same,
could be a logo for the butter they've no-noed,
dismissing a country's living tannery with a sniff:
the hides of rain-slicked cows only acceptable
in the corner of a page by Frank Sargeson.
Corrupt innocence, a young brain, prodded Techtones,
featureless Features, a shot Texan burgerbar,
the list is endless but not one story seems complete
on its own, even tying up the numbered dots proves
less efficient than you might at first think
and, anyway, this absurd reductionist format is one
which can only begin to hint at the complex,
underlying reality.
Gossamer threads in air, truck belting down the drive,
irresistible wind urging on the silver mist threads
over the split, cheap graves and into green Norfolk pines.
During the Vietnam War Against Imperialist Aggression
I was schooled in classrooms near Mangere International Airport
as venerable millennium temples blew into
millions of fragments in lovely orange and black
negatives — in a variation on a theme,
a close study of the status of stainless, chrome, plastic,

superheroes revealed wild discrepancies.
Over the various eye-witness accounts
whirred the blades of gunships trailing and corpses
surfed by on an extravaganza of black Coke.
Later, as I put down another batch of jungle juice,
I began to learn that Man cannot live
on home-baked bread and granola alone.
So much up, I moved closer under the mountain
until I stood inside a convention of car dealers
in an Inglewood hotel.
Young and hopelessly flippant, I felt
I should be in an environment where it was easier
to make a buck and people were more understanding
about 'in' references to tribal totems.
I swan-dived through the sex-shops of Wellington,
reaching towards vibrators in a glass case only
to catch onto a picnic papercup then an electrified fence
as it threw the other way
on an elliptical approach towards the majestic
funereal mountain that figures at the violet centre
of the windscreen, first dotted before being laced
by the rain caught in the drum-machine motion of Jupiter,
spearing the side of a punga with a flaming asteroid,
the cosmos being full of Hau-hau vistas.
In the snowstorm black-visored Samurai rode on
hornet-yellow Yamahas past a chipped, white,
enamel basin on a window ledge,
a plant trained to crawl up that same window,
the richly decayed caskets of autowreckers' yards,
the tea kiosks of tourist stops,
and up the winter volcano to the extinct lip.
From ash to dove to puce to brandy
the undersea turbines smashed the tints
of the glassy waves into sloppy froth and stiff whites.
A litany of rejects from dye vats,
the unwanted energy of their beauty decorated the feet
of the giant for whom the many Victorian explorers
also left souvenirs.
A string tie, cedarwood fan, lace-edged cambric,
saddlestrap, sherryglass, wristwatch, nightgown, velvet ribbon.
In the centre of ferns they were given back
the ghost images of sedated depressives in the foetal position.
As I scrubcut my way around a backblock wilderness
as unknown as Europe it was I who began to crack, not it.
The mountain 'Egmont' rained down its ciphers as I slept
until I entered the psychologically tropic world
of heat and fever, lava village of the last upthrust.
Dealing with the giggling mountain, walking it,
you felt you had seen one of the quadrants,
fundament and crotch scored
between the arched legs of the world.
This province began to experience happenings.
A two-headed calf was born at Stratford,
at Bell Block at evening an old age pensioner

hung himself by his shoelaces in a Corporation bus,
Dow Chemical Plant mutated into a radioactive centre,
firing out supernovae.
Sacred sites became fictions and sensitised scraps
of computer card in plastic envelopes were irrevocably
drawn into the throbbing whirlpool of events.
A drudge in a hotel kitchen cornered the market
in replicas of credit cards by fabricating a deception
which played on the public's mounting fears of eruption.
His prolific operation soon saw him zooming
to the top of the money tree.
Bizarre mission for a steamy morning, hunting
through the underbelly's growth canopy
for signs of the tribe as showers sweep down
and a rackety V8 is driven from under
a dilapidated carport overhang with the rain seeping in,
the tribe collapsed like a rusty barbed-wire fence
in front of a wedding-cake house with soft pink icing
spelling out blushes and little tears of joy
in the happy hour.
Scrawny wetas skipping across cushions of green moss
on fallen old totaras. Neat, eh, to see
ragwort, cocksfoot, fennel, catmint growing
round a shagged dinghy on a rusted cradle trailer
as wraiths ascend supplejack and the beekeeper
is rooted to the spot with a curse.
And now with the art that goes through daily life,
the fundamentalist preacher, like a page of old history,
speckled, damp with mildew spots,
his brylcreemed waffle of hair catching the morning sun,
walks in the foreground of cones of gravel,
central and terminal.
Stained stacks of *Truth* newspaper in the skew-whiff shed
adjacent to the off-balance dunny.
In the wool shearers' abandoned quarters
a few stained, bloody mattresses, stuffed with kapok,
have burst.
Cherubim perch on the shingle, ice-cream
types of gentlemen swing their partners
like candyfloss in a spin.
A bruised young mother
with her mother in a trouser suit
and upswept wings of punished hair
recalls knitting needles of the circle clicking
like train wheels
in the pink-wafer light that reminiscing imposes.
Quattrocento fanatics didn't have it like this.
From them we borrowed cardinal red and pageboy hairstyles,
our larders and pantries stuffed with wholemeal loaves
on the rise, in ferment.
Beans swelling, sprouting out of their jars.
Nuts pouring from plastic sacks.
The stillness leads on into a chapel hush.
Grated carrot bristles. The dinner guests shrunk

back from the gurgling wine like tarnished coins
thrown into a pocket
the questing forefinger seeks.
A Model-T Ford carhulk planted
in front of the mind like a zombie chariot before the cult of skis.
A battery of children
winding in a crocodile, candles aloft,
their seed teeth bared at the effort of the pilgrimage.
Those ropey arms and flayed legs are not
starved of sensation nor the sharp black/white
as the light snaps on.
Don't knock yourself out,
Taranaki will be there in the morning,
the snow a gunky white blob of brilliantine,
an ornament, a gargoyle for Bat-Stud.
The town hall, pub, gymnasium and squash court cluster
below; everything we have learnt reduces to a search
for the pyramid they burned down.

1986

God Defend New Zealand

When young men no longer pick the peaches at the beaches
and the West Coast coal veins have been taken too far,
when the gold and orange dreams leave the crayfish pots
and supermarkets stop leaking Classical Gas,
        God defend New Zealand.

When the Golden Gorse hums no more with bees
and blue heaven's blackberry delights fail to please,
when old ladies brush their hair into atomic clouds
and Auckland pubs lose their sweating crowds,
        God defend New Zealand.

When teenage yahoos quit going on the razzle
and the Tasman Sea gives up its dazzle,
when the cow-nipple of green Taranaki ceases to spout
and the neon sky-writing of Newmarket goes out,
        God defend New Zealand.

When Henderson's purple river of wine won't flow
and the waving wheat carpets of Canterbury don't grow,
when the fruit machine of juicy Nelson breaks down
and bobby-calf trucks buzz off from one-horse towns,
        God defend New Zealand.

When the salt lake vanishes from lonesome Marlborough
and Otago's blooming cherry trees no longer bother,
when Japanese power tools blow up as they shape the land
and kids will not play on the crystal sand,
        God defend New Zealand.

1989

ALAN RIACH

Born in Scotland in 1957, Alan Riach came to New Zealand in 1986. A noted poet and critic both in New Zealand and abroad, he is editor of the Carcanet edition of Hugh MacDiarmid's Collected Works. He lives in Hamilton and teaches English at the University of Waikato.

from An Open Return

The Blues

The lights are on all over Hamilton.
The sky is dark, blue
as a stained glass window in an unfrequented church
say, by Chagall, with grand and glorious chinks
of pinks and purples,
glittering jewels on those glass fronted buildings
where the lifts are all descending
and the doors are
being closed.
　　　　You're out there somewhere,
going to a concert in wide company or maybe
sitting somewhere weaving a carpet
like a giant tapestry, coloured grey,
pale brown, weaving the wool
back in at the edges of the frame, your
fingers deft as they turn the wool in tight and
gentle curves.
　　　　Or somewhere else.
　　　　What do I do
　　　　except imagine you?
　　　　The river I keep crossing
　　　　keeps going north. The trains
　　　　in the night cross it too.
　　　　Their silver carriages are blue.

The seabirds are dying

The seabirds are dying,
　　　on the wing, on the water.
The sea isn't hungry
but it swallows them
without thinking.
　　　A bee's wings
　　the wheels of your bicycle, or
　　　　the long roads
all move without thinking
　　　Herons, those long and longwinged birds
(I remember one flying below the road beside the mountain
　　over the river's silver, in
　　the rapidly darkening valley, from

Loch Snizort, towards
the sea)
them too, I'm telling you, sometimes get lost
in the 'aimless air'

At Spirits Bay, the Empty Sea

'You cannot miss the ships that miss each other
ships that the wide earth parts'
the sliding waters meet
them all, and all the ships come in.
The Tasman nudges off the Cape
the sallow stern of long Pacific slants.
The Cape runs ragged down the land
and susurrates into the oceans;
Auratic, yet the sand is scald, is
beaten gold, the rocks as black,
the grasstopped hill
bright emerald, the lighthouse
lighthouse-white.
'Have I come these 20,000 miles
to be beaten by an empty wind?'
(The ruin or the blank in our own eye.
The axis of vision is not coincident
with the axis of things. Therefore the words (world)
lacks unity. Said Emerson. He sang:
Don't fence me in.) The palisades
surround the lighthouse.
Even out there
where the 2 seas say hello
to each other they're shaking hands
with rippling knuckles, as
white as waves are
on cobalt.

Waldo Waved his Knife

Waldo waved his knife over the plate. 'That's
Maori bread,' he grinned. I was
taking some. 'I see,'
I said. 'What
makes it different?'
'Absolutely nothing!' I was reaching for the butter.
'But there is,' says the Pakeha man
on my right. 'It's baked
differently.'
Waldo is eating (and smiling)
raw fish and paua sauce, as I will,
in a moment.
'It's good' (I said) 'I hope
that you won't mind now
if I eat it.'

1991

JOHN DICKSON

Born in 1944, John Dickson lives in Dunedin where he works as a librarian at the Otago Polytechnic.

from Jonah

1

'World news in your hands —
history in the making.'

That's Newsweek's claim
not mine, for the news from me

isn't so grand, like
I've had a drink or two

and right now
I'm where I was before

inside the belly
of a monstrous fish

2

           there's
not much of a view / in today's Newsweek

there's photos of bodies
lying in a ditch.

A massacre? an execution? Whatever
you choose

the photographer's hands
weren't too steady — the shots blur

aren't so well defined as those
for Singapore Stopovers

3

this one
has a hole in his head — at least

I can't see his eyes — this one
clutches at the earth

and this one and this one and this one
all of them together

having passed right through
without cameras, without traveller's cheques

without the pulse of blood
as mine beneath my wrists

4

the worst thing
about the belly of the fish   is that

in here it's not that bad. I mean
I won't start wearing sackcloth and ashes

nor will I cry for the vengeance of the Lord.
Instead, I shall grin

I shall saunter through all the streets
I shall cruise for whatever comes my way

because I, like you
can get used to stinking fish

8

up here on Highgate where the Mercedes
and Daimlers slide past

on their axles of grease, you can see
the economic miracle is working: and the sign

is not the cars, it's processed
food. On an evening, if you walk

towards the houses of the rich, step with care
for as you approach you will notice

a marked increase per square metre
of the size and amount of dog shit

11

poppy day

'we all know that Major Tom is a junkie'
but the young Maori woman slumped

against the juke box is somewhere else
her eyes gazing inwards as though

she's dreaming of a light more radiant
than 10,000 suns. She doesn't care

that merchants have sold her to a field
in Thailand. She doesn't care

that as she works the streets
the dark earth is filling her veins

1986

JOHN NEWTON

John Newton was born in 1959. His Tales from the Angler's Eldorado *appeared in 1985. His poetry has moved from its earlier purposeful revision of New Zealand's pastoral tradition to a more theoretical base.*

Lunch

Shorn in this weather the sheep get burnt
so they're trapped in clusters,
piled in the shade.
They'll wait for dipping until they get
patched up, comb-furrows
rust brown, mending black, and troubled with lice still
they work their backs
against the rutted trunk of the big macrocarpa.

Twelve o'clock.
When the shearing machines and the tractor
go off it seems silent
at first: then you pick up the sound of a chain
being wrapped around a fuel-drum kennel,
the thump of surf,
the blare of cicadas, the squeal
of hinges on a gate swinging open.

Or you do if you listen. And the high
square door of the woolshed frames
the breathless glare outside
in shade, a vehicle closing in down the hillside
trailing its balloon of dust.
The powerlines catch the sun like water.
Packed in the shade of the big macrocarpa
this morning's shorn sheep heal
and rock in the heat.

1985

Ferret Trap

A white hen sitting under the house
butchered, the nest cleaned out:
with a ferret about
the nights are full of noises.

They may show up in possum traps
but you're never ready, you never get
used to the noise they make when you
corner them, the smell, the coldness
of the fur to touch,
the body like a cat's surprisingly
heavy. The blood

on bait or the plate of a trap
seems darker than it ought to be,
darker than possum blood,
darker than the blood of a hen.

The dogs bark at a pair of headlights
creeping down across the black hill,
the chooks in the macrocarpa shift with unease

as you staple the trap to a wooden pile
and set it, sheep's heart jammed on a nail
for bait. You wash up, watch T.V.
and wait for the smash and the cold shrill chatter
an arm's length away from you
under the floor.

1985

Opening the Book

You open the book
& there unfolds a road   its skin is blue, it is summer
the heat   that dances in its hollows turns

into water. You ride it in the vehicles of strangers:
homesteads & haybarns   dusty yellow sheeptrucks
convoy of soldiers in jungle greens returning

from an exercise
slipping past their polarised windscreens;
you draw from them splinters   of lives made of words

though you never take your eyes off the mountains.
The mountains reach out to embrace you
they fold their blue ankles

they give birth to rivers, they
can even crouch like tigers if that's the way you
want them: they are a story you tell

about yourself, a story you are journeying
into, which swallows you.   You leave
the road, then   you honour the logic of ridges

& gorges, of funnels, of slotted
stone chimneys   You startle a huge bird
nesting in the riverbed, climbing on slow

cream & ash coloured wings   & you follow
as it disappears
inland, you tunnel to the spine of the island

& bury yourself   alive, with your possessions, this
curved sky, this whisper of ice-cloud
this magic mountain slamming shut behind you.

(1985)

Blood Poisoning

Cold-start mornings   tractor coughing blue smoke
a child's landscape blanketed in frost

Trailer   rocking
haybale, chainsaw, two-stroke fuel in a Gordon's bottle;
animals in blithe
possession of their element, the way that sheepdogs
sidle out of the path of a moving vehicle

Tractorbox:
rubber rings, long-handled pliers,
penicillin, pocket-knife, amyl nitrate, Park Drive

Hot greasy naked
skin of a ewe's armpit:
blunt needle, angry purple udder

A child's landscape: forest of frost
seagull sideways at a safe distance   head cocked

Watchfulness, hunger, bloodlust,
greed: percussion in a dog's throat
gulping   afterbirth

(1989)

KIM EGGLESTON

Born in 1960 in Picton where she presently lives, Kim Eggleston has published three collections of poetry: From the Face to the Bin, 25 Poems and, with others, The Whole Crack.

This Heart of Mine

My cigarette tastes like a cypress
bending cool over the lagoon
My legs are long enough
to circle the moon

I am Paris
the avenue
the gargoyle over the door

the gull on the roof
the ripped fish net
the dancer bleeding raw

Buy me drinks
Sweep me off my feet
All the casking in the world
will never put you close to me

You can stand at the entrance
to this heart of mine

But these glasses
will not wash themselves
for that wine.

                    1984

Invisible

When a dry wind scrapes
in over low shoulders
of sea, bangs into the house rattling

quills, knots of Chinese
cooking pots, cards
from people gone
to Glasgow, Tokyo
or just disappeared
under dancing sand
and the kitchen is filled
with burnt chicken bones

and African violets,
she stands naked
at the window
reciting dates and places.

She wanders through water
fuchsias, nikau,
banana palms

spilling wine for the dog.
Keeps her back to the wall
like Delmore Schwartz
in a restaurant, her arm

holding the glass
wide as helicopter blades.

                    (1992)

LEIGH DAVIS

Born in 1955, Leigh Davis edited, with Alex Calder and Roger Horrocks, the icono-clastic literary journal AND during the mid-1980s. Since then he has worked as a merchant banker and has published little poetry.

from Willy's Gazette

You're a big ghost, Jim St. John,
nice sheen on your forehead and noseridge's catchy,
spread over the billboard, nine years later . . .
I was in the mind for Jerusalem, but early Willy's like
a 1972 *Listener*. Barefoot for forty miles in the rain,
kenosis, (who were you reading?) . . .
Then our literati were known for their sandals,
their misery . . . & talent, leisure, demography,

capital markets, blew old icons up
into large collected poems, where the audience knew
the hagiography, or were instructed: 'What is the inward
part, or thing signified? The Body of Christ, taken indeed . . .'

Who was Gaudier-Brzeska? (For what Willy assumes
you shall assume, take it upon yourself).

*

. . . such white details, such chickenwire . . .
I'm closer to Pearse than before,
S is a relation, Willy's a relation
to speak of, a marionette, a boundary,
mundane without clogs embroidery
or land his own Dakota
like Pearse, who was the first to fly —
which is not complex but circles a simple stance,
hot goats on the hill, there is a frontier
for Willy to cross, lumbering surfcast
to repeat, the elements are all there —
I'm describing what is fundamentally my own,
a huge pole, a ridge, over Mahia,
which is like Morocco

*

Big loose Perry Ellis blazers and pumpkin
sashes, flared skirts — these are
the currents the summer's political gestures
Paris off beam a moue a fichu
on the young woman that blooms
left in the photograph upon a slow draft,
somebody puts a flag together . . .
cunningly ruched their mustard/royal
blue shoulders . . . Turn up on any day
take in the chalk of raw cottons
with your papers in the park rough
cummerbunds touches like that Willis around
Mykonos its brindled landscape of plasterhouses
and blue bleached cambric

*

years rising in the early morning
as anonymous dancers like croci
yellow and blue with round thighs
and small wrists these cutouts
pacing endlessly over the background,
dans les magasins / it's very artistic downtown.

says Willy, carrying hs thoughts like a
pubblicazione about unfurled but
manifold as bonbons paper is bliss
the way it curves back the magazine a
strange warehouse behind enemy lines,
these ideas (but my fear of reading, Giovanni,

when Jamayca is in the library) a cache . . . &
de novo, le pa-twah de l'oiseaux

*

The patois de birds in the tree's
getting free and loose with their English
off any way, broadcast from green
wattle station and Willy
his toast and eggs and coffee
also conferring plaudits plus dits
too wry eh and the morning is
attractive, non-paginal. All he does
is rise over the Reserve Bank
crying and hanging like a bird
himself silly in the updraft this exercise must
loosen look across you lovely Mount Victoria
houses your flat planes and two
radio masts fire your retro rockets

*

December 1979 in Paris was a bad time
to step before a Renault or a Citroen
when late in the month or the winter
you were feeling particularly
buoyant and the plane trees
had an attractive appearance
& you were considering a diagram that's got
giant spokes and guywires wheels and
turned pulleys that's attached to
Leonardo and his hazardous
design for a drive . . . it's a formerly
graceful vehicle longhand at various points
propped up as I recall with a man's image underneath . . .
Barthes was better than ten Frank Wrights.

*

Marking the occasional paper
indian file, so formal, peering
after the liner (the daisywheel)
in the common way, how it lowers
into the blue sea . . . still there you find
him, so textile end on, flat as that
& so transferred, taking a shiver
down his spine, and the cabbage tree claps
its swords over the setting sun
turning as if to say
mouth open, exclamatory
so armature you were so ready
so gestetner, old and dizzy,
& your line so charcoal grey and endless

1983

J. C. STURM

J. C. Sturm was born in 1927 in Taranaki. After working most of her life as a librarian in Wellington, she retired recently to Paekakariki. During the 1950s and 60s she published short stories which were eventually collected in The House of the Talking Cat *(1983). More recently, she has published poetry in* Landfall, Te Ao Marama 1, Kapiti Poems, Hecate *and other publications.*

Maori to Pakeha

You there
I mean you
Beak-nosed hairy-limbed narrow-footed
Pakeha you
Milton directing your head
Donne pumping your heart
You singing
Some old English folksong
Meanwhile trampling Persia
Or is it India, underfoot
With such care less feet.

Where do you think you're going?
You must be colour blind.
Can't you see you've strayed
Into another colour zone?
This is brown country, man
Brown on the inside
As well as the outside
Brown through and through
Even the music is brown
Like us.

So what are you after?
All the land has long gone
With the tupuna.
Nothing left to colonise now
Except the people.
Do you plan to play
Antony to my Cleopatra?
I mean
Who do you think you are?

Tell me all I want to know
Before you crook that finger again
Smile me another crooked smile.
Give your mihi tonight
Korero mai
Till dawn breaks with a waiata
Meanwhile holding me gently
Firmly captive
Here, in the tight curve
Of your alien arm
My dear

Oh my dear.   (1992)

Splitting the Stone

(for John)

You brought back
Carefully, nervously
A heavy grey boulder
From that other beach
Up north —
The place I call home
When I feel inclined —
A narrow iron strip
Between land and sea
With several old battlefields
Close by
And a guardian mountain.

On a clear day
If you are lucky
And really quick
You may see him
Even from here,
A small opal cone
On a blue horizon
Northwest of Kāpiti.

And then
As I had dreamed
The night before,
You started to make
According to instructions
A flax pounder
Like the Old Ones
Used to use
(Some can still be found
With other missing things
In various museums)

Striking stone on stone
Carefully, patiently
While I kept away
As I knew I should
Waiting for the stone
To split
As I knew it would
And let the Mauri through.

And after
Your amazed silence
I watched you set to,
Forgetting the pounder
And all those
Sad museum pieces,
And make instead
Like the Old Ones used to

A stone dwelling
For the newcomer —
A place to call home
When he feels inclined —

Carving it
Steel on stone
Carefully, lovingly
In his image
So the world will know
It is meant for him
And him only.

And when it was finished
You stood there
In the small space between
The roses and the taupata,
Heavy grey rain
Soaking through your clothes
And the pores of your skin,
And looked in wonder
At what you had done,
Nursing a bruised hand.

(1992)

CILLA McQUEEN

Born in England in 1949, Cilla McQueen has spent most of her life in Dunedin, where she currently writes full-time. She has been involved in numerous multi-media projects involving actors, musicians and artists including Ralph Hotere.

Homing In

Here again.
Darks falling. Stand
on the corner of the verandah
in the glass cold clear
night, looking out
to emerald and ruby harbour
lights:
                too sharp to stay
out long,
                enough just to
greet the bones lying
on the moon
and two fishing boats
homing in.

1982

Matinal

Alice on the croquet lawn
is nibbling   at the morning
high   as a tree she is
appropriately placed for
contemplation.
            In the garden
held down by webs
                anchored on
leaves,
    quiet as trickling
the wind unknots its branches.
Alice goes in to the garden
leaf by   leaf:
            such small things
as transparency in the sun's light
move her.
            The blackbird directs an eye
at veins   under the
skin: she watches a moment, and
laughs her
            disappearing laugh, unpicking
nets of shadows.
            Alice's balance
is delicate;
        yet see
the quiet spider journeying
from point to point,
repairing her small wounds.

                                    1982

To Ben, at the Lake

See, Ben, the water
has a strong soft skin,
and all the insects dance
and jump about on it —
for them it's safe as
springy turf. You see,
it is a matter of ensuring
that you are lighter
than the medium you
walk on: in other words,
first check your meniscus
And also, to hell with the
trout — you can't afford
to look down, anyway.
You and I have lots of
golden sticky clay on our
gumboots — the world
is holding us up
very well, today.

                1982

Living Here

Well you have to remember this place
is just one big city with 3 million people with
a little flock of sheep each so we're all sort of
shepherds
               little human centres each within an outer
circle of sheep around us like a ring of
covered wagons   we all know we'll probably
be safe when the Indians finally come
down from the hills   (comfortable to live
in the Safest Place in the World)
                                        sheep being
very thick and made of wool and leather
being a very effective shield as ancient
soldiers would agree.

               And you can also
sit on them of course and wear them and eat them
so after all we are lucky to have these
sheep in abundance   they might
have been hedgehogs — Then we'd all be
used to hedgehogs and clothed in prickles
rather than fluff
                      and the little sheep would
come out sometimes at night under the moon
and we'd leave them saucers of milk   and feel sad
seeing them squashed on the road
Well anyway here we are with all this
cushioning in the biggest city in the world
its suburbs strung out in a long line
and the civic centre at the bottom of
Cook Strait   some of them Hill Suburbs
and some Flat Suburbs and some more prosperous
than others
               some with a climate that embarrasses
them and a tendency to grow strange small fruit
some temperate and leafy   whose hot streets lull

So here we are again in the biggest
safest city in the world   all strung out
over 1500 miles one way   and a little bit
the other
          each in his woolly protection
so sometimes it's difficult to see out
the eyes   let alone call to each other
which is the reason for the loneliness some
of us feel
               and for our particular relations
with the landscape   that we trample
or stroke with our toes or eat or lick
tenderly or pull apart
               and love   like an

old familiar lover who fits us
curve to curve   and hate because it
knows us and knows our weakness
We're calling fiercely to each other
through the muffled spaces   grateful for
any wrist-brush
        cut of mind or touch of music,
lightning in the intimate weather of the soul.

1982

Vegetable Garden Poem I

The hardest thing is seeing
straight and saying plainly.
Some of this grass goes up
four feet without a kink. Then
there's the heads on top of that.
The thistle beside me is a city
of prickles and flowers visited
by bees. There is a lot going on
here. The sounds are: the gum trees
by the graveyard catching the wind
Mr and Mrs Potter's cabbage trees
a cock
a cicada
a faint radio
voices in backyards
the sea below the threshold
all the birds
leaves sliding apart and together
in the close trees.
Things are easily distorted and made
more complicated than they are.
The railway crossing bells ring
and a train comes out of the tunnel.
It toots. It is the blue train with
passengers looking down. I hide behind
the thistle.
A friend of ours shot himself
yesterday.
Imagine.
Sit quiet in the garden and get in
amongst it. The bricks the grass and curly
weeds. The sun is getting down inside the silver
beet. A double helix of white butterflies.
It's as simple as
peas and broccoli.
Growing is holding up your enormous green
arms to all the light and water, being
hauled upwards by the sun.

The solo cicada stitches all the little
bits of the day together diligently.
I can hear Margreta practising
her soprano in her kitchen.
Bellbird.
One drop.
A breeze.
The grass nods.
All day I am sitting in the vegetable garden
in the sun, trying to get things straight.
Trying to write.
Trying to disappear.

1982

Vegetable Garden Poem IV

(*On this side of the house*)

On this side of the house
there is no wind
the garden is warm   the broccoli
has turned into immense pale yellow
bouquets   and the spinach is going
to seed   the place zipped through
with cicadas and yellow and white stars
You know words have a lot
to answer for
                        when the subtle illusion
of meaning slips away
                        this vegetable
garden released from its designation
becomes a riot of architecture
carrots underground missile sites
thistles explosions cabbages immense
veiny roses
                        and overhead a creaky whirr
of woodpigeon and bees
homing in on softly blue
sun through short staple
cloud
                        Now I am listening very carefully
to these new dialects of earth and air

1984

Dogwobble

wobble bark wobble bark
wobble wobble bark wag wobble wobble
wag wag wobble bark wag
wobble wag wag wobble wobble

bark bark wobble wag
one two three a
doga doga doga doga doga doga doga doga
wag dog wobble wobble
one two three a
jellyfish dog in a toothbrush tree.

1988

Recipe for One

Take a Dunedin winter's afternoon,
a woman blown along the road,
a leaf, a russet umbrella
Take heed of the weather:

Take the washing off the line
and listen under the tree
to the storm coming seawards
over the mountain, cold taffeta

Take into consideration
the blackbird and the worm,
the world beyond the surface:
a jump through the meniscus

A glance, a chance, a step, a risk
a fancy, care, the liberty;
a moment held for time enough
to let the tones untangle.

Take all of this to heart.

Now,
take the rain

1988

The Mess We Made at Port Chalmers

Tongue-stump of headland bandaged with concrete,
Obliterated beaches stacked with chopsticks.

All of this takes place in shallow time.

In deep time, the trees have already recovered the hills
and the machines rust, immobile, flaking away.
Healing, the land has shifted in its sleep.

All we would see if we were here
is seed-pods moving on the water.

1994

KERI HULME

Author of the Booker Prize-winning novel the bone people, *Keri Hulme has published short stories, non-fiction and two collections of poetry. Of mixed Maori, English and Scots descent, she was born in 1947 and currently lives at Okarito, Westland.*

from Fishing the Olearia Tree

The lagoon is on the maps. Stars fall into its waters: wounded
fish shelter there. People live on its margins, and crabs. Boats
drift across the water-top, and over all, the birds —

You grow with the stories and the stories say:
a bird from the other side, the twelfth heaven,
a bird which left reality with Rehua and now flies,
its own shadow, between here and hereafter

you get hints and shadows of the pattern but never
a complete and steady sighting.

The royal spoonbill is here, really a beak with a bird
attached, kotuku-ngutupapa as the naming goes, 'a bare
black face and baleful yellow eyelids'. The little shag is here,
dancing clown attendance. And in August, the others come.

The lagoon is on the maps. The others build nests and rear
their chicks from bluish-green eggs, all the while elegant
        themselves
in dorsal aigrettes, nuptial plumage. They are not
many: the survivor chicks are also few.

We dreamed we won the land . . .
now we wake, and know
the land won us a long long time
an age ago.

It stands, a yard of bird in its adult pride. The family is flown
throughout the land: here the strangers, in green squeaking flocks
flutter and glean and ripen all autumn.

The heron is perched on my roof. It is crouched against the
wind, the precision feathering blown awry, crowded into
sharp-edged ridges. The heron stares with a cold eye at the
blood by its feet. The blood is from a shot possum. It would
affect the heron no more no less if it came from me.

    I bury the carcass in the compost pit — taihoa
    calling it carcass brutalises both:
    a corpse, is a corpse is a corpse
    — I mean, god help us all if I start looking on the world
    with a heron's eye.

The Chatham Islands olearia tree feeds well from the pit. It
stands twelve feet tall now, grown from the mere bush of five
years back. Yes, that tree is truly on the map.

The lagoon is under my roof.

The birdwoman hunts the lagoon. She stalks us all with her
    yard-long ivory nails.
She continues, hungry, you know the end
in your back, sudden as the heron's bill
exact through the water-top — you thought
you were safe in this air of reality?
She snaps through the crack, you are not Hatupatu, you do
    not escape.

The tree holds up my roof:
I have these things on my tree;
a paper kite in the shape of a tropic dragonfly
such as Chinese children flew;
a barometer shaped like a porthole in brass & glass
such as old ships never carried;
borer holes, much greenery, and a crucifix the spiders
have nearly succeeded in shrouding.
It is made of some dark foreign wood, and the corpus is silver.
The nails in the hands got lost in an earthquake.
I replaced them long ago with chitinous slivers I carved from a
    feather.
Highly symbolic, for me, at the time.

    'For that which befalleth humanity, befalleth beasts;
    as one dieth, so dieth the other . . . so that no one
    hath pre-eminence above a beast.'

Ahh, Ecclesiastes: we dreamed
                    you get hints
                    there are maps.
(You take a black path to my house
— that fantail flicking   there
            there
here   knows it.)

. . . .

My house lies
equidistant between Antarctica and Australia:
I can't hear a call from either
but a thousand miles a thousand years away
a wave rises in Hawaiki-nui Hawaiki-pamamao
and breaks here

on the rocks in the dark, the rocks at the far end
are fat with mussels: select some dozens
and steal them away.
Young shellfish, I scrape you so easily out of your shells ... aue!
so rich with the possibilities of life! Ka tangi ahau with tears of
    steam

but it's just a shame and your damnation you taste so sweet
   — and these extras,
peacrabs tucked in the soft security of mussel mantle;
   peacrabs loaded
with ochre-red eggs, taste a bit gritty but taste pretty good, as
   does a sea-spider
couched away here in the steamed mantle erstwhile cool home,
the little toil now still
of chitinous candy-glass legs, crunch. Ah well, we all
should make such sweetness, such douce noise at our going

'the sea hath fish for everyone'
      and so it is:

          What luck!
          A hen-crab, in berry
          and me with pot and appetite
          just sitting here
          ready!

A Taoist sage-of-the-beaches
supplementing the chancy gifts
with seaweed
and sad mutants that crawl ashore
. . . o they shout in chorus
     stick her in the iron pot
     try her out —

I go fishing with spiders
I go fishing with flies
sometimes I catch fish but
there is more to fishing than catching

the cloud of terns glitters blacks flickers glints as they wheel
foil and white wing and dark cap and reel

     so the bush is grey, grey the lake
     and the hills retreating greyly
     from the eyes
     and the rain falls unceasingly
     from grey and sodden skies
     while the steely bladed flax
     flexes and shines with/unholy sparking pride

the drone of days coming
     going going

and the black brooding bulls in Flanagan's paddocks

and the still white bird at the water's edge

. . . .

If this was anywhere else I would be worried by the presence,
   by the stillness.
But he isn't any kind of aitua: he has just finished spearing
   the daily ration
of waxeyes in the Chatham Islands olearia, fishing the bush

like he was fishing
an upriver pool.

    There was one tauhou preternaturally wary and,
      somehow, knowing:
as yet another bird was jabbed and defeathered while
    shrilling despair
it would whistle a single sad pipe.
It is the counter of kin-dead? The flock-heart? The one who is
    aware?

. . . .

There's a new moon tugging this tide
urgently upriver:
watch her rouse and swell
and burst the bulrush border — watch her now
over she comes!
fleet fleet fast towards you —

It's been Welcome! the rich feasts of winter
pink flesh of smoked eels, the tangy succulence of oysters,
muttonbirds grilled so their skin crackles and the sweet fat bastes
the kumara, the baked yams, the wrinkled salmon-pink yams,
and the tongue is tingled by a quintessential southern salad
pale cabbage and the glory of tamarillo — such shared feasts
lap these curves these sturdy bones with another inch of warmth
against the leaner spring —

so let us dance   let us dance

let us dream a tauhou: the mossgreen back, greyish breast
    and russet flanks;
the matchstick legs that can look pink, and the bright white-
    rimmed eyes.
A flick-quick yet plump little bird, seeming all feathers and
    squeak,
driven in winter by the fire in its belly
— must eat   must eat   must eat —
even after I cease composting the pit by the olearia tree
they visit, full of hunger and twittering hope

let us dance   let us dance

    but who can dance with the shades?
    Who can dance/without a head?
    — the music is no matter —
        It can stand leant forward, dagger beak poised
        so intent you hold your breath, so long you gulp air
        and lose it and wait breathless again
        the heron is not real, the heron is carved, an S-curve,
        immobile
        it must topple a wind eddy will the moment is forever
        the stab is faster   than vision
        blurs even a camera's eye
        the strangers see it coming

and dodge into thin air
except the one, the eyed, the paralysed,
that which is pierced and briskly shaken
from its skin and gulped
raw and squeaking still

sometimes the heron will commence to sway
a slow slow side-to-side sinuosity
and a hypnotised tauhou joins this deadly reel
feet glued to branch and minute shaking head full
of fixed and rigid eye

    as it dies
    they panic for a moment distressing the air
    they settle a moment later
    the heron waits, a moment.

1992

He Hōhā

    Bones tuned, the body sings —

See me,
I am wide with swimmer's muscle, and a bulk and luggage I
    carry curdled on hips;
I am as fat-rich as a titi-chick, ready for the far ocean flight.

See me,
I have skilled fingers with minimal scars, broad feet that
    caress beaches,
ears that catch the music of ghosts, eyes that see the
    landlight, a pristine womb
untouched except by years of bleeding, a tame unsteady
    heart.

See me,
I am a swamp, a boozy brain with stinking breath, a sour
sweatened flesh;
I am riddled with kidneyrot, brainburn, torn gut, liverfat,
scaled with wrinkles,
day by day I am leached, even between smiles, of that
strange water, electricity.

See me,
I am my earth's child,

    and she, humming
    considers her cuts and scars, and debates our death.
    Mean the land's breast, hard her spine when turned against you;
    jade her heart.

Picture me a long way from here —
back bush, a rainbird calling,
the sea knocking shore.

It is a cliché that once a month, the moon stalks through my
    body,

rendering me frail and still more susceptible to brain spin;
it is truth that cramp and clot and tender breast beset — but then
it is the tide of potency, another chance to walk through the
    crack between worlds.

What shall I do when I dry, when there is no more turning
    with the circling moon?
Ah, suck tears from the wind, close the world's eye;
Papatuanuku still hums.

But picture me a long way from here.

    Waves tuned, the mind-deep sings —

    She forgot self in the city, in the flats full of dust and
        spider-kibbled flies;
    she forgot the sweetness of silence in the rush and roar
        of metal nights;
    no song fitted her until she discovered her kin, all
        swimmers in the heavy air of sea;

    she had lost the supple molten words, the rolling thunder,
    the night hush her mother's tongue;
    she had lost the way home, the bright road, the trodden
        beach, the mewling gulls,
    the lean grey toe of land.
    In the lottery of dreams, she gained prize of a
        nightmare, a singular dark.

But picture her a long way from there,
growing quiet until she heard herself whispered by the sea on
    the blackest night,
and echoed in the birds of morning.

    Keening, crooning, the untuned spirit —

I am a map of Orion scattered in moles across this
    firmament of body;
I am the black hole, the den where katipo are busy spinning
    deadhavens,
and he won't go, the cuckoo child.
Jolted by the sudden thud and shatter, I have gone outside to find
the bird too ruffled, too quiet, the barred breast broken, an
    end of the far travelling.

Tutara-kauika, you father of whales, you servant of Tangaroa,
your little rolling eye espies the far traveller — quick!
whistle to him, distract, send him back to the other island;
I don't mind ever-winter if summer's harbinger is so
    damaged, damaging.

He turned full to face me, with a cry to come home —
do you know the language of silence, can you read eyes?

When I think of my other bones, I bleed inside,
and he won't go, the cuckoo-child.

It is not born; it is not live; it is not dead;
it haunts all my singing, lingers greyly, hates and hurts and
    hopes impossible things.
And Papatuanuku is beginning her ngeri, her anger is growing
    thrumming in quakes and tsunami,

and he won't go, the cuckoo's child.

        O, picture me a long way from here;
        tune the bones, the body sings;
    quiet the mind, the spirit hums,
        and Papatuanuku trembles, sighs;
        till then among the blood and dark
        the shining cuckoo spreads it wings
        and flies this hoha, this buzz and fright,
        this wave and sweat and flood,
        this life.

                1992

HILAIRE KIRKLAND

An accomplished young poet and literary figure at the University of Otago in the 1960s, Hilaire Kirkland (1941–1975) travelled overseas before returning to New Zealand. She died in Wellington after a debilitating illness.

Observations ii

daily the neighbour's dog is withdrawn to the park
ignores his mistress and courts her
the mongrel in a canine pas-de-deux
I have a dog most like to this which bites the heels of men

I must subdue it then.

my old dog blindly whimpers in the dark
hunts for its bounding hare in dreams
through my thorned channels and deep streams
and twitches bloodwet at my feet till I am rudely woken

so I shall whip it then.

I have a hound too weak and too afraid to bark
which cringes for the flesh that I withhold
and aching nuzzles me when nights are cold
till I allow my animal to feed and thrive again

it will devour me then.

                1981

Aubade

no white and coppermolten sky
could scorch my limbs

like the dry furnace of your body,
this hour before morning.

I need no false dawn for vision —
my blinded flesh shouting
sways up and burns with yours,
and knows its slow familiar aching.

but wake and see poor girl.
only sun warms your pillow
you are sheet-knotted and solitary
— and dawn came long ago.

1981

Clotho, Lachesis, Atropos

1 Clotho

I learn you were hurt my sweet and hurt again
    from loving too much
and of this wound and loss regretted nothing —

a slave in subject to voluptuous pain
    which caused you such
an ecstasy of bewildered weeping.

I the animal whose quick teeth nipped your vein
    now seize a bolder clutch —
lie down my whore you are not finished bleeding.

2 Lachesis

look at me sleeping I am somewhat disfigured
    like a statue from malice
with strong wrists and proud lips broken.

you the vandal in my private park who fled
    from mutilating this
creep back to gape at love so quaintly stricken.

oh then I grope blind arms across my empty bed
    and sadly wait your kiss —
and smile to think it is my hate you'll waken.

3 Atropos

I whom you touched am other things beside
    your only mourner trailing
an infamous coffin through each sullen rank,

friend you are dead your flesh is putrefied
    and no clean-smelling thing
nor memory obliterates the stink.

As for convention I have wept dry-eyed
   from numbness having
greatly loved you for a time, I think.

1981

MEG CAMPBELL

Born in 1937 at Palmerston North, Meg Campbell now lives at Pukerua Bay, just north of Wellington.

The Ancestors

They did not survive
by trading old grievances for new:
caught in Earth's pull
they put on flesh like widows' weeds,
making their poems in an ancient tongue.
Now, they protect us with their bones
just as dead branches shield
new growth from the wind.
Soon we will lift their weight
gently from ourselves, and,
begging them to watch over us,
but not to obstruct us,
we will nail them back again
to these rafters that are painted
black as night and red as ovens —
we know there is to be change.

1981

Calvary Hospital

for John Beaumont

That is the hospital, suddenly
looming over tired old houses
that shed their paint
and corner shops with absurdly
grand façades: Calvary beckons
its grim concrete cross high
on the gabled end wall,
and in the cramped garden
flowers and flowering shrubs
tenaciously stay alive.
You are in the hospice,
cheerful and laughing
at our idiotic jokes, though
it's difficult for you to speak.
You are going away, though we
have tried all ways to keep you.
Now, the graceful nuns

have made you glow like a choirboy!
We've brought our daughter
to say goodbye — today
she leaves for Australia —
and she smiles softly at you
knowing, perhaps, that you and she
are both travellers.

1981

Concession

for John Orsman

By a small concession
the dead are always with us,
like the outline of a missing limb,
an aching, recognisable shape
through which we watch rocks and rain.

1981

After Loving

While we lie hidden in ourselves
a moment longer, two colours
light up a world within.
At first, Chinese red
because we are happy,
and then emerald,
the god-green of peace
that follows when you follow me
while my hands
wing their separate flights
along your gullies.

1981

Aftermath

On a narrow shelf,
between steep hillside and sea,
small stones pack flat
forming a track where we walk
as the storm lessens,
and hear waves gushing
as though they scold the beach
above a deeper roar.
Cicadas rasp endless
questions at the trees

as the day grows hot
and the hills more overbearing
in their spinning heights.
You walk ahead,
past wild poppies and sedge,
your thoughts too widely cast,
your steps too brisk
for me to stay at your side
as separately we search
the flotsam above a boiling tide.
When we turn for home,
though comforted at meeting again,
our words are wind-driven
and stark as these cliffs
where no quarter is asked,
no real shelter given.

1981

Tess

for a grand-daughter

She is my swallow
curved in yellow light,
this child, reared
in the red glow of her birth;
there is no pain today
for her or us.
May our words form
a canopy over her living,
though books will tell her
less than a sky whose colours
gather to the west.
The earth is her lost bell,
whose ring makes all
sorrow recede. Being new-born,
she is laid bare to herself,
knowing the world's worth
and what to love,
seeing the truth
as a blind girl the wind.
She laughs with us,
not because we are virtuous,
but because she understands us
at this moment.
Dear heart, it is enough.

1982

IAIN SHARP

Born in Glasgow in 1953, Iain Sharp emigrated with his family to New Zealand in 1961. While completing a doctorate in English at the University of Auckland, he trained as a librarian. Having published three collections of poems in the mid-1980s, he has in recent years devoted most of his time to journalism and literary criticism.

Air

Air can do anything. It has that kind
of flexibility. You know this because
you live in it. You live in the air
and you peek out your window,
you hold out a feather,
you wait for special announcements
that come to you over the air,
you attend to the wires,
you breathe it in,
and check for evidence of tempests,
such as runaway trees, truant windows,
your neighbours' rooftops puffed abroad,
or your neighbours borne aloft.

When the air is well-disposed,
when it zigzags,
when it entertains bright insects
I suggest you go and meet it.
Be bold. Take off your cardigan.
Tango in a backless gown
with the air against your
vertebrae. Send up a kite.
Send up your legs
like Nini Paws-in-the-Air.
Feel the sky. Filter the breeze.
Fill a polythene bag
with your exhalation
and post it by sea to a blue whale
as a gesture of fellowship,
an emergency aqualung.

Then proceed to an airy spot
and build with a nonchalant air
a white dome which doubles
as a bust of C. K. Stead.
Perch on its summit and part
your hair with a silver comb.
Lean back. Wave to the whales.
Drop a paper helicopter
down through the atmosphere. Smile.
Smile like a Hollywood Pharaoh.
The world is unruly but it's yours.
You're its heir.

1985

A Game for Children

Animal. Mineral. Vegetable.
The same breath sings in them all
and once the singing's over
who can distinguish the dust?

I told my sister's dog,
'Hey, dog, brush your teeth.
Wash behind your ears.
Trim your toenails.'
I warned the wedding ring,
'The game's up, you rake, you hussy!
Confess your promiscuous past.'
I stomped through Albert Park
and instructed the English trees
to pick up their messy leaves.

I threw back my shoulders.
I stood proud and erect.
I used my mussolini howl.
But all of them ignored me.
They paid no heed.
They were busy.

Animal. Mineral. Vegetable.
What does it matter?
My hair is tussock.
My bones are long stones.
I do as the dog does.

1985

The Sanctuary

I keep dreaming of a high country
where I live in brisk blue sunlight
with a wise dog and a few good friends.
I couldn't name the place or map it,
but we own an adobe cottage
and on our bare wooden table
there's a bowl of tangerines.

No-one dares to visit
for a vast precipice shields us
from the far hubbub of cities
and there are no roads, no tunnels,
no signs, no radio contact,
no cinema, no moving pictures
except the fine shadows of insects
against the whitewashed walls.

We communicate by music.
We never read the papers.
We pass the days shelling peanuts
and watching our fingernails grow.

1985

The Iain Sharp Poem

Iain Sharp is a fat parcel
of mixed groceries
tied with a clumsy knot.

Iain Sharp is a black kite
adrift on changeable winds.

Iain Sharp is a pile of scoria
trickling softly to the sea.

Whenever I peep in mirrors
Iain Sharp frowns back at me.
It's terrifying.

Iain Sharp is a runaway tramcar.
Iain Sharp is a chunk of moonrock.

Iain Sharp is nine letters
wrenched from the Roman Alphabet.

Look there and there!
Bits of bright confetti
blow from chapel to chapel.
I chase them with outstretched hands.
They might be Iain Sharp.

1985

RIEMKE ENSING

Born in the Netherlands in 1939, Riemke Ensing now teaches at the University of Auckland. She edited the groundbreaking anthology of New Zealand women's writing, Private Gardens, *in 1977. Two volumes of her poetry were published in 1995:* Dear Mr Sargeson *and* Like I Have Seen the Dark Green Ladder Climbing. *She also writes extensively about art.*

from Topographies

Obsidian for instance. Certainly
this is a violent country
and artifacts were found.
Adzes, weapons. Also fish
hooks and in another place
down at Takatu Point
a necklace of human teeth.
*

Already 5 drownings 32
rescues & various mishaps this season.

On the older map there are two houses.
Pine trees are also indicated.
Some things are constant
for a while.

Clouds scud past the moment-
ary sun. We are caught
up in the drift of things.

This is the second Sunday after
Epiphany. You are locked in the sky
on your journey east. I'm walking
west into the sun. The hills leave
awesome shapes against the red.

There is someone down there
weaving on the loom of the sea.
The currents shoot back and forth
the undertow shuttles in three
directions to pattern a fabric
of terror & joy.

What do you think of the weaving
I ask James. From where I stand
the foam & water crashes
an amazing spread of crochet.
I like his image. He tells me
use it.

You note the Greeks keep appearing oddly
congruous in this landscape.
Penelope & Orpheus. The memories
of Odysseus haunting rock
& shadows. Something old
here. Older.

*

The poem has been held up
by domestic detail one might feel
at home with. The scraping of a door
back to the bare wood.
Uncovering it of layers of paint/
discovering it in the fine gold
grain we call kauri.

This tells me nothing of giants
with heads green in the sky
so high. Nothing about twenty men
circling one tree and the saws
ripping for weeks before the tear /
ing timber scarred the hill, falling.

Nothing of that dreadful silence
after   and the burning.

*

One tree to build a settlement /
church and all.

1984

Naming

The son is named after his mother's
father. Theo for short. Gift from God. His
sons carry the respective names
of grand and great-grand fathers. Men
are important.
Hendrik Joseph
Theodorus Dirk
One way of keeping close
to family we'll never see again
except in photographs. Two
for Calvin, one Catholic
and a communist who rolled ball-bearings
down the street during the union strikes. He lost
an eye on a wharf loading timber and didn't
smile much. Our son too bears the weight
of history. Generations of settlement
here and elsewhere across oceans/all leaving
their small stories on the postage stamp
landscape of our existence. All scattered
and gone/on journeys into pages
of mythology.
The younger branch opts for modernity.
They are not migrants.
They name their children after clowns, gods,
a Russian princess counting pence
in Woolworths after the Revolution. Anything
not to hear those schmaltzy songs
expatriates might sing, hand over bleeding
heart in postures of melancholy. Everything
to avoid the pain of past/images of eyes
asking too many questions/arms raised
in wavering
farewells.

                                                    (1989)

A P I R A N A   T A Y L O R

*Apriana Taylor was born in 1955 in Wellington. Of Te Whānau-ā-Apanui, Ngāti
Porou and Ngāti Ruanui descent, he spent part of his childhood in Bangkok. After
studying at Massey University, he worked variously as a carpenter, journalist, fisherman and actor. He is currently based in Wellington where he is involved in Maori theatre initiatives. He is best known for his two short story collections,* He Rau Aroha: A
Hundred Leaves of Love *(1986) and* Ki te Ao: New Stories *(1990).*

Sad Joke on a Marae

Tihei Mauriora I called
Kupe Paikea Te Kooti
Rewi and Te Rauparaha
I saw them

grim death and wooden ghosts
carved on the meeting house wall.

In the only Māori I knew
I called
Tihei Mauriora.
Above me the tekoteko raged.
He ripped his tongue from his mouth
and threw it at my feet.

Then I spoke.
My name is Tu the freezing worker.
Ngati D. B. is my tribe.
The pub is my Marae.
My fist is my Taiaha.
Jail is my home.

Tihei Mauriora I cried.
They understood
the tekoteko and the ghosts
though I said nothing but
Tihei Mauriora
for that's all I knew.

1979

Te Kooti

Once hāngi grew
like melon pregnant bellies
full of black and white flesh.

Now the stones are cold.
Te Kooti is dead
under incubus earth.

We are ashes of his fire
dead a hundred years.

Safe in our houses
we have stripped him
to a feather in the wind
as distant as a morepork
that calls in the night.

1979

A Departure

The sea lashed rocks
like broken teeth
where alone he stood
with waves crashing
the song of time's whiplash tongue.

Alone on the beach
he watched the sun

plunge into the sea.
And felt his life
like a river bleed dry.

He saw a fish
stripped tossed and speared
by the beak
of a flesh-gobbling gull.

His mind snapped.
His heart thumped memories
from the spring of his days.

Then later in the morning light
with the sun
flung skywards from the sea
he visioned life and death
bodylocked like Siamese twins.

He saw an Island born
to the storm's swirl and thrust
and felt the ocean suck
the marrow
from his mountain bones.

And without fear
he released eighty years
to the outgoing tide
for he understood
his journey uncurled
the fish the sea
the Island and the sun.

1979

Taiaha Haka Poem

I am Te-ngau-reka-a-tu
I once danced with killers
who followed the War God
beyond the gates of hell
to kill in the gardens of pleasure

I am the taiaha left among people
who dance and twirl poi
in gaudy halls
of plastic Maoridom

Father give me guts
Evil one why
have you forsaken me

1979

The Womb

Your fires burnt my forests
leaving only the charred bones

of totara rimu and kahikatea

Your ploughs like the fingernails
of a woman scarred my face
It seems I became a domestic giant

But in death
you settlers and farmers
return to me
and I suck on your bodies
as if they are lollipops

I am the land
the womb of life and death
Ruamoko the unborn god
rumbles within me
and the fires of Ruapehu still live

1979

B R I A N   T U R N E R

Born in 1944 in Dunedin, where he still lives, Brian Turner works as a freelance
writer and editor. As well as poetry, he has written widely on sports, recreation and
environmental issues.

The Initiation

Use a decent length of No. 8:

make sure you get it in deep, right
to the back of the burrow
if you have to.

Push and probe
until you feel the bastard
trying to squirm out of the way

then when you feel you've got it cornered
shove it in
and twist like hell
until you've got the bastard
really wound up
tight (it'll

squeal a bit) then
pull it out slowly
like you were pulling a lamb
from an old ewe's cunt,

then grab it
and break the bastard's neck

the foreman said.
It wasn't *that* easy.

1978

Drain

(after William Gass)

A drain
is real, no argument
there. The water's muddy
and stinks; no argument there,
either, and the clay's shot
through with blue and gold
that catches
the eye, but your back
aches and the smell's
too much, eventually, so
you call it a day

and go inside, make a pot
of tea and a sandwich
and sit outside on the porch
you built forgotten, mostly, years
ago. You watch and listen
to the birds, and the nesty
clouds drift this way
and that and, on the other side
of the neighbours' deer fence
their latest acquisition, Pepper,
a month-old orangy-brown wild pig
assiduously roots and
snuffles, and you think

one needs to slip in to
a private space that's yours
and yours alone, sometimes; one needs
the lulling solace — is it? — of something
like serenity, which is — yes? — music,
naturally, and blue, blue that roves
over the sea as cloud burns, the blue-edged
flame of a spirit fire, the blue
that radiates out from
summer's Cyclopean eye, and the blue wind
that rivals the blue of the sky
that's bluer than a peacock's
when it flaunts and parades,
its blue
smouldering.

Blue's the word for the feeling we want
when blue's the meaning we need.
Longing is the blue of
beauty unassuaged and serenity's blue
is a hollow, airy place
where the spirit seems to levitate,
and a voice that could be the spirit
talking, says, That's paradise, that's where

you can 'Rest in the present'.

The sun glints through the trees
and the sky is suddenly blue, not
blue, then blue again; and
close to tears, you remember
you used to think
that you were lost. Back

you go, back to
the drain
before it fills again
with all that isn't blue
and can't be
if you are
all that blue can be.

1989

Chevy

Just what you've come to expect
of civilization, beside
the road, down a bank,
veined with vines

and a net of old man's beard,
a rusting wreck, a
Chevy of the kind
we used to ride in

over 30 years ago — Mum,
Dad, me, and my younger
brother. We felt we'd
arrived; it gave us

the novelty of status,
America's showy opulence
revealing itself to us,
slow starters, hicks

way down in the remotest
reaches of the South Pacific.
It was a key, a chariot
of the real world.

So there was a great old
Chevy, two doors
missing, windscreen gone
leaving one wiper blade

like a feeler
waving. Only one rear wheel
remained and the upholstery
gaped at us.

On the back seat
my son found
a yellowy paperback Western
about Zane Croker

and a whole heap of trouble
at the B-Bar-B; and also
a condom that had seen
better days. He smiled,

picked it up, and
asked me what it was.
He looked me straight in the eye
while I told him.

1989

Wilson Boys' Boat

(after a painting by Grahame Sydney)

I own it now. It is my visual,
my imaginary possession, more real
than real, and what's felt
as much, or more, than what's seen
combine to arrest both mind and eye
which wander and return
stirred as much by what's left out
as by what's put in . . .

which is, for instance, the washed-out,
exhausted, exclusive blue vanity
of the sky; the deeper, greedier blue
of a near-flat sea
swelling into the semi-translucence
of the one wave; and above all
there's the scallop-shelled
pale bluish lines of the clinkered
'Wilson Boys' Boat' on its black
rubber-tyred metal trailer, unattended
on smooth orange and yellow sand.

Tension lines the timbers
of such almost-perfection
and the boat's sheer symmetry
distracts, conceals the injustice
of its predicament,
and frustration's the space
between where it sits
and where it was made
and is aching to be.

1992

Fish

The child
asks me

Is it wet
inside a fish

and I say No
and he says

Then what is it
and I say

It's red and pink
and cool

as a tomb
in the morning

and he says
How do you

know except
when it's dead

1992

JOANNA MARGARET PAUL

Born in Hamilton in 1945, Joanna Margaret Paul now lives in Wanganui. Highly regarded as a painter, she is also known for her short films and photographic work.

from Imogen

in the green garden
a purple hose
streaks the grass
I hold on
to the face
of a rose

those distinct pinks
of almost trivial roses
in the room
began
to run
became
membrane tissue
palp pulp of flesh
the colours of inside
unseen.

(IMOGENS)

mouth
        like
a goldfish mouth is
             working at the breast
blue/wet & slippery
the milk
     flows
           down
in the blue wet/mouth
         lights shine
from the yellow shade   in the blue room
        here / now
that loose white ear
        like an (orange) oyster
           (smoked)
& the (lamp lit) tongue flashes out & in
        the corner of her codfish mouth

     like

hand (not by the eye) seen
        tongues
           of
shellfish (cockle) under the sand as the tide slips over
             at dusk

little fish
     (baby)
dont learn
    to
    walk
    on
    knives
      !

                OMENS
                      rose &
                The wood-pigeon / fell

                small boys flew comets
                in the park

       small

                a blue-veined rose

I scan girls faces for her
high round forehead,
& the soft pale limbs of
young children
new white bodies of
shorn sheep
enthrall me

for Bill & Marion

The flowers swell & swell at me
across the hospital room
across
greased lino
swell
yellow & blue;
next
a brown paper rubbish
bag
a white striped
towel a
stainless steel
sink in
fluorescent light
fluoresce
yellow chrysanthemums
yellow carnations
the yellow lobes of
irises
that are altogether
blue
& keep saying it:
their silence is inexhaustible —
this kind of conversation
I have never quite had with you, my friends
before
(the leaves are very cool and dark & smell good)
        yellow, yellow
          & blue.
. . . .

                              1978

ALBERT WENDT

Born in Western Samoa in 1939, Albert Wendt is currently Professor of English at Auckland University. A crucial force in the evolving literature of the Pacific region, he is best known for novels such as Sons for the Return Home *and* Leaves of the Banyan Tree, *and for his story collections including* Flying Fox in a Freedom Tree.

I, God Uphere

The land, it here,
The sea, it over there,
The sky, it way upthere,
And Man, he claim he everywhere.

But I, God uphere, know better
I know the land, it will be here,
   the sea, it will be there,
   the sky, it will be upthere.
But Man, he rise, he shine, then
   he fall to rise nomore.

So, sing now,
   sing now of land, of sea, of sky,
   sing now of Me uphere!
   But for Man, just weep,
   just weep for him
   cause there no other thing,
   no other thing he do
   but earn,
   but earn his sunset death.

1976

Town and Village

A town is made
of iron, stone, and wood.
A village is made
of palm frond, people, and great silences.

I am attracted to the villages
but I live in the town.
Why is this? I always
ask myself.

In the town I can hide
from the great silences
that fall at evening.

1976

Colonialism: Independence

The palagi Governor, he gave
to me an axe and some nails
of steel. He tell me
for to use them to build
a strong house.
I did that.

The palagi Governor, he teach
me the white face of his God
and Government.
I learnt that.

Then the palagi Governor, he reward
me with a musket,
and, when he refused
for to leave my house,

I shot to him
and he is dead.

1976

from Short Songs

Hands

In my sleep hands aglitter with rainbow rings,
hard immaculate hands which sell other hands.
I couldn't wash my dreams
clean of those hands.

Night

The night is a white song.
You turn in your sleep
and suck it through your mouth.
Inside you it grows like a child.

Parrot Fish

As the dawn pours through my window
I want to open to it
like a parrot fish slit open and gutted.
An emptiness to fill with light.

1984

No Return

Our village is reefed on the night's edge
under the heels of the sky.
Hungry mongrels snap at the wind's tail.
From the sea the stench of a sun
drowned among unknown islands.
No name for the creature howling
soundlessly inside my head.
Cocooned in their mosquito net
my children dream of their mother,
but the night holds no hope for her return:
her journey to Pulotu* has no dawn.

I feed on the creature in my head.

1984

---

* Pulotu: the Spirit World

My Mother Dances

Through the shadows cast by the moon tonight
the memory of my mother dances
like the flame-red carp I watched
in the black waters of the lake
of the Golden Pavilion in Kyoto.
Such burning grace.

Though I am ill with my future
and want to confess it to her
I won't. Not tonight.
For my mother dances
in the Golden Pavilion
of my heart.

How she can dance.
Even the moon is spellbound
with her grace.

1984

The Mountains of Ta'ú

Mountains wouldn't be
mountains without the valleys   ravines
and sea level they rise up from
They are
the rising high of sight propped up by stone
earth and sky
They can't be
any other thing (and they know it)
They are
the eyes of earth   gazing out
gazing inwards   contemplating the future
on the horizon line and in the depths
of the whirling retina

These mountains   the mountains of Ta'ú   are
locked arm to arm   blood to blood
and live in one another's thoughts

They hum
like spinning tops or Maui's endlessly
inventing mind   on fine mornings
when the mist lifts and the horizons open
to the promise of what may be

They creak and crack
like old aoa trees   as they dry in the sun
and the river dives and digs
for its roots   and
fat pigeons nibble the day away on
the sweet black berries of mosooi   and
in cold rock pools atua wash off

the night's stale smell of sex and perfume
their twisting hair with laumaile leaves and
for dear life trees and creeper cling onto
sharp slope and cliff and the air
is thick with long messages of death
in the falling

They whisper together in the evenings
in talk only they can hear
as the dark turns all languages
into one shape of the tongue   and
the ravenous flying fox chases
the ripe-papaya moon   and
comic aitu squeal in the waterfall

They sleep best
on stormy nights when they can't hear
one another's sleep-chatter
and the wind massages their aching spines
with tender hands

These mountains   the mountains of Ta'ú   are
above the violence of arrogant men
They now fit my eyes and heart exactly
like a calm river is snug in the hand
of its bed
I am of their rising
I am of their dreaming
and they of mine

These mountains   the mountains of Ta'ú

(1986)

GRAHAM LINDSAY

Currently living in Christchurch, where he teaches and drives a taxi part-time, Lindsay was born in Wellington in 1952. He edited the short-lived but influential journal Morepork *in the late 1970s.*

Big Boy

Oh ah yeah there's this little boy
(actually, grown man) standing at the gate

ostensibly gone to get the milk in
and god knows what for but the eyes of neighbours

are staring out their front windows
at seven a.m. at him

he's standing there
twitching his toes in the gravel in the builder's sand

imagining he's on holiday
it's really the beach it really is

summer! a crib he's at
this is the promise

pretty soon he's going to make a pot of tea
he's going to make a smoke pretty

soon he's going to blow it
he shuffles at the gate

lingering in the enlargement of the whole
misty-eyed length of the street

the blue breath of the bush
the peninsula's pink horizon

there's a cool water feeling of air
fresh on his face

and if anything's rooting it right now
it's those imaginary neighbours

peering out the portals of their urban warfare tanks
telling him, telepathetically

that you just can't stand there, pretending you're a boy
when you're a man, fuck it!

1986

Playground

The sun's hot on the playground
the bell has rung and what have we learned?

Maybe this one thing, maybe some other
pebble-weights in our brain!

Only a few things are for sure
mostly to do with time.

So we got out of that classroom at the end of primary school
and we got out of that classroom at the end of high school

and where are we?
Epochs have passed

the spring of morning, autumn of afternoon
midday's shadowless mysteries

on the fencerail overlooking the playground
two five-year-olds rolling down a bank kissing

Flagstaff sinking in mist and dusk
we are here and we don't know how.

1986

White Cherry

It's certainly amazing being alive
it's not going to last that's for sure.

Crossing the polished metal of Eglinton Road
watching for cars coming out of the sun
looking down at the brown and grey patches in the cemetery amidst
     the green
out over the roadstead of the harbour where the ocean-going
     peninsula is moored.
Watching the stairway's erratic descent
watching out for people
sitting on the grey.
The cemetery like a quiet model of the city
not the names on the stones so imposing as the shapes of the stones
their bearing on these hills.
And ships with sail, sails furled
masts cross-referencing the harbour
waters beamy under north-west breeze.
The wake of a white cherry
springing against the sky.

                                                                1986

Zero

One needs to have many different lives
one needs to live all lives
a house in every suburb in every town in every country.
How different the world is
how different you are
don't go back.

This seaside resort —
a harbour, the open sea, with a ship coming in
out over the Pacific;
white tower among red roofs on a promontory.
You have disappeared, you are new
there is nothing to hold to

just the hole, and the noise of it.
The terrace house with their engines smouldering
the enormous chasm on the edge of a world wilderness
LIFT OFF
from the hills' silhouette into the pale gleaming universe
you world full of possibility.

                                                                1986

Seeing As How

The cups ring
                    my father sings
staggering out of the lemon tree
eyes brilliant

with song
arms bloodied by thorns drunk
with the scent of lemon flower

like a sparrow in a dustbath dancing
in the work
of selecting wood
and pruning it
giving the tree

room to breathe

now he's silent
since I called him '*Coffee!*'
recalling him
from his reverie

he begins again
talking to himself
in the bathroom mirror putting on
a sticking plaster

and in the lemon tree
where he goes back
to replace a ladybug, tilting it
on his little finger hatching its light
sometimes blue sometimes green
'It's sort of metallic isn't it?' he says
showing me how

1991

Actually

As if there was a radio

on in the back of our heads, to which we

had to be faithful.
Peeling layers back

to original recording
to begin with

nothing.
Sheepshit and grass and

hills and magpies and stones, 'you' and 'I'
thinly disguised, pretending there's
someone

1994

Context of Words

A hat is a sort of a house

like a derelict set for a western
Step right this way, ma'am, touching

brim.
Looking for a lover to

let the other
out. 'Love don't come around here no more'
sings the worm
skilfully.

       She stays inside the window
reading her book. She doesn't want to go
where he goes, doesn't want him to go
there either.

       Air's granular flow
over mudflats crabs
scuttle for their hangars
'Love don't come around here no more' Tom
Petty's seductive
voice like a snake.

Art is your lover, art is who

you tell your secrets to
putting the notebook away

till you have something
to say
      telling pictures

in a lighthearted
deep sort of way

like water at a jetty
talking endlessly

           (1994)

Gull's Eye

Gulls yell

above a tiny hill crowded
with untidy houses
where a rubbish truck climbs

steep winding streets
river valleys fall

away west away east
an aeroplane engine

is almost obliterated
by the grunt and holler and catcall
of sirens out

      over the reclamation
the seagulls circle
like balsa models

high over the city
the tiny smoking city
like a rubbish dump

1994

GEOFF COCHRANE

Born in Wellington in 1951, Geoff Cochrane published five small books of verse before a collection of his new and selected poems, Aztec Noon, *appeared in 1992. He has also published a novel,* Tin Nimbus *(Victoria University Press, 1995).*

Aztec Noon

This I had thought forgotten
I recall now almost perfectly
In the gloom of winter:

Past a cloacal wall whose posters
Decayed like leonine faces,
I took you home up steps,

Strewn with crates and cabbage,
To a room which seemed a tank of light
At the very top of the world.

All summer was a gala Aztec noon
We walked in, hip to hip,
Through odour of the sea's green cistern.

1992

Suicide Abroad

You buy bullets
Which lie on your palm like money.
You owe them nothing.

To release a captive sparrow
Is prayer. You meet your agent at dawn
Amid fragile cages of song.

1992

An Ambulance

Between hospital and zoo
asterisks of rain fall audibly
on the many old tin awnings.

Through cool blue air arrives
a siren's pure ambulance. Someone
is dying of too much afternoon,
of fennel and cats and clothes props.

1992

A Lyric

Autumn is dusk, brings dusk,
Dusk's grave adjustment of tones.

I have bathed, my fingers smell of money.

Greyness, stillness, chill —
Each is rich in itself.

The sea has fingers like these smallnesses,
These notes; those who are cold
It touches with odours.

Behind you hung a vast fund of cloud.

There dwindles on my eye
Your eye, the charm of clavicles.

You were as real as meat, as thunder.

(1993)

Polygon Wood

(Polygon Wood gave its name to the second of the three Battles of Ypres. My grandfather survived it.)

'From tents on a plain
We were tempted out. To embark for this,
Not yet all mud.

'Mother, I am lost,
Am lost inside a map you enter through
A hole in a hedge.'

Soon winter will come and snow seem to repair
This medieval convent.

Because he is clad he is ready.

Because he is clad he deflects.

He will move forward untouched
Through all that is neutered and still.

(1993)

The Maritime Cook

Here lupin hides lost items
of the ocean's rusting tackle.
Beyond these chains and flukes
is a bach I have my eye on,
a shed built into clay
and roosted in drab flax.

Feeney was once in a film
with Ustinov and Mitchum.
When he came into The Grand
it was with a toey shuffle
he made seem heroic.
Black Irish, square-templed,
he had a broken nose
the shape of a pawn or key.

He burned himself to death
with magnificent negligence.
Among the many things I seek,
the many reliefs I crave,
is illusion of the imminence of rain,
the first scant scratches of drizzle
on asphalt or pane.

(1994)

JAN KEMP

Born in Hamilton in 1949, Jan Kemp became prominent as a poet in the 1970s. She was the only woman poet to be included in Arthur Baysting's 1973 anthology The Young New Zealand Poets. *She now studies in Germany, after teaching for fourteen years in the South Pacific and South East Asia.*

Poem

A puriri moth's wing
lies light in my hand —

my breath can lift it

light as this torn wing
we lie on love's breath.

1976

Paperboygirl

paperboygirl paperboygirl paperboygirl
globe 'n mayyyll
globe 'n mayyyll

zip zip zip zip
here i come
globe 'n mayyyll
globe 'n mayyyll

thunk — on yr doorstep
thunk — on yr doormat
thunk thunk thunk down the zigzag street
in the early sidewalks
    early dogs
    early skies
    early morning treeeeeeeeeeeeeeeeeeeeeeeeeeeeeeeeeeeeees

wanna hear how general abey massacred the students of yuzele
wanna hear how women were raped their men skunked their breasts
lopped off like coconuts & they lay nightlong screaming

wanna hear the latest wanna hear the latest
wanna book yr seats for the fight of the lions
mecca jerusalem mecca jerusalem gentle mecca gentle jerusalem
split down the middle of faith like chopped palms
smeared moslems smeared christians like smeared dates
on the road the blood coagulate & brown in the dust

and that ain't all no that ain't all

catholic children know which end of a gun is orange
which green before they can read the writing on the wall

rusky chinchin & merigo went down to the river to bathe
all three were drowned & who do you think was saved

is this the news i bring to waken the world is this is this

maples fall yellow crows' tracks at my feet
rain tunnels down my face
i run outside myself wet slick
                flat stick
                zip zip
        trousers flap
            slap stick
thonk thonk the papers are heavy

zap zap zap zap
this is what i bring BLANK NEWSPRINT blank newsprint blank
newsprint blank newsprint all folded up all neatly folded up
all un-paged BLANK NEWSPRINT
THONK on yr doorstep
globe 'n mayyyll
globe 'n mayyyll

inside my dreaming eyes wake up on the world so still
black tree bark against sky-peach
wet grass
the leaves in light

sun arise sun arise trees so green so yellow sky so new
sun arise
waken the world waken the world waken the world

paperboygirl paperboygirl paperboygirl
i say let me bring you this sunrise
today & today & today & today & today

(1980)

MICHAEL JACKSON

Born in 1940, Jackson is a distinguished anthropologist who, after seven years in the USA, now lives in Sydney, Australia. He has published five collections of poetry, three works of fiction and several ethnographies.

Pioneers

Someone took a photograph of them
standing in a clay track,
a winter frontier town
a hundred years ago.

Surrounded by forest
in an archive of silences
I cannot believe them gone.

I have imagined a grave
marked by a pine slab
and run my fingers over the rain-blurred
braille of their origins.

I have woken to the traffic
of the rain, pine branches
waved like river water
and a workman shovelling in the dark

And I have seen them again
the sepia of their expressionless faces
in the bush they cleared.

What do they want me for?

I am theirs and of them and for them speak.
My hands have gone over the roofs and gullies
of their names.
These hills I live under are their doing.
I have been given what they got.
I am what they became.

1980

The Moths

Our house had filled with moths,
a slow silting of lintel and architrave

a cupboard dust,
until I looked much closer
and found the wood-grain one,
the white quill paperbark, the blotched
shadow of a patch of bush,
an elbowing riverbank that had gone deep blue.

The soft perimeter of forests
had entered our house
fluttering around the moon.

Then for five days they drowned
in sinks and pools or seemed to wane
into sanded wood or ash on windowsills
until they became
what they were when I first noticed them:
fragments of a dull interior.

1980

Nightmare of Mushrooms

On the other side of the wall
mushrooms are growing.

An occasional soft bump —
another is pushing through a wiry skein
of clover root —
a pale bulb looking for the light.

All night I have heard them
and hardly slept;
hills in soft rain
bare feet on cold grass
a basket smudged with their black spoor.

They are measuring something
I can't explain,
bubbling up in rows and rings
to spread like a wild calendar
rumours of death
someone I love's name.

1982

Seven Mysteries

Now write down
the seven mysteries:
why you so young and beautiful should die;
why consciousness prevents
escape into the chestnut branches where
foliage goes soft
with God's vermilion;
why what is said is seldom what was meant;
why men and women work, come home,

cook meals, argue and renew
their vows of silence or revenge;
why we were different;
why there are seven of everything;
why I go on
broken-winded like that horse we saw
on the ridge above Waipatiki
by a bent tree
watching the waves roll in.

1982

Stone

Jedes Dasein scheint in sich rund
(Every Being seems in itself round)
—Karl Jaspers

Life is probably round
—Vincent Van Gogh

Das Dasein ist rund
(Being is round)
—Gaston Bachelard

Oglala Dakota

In the beginning everything was made round
except stone.

Sun, earth, moon are round
like shields; the sky
                        a deep bowl.

Everything that breathes is round
like a plant's stem.

The circle stands for everything but stone:
the four winds travelling
at the world's edge,
for day and night when the moon
goes round the sky.

Therefore
we made our houses round,
our campsites circular,
and sat in circles when we ate.

I used to shut my ears when old men
        passed the sweetgrass round
            and spoke of stone;
it was the heart of those who ruined us.

We were deceived
        by their sky-blue skins
            and uniforms of indigo;
watching them in their tents and yards
        all edged with stone
we wondered why they rode in lines

and laid down iron roads
     on plains
    that flowed with game and wind.

Maori

Like wind far off
with great grave steps
came the rain.

Across the river
men with guns
slipped darkly on horseback
down the scree.

I called out to them
but the river drowned my voice.

I wanted you to tell me the darkness
was merely dark green,

our salvation the silver light
       along the ridge,
that it was you we glimpsed
   at the edge of the clearing
      through the rain,
that your love would come to us unbidden,
the circle be closed again.

I wanted to hear that the darkness
   was filled with snow-fed streams,
that our broken staves our fences
our plough lines our language
our songs our plantings
our selves
would soon be mended
by your words your promises
by a carved house
by the five voices
by the clover leaf, the diamonds, and the stars

Mihaia,

yes, and I hoped your voice
would recall for me,
my mother singing
      in the rainbow room,
wild plums under windows
      where we threw the stones,
women with lacebark kits
      bringing flowers and evergreens,
card players on a grey blanket
sheltering under a lean-to from the snow.

Achaea

The chorus began
in the noise of a threshing floor;
the navel of the earth
was a net of grain
flung round a stone.

A snake like a necklace
of onyx and emerald
drank at the air
then slipped through the ruins
at my feet.

By a cold spring
in a handhold in the hills
surrounded by cypresses,
the inarticulate syllables
of a wild girl.

At Epidauros
crushed laurel and sage
in a cupped hand

In the labyrinth
fat and limping citizens
dream their therapies

The scored bark of pines
bleeds resin
for wine

A mason's mallet echoing

Rain water collects
in a stone bowl.

                              1980

ELIZABETH SMITHER

*Born in 1941 in New Plymouth, where she still lives and works as a librarian,
Elizabeth Smither has published twelve collections of poetry as well as novels, short
stories and a collection of journals. Her selected poems,* The Tudor Style, *was published in 1993.*

Here Come the Clouds

Here come the clouds the same as last June
Puffy like the breasts of birds, one . . . two . . . three . . .
They have circumnavigated the world
Birds heavy from flight, home again.

A year has passed. Now they fill the sky
Thicker and thicker having no other place to go.
What is the end of navigation then? They seem
Swollen as though their arteries of air

Ached from memory as well and
Dilated their hearts so they come
Weighed with longing for their homeland.
And here they are. Is this it then?
This empty sky, waiting.

1975

Casanova's Ankle

Casanova was turned by an ankle
Over and over. His glance ascended
To towers of conquest, snares set
In the shade of trees. Too bad
He had to toil as well in the trap
To free the booty used
And stained by capture. Distasteful
Somehow what he possessed
When the time for possession came.
It was better in the stalking light
With the moon half-hid
Following the scented glove, the ankle.

1981

The Legend of Marcello Mastroianni's Wife

All summer in the shallow sea
She lay on a lilo waiting
Dangling a hand, primed to embrace
And bless the demi-god.
She would cook from the freezer
Breasts of pasta, sauces like milk
Spoon-feed him, flirt
Mountainously and save herself.
In bed while she ministered
Territories of herself she spoke
Into the darkness the litany she'd learnt:
Whales, dolphins, the dove-like sea.

1981

Fr Anselm Williams and Br Leander Neville hanged by Lutheran mercenaries in 1636 while out of their monastery on a local errand of charity — from the guidebook to Ampleforth Abbey and College

'We'll see who can stick
Their tongue out first for God
Out of you two,' binding the hands
The flowers in the hedgerows starting

The sky turning over with a lurch
As when Brother Leander dropped the eggs.
They wouldn't be back to Compline
The hedgeroses looked askance now.
A swallow passed. Their hands touched
Just the fingertips like passing a note.
The tongues would come out later
Into an air gone blue, a world.
                    from 'an English notebook'

                                        1981

Temptations of St Antony by His Housekeeper

Once or twice he eyed me oddly. Once
He said Thank God you're a normal woman
As though he meant a wardrobe and went off
Humming to tell his beads. He keeps
A notebook, full of squiggles I thought, some
Symbolism for something, I think I've seen
It on lavatory walls, objects like chickens' necks
Wrung but not dead, the squawking
Still in the design, the murderer running.
He's harmless, God knows. I could tell him
If he asked, he terrifies himself.
I think it makes him pray better, or at least
He spends longer and longer on his knees.

                                        1981

Visiting Juliet Street

All the streets are named after Shakespeare.
Hamlet and Juliet are separated by an intersection
Down which floats Ophelia Street, very sleepy.
They are all such demanding people
Which lends the town an air of tragedy
As though Mercutio coming home after a party
Failed to dip his lights and ran over
Polonius Street right up onto the sidewalk.
Even Shakespeare thought it best to keep them separated.
At the end of long girlish Juliet Street
With limbs like Twiggy the air grows
Sleepier and sleepier as though
Juliet had anorexia nervosa and could hardly bear
A morsel of blossoms or any sap.

                                        1981

I Think Joan Didion Has Died

for Ursula

I think Joan Didion has died
I think I read it somewhere
And something about her face
Leads one to add two and two.

She smoked too much, was too skinny
And words were brutal, she said
She finished each book at her mother's
Sleeping in her girlhood bed.

I'm sure there was something beckoning
It could have been the Hollywood guests
She hosted with brittle conversation
Brutality's weekend off.

Words are so awfully menacing
Only a fool takes glee
And uses them up like a spray can
Of gardenia or lily of the valley.

Real words are the Valley of Death
They leave such awful imprints
Worse than a snow rabbit makes
And he is harmless, God knows.

So I think Joan Didion's dead
It's just natural to suppose
That her combination and death's
Would meet, as it were, nose to nose.

1983

The O in Shakespeare Explained

Sometimes a writer turns
His eye to the whole of his subject
Or a whole subject apart from it
O is the word for it.

This book against a stream, a flood
A sky of stars that process
Any digression as long as it is large
O is the word for it.

A hundred thousand blades of field
And it held whole in all detail
A wheel of birds that sagas make
O is the word for it.

And Shakespeare's head beginning to ache
For sure the play is a sandwich
And slippery as eel or heart
O is the word for it.

1985

Finger to Finger

People comment on my cold fingers
But they are warm. They lay between
His that were white and translucent
In which the small injuries his fingers always had
Small bleedings, missing with nails, cuts

All his large economies, savings
My school shoes, ballet lessons, wasted music
Look up at me, like a leaf looks up at autumn.
                    from 'To my father, E.R.H., 1904–1984'.

                                        1986

The Veronica's Veil Technique

Certain that something's happening but what?
Press a convenient bit of cloth
Against the nearest obvious manifestation.
You should come away with a print in your hands
Which will be useful later when they're trying to put
A name to it, the event that was unfolding
Which you took part in while they only watched.

                                        1986

Error on a Quiz Programme

for David Hill

'Give me the names of three lady violinists
Who lived at Haworth Parsonage?'
Charlotte on the violin, Anne the viola
And Emily on the violoncello.
Each evening in the dark drawing room
They drew up their instruments and played
With the wind above the graves.

Charlotte was most in demand as a soloist
Anne was too shy and with a limited repertoire
The violoncello takes up too much room in a carriage
If anyone was asked out it was usually Charlotte.
Emily carried the violoncello on her back
As she tramped the moors. Sometimes
She laid it across a stream and jumped over it.

                                        1986

A Cortège of Daughters

A quite ordinary funeral: the corpse
Unknown to the priest. The twenty-third psalm.
The readings by serious businessmen
One who nearly tripped on the unaccustomed pew.
The kneelers and the sitters like sheep and goats.

But by some prior determination a row
Of daughters and daughters-in-law rose
To act as pallbearers instead of men
All of even height and beautiful.
One wore in her hair a black and white striped bow.

And in the midst of their queenliness
One in dark flowered silk, the corpse

Had become a man before they reached the porch
So loved he had his own dark barge
Which their slow moving steps rowed
As a dark lake is sometimes surrounded by irises.

(1986)

from Swimming

The Meeting of Ocean and Air

Of all the beautiful equal edges
Which are everywhere observed: the edge
Of this plank decking and the air for instance,
A leaf edge/air, an air/wing of bird,

This bubbling, live, taut, vivacious edge
Of underwater ocean's edge and air
Is the best example to be immersed in
To open eyes in and ride to surface.

Where else can be so graphically illustrated
How, in what manner, two elements meet
Like Stanley and Livingstone, only better
For this handshake goes on for the length of a beach

And all around the earth is transmitted
To anyone surfacing: a diver, a fish
A porpoise, an inept swimmer, gasping
Streaming in the streaming that overcomes

Even the fear of drowning: this perfect
Sharp, soft, limber, rigorous, two-doctrine edge
Like the Pope and the Dalai Lama meeting
Under dissolving mosques and steeples and bells.

The Safe Beach

Beauty does not swim here. It's utilitarian
That beauty (grown) will take energetic styles
Like its own curves: curve calls to curve
The flat safe beach to those whose shapes are mild.

And flabby, overflowing, crinkled, run wild
(A means of saying, merely) those who wear
Old-fashioned bathing hats and last-minute towels
And converse as though it was a social occasion

Since their heads are never in the water as they swim
(If one can call it that). It's not a crawl
Or backstroke exactly, more like going to sleep
With gentle arm movements to check the mattress.

Swimming with the Dead Woman

In the shelter of a sandbank lay
A still flat-bodiced body under a hat
Trimmed with black ribbon. A black mouth
Gaped, sideways, like a mollusc.

Asleep, we thought, drying ourselves
After our swim. That day the sea
Had noticeable cold currents.
The day before sea lettuce

In the lowest waves was crepe
To hang on doors. We swam
In spots as warm as blood
Like small rooms or vestibules.

One stroke took us out of them
Into chill corridors. They wound
Around our feet like ribbons.
'I've swum into a refrigerator,' you called

Or at least away from a small town where light
And warmth bubbled underground.
Absurd. But when we saw
The flat chest underneath the hat

Not appearing to rise we passed
From another cold spot to the heat
And remarked we'd often seen
Black mouths in hospital like that

On sleepers who would tomorrow
Breakfast and joke and converse normally
And not know that they talked or gaped
Horribly when unconscious.

Last night though both of us searched
The small print in the paper for
'Woman's body discovered on beach'
And an article beginning

'It seems quite odd with bathers coming and going
Some quite close to where she sat . . .'
And on our next swim, in circles,
You mentioned an anonymous call to the police.

At least, if she was dead, the beach was bare
And it would have been a good way to go:
A commodious basket, drinks, a book
A favourite hat, warm cooling sand.

We hadn't yet discovered how the sea
Relates each day to steady heat or wind
Not how we expect but according to
Its own undoubtedly logical whims.

The dead woman would have given all that
A miss. Perhaps decided the sea was a bad hat
Like an errant husband. No really warm depths
Until twenty-eight warm days of February.

Then we forgot her, swimming on our backs
The laziest stroke, the most philosophical
The stroke of those carried on a stretcher
D O A, the big toe with the luggage label

And then, facing the shore, we saw her
Coming in to bathe. We recognised the nose
Outlined in purple zinc, the thin mouth
Which closed the cavern. She even had the hat

On until the last minute. She placed it on the sand.
The tide was going out. She weighted it with a stone.
Her chest was flat and hardly rising
But she looked as if she could swim.

Her bony arms splashed water on her shoulders.
As she came closer she called us, 'Ladies'
And called out 'Is it warmer today?'
And 'Are you getting out already?'

Luckily bathing in salt does something to the face
(The reason for total immersion). We looked
We hope, innocent and friendly, praised
The sea and said it was improving

Hoped she enjoyed her swim. Lay some moments
In the shallows, always warm, no matter
How gingerly we get in. Does the sea
Have this morality to welcome mariners

And castaways, those who summon
Faithful eighty-year-old swimmers from their sleep
After being beached and crawling for the sand
And reaching in their bags for hats with bands?

1993

The Sea Question

The sea asks 'How is your life now?'
It does so obliquely, changing colour.
It is never the same on any two visits.

It is never the same in any particular
Only in generalities: tide and such matters
Wave height and suction, pebbles that rattle.

It doesn't presume to wear a white coat
But it questions you like a psychologist
As you walk beside it on its long couch.

1993

RACHEL MCALPINE

Born 1940 in South Canterbury, Rachel McAlpine now lives in Wellington after a sojourn in Kyoto, Japan. As well as seven collections of poetry, McAlpine has written radio plays, stage plays, textbooks and three novels, the most recent of which is Farewell Speech.

Zig-Zag Up a Thistle

I

A lot has changed here since the day
he left.
Fig trees have thrust up
their chubby fists,
tiny thumbs are dangling
from the sycamores,
cabbage tree's rococo
in her blonde embroidered plaits,
fuschia bleeding pointedly
from every joint.

Some things remain the same:
the cat is happy.

And my fridge is over-full
of half-forgotten love,
marbled with islands of mould.

II

It's hard to fix your pronouns.
I was happy with 'me'.
Then we made an effort to be 'us'.
He retreated. I had to learn
'you' and 'him'.

I still say 'There are fig trees
in our street.'
I belong to many an us:
the family long and wide,
the human race.
Nobody lives alone.

Romans began their verbs incognito.
I (a part of us) got
two Christmas presents.
A Latin grammar once belonging
to my mother's grandmother.
A four-leafed clover
which I keep between
'idem, alius, alter, ceteri'
and 'hic, iste, ille, is'.

III

I used to have a friend and people said
how strong she was. I sanded
the banisters yesterday.
If only she were here! Her eyes
are nimble and her fingers slick
with putty, brush, plaster.

Today you touched my breast and so
I must be near. Thank you, thank you.
If I could find my friend
I might supervise your loving.

A final decision every day.
I check the calendar —
so far, thirty-two: nil.
Poetry's algebra,
love is arithmetic.
Some people say we are living
lives with a shape.

IV

Sometimes you forget your lines
and have to act them out
again. This time,
should I flatter him, or cringe?

I have had such an urge to tidy up.
But I can work in a mess
and I usually do.

There is no
single perfect gesture,
and there is no amen.
The world will ad lib without end.

V

On a dry hill I look
at small brave lives.

A lark aspires to the orgasm
of a Pegasus. A ladybird
uses cocksfoot
for tightrope and trapeze.
Spiders zig-zag up a thistle.
Butterflies rely entirely
on their buoyant colours.

No one but the skylark travels
in a straight line.
The rest of us polka and pussyfoot.

VI

The dandelion opens twice,
first to a dominant gold.
Then discarding petals
it clamps up tight,
and leggy seeds develop
in its grip.
And later — froth.

Love must change or die.
The future needs no feeding,
no permission.
It is white.
It happens somewhere else.

Love, work, children.
Angels fly on
two wings.

VII

A good decision, that,
deciding to live, and properly.
Down on the beach it's hard to play
the tragedy queen for long.
Fathers watch their toddlers waddle,
lollipops laze in candy togs,
the sea explodes with kids
and yellow canoes.
You popping seed-pod of a world,
I love you, I love you,
let me come in!

1983

Before the Fall

After the bath with ragged towels
my Dad
would dry us very carefully:
six little wriggly girls,
each with foamy pigtails,
two rainy legs,
the invisible back we couldn't reach,
a small wet heart
and toes, ten each.

He dried us all
the way he gave the parish
Morning Prayer:
as if it was important,
as if God was fair,
as if it was really simple
if you would just be still
and bare.

1983

LAURIS EDMOND

Born in Hawke's Bay in 1924, Lauris Edmond raised six children before becoming a full-time writer. She has written poems, plays, a novel and a celebrated autobiography. Her Selected Poems won the Commonwealth Poetry Prize in 1985.

Before a Funeral

The great bright leaves have fallen
outside your window
they lie about
torn by the season from
the beggared cherry trees.
In your room, alone,
I fold and hide away
absurd, unnecessary things —
your books, still ready and alert,
it seems, for understanding,
clothes, dry and cold,
surprised in holding still
to hairs upon the collars,
handkerchiefs in pockets,
socks, awry, not ready for
the queer neglect of death.

Mechanically useful, I make
preparations for some possible
impossible journey no one
will ever take; work will help
they tell me, and indeed
your room is now nothing
but things, and tidy.
I have put away your life.

Out in the autumn garden
a sharp rapacious wind
snatches the brilliant booty
of the leaves. The blackened branches
groan. They knot, and hold.
And yet the cold will come.

1975

Ohakune Fires

There were bonfires on the hillsides
in those days, high
above the raw-boned town
and trees and men giants against the sky
grappling for mastery — not men but bushmen took
their slashers in to hack
blazes on the beech trunks
smacking up a track of sorts,
forced a way to the ridge and stood

straight up to breast the trees
defeated, famished
in the thinning air.

Back on the farm on milder hills
they clubbed second growth
and lit their necessary fires;
women came — sometimes a child
screaming when the blazing
raced up close.
                   Dark, and
the booze began, tall tales
of men and bullocks gulped down
in twenty feet of mud, or some
such thing, in grandad's roaring time.
Round them the spit and snore
of logs' red bodies,
later the blundering
journey home (one, a neighbour,
drunken-drowned in the freezing stream).
And all the time
the hard stars riding by.

Time, it's a moving stage —
bonfires still blaze
and we hold out our hands
across a widening space
calling, hearing now only
the faint snap of the burning
and the far-off pack-a-pack
of the axes.
                                        1975

The Pear Tree

Pear tree like snow blowing across the sunlight:
spring this year is not for love, nor hope,
nor passion, but something with which we are to be
reconciled. I remember the winter tree,
its bare branches entwined in the hieroglyphics
of a message too hard for us to comprehend,
a language of defeat.

Yesterday I saw the first green swellings
and a green shadow over the fallen husks
of bark shredded by weather in a winter
that brought death to the house — a bleak time
when frost blackened the geraniums, so
indestructibly scarlet last autumn;
sap was low and the cracked shell of the pear
tree promised nothing. We had so little
force or fibre, the numb days when
we sat together, pain like a blight
withering our understanding, and the dark arms

of the tree lifted across the window
as if in supplication for us.

Now the thousand faces of spring shake
their white light across the glass; in us
too there is a stirring, of force or feeling —
but this is no simple flowering, no ordered season;
the hard grind of grief still holds,
a bitter sap in the wood blurring the break
of the season. No spring can restore to her the changes
of sun and rain, the quiver of wind in the blossom
the morning's tender sky; her sleep is unshakeable
beyond all seasons. We must make alone what sense of this
we can. Spring is a reckoning.

                                            1977

from Wellington Letter

I

Five o'clock; the winter morning's
no more than a bleak frontier
of the night. This rough hill, where
houses tilt to the tides of the rowdy
dark, gives just a hand-hold; we're
tossed among squally showers 'moderate
swell to the west, wind 20 to 30 knots'
— the marine forecaster's voice brings
a map of rainy seas, Kapiti to Cape
Palliser, Cape Palliser to Puysegur
Point, visibility 4 knots (from Stephens
Island to Jackson Bay the seas are
slight). And Nugget Point? He burrs,
knobbed as a knotted rope, a chunk
of cliff chops into the misty vision
slapped by a moderate southerly swell.
We rock into the windy morning. Yesterday
Evans Bay was a city of slim white ships.
I thought of you. Voices. Voices.

II

You are the smiling photo beside
the telephone, the laughter stilled
on a tape casually recorded. There are
other exact presences; it's true death's
winter passes, we meet in a new spring
and I walk your green aisles of silence
in a remembered confiding. In four years
I have given up straining, have learned
to stand still, unprotesting as forlorn
couples do when the train's gone, taking
a child to the dangerous city. Through

breaking clouds I see there was a true
madness in you — 'I'll eat a lily' only
you could say, and laugh, and do it
despite expostulations; poisonous?
You didn't care, taking yourself too
lightly even then. Four years. It's
hardly time, yet this is the work
grief gives, to set about composing
the lifetime that we thought we knew,
without falsity or fear to try to make
it whole. One remains accountable.

Death's an explosion in the mine
of love; this letter tells of
reconstruction, failed attempts,
of gifts, of visitations from those
who come like neighbours bringing
soup and clothes to families made
homeless by disaster; so love
returns, limps in, is recognised.

III

Thomas Hardy leaned
against the trunk
of an oak and said
with the deep-reaching
whimsy of the man
of earth and education
'This tree is
a man I knew'.

        Ten
feet down the bank
where last year's
storm has gouged
a niche of clay
I planted a totara
for you, its tough
sprigs to contain
your delicacy,
your grace, Rachel.

            1980

The Distaff Line

So late your letter comes — forty years
and now this wild face, round-eyed child
crossing the dark field of consciousness
and closer, suddenly old, holding me with
a fierce mnemonic stare. How shall I learn
a lifetime in an instant? Turn back, we'll
go together down a lengthening road, find

the orchard, the track of spongy elephant
grass that leads to the apricot tree.

Look, here's the raffish village, here
the ha'penny store, the bar hump-backed
like a whale that crammed with mud the green
throat of the river; and here the trees,
apples, pears, spindly plums, last and best
the apricot, grey grandfather drowsing
in a dusty light. Now see a familiar shadow
fall upon the grass as those formidable
women — your mother, midwife to a hundred
Maori families, mine their children's
teacher — country women, tall as scarecrows,
arrive to summon us to evening rituals
ordered by their brisk instruction.

Old friend, cousin, let us say the secret
creatures behind our eyes have not grown
old (and were they ever young?) — come,
lay your cheek against the green skin
of the river, grasp the branch that
holds the ripest fruit, we'll sit here
as we did before through endless amber
afternoons of childhood's summer.

But there's your letter — which I shall not
answer, guessing your reticences well enough.
It shows you, as I would have thought,
straight-backed and calm, a little stately,
looking Master Death severely in the eye,
never doubting that the only failure is
a loss of nerve. So it's to be. The ripeness
now has fallen from the trees and in the dusk
your face puts on its mask, rubric of
a resolute clan whose women's voices,
unshaken, ever spoke the word that called
us in and put an end to all our playing.

1980

The Names

Six o'clock, the morning still and
the moon up, cool profile of the night;
time small and flat as an envelope —
see, you slip out easily: do I know you?
Your names have still their old power,
they sing softly like voices across water.

Virginia Frances Martin Rachel Stephanie
Katherine — the sounds blend and chant
in some closed chamber of the ear, poised
in the early air before echoes formed.

Suddenly a door flies open, the music
breaks into a roar, it is everywhere;

now it's laughter and screaming, the crack
of a branch in the plum tree, the gasping
and blood on the ground; it is sea-surge
and summer, 'Watch me!' sucked under
the breakers; the hum of the lupins, through
sleepy popping of pods the saying of names.

And all the time the wind that creaked in
the black macrocarpas and whined in the wires
was waiting to sweep us away; my children who
were my blood and breathing I do not know you:
we are friends, we write often, there are
occasions, news from abroad. One of you is dead.

I do not listen fearfully for you in the night,
exasperating you with my concern,
I scarcely call this old habit love —
yet you have come to me this white morning,
and remind me that to name a child is brave,
or foolhardy; even now it shakes me.

The small opaque moon, wafer of light,
grows fainter and disappears; but
the names will never leave me, I hear
them calling like boatmen far over
the harbour at first light. They will sound
in the dreams of your children's children.

1980

Going to Moscow

The raspberries they gave us for dessert
were delicious, sharp-tasting and furry,
served in tiny white bowls; you spooned cream
on to mine explaining I'd find it sour.

The waitress with huge eyes and a tuft
of hair pinched like a kewpie so wanted
to please us she dropped two plates as
she swooped through the kitchen door.
No one could reassure her. Snow was falling;
when you spoke, across the narrow white
cloth I could scarcely hear for the distance
nor see you through floating drifts.

Then the tall aunt brought out her dog,
a small prickly sprig like a toy; we put on
our coats and in the doomed silence Chekhov
the old master nodded at us from the wings.
At the last my frozen lips would not
kiss you, I could do nothing but talk
to the terrible little dog: but you

stood still, your polished shoes swelling up
like farm boots. There are always some
who must stay in the country when others
are going to Moscow. Your eyes were
a dark lake bruised by the winter trees.

1983

The Ghost Moth

Once we lived so close to the bush
each day wore the beech trees' rangy profile,
all night the creek purred, brushing
the antennae of our sleep; in the evening
moths came pouring into the lamplight,
some small, blue-sheened, as though it was
light itself combed to dust on their wings

or a ghost moth stared from the doorway
sheathed in its gentle shallow gaze;
and we ourselves seemed diffused like
the light, and would wander away
past the moths to the leaf-shivering trees
as though summoned in secret
by the morepork's comfortless cry.

That earthy unearthly life is over now
but sometimes still when you come in
from the purposeful street and hesitate,
blinking, I think of the moths
how they wheeled into the lamp's bright
aureole and turned and turned, dazzled
by something they never really saw.

1986

Things

Yes, I like it here,
things have their place;
at night there are lights in the water;
if you offered me something unexpected —
a fast car, a bantam hen,
a small bunch of violets
purple velvet and looking authentic,
I would be touched
though I could easily refuse.

I have choices galore
but the same grey trees lean to the wind
at my window,
the same unwary bird is killed
every day on the grass,
and I long to long for something attainable
by sheer hard work
   — like cars or clothes —

whatever would not, when achieved,
stay in its place looking perfect
with death's shadow
slowly deepening
behind it.

1987

Camping

Do you remember how we woke
to the first bird in that awkward pine

behind the ablution block, and leaned
across the knotted ground to lift
the canvas as though it was
the wall of the world
and ourselves at the heart of it
lying together
with the fresh grass against our faces
and the early air sweet beyond all telling —

do you sometimes look still
into that startled darkness
and hear the bird,
as I do?

When we drove away I looked back always
to the flattened yellow grass
to see the exact map of our imagining
our built universe
for a week
and saw that it was just earth
and faced the natural sky.

We took with us the dark pine
and the blackbird
and the dew beside our foreheads
as we woke

and now we live apart
and I don't know where they are.

1991

FIONA KIDMAN

Born in 1940, Fiona Kidman is best known for her novels, which include A Breed of Women and The Book of Secrets. Kidman has also written plays and non-fiction. Her selected poems, Wakeful Nights, was published in 1991.

Earthquake Weather

For three days now, the air
has been quiet and still.
Yesterday, a vase walked across
the mantelpiece. A friend and I

have traced the fault line
along a map. It is very close.
There is neither sun, nor yet rain,
and the wind has departed too.
The crickets have stopped singing
and the children's quarrels grown bitter.
We wait, sealed in this
grey vacuum.

And when we went to bed
last night, the moon slanted
between the curtains (yes,
we still have a moon),
catching your white smile
in a dazzling glitter. We
who have known rage and lust,
regrets and promises, have come
to understand love. I was afraid
you were about to devour me.
I wish this weather
would break soon.

1978

Makara Beach, Spring

It's this skin of happiness that holds
me together. Like an olive round an anchovy's
body. More loosely, like Maggie's neck
collected in folds over her collar bone
sliding about, no special grip on the world.
A dog's life all right. But god, it's good, beside
the sea collecting wild flowers and weeds
of new zealand. Blue eyed daisies, white as foam
and dark as the sea's centre, the middle's
what counts, and yellow, there's yellow
flora all over the place. I've even got you
collecting the encroaching cream off
the land, and a smudge of silver edged
leaf. A heron
bows, arches, stalks across
stones. A bunch of overland cyclists stand
aside, smile. Indians picnic in the shade
of a cliff. A Vietnamese child lies down
waiting to be rescued on the round
rocks. A tide of gorse
flows over the hills flushed at the seams
with orange broom. We agree to share botulism
if the crayfish roll at the tearooms
should fail us. Well yes. This is certainly
short enough to be happiness.
The morning's a ball
of silk unwound about us. You gather
it back with me at its centre.

1985

MICHAEL HARLOW

Michael Harlow was born in America of Greek and Ukrainian parents, in 1937. In the 1980s he was an editor of Landfall *and of the Caxton Press Poetry Series. As well as publishing five collections of poetry and a book on teaching poetry, Harlow has collaborated extensively with the composer Kit Powell. Currently living in Christchurch, he divides his time between writing and practising as a Jungian psychoanalytic psychotherapist.*

Today is the Piano's Birthday

Today is the piano's birthday. Yesterday it was found weeping in the garden. Mother was not there, father was gone. But today is the piano's birthday . . .

Under the balalaika tree the children touch it. The piano's foot-pedals hum.

Hurrah! shout the children. The piano is on holiday! They sing the birthday song. They bound up and down. They strike the exact note without looking, without looking the piano writes a song for the children . . .

Plinking, planking, plonk — the piano conducts the children through a small wood of ivory. The children sing with their feet. They call to mother who is dreaming on the lawn, to father who is at the office polishing his machines . . .

The piano falls into a dream. The children listen. From far off, birds with the faces of women enter the garden. They lie down. They call to the children. The children listen. They lean into the darkness. They decide. They curl inside the piano's birthday. The children are the size of a crotchet. The piano grows around them.

The piano is being dreamed. The children are the stories. They are listening . . . to mother wake on the lawn and touch the space around her . . . to father close the office door . . . And today is the piano's birthday.

If we listen — we can hear mother call them, we can hear father enter the house, carefully. If we listen — we can hear the very first song the children sing, the very first dream the piano dreams . . . we can hear . . . mother and father touch each other with wonder . . .

1981

Poem Then, for Love

1 Always you are there

Always you are there — standing
outside the door when someone
shakes the house down, packs
the children away. You appear
at the bedsides of friends who
are leaving town, and finally.
Shadows grow out of your hands;
you bring hills into a room.

There is no question of regret,
you are busy with the secret
joy of one who is inconsolable.
Tomorrow, we may swing on the
bell of the sun, hang by a song;
we may sing. Oh, there is some
small promise when you say *I do
not believe, I know*. When I
touch your body there is light
buried in my hands; there is the
distinct possibility of romance.

2 *And just now*

The way light swarms over
your shoulders.
The day is remarkable that lifts
the town to walk on stilts.
The sun wheels down,
windows shine.

In the crowns of flowers
small fires leap; seeds spill
in the bright air.
Like planets spinning
into sight, passatempo our bodies
turn the hours.

For love your hair sings,
and earth's curve.
For love I pour light
into your body like this —
oh, there is music to be heard,
and just now.

3 *The arrangement*

Your letters arrive
almost daily, and on time;
there may be songs filled
with light, there may be none.
'When you appear on the balcony
like spring undressing, I will fly
through the points of your eyes.'
And what about that fine calligraphy
of sky?, I add as if to meet you
in the middle of a story that's
half gone: oh, we are happy, love
to make use of words even
if it is a trial.

Of course there is an
arrangement. When you say
it's time to move on; that your body

is a heave of old desires you are
ready to shake down — I can see
we are on the way to a fine future,
even if I refuse to know what comes
next (à cause de ma folie). Oh well,
somewhere there is a sentence
chasing time; there is a story
we may need to sleep on,
and always.

4 The right touch

You undress
by moonlight; your body is an adventure.
The mirror goes on
forever. I begin to suspect
you are leaving the story
I have been holding in my arms
all these years, or almost.

If I walk
from this room, return with a
small song for company
and the right touch to write in
the ending, will I find
the mirror may be taking you
away — the moon
a perfect accomplice?

Will I hear that cry
in the dark space
behind you?

5 My love in bed I will not lie

My love in bed I will not lie
You take off in the middle of it all;
Of course the moon is right on time.

I would wrap my legs around your waist
On point in air pin you against the light,
But too much is happening elsewhere.

When you fall, if you have that
In mind, I will not be here despite
The pleasures of an old regard; there is
A boisterous affection in how we hate, and lately.

It is a comfort to know this speech
You make on leaving is also
About love, and clearly.

6 Leave it

Leave it:
on the table
with these small
islands of stones,
and that fine Bakubu king
in ebony, his plum-coloured belly
a wishing-ring.

On the way out
you may be looking for words
to sing the perfect pitch
of morning; unriddle why last night
certain stars light years
from here were discovered
leaving town. Let be
what is, love, you know
every/thing that is
in the world changes
what is real.

Leave it:
but keep in mind,
no doubt you will,
these chevrons of lavender
shedding their points,
that there is of course
no 'commercial outlet'
even if it is
invisible.

                    1985

Vlaminck's Tie / *the persistent imaginal*

Vlaminck's tie survives.
It is made of wood & painted yellow;
it has purple polka-dot moons
that once were sighted floating around
the town, walking Vlaminck in every
direction.
                    When I tell my son
it is resting now in a glass case,
it looks like, say, the beginning
of the world, he says, measuring
the space between his outstretched
hands, oh — like a crusader's sword
you mean.

                    Yes, perhaps that's it
I reply, looking out over the yellow

fields, the tall sword-grass battling
the air. I see: now I see Vlaminck
in his wooden tie sailing right by
the day-moon, milky & far.

1985

MURRAY EDMOND

Born in Hamilton in 1949, Murray Edmond has worked extensively in educational and experimental theatre. He currently teaches drama at the University of Auckland. In 1987 he and Mary Paul edited an anthology, The New Poets.

Shack

I read the word shack.
I like it.
It is a good solid small word.
It would be good to live in a shack.
In inflationary times a shack
would be a good place to live.
Welcome to the shack.
It hardly exists.
You are out the exit
before you are in the entrance.
Turn it sideways —
                    it disappears.
Just a few upright bones hung with flesh.
The beating brain like a soft bunch
of kapok tossed on a derelict floor.
Love this shack, take it to your breast,
wrap your legs around it, it is the best you'll get
this year, next year, never.
Come, let us put ourselves out on the hillside,
let sunbeat drain and dry us,
windbeat drive out the loving heat,
there's more we can make
when we light up the fierce furnaces
of this rusty shack.
Let us be done with concrete and steel,
plastic and formica and all the festoonings
of luxury and comfort, all the false triptrap
gadgetry of glamour.
We can boil potatoes in the middle of the floor.
We can stoke the fire.
We can shack it.
This glorious tiny unstable living heap
which hugs the hillside.
In a week of looking for the cheapest
chintziest, ritziest, ripoff place to live in town
I got sick in the mind, sick at the heart
like Lord Randall returning to his mother
from all the agencies who own the land,

I was sick in the balls
from the way this city was dressed up,
a series of Christmas treats under the richman's
tree I wasn't allowed to unwrap.
Until I found this word shack.
I took a good bath in the word,
washed myself clean with it,
let its pure language force pour down over me
and give me back the smell
of salt and earth and iron
and the sweet wood smell burned grey by the sun.

1981

from Poems of the End Wall

House

Last night as I lay beside you all the desire had gone out of me
and I was cast up like a heap of sand, porous, shapeless,
    shifting,
a thing of shape, an entity, only by virtue of its million parts.

Here I live on a cliff in a house at the end of the island
and in the face of the wind from the north and the wind from
    the south
I surround myself with this thin wall of wood, this shape in
    space

and you are there asleep in the bed, curled to the end wall of
    the house,
your breathing blowing shapes in the cold air, your dreams
    dreaming,
your dreaming holding up the whole fabric of paint and wood
    and tin.

If you stop wanting to dream it will collapse. Your desire to
    dream holds it up,
all the bare longing of the imagination holds it up, the desire
    of the nail

to enter the wood, the desire of the wood to embrace the nail,
the desire of the paint to hide the wood and reflect the light,
the desire of the roof to contain a secret shape of darkness,
the desire of the glass to shine like the sun in the face of the
    sun.

And the earth desires to lie asleep under the house and dream,
it dreams the very shape of the house as though it was
    something organic,
whole as a body, breathing and seeing and standing cold in
    the wind.

The house is the container and you are the thing contained.
Its membrane protects you and your life gives it energy

and stops the walls from collapse. And the moment of seeing
　this

and the moment of saying this are two separate moments:
the first, the moment of seeing is a moment without desire,
at night, by the bed watching you sleep, alone, still, chill,

but not cold, watching, as the silence of space watches the
　grinding earth,
when all the desire has gone out of me and I get up,
get up out of the bed, go out the door, out through the end
　wall,

and grasp hold of the string on the balloon and rise slowly,
　steadily,
shimmering like a giant eye over the house, the whole town,
　the capital city,
rising over the island and the ocean, the earth opening like a
　flower.

But the second, the moment of saying, involves me in the
　grammar of desire.
I have to touch you with my speech to be heard.
And grammar itself is a thing of desire, announcing its
　capacity

to evolve infinitely more complex systems out of bits of
　nothing,
to put together the grains of sand to make rock and the rock
　to build
a cliff and the cliff to hold a house, many houses, a city

to stand at the end wall of the island, the end wall of the land
turned like smooth wood in the yielding shape of the bay
to embrace the random desiring waves of the sea.

Somewhere a child is sacrificed and buried at the foot of the
　posthole
which comes to hold up the whole house. Building walls for
　the compost heap
I smash a post in half and in its rotted core a weta lies, soft
　and sleepy,

hiding until its new exoskeleton hardens enough to let it safely
　live,
to let it grow vulnerable, as earth to light, as sand to sea.
Tonight I embrace you and trust the roof will hold up till
　morning.

　　　　　　　　　　　　　　　　　　　　　　　1981

A Letter about Cars

(*to Russell Haley*)

It started with the implant of the poem about the hat
and came back suddenly to what we used to call,
'Mum's House' — standing, or swimming, feet deep

in the green Waikato flood, a dinghy roped to its steps,
just off the Rangiriri straight, the place which always prompted
Mother to say, 'That's where I wouldn't like to live' —

which gives you the historic logic behind the way we christened it,
'Mum's House', while you, with your dreams of owning
a pair of maroon slacks and a grey blazer were haunting Trafalgar

Square dressed in a death's head mask. A foreign woman came up
to you — 'Young man, you have made a lot of people very happy
tonight.' I connect us by this quality of being coeval —

like Malvern Hill and Rangiriri. Last year I stopped the Triumph
on the gravel-chip carpark ironed out for tourists like myself
below the battle hill — you can picture me, an apprehensive blur

half-turned towards the shot, receding against the 1960 National
Geographic green of the yet-to-be-turned-into-butter grass
and the white handrail climbing you up to the top where a noticeboard

orders you with military precision to gaze southeast and pick up
the low ambience of another fortified position while averting your gaze
from the southwest aspect across the river where the willows tangle

with the bank and begin the land Tawhiao sought back one hundred
     years ago
last year, coming up this road (or perhaps by train) to catch the
     London boat.
Or thirty years ago next year I took the road with my father, driving

the Springboks out to welcome by Koroki. We came year after year,
first in a Plymouth with tartan seats and then in a '56 model with
small fins, then a '58 Dodge, slender-waisted, black and yellow

with huge fins and a sting in the tail, with flags and hats
(the hat in the poem) and red, yellow and black ribbons streaming,
always with a nod to Mum's House — you were emigrating to
     Australia —

the implant of the image flares up out of the water as words form
across a page of white sound — as though meaning meant
     accumulating loss —
the whiteness dropping piece by piece down spontaneous holes

forming the memory, always, in negative. He takes it this way when
writing about Mum's House which he carries as a residue of the
    incredible,
the impossible, a Ripley's sketch of local significance.

They both realise, in telling tales, they have been constructing
themselves backwards for the other in order to increase the level
of negative feedback, to push the print towards blackness without

complete loss of image. The history of seeing is contained in the
deceptively facile surface of this photo of his wife standing by
an unknown car in front of a house where both of them

used to live. At a certain point the history of a place
capitulates to its dreams — they are both far past that point —
he has inhabited two places already in this way — and so too

a narrative of beginning which goes on far enough begins to
contain another beginning. The text will alter subtly under weight —
as snow released from a branch for you — for me, the river over
    banks —

the house awash, isolated, dreaming of a car full of family
driving past. It is the way you inhabit character — coming out
of the airport and noticing the Triumph parked and the disbelief

on your face — allows the shared thought. We test drove it
down Taranaki St, into Abel Smith, up the top of Willis and across
Webb, and, back at the yard, the shared thought — 'It's too good

for us'. But already we had begun to inhabit a new origin.
Shifting the weight from foot to foot, reading the precise
    noticeboard,
becoming tourist, the hat becomes poem. I touch the back of

the earth with the nape of my sole. You lean forward to read the
    line.
Inside the letter is sealed another letter, and, on opening it,
another is found. Each allows you to understand more and more

of a rapidly moving, accumulative fiction. But memory strains and
multiplying versions of origin confound synopsis,
From time to time the river floods its banks and leaves the house

to stand like an island. The Triumph, grinning slightly, draws out
into the stream of cars on the Prussian blue seal. You can follow it
from your hill but it turns aside before becoming like a dot.

                                        1987

About Wasps

for Ian Wedde

In pipes, in tins
            in broken clay,
under a ledge of brick or wood,
        hung from a tree,

anywhere
         a cavity is formed,
hidden, secret,
             now, at this time,
October,
          the dormant queens begin
to sniff the wind,
            twelve degrees
expected maximum
        in Wellington today,
along the cliffs
         of Maida Vale
and Lyall Bay
           Vespula germanica is seeking
out a place,
        those brittle mothers
with ten thousand, maybe
     more eggs ranged
              inside the abdomen.
       Not this winter
but the one before
        in my house above
the sea I turned the bricks
            I'd stacked
for paving and retaining
     in my crumbling
  garden
       and found them there, a dozen
or so
      of the hibernating queens, huge,
       yellow, sluggish,
  cold, stiff as ancient metal rusted up
(the first one blundered
     in my Christchurch kitchen
  yesterday. I hammered
it with a rolled-up
     newspaper). Those
rigid winter queens
       I rolled out in the wind
and let them die,
        feeling
more part of the natural
      cycle of
the garden for
      doing so.
        The nest
by March or April
         brims
     with workers, queens and
drones, the cells
        are packed
  with pupae, larvae
and sweet food,

                              royal jelly
          culled from aphids, jam
                         and fruit,
          but by late May
                         or early June
          after the workers have
                    cannibalised the nest
              and gorged themselves
          and ceased to come back
                                   home
          and the queens have
                    danced above the trees
                    and mated,
          the rats and mice move in
                         and rip the nest apart
              and shred
          the paper honeycomb
                         to line
          their own dark holes.
                    And now, today,
          those queens who made it
              through the winter,
                                   they
          begin to venture out
                                   in
                    slow cumbersome
          flight,
                    they test
                         the equinoctial wind
          not knowing yet
              what is happening
                    on the updraught and the down,
                                             why even
          sleep has stopped
                              and they
              fly at all,
                         yet in this state
                    one will clip
          herself
                    to the grey, splintered
          side of a lamppost
                    and with her jaws
                                   scrape off
              small wood
          and chew it up
                         and swallow it
                    and regurgitate the mash,
                    a pulp for making
          paper,
                    the first stutter
                         of the new

                         1987

The Blue Boy

What manner of child was this
who turned the heads in Milne and Choyce
at the quality of cloth he wore,
the fine bone china of his hand,

the way a cricket ball would roll
with linseed touch across his palm
and devilishly elude the batsman's
prod? The mothers all swooned

when he drew his dirk and foil
and danced at Christmas time
in the forecourt of the petrol station.
Fathers were not so taken

with his *jouissance*.
For one thing, growing up
wasn't on his purposeful agenda.
His body language told them something

they pretended not to want to hear.
And in space he hybridised
the Victorian and the Continental:
chasms vast of cliff and crag

floating in sublimity of storm and sea
were melded with the café corner,
enclave with absinthe and a dream.
He was the boy you were born to fall

in love with, the child every mother
ached to hang upon her wall.
He drove that kind of 1930s sportscar,
had a library of erotica,

smelt as other men then did not smell
and got away with it
because his Dickensian offsider, the Red Boy,
took the rap.

          That such a spiv as that Blue Boy
was living in the lounge, a room
parlous with dignity where you were taken
when the doctor came, a ripe needle
in a whack of buttock, standing on a chair

so the doctor didn't have to bend,
this was his enchantment.
From his rock settle he looked across
a tuneless piano to a glass flamingo.

1992

ALAN BRUNTON

Born in 1946 in Hamilton, Alan Brunton was co-founder of the influential 1970s periodicals Freed *and* Spleen. *He also founded the still-running theatrical troupe Red Mole and a selection of his work as playwright,* A Red Mole Sketchbook, *was published in 1991. He lives in Island Bay, Wellington.*

It Was Night in the Lonesome October

IT IS RAINING
(il pleut   pleut   pleut)
! ! ! ! ! ! ! ! ! ! !
at Fayette St and Green
! ! ! ! ! ! ! ! ! ! !
(mon dieu —
il pleut some more)(!)
in Baltimore
where Kravitz and Rothbard
merchandisers of carnival oddities
(for showfolks that they know) like
calico clowns, mechanical pencils,
3-dimensional views of the holy grot at Lourdes
and parasols cut out of cheap organzas
are liquidating
(this) Kravitz and (this) Rothbard
their whole crazy business —
perhaps it rains for them
(!)(il pleut
some more) in Baltimore
where the Poet's mother starved to death
and he danced in the flames
of the Broad Street Theatre burning down
where whisky had kept him quiet
night after night
while she drummed up a riot —
she was The Darling of the Gods! —
and (counting unicorns) Kravitz asks
this your first time in Baltimore?
I say *oh yes*
too bad it's ah raining says Rothbard
and I say *too bad* yes it's too bad it's raining
over Baltimore
and over the road there, why ...

WHAT MADNESS DRIVES POETS TO ENLIST IN ARMIES
I THINK
even this Poet
one day elected sergeant-major by the troopers
he fell off his horse(!)
(whisky rained *Encore!*
and opium: *Encore!* too) (in his heart)
and jailed for public drunkenness
and disgrace in St Petersburg he scrawled

MY WHOLE NATURE REVOLTS AT THE IDEA THAT THERE
IS ANY BEING IN THE UNIVERSE SUPERIOR TO MYSELF
but that was after
Kravitz and Rothbard
ancestors of (this) Kravitz and (this) Rothbard
came ritzing into this same Bay
on some hell-boat out of Varna
speaking no English at all
except the name of a dream: *Amerika! Amerika!*
and the first thing they saw was a cortege of paupers
for Virginia had died
(she was the Poet's bride)
warmed only by his Army coat
the coat he wore that day to her funeral

*IS THAT UM THE WESTMINSTER PRESBYTERIAN
CHURCH OVER THERE?*
I ask Kravitz
but Rothbard *yes* says
and Kravitz too *too bad it's raining*
I say *yes* (too bad
it's raining I think)
yes there were two men talking one afternoon
one said to the other coming upon the Poet
about to jump from a bridge
one said *who is that?*
the other *why* replied *this is Poe* aha *the Poet!*
and lying at their feet the Poet yet
speaking gave vent to this lament:
MY BEST FRIEND IS THE ONE WHO WOULD BLOW OUT
MY BRAINS
so I guess it's right it should be raining
! ! ! ! ! ! ! ! ! ! !
(au-delà) like (this)
atramentously (this) day (this) October 7
(this) day (this) Poet discharged himself from pain
LORD HELP MY SOUL
he said as morticians lagged his legs
so he'd not rise again from his coffin
Lot Number 80
it was unclaimed for years
we shall never open these doors again sighs Kravitz
and Rothbard *never* agrees
it can rain forever more in Baltimore
and he spit
!

SO OVER THE ROAD TO THE CHURCH I GO
where an albino bone
of cold limestone
sits on the bones
of Edgar Allan Poe and Virginia Allan Poe
and upon that sits an ebon cat
and as I place there a paper rose

(courtesy of Kravitz)
and a postcard (from Rothbard)
a raven unravels from the sky
and sallies *nevermore*
and just like that (!) it's raining somewhere else
(le ciel est bleu)
no more (il pleut) over Baltimore

. . . .

POE? KRAVITZ HAD PONDERED
and Rothbard too *oh*
I *yes* had replied
he's buried there next door
Poe the Poet
at Fayette St and Green
and *gentlemen* I had wished them *happy disestablishment*
right there
in Baltimore

1984–1991

K. O. ARVIDSON

Born in Hamilton in 1938, K. O. Arvidson currently works in the English Department at the University of Waikato. He has also taught in universities in Australia and at the University of the South Pacific.

The Tall Wind

He said to them, Look at this: you see
where the tall wind leans against your window-pane?
And they said Yes; the cold has come again.
Which being true, he dared not disagree.

Instead he said, If that wind once more blows
like that, your house will fly away like straw.
But they, of course, had thought of that before.
And also, though he did not dare suppose

they might have done, they'd seen a dead man lain
for laundering on half a fallen tree.
He thought, How strangely that man looks like me;
and said aloud, With luck there'll be no rain ...

and just as he spoke, it started in to pour.
One of them laughed, and one said, Thar she blows:
we'll find out now what this young charlie knows.
There's a tall wind out there, leaning on our door.

1973

Fish and Chips on the Merry-Go-Round

In caves with a single purpose
fish were drawn deliberately
from room to room.
Pallid Romans employed them
in a kind of masonry.
They even had their own day of the week.
Before that, though,
presumably,
before the nails from Calvary went back
like bullets into the dove on Ararat,
there must have been a fish or two
sharked many a household bare,
great bloated sunfish, ogling octopi,
between the bedstead and the hearth with relish
tearing apart all shining, arkless men,
competing for the viscous eyeballs loose
like opals on the suffocated floor.

A seasonable peripety assures
contemporary hygiene,
symbol and ancestor alike
hosed out, or splintered off.
Little, or large as eels, fish
fodder us; best of all
on the six days in between.
They build us up.

Still,
on a slow wheel, sharpening fins
give glints.

1973

The Four Last Songs of Richard Strauss at Takahe Creek above the Kaipara

1. *Frühling*
      (Hesse)

Waking's urgency, that sets
the day's track of desire, I deem
instinctive, right as the opening flower.
It surely leads me. Newer the sense of sky,
of skittering cloud, of new winds in the marram
murmuring. Gulls go blithely. And on the terrace,
north, and over the formal lawn,
the air itself sings freshly of my love,
its sweet betokenings, its fierce and morning
certainty.
         In what sense is it I regret
the harbour's tranquility? Sun upon water,

and small lights murderously encroach
of elements at ease, in subtle harmony.
Eyes against eyes. And my eyes briefly wish
the whips of wind back, and the speed of rain,
the water's winter trepidation. Peace,
and the promise of this rising tide,
betray me; even in such a morning;
even in all this complement I find
to my conviction, fixity of dear pain,
anguish of the rose unfolding
in beauty once again.
                              But the time
does lead me; and I breathe
consuming fragrances.

2. *September*

  (Hesse)

I am assembled here, at ease
in foreboding. I have measured the shadow
dying, and the brilliant wind
is alive with new things, lambs and petals and light,
asserting permanence. And yet,
this little thrush, that madly
flew through the scents of newness, now
grows cold within my hand. Strange noon,
to smite so casually, to freeze so small a thing
and drop it on warm grass!
I watched this little bird. It sped like a thistle
recklessly, bucketing on the air,
and very loud: implying, I think,
mortality, because I watched it all the way
from the long soft grass through that abandonment
to the tree so landmark-large, to the last and sudden
blindness, staggering ecstasy, light
singing
          death.
                      I am assembled here, at ease
in foreboding. And my desire?
My love should bury this with love.

My love would not. My love would
toss it in the air.

3. *Im Abendrot*

  (von Eichendorff)

The far Brynderwyns heave across the harbour,
rising upon the second tide, mountains
in mangrove moving, weaving
the last complexities of the sun. These
are a tangle of reflections. Over them,
the next peninsula shines yellow,

pastoral century of slow change,
and the roofs of pioneers, like beacons, prophesy
the imminence of fishermen, their lights
alive and casting, quick
to be out before the strong tide sucks and runs.

> I sing of our long voyaging,
> and you who led me, at my side;
> I sing the saddest of all things;
> I sing the unaccomplished bride.

The hills will cease to float soon, and the mangroves
ripple themselves away.
The wandering flames of grass will calm, and the cattle
boom night's gullies up and down. My lights
will anchor a headland. Boats will take bearings,
seeking the channel; and then,
the Kaipara will move out.
A shag clap-claps in shallows.
I point the way to an open sea,
though all my doors are closed,
and I within.

> Go slowly, sun. A gentle death
> of day is in the birds that wheel
> in clouds to their accustomed rest,
> and in the racing of the keel
>
> before the racing of the tide,
> and in the crowding of dark trees.
> I sing the unaccomplished bride.
> I sing my death in all of these.

4. *Beim Schlafengehen*

> (Hesse)

The fire of darkness, battle and desire,
the rising blood. Without, within,
sounds of continuance. The cattle do not sleep;
a lost bird quavers over the water, cautious,
ill at ease; the sheep in random companies huddle,
munching. Music overwhelms me, builds
and dissipates; my harbour, rising and falling,
song and ambience,
            Strange old man, man of my hemisphere,
spinning your daughters still, in such age,
deftly out of time and the lapse of time!
Tainted in wars, surviving; cause and cure;
your face unchanging — love alone, there? or music
richly ambiguous? — beauty with burden, beast
fulfilled and not fulfilled
in yearning. So am I.
            Northern, I think
you did not care for the dog-star greatly,

or else it rose in one eye, set in the other.
Here, still paradox, smiling and murdering,
restless lights locked in a softening cave
with sound that kills. Alarming spectre;
the sweetness of despair, the sandstone washed
and falling all aflame, its granite change,
and caught in fondling only, like a flower.

Of love elector and disposer,
of war creator and composer,
this music evades the season and month and hour.

1973

PETER OLDS

Born in 1944, Peter Olds lives in Dunedin. His poetry encapsulates a gritty, urban-realist strand in recent New Zealand poetry.

My Mother Spinning

Sit too close
& the spinning bobbin cools you.
Leave the room
& the foot pedal beats
on a raw nerve.
Leave the house

& a thread of wool follows.

1976

Thoughts of Jack Kerouac — & Other Things

I work nights at the University Bookshop:
Junior, Intermediate, Headman, Honorary Caretaker,
Master Cleaner. I work in every conceivable position
from toilets, Foreign Language to Herbal Cookery,

sometimes singing 'Oh What a Beautiful Evening' and
sometimes not. Mostly, I just race about like
Neal Cassady with an overstuffed vacuum
cleaner snarling on my tail, cornering fast on one

sneaker past SUPERWOMAN and gassing like a madman up the BIOGRAPHY Oneway Section — chewing-gum,
cigarette-butts, paper-clips and brains dissolving before
my foaming fury . . . . Zap, out the back, empty a tin,

grab a bucket one mop one broom, flash back
past LAW, Modern PSYCHOLOGICAL Medicine, Heavy
Granite Colour-filled Graffito ART, Sex Cornered
PAMPHLETS, miles of wrapping paper and up the stairs

to the staff room for a coffee break at 8. Ten
minutes only. Into the toilets, scrub shine wipe

on hands and knees, sometimes thinking 'The Closest
I Come To God and Other Things' and sometimes not.

Mostly, I just thank the Lord for the Detention
Centre Experience many Rocky Youthful Years back
and get the hell out of there down the stairs (4 at
a time), jump over a hot PAN Paperback, switch off

the lights (5 second silence by the NZ POETRY
Section), scratch my backside, straighten the doormat,
lock up, slam the outside door tight, run to the pub
(9PM), sweat, feel proud, get half drunk,

crawl home, sit down, try to write a love poem
to a girl who works in the Bookshop Office . . . .
Her typewriter and hairpin, her mystery yoghurt containers, her tiny footscuffed secrets and solitary chair.

1980

DAVID MITCHELL

*Born in 1940, David Mitchell was an important figure in the live poetry scene in
Auckland during the 1970s.*

My Lai / Remuera / Ponsonby

she
holds th mirror to her eye

whole villages burn.

2 million years have proved nothing
she

did not already know.

th lines on hr hand
speak out clear   &

serene

also those beneath her eyes
& in between ...

she
sits in th kitchen
'boiling an egg'

she
inverts th tiny
'hourglass'   &

30 seconds pass   &

she
contemplates th sand
                &

she
holds a hand over each dark eye
in turn
        &

children burn.

                        1972

Olive Grove / Noon

(*for Garcia Lorca*)

deliver me
olive tree

from my hard silence . . .

an old woman carries fruit
an old dog crosses the square
diagonally
                the wind blows . . .

deliver me o sacred tree
from the eye of the storm —

my houses are razed
my armies imaginary

my ladies are ghosts
my friends
              enemies

my gardens are devoured
by the sea . . .

my times are treacherous

my dreams cowards —
they turn

they turn
& flee . . .
    deliver me o sacred
    tree

    from my hard silence.

an old man carries himself
across the square
in agony

the times are treacherous —
his brothers have seen
to that

they are dead
his brothers

still he carries them
across this square

they are my brothers

deliver them from their hard silence
    o sacred tree

an old woman carries flowers
she crosses the square

silently, silently.

(1980)

IAN WEDDE

Born in Blenheim in 1946, Ian Wedde spent his childhood in East Pakistan and England as well as New Zealand. After graduating from the University of Auckland, he travelled extensively, living for a year in Amman, Jordan. In 1985 he co-edited the influential Penguin Book of New Zealand Verse *with Harvey McQueen. Wedde has published poetry, three novels, a collection of stories and a substantial body of literary and art criticism. He is currently Concept Leader, Art, at the Museum of New Zealand Te Papa Tongarewa.*

Ruth

1

If I call you Ruth. She lay
at the big man's
feet & covered them.
Charity flowed from him
like good sense. He had cut
corn all day, dirt
filled his body's flaws, he
snored. I have not

so much as stepped
outside the front door.
The sound of wind in the cypress trees
is like you turning over.
If your breath
touched my face now I would
not call you Ruth. You
are not here. You are Ruth.

You looked back two or
three times trying
not to cry. This vacant image

is with me, the
knowledge of your absence,
a space you turn towards
doubtfully, having no choice.
The rest I

grope my hands through
like latticework, the negative

light in which my eyes
blaze, pearly cataracts.
There are things you
touched, they have gone.
My lips move upon a word, *Ruth*.
You are trees, a sound. You turn
to me with a sound
of wind stirring the cypress trees.
Your breath touches my face.

2

The blood rose out of me
for some who had not died
in makeshift ambulances along the
pitted Damascus road. I remembered

an evening in that white city
when my blood rose towards
you. Kites hung in the summer convections.
Your pale body on the white bed, long

scars across it, green jalousie shadows.
My life crowds up in me.
My thoughts tug like
kites above the dry upward currents.

3

Night wind in the dusty
cypress trees. No part of you
is whole to me, my blood rises for the wind
turning in my bed. Ideograms

of the blind, the violence of memory.
In the light cast upward
beyond your white body your tongue
is a dark fuse your eyes are
touched with red. You grip
me & tread my body drawing
blood. Each dove-twilight, each
morning they have brought up
mangonels against your tower-cote.
You turned sadly towards a
space, each morning
something more of you has gone.
It does not atrophy, I

cannot hold it, your image grows
into what surrounds me. *Ruth*
Ruth how long before

you cover me again,
simple & small as something done.
The red factor canary turns
out its wings, the cat goes daintily
across the garden, the
wind touches my face.

1974

from Earthly: Sonnets for Carlos

2 for Rose

9

'If thy wife is small bend down to her &
whisper in her ear' (Talmud)

                                    — what shall I
whisper?   that I dream it's no use any
more trying to hide my follies. If trees &

suchlike don't tell on me I understand
my son will & soon, too. His new blue eyes
see everything. Soon he'll learn to see
less. O the whole great foundation is sand.

But the drought has broken today, this rain!
pecks neat holes in the world's salty fabu-
lous diamond-backed carapace & doubt comes
out, a swampy stink of old terrapin.

What shall I say? 'I hid nothing from you,
but from myself. That I dream, little one,

10

by day & also by night & you are
always in the dream . . .' Oh you can get no
peace, will get none from me. The flower smells so
sweet who needs the beans? We should move house there
into the middle of the bean-patch: a
green & fragrant mansion, why not! Let's do
it all this summer & eat next year. O

let's tear off a piece. It's too hard & far
to any other dreamt-of paradise
& paradise is earthly anyway,
earthly & difficult & full of doubt.

I'm not good I'm not peaceful I'm not wise
but I love you. What more is there to say.
My fumbling voices clap their hands & shout.

20 *a sonnet for Carlos*

His new blue eyes see everything   to live
with the dream & have the world come on in!
because I believe it's happened again . . .
O their perfect intentions, all that love,
indifference he'll lose the knack of.
There's no date on the precious token
but I know it (huh!) november nineteen-
seventy-two, in time . . . while the dream heaves,
tilting heart true again on its fulcrum
among the unruly facts & fragments.
My fumbling voices clap their hands & shout
out, a swampy stink of old terrapin,
& for thanks, within this small settlement,
earthly & difficult & full of doubt!

26 *power transformer*

Dozens of wrangling sparrows have built their
shitty serviceable nests high up Three
Mile Hill in a power transformer. I see
them every day unscorched & lusty where
they're getting on with it in that airy
crass penthouse with its fine view of the sea,
shouting & breeding among the deadly
grey buzzing conduits . . . oh you were born there

first of all little Carlos, in the mind,
& there you live now in faith & in hope
before a horizon that could skate right
up to you! (closer than *this*, than these lines,
& closer than the thought of love, the 'shape
of things to come')
                            — let them see/
                                        who have sight.

27

Precocious spring how beautiful you are!

Let them see
                who can.
                            Barberry puts out
fiery buds early flowers prepare to shout
cold sere hills exhale the yellow colour
of births & marriages: spring, piss, sulphur!
Io Hymen! gorse, broom, lupin, ragwort:
the tough surviving 'noxious weeds' hang out
their crass banners all around the harbour
where this time last year seabirds crashed into
frozen slush

                    when memory, a former
lover come to wish you well, left early

went home & wept alone . . . you never knew . . .
you forgot!
        O these battered weeds have flowers
as delicate
      & sweet
          as any

31

Diesel trucks past the Scrovegni chapel
Catherine Deneuve farting onion fritters
The world's greedy anarchy, I love it!
Hearts that break, garlic fervent in hot oil
Jittery exultation of the soul
Minds that are tough & have good appetites
Everything in love with its opposite
I love it! O how I love it! (It's all

I've got
        plus Carlos: a wide dreaming eye
above her breast,
          a hand tangling her hair,
breath filling the room as blood does the heart.

We must amend our lives murmured Rilke
gagging on his legacy of air.
Hang on to yours Carlos it's all you've got.

32 dawn friday 17 august 1973 /American bombing
   halt in Cambodia

The sky bellies
      in the east
             mouths of hills
spill thin milk, the Pleiades depart leading
their bull by the snout . . .
           great Taurus drooling
for your Pasiphae
         winched up on the sill
of Daedalus' weird machine, bollock-full
& red-eyed you gored & bellowed plunging
yourself asleep. Ah she was a strange thing

so foreign & delicate:
       maddening you . . .
& that crazy egghead strapping you in . . .

Later you woke & saw monstrous children,
the cities crashing down. You were meant for
a gift, Bull, but you were hoarded & then
your huge   poison shot out into the world . . .

These are old tales Carlos
        & there are more

37 land-mine casualty Amman 1970

Because he was a man he retreated
instantly 'inside'/
                            His extremities
flipped off: feet genitals chin fingers nose.
Then he was sealed in what was left, a kind
of atavic stump. He had been erased
from the personal familiar surface
of his skin. I couldn't look him in the face.
When to greet him I took him by the hand
or what was left of it it was glossy

as though the gorgeous facets of minerals
were cicatrices.
                   He'd become stone
warmed by the sun. It was the kite season.
Above scorching hillsides whose flint scars blazed
his children's weightless toys quivered & spun.

50 for Robin & Lois

Cast off   earth-ferry! forever into
your own presence
                            under the shining sails
of your firmament
                            among galaxies
archipelagos the colour of stars
endless oceans continents star-harbours . . .

au revoir
            so long
                   bon voyage Charlie
have a wonderful time. Planets also
are lofted by those convections   they are
kites carried by your breath Carlos   the sail
sings in the updraughts of your blood   forever!

into *this* presence
                   where you are sleeping
& dreaming under Robin's plum tree, small
& mysterious as well, a traveller
like the rest of us
                   dreaming of travelling.
                                          1975

Pathway to the Sea

to A. R. Ammons

I started late summer-before-last
    digging for a
        field-tile drain

at the bottom of the garden
   where below
      topsoil that leached away
as fast as I mulched &
   fed it was
      a puggy clay

slick turning rainwater
   frost dew snow sparrow-
      piss & other seepage & drainage down
under an old shed
   in the lower adjoining
      section: here the water
bogged foundations & floorboards
   till the whole crazy
      edifice began to

settle sideways &
   slide on greased clay
      downward
taking a fouldrain with it:
   visions of 'faecal matter'
      bubbling up from clogged
overflow traps bothered
   me & some
      others too: it was time

to act! especially since
   in addition to ordure getting
      spread around &
putting its soft mouths in
   deep cloacal
      kisses to our
livers any obvious
   breakdown in the system for
      disposal of this shit

(*ours* in fact) would
   bring the council inspectors round
      like flies
aptly, & *that* would mean
   they'd get to look at
      other aspects of how
we choose to
   live which might strike them as
      unorthodox or even

illegal: for example there's
   lots being done round here
      with demolition
timber, & that's illegal, you gotta
   use *new* timber,
      citizen, the old stuff

which was once forests of kauri &
    totara & rimu took oh
        hundreds of years to get to

where it was when it was
    milled, the houses it knit
        together stood & with-
stood 'better' than the forests
    I suppose: the timber
        served, anyway, it
did that for whoever watched
    the process through, &
        now that the houses're out

of phase much as the forests once
    were, though like the
        forests the fibre of the brittle
timber can still spring
    & ring . . . anyhow,
        now it's time
to go, it has to be stamped down, splintered
    by a dozer's tracks & what's
        left of fibre knot

& resin has a match
    put to
        it: it goes 'up
in smoke' — but round
    here we hoard the stuff &
        use it, it easily bends
nails, it splits & you
    belt your thumb often enough
        to know all about that

but the structures
    stay put! & the inspectors
        would say 'Down
with them' — well down with
    them! . . . I like the way you
        have to compromise with brittle
demolition timber: what gets
    built has bent the
        builder as well as his

nails & nerves: he's
    learnt something about
        service, the toughness of the
medium may have taught him
    that ease is no grateful
        index to dispensability
or availability: like
    who wants a companion for
        life or whatever span

you fancy (they're all 'for life') who can't
   put some juice
      back in your
systems? — ah how you value
   the tough lover who
      keeps you up
to the mark, whose head
   eyes language hands
      loins *en-*

gage you, give you
   elevation, a prospect, with whom you ride
      up the up &
up like birds beating on in
   the mutual updraughts of
      each other's wings — *birds*, a
subject I'll come back to later
   when I'm through with this
      drain: what needs

to be noted here, though, is that even if
   some things don't fight
      back at once or
obviously, you can still
   bet your 'sweet' (for)
      'life'
they fight back all right & your children & children's
   children will be paying *your*
      blood-money, citizen —

well, meanwhile, we agreed, let's
   keep our shit out
      of the public eye & let's
keep our friendly sheds, our lovely slums,
   our righteous brittle screwy
      inspired constructs
up: & then
   let's add some
      flourishes, decoration in this kind

of setting doesn't coddle
   anyone, least of all the chickens
      whose coop's
included in the drainage
   problem threatening to
      overwhelm us
all: besides, we'll all
   benefit: chickens with dry
      feet lay more eggs

because they're happy: happiness
   as a concept may be
      about as brittle as
demolition timber when the latter's traced
   back to its
      forest & the former

to its causes, but it
    serves likewise, it teaches us
        'for life': if you're

for life you're for its crazy outhouses,
    the corners of happiness that don't
        square: right,
there were lots
    of reasons, the practical & the
        ideal didn't separate out,
the forests & the brittle planks
    were one, we
        were *engaged*, we wanted

to convert our drainage problem,
    transform it, *tran-*
        substantiate it, assume it into
the causes of our happiness & the
    happiness of our
        chickens whose wet feet
& poor laying rates
    rebuked us daily — we picked
        up shovels, backed off somewhat,

then we started digging fast, we went at it, we went
    down four feet & then
        two more, there was
all kinds of trash, bottles & old
    sofa springs & broken
        masonry & bricks
& unusual quantities of bones dating
    from a previous owner who'd bred
        dogs, Dobermans (-men?) I

heard, then we began to get
    into the clay
        pug, we were out of
sight by now, the shovels hove
    into view at
        rare intervals,
shaken by
    buried handlers
        to loose the sticky glup:

a comic & as time went by
    popular spectacle: for those
        down in the drain
the strain began to
    tell: some quit, some
        hid, some developed rheums
blisters & trenchfoot, streptococci
    swarmed upon their tonsils,
        they pissed

chills straight from the kidney (it was
        now winter, autumn had
            dallied by among
the easy wreckage of an
        earlier level)
            they defected, deserted,
they offered their apologies, they
        fucked off, the practical &
            the ideal

sprang apart like
        warping unseasoned
            timber, boiiiinngg-
ggg . . . a sound, I
        thought, not
            unlike a drop
on a long rope: what
        deserters got once, & I found myself
            wishing it on them

again as I
        plied my lone shovel, bucket,
            grout, mattock, axe & spade,
baling out the boggy trench
        as the 'drainage problem' halted
            right there, hacking
through roots (that deep!) shoring
        up avalanching walls (the drain — huh! — was
            by now fifty yards

long & in some
        places twelve feet
            deep! impressive even
if left at that) & shaving
        out gummy scoops
            of clay which grunting
I then flicked heaven-
        ward into the blue
            icy sky or

alternatively into the sky
        the low colour
            of clay: clay
anyway, clay & more
        clay, the gobs landed up
            there pretty
randomly after a while, & sometimes
        they got washed
            down again by the late winter

rain, heavy rain, which the
        roots of trees were
            sucking at, sap

beginning to rise in them,
    refreshed by those
        surface-feeding tendrils, those deep
tap-roots, & it's here the
    story really
        starts: not

that what's been said so far's
    irrelevant, though I apologise for its
        disorderly development &
the large number of
    seeming non-sequiturs — things
        do
follow I assure you, they
    proceed, citizen, they practically hunt
        you down, & me, who've

just been enjoying the way
    these lines unfold, much
        more easily than how the pug
& clodded
    marl left that
        drain, landing up there
out of sight & almost
    burying one
        of three baby

fruit trees (we're here) which
    therefore didn't get its tiny
        branches cut
back before the
    sap rose in them as spring came
        on gravely, gaily, with me still down
there in the trench
    still chucking the odd
        clod up & still

covering that pear tree: finally
    a retaining wall
        got built (use
was made of
    used materials) & then a truck
        came with field tiles
& another with shingle & we got
    together some
        used roofing-iron

& we had a drain! Yeah! there
    was enough fall in it to get
        'the problem' drainage
away & out of our way, the chickens
    basked & laid, the clammy surfaces
        of seeping banks
dried up, the rotting
    structures with their feet in
        clay delayed their

inevitable demise, miasmal
   damps & soaks breathed
      out their last stinks of mould
& fungus, artesian
   cheeps & kisses of surfacing
      wet were drowned in
birdsong, when the sun shone it
   dried & when the rain fell it ran away
      the way

we wanted: it was
   summer, the leaf
      uncrinkled from the bud
blossom fell, fruit
   spurs plumped out,
      sap circulated with its natural zest,
& one small
   pear tree, un-
      pruned, went

crazy! was a mares-nest
   of wild growth, capillary
      maze of shoots & tangled
twigs gobbling the provisions
   of root & leaf, starch
      & water, sweet open
sandwiches of rotted
   stackbottom & whatnot,
      bonbons

& snacks broken & tasted
   by those bon-vivants the
      earthworms: the whole gusty
catering-service
   served
      that tree whose clusters
congested & grew
   together with ungainly health
      while nearby

the other two grew
   straight sturdy
      & slim, sunlight
entered their hearts,
   they reached up
      heavenwards: 'benighted' is
a word we should have
   the use of
      more often: oh pear tree! in

that condition you'd never
   score a single
      shriveled product: well
come autumn I cut you
   back till there was almost
      nothing left: the lesson

is, effort's got to be directed . . .
   yeah, I heard
      they wanted to build an

ALUMINIUM
  SMELTER
    at
Aramoana, the sea-gate, & someone's bound to direct
  more effort that
    way soon: listen, there's
birds out there, we're
   back with those lovers, the buoyancy
    & updraught of some kind of

mutual understanding of what
   service is, of the fact that
    a thing being easy doesn't
make it available or passive:
   listen, effort's got to be right
    directed, that's
all, the catering's amazing, everything
  proceeds, citizen, sometimes
    it's hard work, but you're

engaged, you want
   to keep practical & ideal
    together, you're
for life, you know that happiness
  has to do with yes
    drains & that nature
like a pear tree
  must be served before
   it'll serve you, you

don't want your children's
   children paying
    your blood-
money, citizen, you're
  for a different sort
   of continuity, you want
to live the way
  you want
    to, you want to keep

your structures up, you
  want elevation,
   you're ready to do
your share, you'll dig your field-
  drain & you'll
   keep your shit out
of the water supply:
  you want to
    serve & to be left alone

to serve & be served,
   understanding tough
      materials, marl & old timber,
the rich claggy rind
   of the world where
      dinosaurs once
were kings: well they're gone now though
   they survived longer
      than we have

yet, but then we know, don't we,
   citizen, that there's nowhere
      to defect to, & that
living in the
   universe doesn't
      leave you
any place to chuck
   stuff off
      of.

              1975

Mahia April 1978

1

The amazing stars! they
still burned through the pines.

The sea rushed in
with its stellar sound.

I thought, This is it.

The whole firmament was whirling like a kaleidoscope.
I nearly broke my neck looking at it.

I was getting good at being lonely.
I had the the 'whole' experience to myself.

2

The Age of Aquarius was short. The two hundred
Vietnamese orphans snuffed in that plane crash
in, when was it? that

was it. Howard Hughes & the CIA,
a poor choice for godparents.

Bad PR for an age.

Let's not try to talk anybody into anything.

In 1978 I consider the air I breathe
and I refuse to thank anyone for it.

I pick tuatua and pipi along Mahia Beach.
A la Frank Sargeson I scatter bread

persuading them to come clean.

There is plenty of space for my lonely joy.
I walked all of eight miles & met nobody.

Swimming naked in a channel the tide
was filling, thought
it would be sweet to fuck like dolphins.

Makotahi Headland stood up there like a burning mirror.

Now I sit in my cabin and listen
to the sea beyond the pines. Near me
the shellfish are sucking at my bread on their water.

And I miss you so badly.
And I feel so far from my borders.
Will you barter with me for my solitude.

3

I used to think, poetry
was what you did when people stopped listening.

Now I guess it's what you do when there's nobody.

Message in bottle: Send help!
They arrive and collect the bones.
All around the evidence of an ordered life.

Immortality is a longterm currency.

The poor bastard could have done with a trip to town,
something of ready exchange.

4

Pausing to read bird encounters in the sand:
two landing tracks, some circles and chalky turds,
two flightpaths off. And we construct

whole epistemologies with these
vicious toughs. Even allowing for 'Percival Gull Six'

Jonathan Livingston Seagull gulped worms and shit.

Oh certainly he could fly.

Don't look up to things because
they're beautiful. Some very famous actresses
have been known to kick & fire.

5

I watch a family come down
to collect pipi. One man
with a walk-on part

is overcome by greed

and takes too many.
A seagull chooses one, flies up
& smashes it.

I watch the waves run and fall,
and the sky
rising through mauve to blue . . . What kind of

predator am I
lying back here on a dune thinking about Goethe.

I should go & talk to someone who knows.

But look at these hundreds of curious

hairballs, maybe
the fibrous skeletons of horseturds,
maybe things a whale coughs.

And always the sensation of there being something important
to say

but no one to say it to, worse still
nothing is clear

finally. Description is only
an endless means. And sometimes

you want to say stop.

Action could hurry the moment to you.

This loneliness that runs falling over itself
coast after coast.

This endless hunt for meanings,
finally a kind of curious greed.

1984

Barbary Coast

When the people emerge from the water
who can tell if it's brine or tears
that streams from them, purple sea
or the bruises of their long immersion?

They seem to weep for the dreams they had
which now the light slices into buildings
of blinding concrete along the Corniche.
Is it music or news the dark windows utter?

Day-long dazzle of the shallows
and at night the moon trails her tipsy sleeves
past the windows of raffish diners.
The hectic brake-lights of lovers

jam the streets. My place or your place.
They lose the way again and again.

At dawn the birds leave the trees in clouds,
they petition the city for its crumbs.

The diners are cheap and the food is bad
but you'd sail a long way to find anything
as convenient. Pretty soon, sailor boy,
you'll lose your bearings on language.

Language with no tongue
to lash it to the teller.
Stern-slither of dogfish guttings.
Sinbad's sail swaying in the desert.

Only those given words can say what they want.
Out there the velvet lady runs her tongue
over them. And she is queen of the night —
her shadow flutters in the alleys.

And young sailors, speechless, lean
on the taffrail. They gaze at the queen's amber
but see simple lamps their girls hang in sash windows.
Thud of drums. Beach-fires. Salt wind in the ratlines.

Takes more than one nice green kawakawa
leaf, chewed, to freshen the mouth
that's kissed the wooden lips of the figurehead
above history's cut-water

in the barbarous isles'
virgin harbours. That hulk shunned by rats
bursts into flames.
And now the smoky lattice of spars

casts upon the beach
the shadow-grid of your enlightened city.
And now I reach through them — I reach
through the eyes of dreaming sailors.

Faces inches from the sweating bulkheads,
blankets drenched in brine and sperm.
Trailing blood across the moon's wake
the ship bore out of Boka Bay.

Trailing sharks, she sailed
for Port Destruction. In Saint Van le Mar,
Jamaica, Bligh's breadfruit trees grew tall.
In Callao on the coast of Peru

geraniums bloomed like sores
against whitewashed walls.
The dock tarts' parrots jabbering
cut-rates in six tongues.

The eroding heartland, inland cordillera
flashing with snow — these the voyager forgets.
His briny eyes
flood with chimerical horizons.

'I would tell you if I could — if I could
remember, I would tell you.
All around us the horizons
are turning air into water

and I can't remember
where the silence ended and speech began,
where vision ended and tears began.
All our promises vanish into thin air.

What I remember are the beaches of that city
whose golden children dance
on broken glass. I remember cold beer
trickling between her breasts as she drank.

But my paper money burned
when she touched it. The ship
clanked up to its bower, the glass towers
of the city burned back there in the sunset glow.'

Cool star foundering in the west.
Coast the dusty colour of lions.
The story navigates by vectors
whose only connection is the story.

The story is told in words
whose only language is the story.
All night the fo'c's'le lamp smokes above the words.
All day the sun counts the hours of the story.

Heave of dark water where something
else turns — the castaway's tongue
clappers like a mission bell.
Unheard his end, and the story's.

Raconteurs in smoky dives
recall his phosphorescent arm
waving in the ship's wake.
Almost gaily. The ship sailed on.

1993

BILL   MANHIRE

Born in Invercargill in 1946, Bill Manhire graduated from Otago University before completing postgraduate studies in Icelandic and Norse at London University. A pivotal figure as poet, short story writer, critic and anthologist, Manhire teaches at Victoria University in Wellington where he runs a creative writing course.

The Old Man's Example

These drifting leaves, for instance
That tap my shoulder
Come along with us, they say
There are one or two questions
We should like to ask you

(1967)

The Elaboration

there was a way out of here:
it went off in the night
licking its lips

the door flaps like a great wing:
I make fists at the air
and long to weaken

ah, to visit you
is the plain thing,
and I shall not come to it

1972

The Prayer

1

What do you take
away with you?

Here is the rain,
a second-hand miracle,
collapsing out of Heaven.

It is the language of
earth, lacking an audience,
but blessing the air.

What light it brings
with it, how far
it is.

*

I stayed a minute
& the garden
was full of voices.

2

I am tired again
while you are crossing

the river, on a bridge
six inches under water.

Small trees grow out of
the planks & shade the water.

Likewise, you are full of
good intentions
& shade the trees with your body.

3
Lord, Lord
in my favourite religion
You would have to be
a succession of dreams.

In each of them
I'd fall asleep,

scarred like a
rainbow, no doubt,
kissing the visible bone.

1972

A Death in the Family

His face is gone golden with the dusk
You would think he burned, he burned

We came without invitation
We did not follow the highways

Trees we went beneath, bending
Then climbed the stone walls

Golden, golden, and he has not spoken
We sent so many missives

Let us go brother, let us go sister
Open the gates, how can we remain?

He will not answer us
His eyes blaze out beyond us

His face is gone golden with the dusk
You would think he burned, he burned

1972

How to Take Off Your Clothes at the Picnic

It is hardly sensuous, but having
Eaten all the cold meat and tomatoes
You forget to remove your trousers

And instead skip stones across the river
With some other man's wife
Until, finally, the movement

Of a small wind, no larger
Than the reach of a finger
& thumb, makes it

Impossible, carefully lifting off
Every item of clothing.
Then you may share an apple and watch

From your side of the river
Shoes & socks coming down
To rest on the other.

1977

On Originality

Poets, I want to follow them all,
out of the forest into the city
or out of the city into the forest.

The first one I throttle.
I remove his dagger
and tape it to my ankle in a shop doorway.
Then I step into the street
picking my nails.

I have a drink with a man
who loves young women.
Each line is a fresh corpse.

There is a girl with whom we make friends.
As he bends over her body
to remove the clothing
I slip the blade between his ribs.

Humming a melody, I take his gun.
I knot his scarf carelessly at my neck, and

I trail the next one into the country.
On the bank of a river I drill
a clean hole in his forehead.

Moved by poetry
I put his wallet in a plain envelope
and mail it to the widow.

I pocket his gun.
This is progress.
For instance, it is nearly dawn.

Now I slide a gun into the gun
and go out looking.

It is a difficult world.
Each word is another bruise.

This is my nest of weapons.
This is my lyrical foliage.

1977

The Pickpocket

We get on well together.
We vie with each other in politeness,
promising no special treatment.
We contradict ourselves constantly.

Look at those people. She leads him
round by the nose, they are always bickering.
He is nurturing a viper in his bosom:
she must have applied for the post.

But, what a day! The favourite lost
by a neck. We lost everything but the clothes
we stood up in! I wish you
good fortune with all my heart.

1977

Children

The likelihood is
the children will die
without you to help them do it.
It will be spring,
the light on the water,
or not.

And though at present
they live together
they will not die together.
They will die one by one
and not think to call you:
they will be old

and you will be gone.
It will be spring,
or not. They may be crossing
the road,
not looking left,
not looking right,

or may simply be afloat at evening
like clouds unable
to make repairs. That
one talks too much, that one
hardly at all: and they both enjoy
the light on the water

much as we enjoy
the sense
of indefinite postponement. Yes
it's a tall story but don't you think
full of promise, and he's just a kid
but watch him grow.

1982

What It Means to Be Naked

As you will know
the hands join hands to sing

and then you are naked.
Under the snow, the hands and chest

are draped, and with them the belly;
the thighs are pure bone

sunk without trace. Likewise
the eyes,

the mouth, the nose
sink in the face, while the teeth

are left surprised
by the pain which has vanished.

Also, as you will know,
the tongue leaves

its voice and taste to the snow
and the room at once

grows chilly. The hair,
of course, stays on the pillow.

Then the penis is removed
and shaved, as you will know,

and is buried subsequently
in snow: and this latter,

covering the earth as always,
as you will know,

and being no more
than the usual snow

under the snow
the snow will eat it.

                    1982

Declining the Naked Horse

The naked horse came into the room.
The naked horse comes into the room.
The naked horse has come into the room.
The naked horse will be coming into the room.
The naked horse is coming into the room.
The naked horse does come into the room.
The naked horse had come into the room.
The naked horse would of come into the room
again if we hadn't of stopped it.

                    1982

The Selenologist

Is gazing at the moon again.
He stares as usual through his optic lens,

The length of tube with glass at either end.
There, as it happens, is the outside cat;
And there are the fox & the flower & the star.
Among all these his life takes place.

There also is the river of light
Which moves past stars with golden rays
Too bright to contemplate or gaze upon.
The river itself begins in snow,
Far out in space. It travels under cloud,
And those who travel in the boat upon the river

Are pleased to hold beneath the cloud
Because there they are always safe.
(Of course, they will never again traverse
The space they have just left
And which they have just deserted forever,
They will never again embrace brothers or sisters:

They are looking for life on another planet.)
Imagine, before the selenologist was born
They were on their way. They dipped their oars
In cloud and thought of water. Even now
They hardly know if they are touching water
Through the cloud — for they are going with

The current anyway. They are unknown life
But not to each other. They know each other
By their voices and the songs they sing; yet
They can only assume the content of these songs,
The golden stars past which they journey,
They can only assume the water.

This is not strictly true
For they can almost guess at death.
They can imagine the faces, growing older;
Also, they know that if one should fall
From the boat, then it is one voice less;
And yet that such a splashing will confirm the water.

It is then they sing with purest pleasure.
The selenologist can hear across all space
The sound that water makes when violently displaced
And fancies he can hear them singing.
He knows that before he was conceived
This noise was on its way; and smiles

And sighs and gives the cat its supper.
He tells the story of the fox & the flower
& the star, he writes how happy all these are.
He sighs and writes: 'Life is motionless
In consequence of all the time it takes.'
He sighs and writes: 'Distance sets limits

Where our vision fails in space.'
He tries to imagine the boat upon the water

But can see only grass in a small field
By the river at the edge of cloud.
It is immense vegetation, fixed in place:
Green as emerald, soft like a lake.

1982

Wingatui

Sit in the car with the headlights off.
Look out there now
where the yellow moon floats silks across the birdcage.
You might have touched that sky you lost.
You might have split that azure violin in two.

1982

A Scottish Bride

Long division and underprivilege,
sweets in a paper twist; or later,
hiking in the hills, days

like the fizz of flowers in a vase
she carried to a neighbour's house,
a war bride with a photograph of home,

and her own house on a single pulse
of stone, lapped by the tidal starlight.
Whose days were those?

A lit hearth, the flames trod water,
and on the dresser a wedding-cake
ascended like a genealogy towards

the two small figures on the top,
standing beside a silver flower
which gave them back a blurred reflection.

Were those the circumstances
which would have to change? A daughter
rehearsed expressions in the mirror,

choosing the face she might prefer to hold,
another touched the perforations
of a stamp, a profile she was saving.

*You cannot imagine, halfway
across the world,* her father wrote,
the sorrow of the undersigned. Was that her mother

then, who made those numbers on a slate?
Were those her children, almost finished eating,
blowing upon their faces in the spoons?

1984

Zoetropes

A starting. Words which begin
with Z alarm the heart:
the eye cuts down at once

then drifts across the page
to other disappointments.

*

Zenana: the women's apartments
in Indian or Persian houses.
Zero is nought, nothing,

nil — the quiet starting point
of any scale of measurement.

*

The land itself is only
smoke at anchor, drifting above
Antarctica's white flower,

tied by a thin red line
(5000 miles) to Valparaiso.
                    London 29.4.81

                              1984

Out West

I was riding one of the best-loved horses in the world.
Hither and yon, we went, here and there,
in and out of the known universe.

'There goes Wild Bill,' people said.
'Look at that varmint go!'
There I went.

I went straight to the dictionary
and looked up varmint.
'What's it say?' said a friend. 'What's it say?'

I thumbed through the pages.
' Vermin,' I said, 'vermin
with an excrescent t.'

'Well doggone,' said someone,
and it's true, the dog was gone,
lost in the gulches and the sages,

leaving just me and the horse,
a couple of ornery critters
who might just as well mosey along,

crossing the ford by starlight,
and miles away, the woman —
lonely and beautiful — waking to find us gone.

1991

Jalopy: The End of Love

Do you drive an old car?
Or a jalopy?
Now where could that word come from?

Somewhere in the world
someone you know
must be driving a jalopy.

As for you, one day you are out
on a country road
miles from the sort of place

that might be miles from anywhere
and your car breaks down.
Well, it's an old car.

And somewhere in the world
someone you used to love
has that ancient photograph of you

sitting behind the wheel
high on the Coromandel.
It's a jalopy.

Just at the moment though
it doesn't want to start.
Whatever it is, it's finished.

1991

Our Father

for Charles Causley

On one trip he brought home
a piece of stone from the river,
shaped like a child's foot

and filled with the weight
of the missing body. Another time
he just walked in

with our lost brother
high on his shoulders
after a two-day absence;

and it seems like only yesterday
he was showing us
the long pole, the one

out there in the yard now,
taller than twice himself,
that still hoists

our mother's washing out of reach.

1991

Magasin

I have brought my father
things to read, *Pix*, *Post*, *People*,
and I tell him how *magazine*

is like the word for shop
in French. I have just started high school,
I am learning a language.

My father lifts his striped
pyjama top so I can see
what looks like the map of Africa

where the doctor has traced
the shape of his liver
for the third-year students.

At the end of the ward
men are listening to the races
and from the next-door bed

the man with one leg,
the bloke my father says
might have to lose the other,

leans across to tell my father
something about
the second leg at Trentham.

1991

Hirohito

*I am like a canary whose cage has been
opened and someone says: 'Fly away!'
Where should I fly to? If I have a song
to sing, why should I waste it on places
where the wind may blow it away?*

To improve his eyesight
the young Hirohito gazes
at the horizon every day.

Birds and clouds: one day
he will be a living god.

*

In the playground
he always has to be leader;
the other kids
line up behind.

Already he knows
about physical fitness,
the importance of the will.

He likes insects, plants and butterflies.
He admires
the delicate protocols of Nature.

*

One day his father went mad:
he peered at his people
through the paper telescope
of his own speech.

Hirohito watched his father
being taken away
and thought of jellyfish.

*

At the age of 20
he travelled to Europe.

In London he sat for Augustus John.
He played golf
with the Prince of Wales.

In Paris his knowledge
of European military history
amazed the generals of France.

The happiest days of his life.

Hirohito went home,
ate eggs and bacon,
and dressed like a Western gentleman.

*

Then there was the war:
about which we know the truth
or do not know the truth,

in which Hirohito either played
the leading part
or he did not.

Perhaps he was
just a puppet of his warlords.

Or perhaps they lined up behind him
while he stared at the horizon

and the sun rose
and the sky filled with planes.

*

Hirohito knew everything
and nothing. 'Let the cry
be vengeance!' cried the allies.
'If you meet this man, don't hesitate.'

Hirohito hid inside the palace air-raid shelter,
a bank vault
with ten-metre thick
ferro-concrete walls.

*

When he announced the surrender
his ministers wept:
the god's voice
being broadcast on the radio.

At first no one could understand Hirohito.
He spoke a language of his own.

And for two days the nation wept —
long enough to let the Emperor's chamberlain
replace the bust of Napoleon
in his study

with one of Lincoln.

*

They say that when he met MacArthur
Hirohito bowed so low
that the handshake took place
high above his head.

So the Son of Heaven was a family man after all —
not in the least divine,
just a quiet marine biologist
able to sign the instruments of surrender.

*

I am writing my book about him,
A Modest History of the Wind,
but I am in difficulty:

chapter after chapter
is being blown away.

There he is: the warrior on a white horse —
blown away.

And there: the Shinto priest
planting rice seedlings
in the palace gardens.

Gone.

And look: there is Hirohito
winding his Mickey Mouse watch.
Tick-tock: the wind takes him.

Petals blown away —
as in a haiku,
as in a tanka.

*

In this final chapter, a funeral:
the powers of the world
have gathered in mourning.

Hirohito —
the 124th occupant
of the Chrysanthemum Throne.

Glancing idly at the news
I catch sight of him through snow,

a man with glasses
staring out of the screen
of my 14-inch Sanyo.

                                        1991

Phar Lap

Unlikely combinations,

Prayer Wheel and Winkie, Sentiment
and Radium: names that contract and expand
like a big heart pumping

till you get an unlikely starter,
this chestnut colt,
foaled in Timaru, October 4 1926,

by Night Raid out of Entreaty,
with Carbine somewhere
in the background.

*

The hide is in Melbourne,
the heart in Canberra.
The bones are in Wellington,

the big delicate skeleton
of a horse
who used to mean business.

*

Can the name
have been planned as a pun?

In English it is one thing.
In Singhalese, Lightning.

And they say it means
something in Egyptian.

*

But he was virtually unbeatable,
the big fellow,
winning race after race in Australia
and never fading,

even after they shot at him,
even after they missed,

*

even after he died in America
of intestinal tympany,
of theory after theory . . .

They say that for five days he ate
pasture sprayed with lead arsenate,

they say that his Australian strapper
gave him Fowler's Solution,
incorrectly mixed,

or maybe even the Mafia . . .

Well, let's say he died in California,
let's say he died of absence

*

and that when they stopped talking
they sent him home,
made him articulate
bone by bone

*

till one day up at the Museum,
it might be fifty years later,

wandering along
past the days of pioneer settlement,

I walk past Cook's cannon
and a case of muskets

and hear a woman sing
in another language

from the far side of Phar Lap's ribcage.

1991

Milky Way Bar

I live at the edge of the universe,
like everybody else. Sometimes I think
congratulations are in order:
I look out at the stars
and my eye merely blinks a little,
my voice settles for a sigh.

But my whole pleasure is the inconspicuous;
I love the unimportant thing.
I go down to the Twilight Arcade
and watch the Martian invaders,
already appalled by our language,
pointing at what they want.

1991

My Sunshine

He sings you are my sunshine
and the skies are grey, she tries
to make him happy, things
just turn out that way.

She'll never know
how much he loves her
and yet he loves her so much
he might lay down his old guitar
and walk her home, musician
singing with the voice alone.

Oh love is sweet and love is all, it's
evening and the purple shadows fall
about the baby and the toddler
on the bed. It's true he loves her
but he should have told her,
he should have, should have said.

Foolish evening, boy with a foolish head.
He sighs like a flower above his instrument
and his sticky fingers stick. He fumbles
a simple chord progression,
then stares at the neck.
He never seems to learn his lesson.

Here comes the rain. Oh if she were only
sweet sixteen and running from the room again,
and if he were a blackbird
he would whistle and sing
and he'd something
something something something.

(1992)

BOB ORR

Born in 1949, Bob Orr has worked on the Auckland waterfront for much of his adult life. He currently lives in Freemans Bay.

Love Poem

In your eyes
there is a balcony

In my heart
there is a hammock

Let's lie
there
& watch those birds
that fly

With wings
like hospital beds
& hope
that they make it into heaven.

1983

Container Terminal

The sun rising
above Rangitoto . . .
there were tracks
across the tide
I stood in sunlight
the colour of containers.
An old freighter with
a beard of rust
lay anchored
in midstream.
Gulls flew between
the masts of moored ships.
Huge wharf cranes
walked the water's edge.
Into my hand they lowered an island.

1991

My Grandmother's Funeral

The last
of the old people —
your shiny coffin
like a horizontal
narrow door.

With your heart attacks
& cigarettes
your Hillcrest house
your loneliness
your whiskey
& your over
fed fox terrier
who could make a party
come alive
like you did
at the piano
when you improvised.
We drive to the cemetery
a stream of cars —
in broad daylight
each one with its
headlights on low beam
as if for something lost
we might be
　　searching

　　　　　　　　　1991

My Father's Bomber Jacket

My father's bomber
jacket still hangs on
a peg beside a squadron photo.
Once I tried it on
but found that it was
far too small.
After all
when he wore it
he was not much more
than a boy —
in his tin machine
with his instruments
& weapons
alone &
far from
land
way out above the Pacific
as the waves beneath
moved like cards
being shuffled.

　　　　　　　1991

SAM HUNT

Born in Castor Bay, Auckland, in 1946, Sam Hunt emerged in the late 1960s and early 1970s as the country's foremost bard and performance poet. Since then he has worked as a full-time writer and performer, touring the country and enjoying immense popularity.

School Policy on Stickmen

It's said that children should not use
stick figures when they draw!
And yet I've lain all night awake
looking at this drawing here
of orange men, stick figures every one of them,
walking up a crayon mountain hand in hand
walking up my wall.

They're edging up a ridge
their backs against the mountain
pinned against my wall.
And every one is smiling.
They know the way a mountain laughs,
especially crayon mountains made of brown.
They know they're not allowed,
these orange men.

                    1971

My Father Scything

My father was sixty when I was born,
twice my mother's age. but he's never been
around very much, neither at the mast
round the world, nor when I wanted him most.
He was somewhere else, like in his upstairs
Dickens-like law office counting the stars;
or sometimes out with his scythe on Sunday
working the path through lupin towards the sea.

And the photograph album I bought myself
on leaving home, lies open on the shelf
at the only photograph I have of him,
my father scything. In the same album
beside him, one of my mother.
I stuck them there on the page together.

                    1972

A Valley Called Moonshine

(for Josh Andersen)

The lights in the farmhouses
go out. The inlet is out.

An iron shack on the shoreline
floats its light on the water.

A grandfather up Moonshine
remembers the first daughter.

Dreams are easy. Wild horses.

1973

Stabat Mater

My mother called my father 'Mr Hunt'
For the first few years of married life.
I learned this from a book she had inscribed:
'To dear Mr Hunt, from his loving wife.'

She was embarrassed when I asked her why
But later on explained how hard it had been
To call him any other name at first, when he —
Her father's elder — made her seem so small.

Now in a different way, still like a girl,
She calls my father every other sort of name;
And guiding him as he roams old age
Sometimes turns to me as if it were a game . . .

That once I stand up straight, I too must learn
To walk away and know there's no return.

1973

You House the Moon

You have moved in upstairs.
I don't know what you do.
Except at night I know you
Sit up late. You watch the stars

About all I know of you.
Merciless as migraine
You pace out my brain.
Maybe you want my view!

Headaches all the more.
I have this dream a load
Of timber's dumped on the road
Right outside my door.

One by one, just your way,
You drag each plank upstairs.

I see nothing for tears.
You hammer away

You house the moon. You join the stars.
You have come to stay

1975

My Father Today

They buried him today
up Schnapper Rock Road,
my father in cold clay.

A heavy south wind towed
the drape of light away.
Friends, men met on the road,

stood round in that dumb way
men stand when lost for words.
There was nothing to say.

I heard the bitchy chords
of magpies in an old-man
pine . . . 'My old man, he's worlds

away — call it Heaven —
no men so elegantly
dressed. His last afternoon,

staring out to sea,
he nods off in his chair.
He wonders what the

yelling's all about up there.
They just about explode!
And now, these magpies here

up Schnapper Rock Road . . . '
They buried him in clay.
He was a heavy load,

my dead father today.

1977

Birth of a Son

My father died nine months before
My first son, Tom, was born:
Those nine months when my woman bore
Our child in her womb, my dad
Kept me awake until the dawn.
He did not like it dead.

Those dreams of him, his crying
'Please let me out love, let me go!'
And then again, of his dying . . .

I am a man who lives each breath
Until the next; not much I know
Of life or death; life-after-death:

Except to say, that when this son
Was born into my arms, his weight
Was my old man's, a bloody ton:

A moment there — it could not stay —
I held them both. Then, worth the wait,
Content at last, my father moved away.

1978

Requiem

They say 'the lighthouse-keeper's world is round'—
The only lighthouse keeper that I know
Inhabits space, his feet well clear of ground.
I say he is of light, of midnight snow.

That other lighthouse keeper — he they say
Whose world is round — is held responsible
For manning his one light by night; by day,
For polishing his lenses, bulb and bell.

My man, my friend who lately leaves, is quite
Another type. He climbs no spiral stairs:
But go he does, for good, to man the night;
To reappear, among his polished stars.

1980

Harold Saunders, Boatbuilder, Tory Channel

A man built a house.
That man years later
became Prime Minister.
I like the idea
of a Prime Minister
being able
to build a house.

Another man,
a man I know,
builds boats.
He builds boats like
Beethoven, say, wrote symphonies or
Henry Moore
cut so deep
to the heart of a stone one day
he discovered, he said,
the sky on the other side.

This man builds boats in his garden.
They're launched from there —
his garden that floats

a step above full tide.

And when the tide is full in Tory Channel
the moon comes to watch.

1989

TONY BEYER

Born in 1948 in Auckland, Tony Beyer has worked in the field of education. He currently lives in Auckland.

Cut Lilac

the dead smell the rain gives
to bunches of cut lilac
in bay windowed living rooms

is another version of the skull
your mouth feels when you kiss
a lover's or a child's clear forehead

but these are impetuous blue
upon the stems that throng
the vase's throat and splay from it

half captive or as free
as wands of light the recent sun
by peering wetly forth outside

has interspersed among them
divining paths like ours in time
that sprawl and gather haltingly

towards the next blind cervix
of the grave the best of us
will shoulder through with joy

1981

Lord Cobham Avenue

a birthday next door
and a visiting
grandmother here

we spend the afternoon
lifting small girls
over the fence

1984

Working Loose

five nights of radiant dreaming
and I am clear
of where the wounded hill

slid rocks and yellow mud
out over the road
confusion of shovels and planks

in the kerosene dark
and you so nearly young again
I was cautious

walking you to shelter
with the leaf rot bickering
under our civilian shoes

I think of you now as one
of the daughters of a fallen emperor
pushed into the room
with the others to be shot

you lie on the floor
and petals of hair close
over your secret face

there are sightings of you
in foreign capitals
and letters come for my children

one with a chain of cut out
paper bears
that hold hands and smile
or turn their backs on us

                    1986

Changing Ground

a path you can see
for miles along
in the middle of the forest
if your eyes are good

or take one step to the side
and you are as lost as anyone
days overdue
who spaces his last
three bullets into the air

go deeper then
among the dismissive gestures
of the ferns and
broken stump ends looming
up from the ground

no one can promise a place
but there are places
quiet and sidelit like
the riven canopy
of your one love's hair
or the room you started from

where you and your tall shadow
with its ankles
fastened to yours will be welcome
1986

Sanctuary

1

on this island
there are insects
heavier than birds or mice

the bush creaks at night
with their tread
and the long heads

of original tree parasites turn
to follow another planet across the dark

2

what can it want
that bird
that talks to the night

the same intuitive
syllables of comfort

3

one dog or one rat let ashore
the legend is altered
1986

Early Weather

1

I was born in a far city
and the speech of trams
and the speech of workmen
grappling out the clay foundations
of a motor parts warehouse
rasped against the windows
of the small brick hospital
where my mother groaned

2

I grew in the house of a man
who had been shot at often
during a long

and singular part of his youth
and couldn't forget

he taught me a wariness
beyond my daily need

it was not easy to be with him
or to watch his love
of the death he had tensed himself
to accept and then mislaid

3

I am one of three brothers
all men now in middle life

our faces are marked by the fingerprints
of our loyalties
our travels and children and lost loves

sometimes we sit together in the sun
and drink beer
and pass around among ourselves
the familiar
wry and insulting language
we invented for another time

                                        1986

IAIN LONIE

Iain Lonie (1932–1988) was born in England and grew up in Scotland and New Zealand before reading Classics at the Universities of Otago and Cambridge. He had a considerable international reputation as an historian of medicine. Lonie published four books of poetry which only since the poet's death have received their due recognition.

By Foreign Hands

You lay in a blue chapel
under blue sheets drawn to the chin
your hands not showing.
Someone else had done your hair
ignorantly parting
it on the wrong side.

Someone else had done your hair
and arranged your hands and tucked you up in bed

and done your hair and done your skin and done your eyes

your long, asymmetrical feet

expertly composing what was to be composed
expertly parting what was to be parted

                                        1984

Point of No Return

We took flight at last
as we said we would
flying westwards, disencumbered

above the thunderclouds
and the turmoil of the elements
in the taut fuselage of our skins

we reached the furthest point
flying six miles high
higher than any condor.

It was what we had come to see
but then you fell to earth:
I watched you, turning over and over

the faintest white speck in the blue
then the many white specks of which blue is made
in the end, only the blue.

1984

The Winter Walk at Morning

Out there where the spilled city began
to crumble at its edges into a spatter of
one-time village names (though any quaint
feature of architecture or sweet natural
touch was now half crusted over or floating in
development, a sort of adaptable
homogeneous flow, vivid like bile)

were first streets without gardens, then with
gardens, creosote-fenced, then allotments
and sheds of iron, though too securely locked
to conceal more than garden tools — so why
should one start to think of raped corpses here, why
should the fluttering loops of surveyor's tape remind
of bloodstained bandages, looped along battlefields? —

dogs, some, perhaps savage. People, no. The time of day,
some TV programme, rush hour, happy hour? No-one.
'Walk, why walk? Nobody goes for walks here.'
Why walk? Either the need
to exercise what whines and snuffles in the heart
walking it out and around, then back again
exhausted, domestic, fit once more to inhabit

cleanly. Or else to recall a memory
of other and earlier walks, their calm patrols
of boundaries, or the heady sense
of voyaging farther out, beyond
Cold Harbour, The Snares, The Noises, Cape
Desolation, though it were only a tree
a telephone pole, a dead end: just touching which

then swinging back to the waiting familiar
would be enough to establish the calm-browed
reasonableness of things. 'Nobody walks here.'
After the allotments, a railway line
then a hawthorn hedge hung with shreds of plastic.
Behind that again, some low changing sheds
and a football ground, also empty; churned mud.

I hesitated, then crossed the field. To souls
no definite place is granted. I was not told
I should find the river, but there it was
flowing, apparently, between low floodbanks
from a bend up there, where were some low trees
to disappear again under the motorway
that came into sight now, barring other progress.

Undeniably a river, with a river's purpose
and the purposes we find for rivers, as: to be the end
of a winter morning's walk, or to sit down
and weep by, or just chuck rubbish into:
about midstream were two cars
like dead crabs upside down exposing shafts
and exhausts. Their celebrated river was nothing, then:

not deep enough even to bury a wrecked car.

1991

Lines on a Photograph

The wind (there's always wind
on this headland) flattens the tussock, makes
the sea's blue bluer even
than your camera could catch it. Still
it's your best photograph to date.
The tussock's golden, flattening
to yellow in the wind, sometimes
to brown. It's like hair.
I'm quite small:
in my red shirt and blue trousers
and what could be a gun in my arms
I'm a small tin soldier standing
in the middle of your photograph.
It's all I know how to do.
If the wind blows any harder
it'll take me with it, melting me
into all that blue.
I'm only a part, but I'm at the centre.
Without me it wouldn't be a photograph.

1991

Proposal at Allans Beach

Basalt capes
thrust into the sea, the sea
curls back intimately

into the land, celebrating
a moody marriage. The wind here
saws into flesh like cord
but just around the sandhills
a small inland sea
dotted with maimais calmly sends
the sun back to heaven.
Even in winter you can lie
on its hard white beach
naked as if you'd just crawled
up from the sea like a fish with legs
and were looking around for a mate.
But up there above the ridges
it's always going on: the air
dividing, and pouring mist
down ngaio gullies, making sheep
get up and move, unveiling contours
taking them away again.
The whole place is a test site.
I've been bringing
people here for 20 years —
sometimes with a hard question
mostly to see how we match up
to its absolute background.
It never fails. Walk with someone
from the flax-hung cliff at one end
to the tidal creek at the other
and you'll know for sure
what's biting both of you
whether you could be friends for life
and lesser domestic truths. Of course
I had to be brought here once myself
on a particularly uninviting day.
Squinting up the dark green slopes
I knew I'd come home. Later
I sat by the lagoon a whole
sunfilled September day and planned
the work of a decade. And once
I came here with a friend and the rain
blew back into our faces and told us
we could never be the lovers
we thought we wanted to be.
I'm never alone here —
the place is full of ghosts.
With luck, you might see one
swimming naked in a rock pool
on the greyest day of the year.
It is a place for strong attachments:
friends, lovers, children.
I can't promise much
but you won't forget having been here
nor who you came with, and all
that followed, if it followed.

1991

Exile

for Bill Sewell

The air will do something to our skin: burn it
and make us young again. We have arrived
and deployed along the lakeshore a variety of things
each with its special use. The slender children
with special needs poise on the edge of boredom
like archaic statues, inscribing with one toe
a question in the sand. How blue the sky
how green the forest! The light of paradise
makes every leaf particular: the number of things
in the world is finite, and each one of us
has his god-given talent. The great cliffs smile down
and guarantee our happiness.

                          Guidebooks describe
the water here as 'pristine': that means free
from imported sludges, but the headland hides
a burial ground where dark roots twist among bones
assembled from three continents. Anyone who arrives
may claim this as his own: two women
who got here first now furiously repack
their rusted Campavan, but the waves
of immigration beating upon the shore
can't be stopped: already an armada
of powerboats is drawn up along the beach
sharp prows in the air. The air is loud
with transistorized warcries: before the day is out
a head will be bloodied on black obsidian.

Noon shimmers, and a smoke of cooking curls
along the shore. The Brownian motion
of human particles is stilled by an artist
recording it at her easel. We shall be viewed
in the halls of some mid-century exhibition
picturesque and anonymous at our point of passage.
Someone calls for sausages. Grasping a spear
a sharkskinned diver lectures his gaping audience
on the typology of tits. This is exile —
being among people one will never understand
however smooth the trunks of trees, renewed
endlessly in the green water, however blue the sky.

Over there on the sand that pale-skinned couple
regard us attentively, as if we might have met
in another country, and exchanged words
heavy with the silt of meaning. But look:
the sun dips and the lake is waiting for us:
where are the thorns on which we must hang our skins?

                                       1991

JANET FRAME

New Zealand's foremost contemporary writer, Janet Frame was born in 1924 in Dunedin and grew up in Oamaru. After time as a student and then schoolteacher, Frame was confined in psychiatric institutions, during which time her first book, The Lagoon and Other Stories, was published. She spent five years in London before returning to New Zealand. She has written novels, an autobiography which has been made into a film by Jane Campion and one book of poems, The Pocket Mirror.

The Dead

I have nothing to say to the dead
unless they approach me first.
It is their right to come to me
with a soft step, singing
or moaning as they please.

The dead cry all night under the trees.
I never tire of listening to them.
Sometimes I want to invite them in
to warm their hands by the fire
but nobody wants the dead inside,
especially not the living. Lock the door,
keep them out, they say,
or the next thing you know
they will overcome you with death,
they will feed from you, rob you,
tap your blood and your preserved memory.
The dead have no memory. A torn scarf
flows in and out of their head, controlled
by the wind of forgetfulness, not by the dead,
and where the end or the beginning may be
the dead do not know
who have no memory, no memory.

1967

O Lung Flowering Like a Tree

O lung flowering like a tree
a shadowy bird bothers thee
a strange bird that will not fly away
or sing at break of day and evening.

I will take my knife
I will cut the branch of the tree
he clings to and will not let go
then the wide sky can look in
and light lay gloss
on the leaves of blood beating with life.

Oh yes, tomorrow I will take my knife
and the light and I will look in,
O plagued lung flowering like a tree,
said the surgeon.

1967

Yet Another Poem About a Dying Child

Poets and parents say he cannot die
so young, so tied to trees and stars.
Their word across his mouth obscures
and cures his murmuring good-bye.
He babbles, *they say*, of spring flowers,

who for six months has lain
his flesh at a touch bruised violet,
his face pale, his hate clearer
than milky love that would smooth over
the pebbles of diseased bone.

Pain spangles him like the sun,
He cries and cannot say why.
His blood blossoms like a pear tree.
He does not want to eat or keep
its ugly windfall fruit.

He does not want to spend or share
the engraved penny of light
that birth put in his hand
telling him to hold it tight.
Will parents and poets not understand?

He must sleep, rocking the web of pain
till the kind furred spider will come
with the night-lamp eyes and soft tread
to wrap him warm and carry him home
to a dark place, and eat him.

1967

Wyndham

The big stick
has given up stirring
the Wyndham pool.

Stones do not move here;
people sleep while
the cows make milk
the sheep make wool

and in the empty
railway houses
no Dad sits each morning
on the satin-smooth
dunny seat.

1967

The Dreams

My brother kept bantams coloured like strawlike copper
    beech leaves;
my sister kept a pet rabbit with a sensitive collapsible nose.

I kept nothing. Nothing stayed with me,
not even snow when I put salt on its glossy white tail
sweeping against the windowpane
with soft floating promises
of obedient captivity,

not even
the snail when I helped it travel a million miles
with one movement of my hand
over dense grass and waste earth
where the robber thistles and highwaymen spiders were lurking,

not even the rescued foreign stamp
when I gave it a family home
a classified accepted understood valued life
on a clean page safe inside a catalogue,
or the dry pressed ragwort
untied with its woolly bear caterpillar in a matchbox.
Nothing stayed.
Dust did not stay, nor shadows. Light,
quietly dissolving the iron bars
sun-melted the key,
splintered the wooden food bowls,
set warm with warning
of inevitable prison.

Then one day my brother's bantams with their heads chopped off
ran in a panic up and down the fowl house;
my sister's pet rabbit escaped and did not know
fear of the hawk and ferret.
The bantams, the rabbit died.
Snow remained free, and snails, caterpillars, stamps, dust,
light entering the sky on its own terms.

I was a child then. I turn the memory
while tonight it snows, but I no longer care
for soft promises, and salt is for rubbing into old wounds,
and it is time, while snow still falls, to feed the dreams
that run in panic up and down my sleep
that escape at last and unwittingly make friends with the hawk.

1967

Impard a Willow-Cell in Sordure

Impard a willow-cell in sordure
chance or chead in fascendure
the sweetable clightly photation
frambling in the quintolution.

Chance or chead in vilitance
a musion briskly appleful
harmworthily impelled
in pulse and mind deeprent
with bountiful irrosement.

1967

Instructions for Bombing with Napalm

naphthalene coconut oil
health
a neat lethal plan
a late net
an alp at panther heap
a pale ten-pin heel lent to plant help
to pelt
at nether halt
at nether halt
hell
concoct ointment
ultimate oil
unction
lotion
count coil
act lout to that tune in loin
toil out then
lick the lion's lap
cut the lint
pal

                                    1967

At Evans Street

I came one day upon a cream-painted wooden house
with a white bargeboard, a red roof, two gates,
two kinds of japonica bushes, one gooseberry bush,
one apple tree lately in blossom; and thus I counted
my fortune in gates and flowers, even in the white
bargeboard and the fallen roofbeam crying religiously to the
     carpenter,
Raise me high! and in this part of the city that would be
high indeed for here my head is level with hills and sky.
It is not unusual to want somewhere to live but the impulse
bears thinking about seriously and it is wise
never to forget the permanent impermanence of the grave,
its clay floor, the molten centre of the earth, its untiled
roof, the rain and sunbeams arrowing through slit
windows and doors too narrow to escape through,
locked by the remote control of death-bed convulsions
in a warm room in a cream-painted wooden house with
a red roof, a white bargeboard, fallen roofbeam ...
          no, it is not unusual
to nest at my time of year and life only it is wisest
to keep the spare room always for that unexpected guest,
     mortality,
whose tall stories, growing taller, tell
of the sea gull dwelling on bare cliffs, of eagles high
where the bailiff mountain wind removes all furniture (had
     eagles known the need
for chairs by the fireside — what fire but the sun?) and strips the
     hangings

from the trees; and the men, also, camouflaged as trees, who
    climb the rock
face and of the skylark
from whose frenzied point of view harvest is hurricane
and when
except in the world of men
did hurricanes provide shelter and food?

In my house I eat bread and wish the guest would go.

1967

The Place

The place where the floured hens
sat laying their breakfast eggs,
frying their bacon-coloured combs in the sun
is gone.

You know the place —
in the hawthorn hedge
by the wattle tree
by the railway line.

I do not remember these things
— they remember me,
not as child or woman but as their last excuse
to stay, not wholly to die.

1967

The Clown

His face is streaked with prepared tears.
I, with others, applaud him, knowing it
is fashionable to approve when a clown cries
and to disapprove when a persistent sourface
does whether or not his tears are paint.
It is also fashionable, between wars,
to say that hate is love and love is hate,
to make out everything is more complex than we dreamed
and then to say we did not dream it,
we knew it all along and are wise.

Dear crying clown dear childlike old man
dear kind murderer dear innocent guilty
dear simplicity I hate you for making me pretend
there are several worlds to one truth when
I know, I know there are not. Dear people like you and me
whose breaths are bad, who sleep in and rumble
their bowels and control it until
they get home into the empty house or among the family
dear family, dear lonely man in a torn world of nobody,
is it for this waste that we have hoarded words over so many
million years since the first sigh, groan,
and look up at the stars. Oh oh the sky is too wide to sleep
    under.

1967

ALISTAIR PATERSON

Alistair Paterson has worked as a tertiary inspector in the New Zealand Education Department, as Dean of General Studies in the New Zealand Police, and in the Royal New Zealand Navy where he reached the rank of Lieutenant Commander. From 1972 to 1982 he edited Mate *magazine (later* Climate) *and in 1980 the anthology* 15 Contemporary New Zealand Poets *(Pilgrims South Press, Grove Press USA). He has published twelve books including a novel, currently writes full time and edits* Poetry NZ.

from Odysseus Rex

The black ships
with their bright shields are gone
                          the warriors & their sword bearers
have fallen into the sea —
into the sunless hollows of the earth.
                                 The wind has taken them
Circe has captured them
the waves have smothered them
                   & Odysseus is left with their silence:
holding to the wreckage of the world
he recognises it —
                            exhausted, he struggles
towards Calypso's island
                  towards a rock-bound coast . . .

. . . .

Meanwhile, somewhere else & far off
                 the tide falls from the mangroves
children wade through the shallows
their thin legs straddling the earth
                      travellers like all of us
           they are fish beneath the water
               clouds above the water
trees whose movement is breathing, growth
        a stretching of leaves, branches, roots.

It is discovery, the dumb
           & particular voices of rocks, stones
the flurry of blood, the flow of the lymph.
They have their directions, they pause
        they run, walk between the dark roots
       the tall grasses & shallow salt pans —
          & with such quizzical eyes
      such curiosity it could be the first
        or the last of their days.

But it's neither of these —
         merely a continuance & a renewal
as natural, spectacular
as the wind's rising, the sun's fall
        the diurnal drift & sweep of clouds
      They are extensions of ourselves

                              travellers with the delicate
                  arms & hands of girls. They go separately
                  follow the dolphin's path, enlarge the world.

. . . .

Four days before Christmas
I sit in my office in Newmarket
                              reading lines from Ginsberg:
'Here in Paris' he says
                                        'I am your guest'
& for the moment I recognise
the reverse is true —
                              he's transported me (miraculously)
to the tomb of Apollinaire
                                        & to the vision of
'Tzara in the Bois de Boulogne
                  explaining the alchemy of machine guns'.

And while he does it
'an ant runs over (his) corduroy sleeve'
                        & I remember Apollinaire dying —
his complaint that there was
                              'still so much to do'
which demonstrates, perhaps needlessly
that most of us don't know when to stop —
                              including Ginsberg
who also reports (being obsessed with death)
                  Jacques Vachè as having invited him
                                        to inspect
                  'a terrible collection of pistols'.

'Pray for me' says Ginsberg
addressing Apollinaire
                        as if they were the closest of friends
'pray for me on the phonograph record
                        of your former existence'
& already his voice
(although he seems unaware of it)
                              sounds like history
as scratchy as his recollections
                        of Paris, Picasso, Cocteau —
'the princes of America' driving
                        towards Montparnasse . . .

*

On the tenth day
                  when he's struggled ashore
Odysseus gathers together
the silence of air & water
                        of the way the light falls
on leaves & grass, on stones
                        & he puts them in a place
where they can't be touched —

not by hand or eye

              or voice in anguish.

The trees decay

            the rocks fall apart —
his blood dribbles out
through the broken pores

                  of his skin

forming quavers & semiquavers
— slow, red beads — of pain

                & it seems

there's no longer either

          night nor day, nor any way
to rekindle the sun

              light the stars.

When the morning comes

          he gathers together
what little remains:
his broken bundle of sticks

           his 'leathern' rope
— a scatter of stones —
& he casts them into the sea

         watches their tumbling fall
away from his hands & down

           into the bay . . .

. . . .

Under
the clean, white sails of childhood

             a boat

moves over still water
& with such certainty, such grace

       one can see the physics behind it:
triangles, hemispheres —

        complementary forces.

It moves
beneath that steep hill

       where, in company with
his fellow townsmen (the last of them)
my grandfather lies under stone —

          lies fugitive
his bones amongst

       long forgotten bones . . .

And soon
there will come a time

      when no one remembers him
who, living, passed his life
a stranger

      moving in front of strangers . . .
He lies with his fellow townsmen

        in the shadows

of hills
& mountains, lies where
                              morning breaks from silence
a tolling of bells
the far crying of gulls —
                                             where boats
move over still water, their sails
                              bent to the sun . . .
                                                          1986

VINCENT O'SULLIVAN

Born in 1937 in Auckland, Vincent O'Sullivan was educated at the Universities of Auckland and Oxford. He has edited An Anthology of Twentieth Century New Zealand Poetry *which appeared in 1971 (updated in 1978 and 1987) and has published eleven collections of poetry, a novel, numerous short story collections and several plays. He now teaches at Victoria University, Wellington, where he is Professor of English.*

Dogknotting in Quezaltenango

In a town with a name as beautiful
as you'll come by, which hand-outs tell you
is known for its hardworking, peaceable
natives, its fragmented cathedral
with provincial baroque façade,
a view of a volcano smooth as an ice-cream,
I witness, for the first time, dogs knotted
as in a dozen jokes — a large, grey
disconsolate mongrel dragging up the street
another, a third its size, which will not screw off.
Appropriate and natural as the weather
in a country which carries parable like a *machete*,
where the divine system of co-ordinates
splays out from each act like pins from their cushion,
where dogs knotted between cinema and church,
observed by mothers, children, an officer
whose pearl butt cheeks the declining sun —
those dogs as much as the vaunted quetzal
yelp of eternal order, the stellar path.
One watches, hears this sad bitch of a country
ridden by the iron hound whom one day will find
taking his turn on the vet's table,
another muzzle to greet you as you cross the border,
the same emblem waiting, one town or another.
                                                          1976

New Delhi — January

I touch an Indian figurine.
It is nothing like her, and yet

I have only her in mind.

She is in a city not my city
near a church I first heard of
as a child, in a song,

a church she sees from her door
and has never mentioned
and when she is walking past it

her steps ring across its pavement.
I cannot claim for her extraordinary ease
with men or cities,

not say she is natural as bird
in the acacia nor oleander
under summer dust.

That kind of talk confuses.
There are only a few words *simple*
direct sensuous complete

and as they're said I doubt them.
I touch a figurine of crude iron,
no more unlike her than the words to say it.

1977

from Brother Jonathan, Brother Kafka

40

Last things:
        the turning leaves slip in the wind
as turning fish; the wind stills and the long branch
outside the window rubs at the late sky,
behind it the library tower, the power poles,

the dead paraphernalia of an ordered world.
The leaves if you like are now spread hands
or clipped identical banners or metaphor
fading against the stalled comparative sky.

The slight ephemeral leaf is the size of night.
The single word swamped in the gob of silence.
There is sky at the window, dark where even dark was.
        The veering fish slip on, there is breeze again
outside …
            an undersea of leaves is schooling,
a branch berths at the wall.
                    One remembers light
as a quaint hook let down
through day's wrack,
            home.

1980

from Butcher and Co

Sinking It

Do *I feel great!* she mutters musky
a matter of earthly minutes
        after galaxies shifted slightly
for *Man, could he feed it!*
          oh amazonian Sheila
her silksac breasts still fog about him
   Great! she says again
and Butcher remarking nothing
         merely feels the runnels
carve down from his armpits
his hair stuck to his scalp itchy with strain
for *Honeyworld of Women,*
                be in on this:
when the Butcher's heart isn't in it
     then it's digging ditches,
even lifting the right word's
           fairly hefty yacker
though he crams his eyes on moonlight,
thinks of starmuff solid.
So now when she *has* to talk
          it's rubbing salt.
Gee Butcher she says at a stretch
        I feel titanic!
And B., mean as a current,
        Call me iceberg.

Still Shines When You Think of It

Stood on the top of a spur once
the grunt before Sheila sharp beside him
a river shining like wire ten miles off
the sky clean as a dentist's mouth
jesus *Was* it lovely!
    and the hills folded and folded
again and the white sky in the west
still part of the earth
        there's not many days like that eh
when your own hand feels a kind of godsweat
fresh on things like they're just uncovered.

And not fifty feet from the spur
a hawk lifted
   and for two turns turned like one wing
was tacked to the air
   and then she's away
beak a glint as she's turning
so the grunt sighs like in church
and even Butcher
         yes Butcher too
thinks *hawkarc curries the eye all right*

gives your blood that push
while the mind corrupts as usual
with 'proportion' 'accuracy' etcetera
those stones we lift with our tongues trying to say
   ah! feathered guts!
And she's closing sweet on something,
death, that perfect hinge.

It still shines when you think of it,
             like that river.

                  1977

from The Butcher Papers

Each Moment May Open Then as a Fan, as Fear

'Remember that day with the hawk?'
   reminisces Butcher.
'The tinny river flaring up from the distance?
The cloth of the Alps pushed into fold after fold?
The sky such brilliant glass
   it burns sort of, to think of?
I think of that now,' he says.
     'It doesn't mean a thing.'

'You expect a day like that,
the snap of delicious cliffs,
   the rake of heights,
turned on for you here and now
   like some bloody switch?'
Sheila whose speech is clear
as high streams are clear
who hates the padlocks of tat
   on her husband's tongue
shocks him more than a touch
   at her sudden turn.

'I mean,' he begins by defence
   'I sense only plains
where I thought there were slopes and views —
   you know, ice in one's veins?'

'Ice' she says 'is an element so pure
the sky hungers towards it, the earth retracts.
And the hawk lifting from ice
or with ice as its height
is a thing beyond you, Butcher,
   beyond me as well —
the hawk as aspiration flies at tricky gates.'

'You thought all that?' asks Butcher.
   He incredules.
'I wasn't there,' says Sheila.
   'That's how I know.'
How the river and the hawk

and the slanting glitters of death
lie between them now on the table
while they talk of toast.

Fish for All That Rise as Rise Wet Stars

Don't get him wrong.
The Butcher when time permits
folds his arms, can lean
lovely as any man in the throes of thought,
shouldering the doorway in summer,
bum on winter's block.

The mind may reel out
pure shining as nylon
what threshes about far out
may be brilliant, sleek;
rising or steeping down
the line still thrills.

Oh it isn't there isn't love
for the grimmest catch
for the flaking shimmer of surface
and the knives of light
but you're simply back always
to eye, to wrist,

to the thread you've inched out
to whatever draws you,
to whatever works its flukes
to a sheaf of foam —
whatever at last ebbs in
decked in light, in blood.

Look Sheila Seeing You've Asked Me

Life is *not* a horse with a winner's garland
on its sweaty neck, across its chugging veins;
not a rosette hung to a pair of agreeable norks
the world pants at like a scrum;
nor *quite* a flushy sunset and its pouring ribbons
from God's theoretic bosom either, lady —
Yet *I don't know what it is* says Butcher
        hardly know what it is
if it isn't this as well —
        which is light walking
the dreamy edge of steel
which is pulse where his wrist lies on complacent death
which is water pure as silence before speech is thought of
from the tap in the back room
        splashed on face, on boots,
so he stands with chin tingling,
        with feet like jewels.

1982

Elegy

Today, because I am not dead,
I notice the red handbasin,
the green curtains,
the knot in the veins behind the leg
of the woman who pours our tea.
I see the world because my eyes are open, thus,
as nothing could stir me, being dead, thus.

Today, as you've guessed, a funeral.
The corpse was my first cousin.
I leaned forward in the cold, kissed my other cousins,
The corpse's daughters.
I said to one, who had lovers,
'There is no answer, no consolation.'
I said to the other, the virginal,
'Perhaps, somewhere, an answer.
We must let time drench us, its river.'

A day of a red bathroom,
of two women I have lied to,
of green curtains in the morning,
of bad weather, hills whose cows
mumble in a paddock next door
while the last prayer promises
the last dream:
the new, the eternal, the shining Jerusalem,
eternity brilliant as cow-spit
in the dripping wind.
The usual slipping of the coffin
into usual earth.

The angels whose wings are paper
we can see the ink through.

1982

Waikato-Taniwha-Rau

We have a fiction that we live by: it is the river
that steps down, always down, from the pale lake
to the open jaws of land where the sea receives it,
where the great body of the sea sucks the river on,
absorbs it, where river ceases as river,
joins the past of rivers:
        and we say as it
slips beneath the fingers of willows,
as it jerks from the narrow gut of white rock,
taniwha rau — good name, eh?
        We see the logs pinned at the bend
the child on the sandbank with a lassoo or a chain
the drowned sheep puffed to a blurred balloon
the old men along the bridge spitting into the current
the pumice's small skulls on the black drift.

We join the men on the bridge, look into the river,
we hear them say *ah* when they say
'Even twenty years back the trout came this far,'
or 'See that brown froth there? That's what gets the fish.'
They talk of 'upstream' as though of a time
when the girls rose as the fish did
and they fall silent for a bit and look down
at the mottled backs of their hands on the rail.
They say 'See you then' when we nod, walk on over the river ...
We have a fiction and the fiction itself is a river,
it has upstream, lake, sea, current, much as this.
We say *taniwha rau* — 'a spirit at every bend.'
We open and close our fists on the edge of the bridge,
raise and lower our eyes to the black water,
its sandbar and sacred mountain, reflected cliffs, the narrows.
We have a fiction to live by, talking of rivers.

1982

Don't Knock the Rawleigh's Man

Don't knock the Rawleigh's Man
when he opens his case and offers you
mixed spices, curry powder, chilblain
ointment, Ready Relief, brilliantine,
don't say *Not now*, don't think
Piss off, but remember:
think of a hill called Tibi Dabo
behind Barcelona and the legend
that up there Satan
showed J.C. just what he was missing.
What he offered was not simply
the vulgar things — the girls
with buttocks like mounded cream
or enough money in brewery shares
to take a Rotarian's mind off mowing lawns
for octogenarian widows,
or the sort of drink we all know
Vice-Chancellors drink when they drink
with other Vice-Chancellors —
not that but more deftly
the luciferic fingers fondled
buttons nostalgic with little anchors
as in the Mansfield story
bits of coloured glass from old houses
and variously, these: good punctuation,
unattainable notes, throaty grunts
at bedtime, the nape of the neck
of lovely ladies caught in lamplight
like the perfect compliance of the pitch
in the last over when the last ball
takes the intransigent wicket —
yes, he did. Satan offered those things,

those were the things turned down,
that's how serious it was.
And what was round the corner as we know
was a tree already chopped
waiting to be a cross and a woman
at home rinsing a cloth white as she could
and Joseph of Arimethea still thinking the rock
he had hollowed at phenomenal expense
was going to be his, forever,
not Some Body Else's, for a spell . . .
So when the bag snaps on *your* doorstep,
flies open like leather wings
and you see instead of feathers
the tucked-in jars, the notched tubes,
the salves the spices
the lovely stuff of the flesh,
ask him in, go on, in for a moment.
There's no telling what else he might show you —
what mountain he has in mind
you may cast yourself from,
what price that your hair shimmer
like a diving hawk.

1982

liberal

Consider this:
    A man who feels for the people.
    A friend to the ill-favoured.
    Never a word against the bar-
barians assuming Roman dress.

Reconcile this:
    A believer in man's potential.
    A voice raised against the games
    where human flesh is sport.
A man whose eyes fill at music.

You might at least concede:
    No man went hungry from my door.
    No woman was molested.
    No child was imposed on.
Humanitas inevitable as breath.

I who might have, have
    never raped, pillaged, extorted;
    abused office or position;
    concealed; interfered with art;
stood between any man and sunset.

And yet as you say,
    I have killed a god. I have made
    of impartiality, a farce.
    I have dabbled in chaos. I,
Pilate. Who vote as you do.

1986

Corner

For 10 years Mr King on the corner section
has been looking for a word like *Andiamo*
or a background with a dago *twang-twang*
to stir up the ladies —
        but has only, Mr King,
his dark half-moon-on-its side eyebrows
to go with the word his tongue
          will never lay to.

All he has to fall back on
is the state-house porch where he stands at sunset,
where he tries the odd *risqué* phrase
to the hurrying-home mums
but Mrs Laracy's bonzer knockers
Mrs Gray's legs which don't quite tally
Mrs Davenport's eyes which sort of look up heavy
as the lid of a mussel surprised in steamy water —
none of them go much on him, somehow.

There are movies & movies
           and some are sad right through.
               1986

Freudiana

First time he saw a swarm of bees in flight
(a veil it made him think of, his mother's
best hat's brown veil that was a sky of spots
if you tried it on, it was that between the trees)
happened as well on the first day
his father's rage bawled at his mother
at what for a week had been waited for
as a picnic. So his father's mouth was the red
exit for a hive. It poured so loudly,
the small brown bees from his father's tongue.
When he thinks now of his father with his mouth
shut the room hums with what could happen.
A single bee is his mother putting her hat on,
for the last time.
              1986

Late Romantic

The moon mightn't be so fat if it wasn't for what we fed it.
The parked car on the lip of a hillside,
the river down there like a spoon raising light . . .

The expanse of January paddocks shaved as a monk,
the expectations of Easter rising and rising,
the Parthenon on a postcard like the skeletons of ten dogs . . .

It slips down the sides of houses easy as a brush.
It pours so a lover on a veranda in Horowhenua
breathes *Christ!* bathed solely in such election.

First time we hold a child while its eyes glitter
with its first puffed moon, we begin to tell it stories.
Someone says 'Aegean' and we fancy night varnished yellow.

Yet raise your hand or both hands so the moon is covered,
so the shape of your hands is edged in pale gloves . . .
darkness pours to fill its absence as though filling a bowl.

Darkness thus becomes a moon we know by touch.
Moon's braille seeps in at our fingers,
our blood sparkles as its lake.

Which is saying once see it, you see it still.
A million after a million after a million see it.
Our adjectives maggot at moonlight till the old bone seethes.

                                                        1986

Surfacing

A boy is standing on the edge of a lake.
(Or a girl is standing. It's not always so
easy at this distance, at that age.)
But a boy, say. He is standing at the doorway
to a room where his parents dispute
or at the corner of a street where he sees blood
maybe for the first time between men
for the mere sake of blood. His hand
raises and brushes over his brow
and along the side of his head,
thinking, is this too far for me
to think of? whose are those voices
scraping against each other? when it comes to it
blood will run simply, won't it,
as water?
                It is an immense lake
to think of crossing, the boy knows that;
the edge of the voices at that moment
is never dulled, for all the palaver
later of what can be absorbed;
as red is red, nothing is more simple.
A boy at the edge of the lake, then,
wanting to go out from the voices,
knowing how all pain but our own is
very distant, feels the water ask
for his ankles, the lake stretched out there
so far its distance is quite another colour.
And his hands moving up across his forehead,
across his hairline. It is the movement
of a boy just before he enters the water.
Or just after he comes out, the water crossed.

                                                        1986

Note from the Gardener

5 red apples grow on that tree
which for the sake of reliable reference
I call Wittgenstein — to turn
as it were the reality we assume
is there before we describe it
into a lovely game which is red,
red 5 times over, of a particular
rondure, even as the tree confirms,
'This is not of course what I was
before you thought of the label,
this is not the complete picture even now,
although you instruct a child, inform the voyeur,
repeat to yourself until you believe it:
Wittgenstein is outside the window,
the one with the branches holding
those things for the words for the things
that make 5 bigger than red,
red less luscious than apple, apple
fatter than 5.'
        When I filch
one of these apples one coming morning,
or the brightness diminishes, say, or its shape
sags mushy, I am ready, believe me,
staked with enough facts to sustain the tree.

                1992

As we say of love, sometimes

By clearing a space for it to grow, by that fact
of a levelled square, say, or an enchanted
circle, or the falling of prayers like Tarot cards
in designs of desire; for the eyes anxious
that the square, the circle, the cards, the prayer
prove fruitful, it is already there,
by consent. So they told each other before
the story quite knew where it was heading,
before the flare of the full stop like a train
in terror movies flashed the end of the sentence,
the signal to jump, run, climb the spidery
steel girders of the bridge (one of many bridges)
that went with lines laid down when the first
card told something about the cleared spaces,
or the talk before the clearing even, the strike
of the primary words burning off the past ...
It is settling in then (the completed story)
it is makeshift beginnings it is conclusions
reluctant as wood when the axe first falls.
It is, as ever, the same story that never

repeats, the notes pure for each performance,
the shadows in polite brackets while the light
cavorts.
   Here's a card for you to turn.

         1992

Hiroshima

The most famous shadow in the world
is the fastest ever made.

The most ordinary of mornings
is the quickest disposed of.

The second hands on the frozen watches
the most accurate of all.

There are speeches, there are prayers.
The seminars and the journalese are endless

on their way to that purest glamour,
the sun close as a mirror while a city shaves.

Light, which is god and father,
Shadow, which is mystery and image,

where have you gone, words, things, we favoured?
You are too close together. You do not exist.

         1992

Matinée

Because the Emperor cannot be sure
that the mouse behind the grain sacks
will not die on the same day as himself,
he buries an army at each quarter
of the wind, he devises a hill for himself.
The mouse with his scattered grains looks lively
among the stars. The Emperor owns all darkness.

         1992

Excellent People

'It is a big box of crockery,' Chekov said.
'Easy to unpack but impossible to . . .'
So easy. So obvious. He was speaking,
at first, of an author's vanity, and then
a character's sister's capacity
to disturb: from a story called
Excellent People — all second-hand as I
read it in another writer's Journal.
Then a clock in a square frame beside the bed
of a woman who writes of the woman
who quotes the Russian. A high white
ceiling sloped with dark beams.
A morepork's stage-effects from the bush

up the hill. A dog with a red scarf
insistent at the door. One story moves
into another story, the characters pass
the windows where they don't belong.
On the same page there is a line
'Countess Julia rowed over the Rhine'.
The lady raises her velvets already drugged
with wet sand. The doctor with his
blank bright glasses notes her sodden
shoe. And so on — why not?
The woman's breast is warm. The woman
who owns the clock, the book to begin with,
who looks too at the sloped beams,
closes her eyes against them all.
Excellent people, but not now.

1992

HONE TUWHARE

Born in 1922 in Kaikohe, Tuwhare belongs to the Ngapuhi hapus Ngati Korokoro, Ngati Tautahi, Te Popoto, and Uri-O-Hau. An active trade-unionist, he worked as a boilermaker before becoming a full-time writer and performer of his poetry. His col- lection No Ordinary Sun *(Blackwood & Janet Paul, 1964) was the first book of poems by a Maori to be published. In recent years he has read his work in Germany and the United States. He has also written a film script, a play and short fiction.*

Monologue

I like working near a door, I like to have my work-bench
    close by, with a locker handy.

Here, the cold creeps in under the big doors, and in the
    summer hot dust swirls, clogging the nose. When the
    big doors open to admit a lorry-load of steel, conditions
    do not improve. Even so, I put up with it, and wouldn't
    care to shift to another bench, away from the big doors.

As one may imagine this is a noisy place with smoke rising,
    machines thumping and thrusting, people kneading,
    shaping, and putting things together. Because I am nearest
    to the big doors I am the farthest away
    from the those who have to come down to shout
    instructions in my ear.

I am the first to greet strangers who drift in through
    the doors looking for work. I give them as much information
    as they require, direct them to the offices, and
    acknowledge the casual recognition that one worker
    signs to another.

I can always tell the look on the faces of the successful
    ones as they hurry away. The look on the faces of the
    unlucky I know also, but cannot easily forget.

I have worked here for fifteen months.
    It's too good to last.
    Orders will fall off
    and there will be a reduction in staff.
    More people than we can cope with
    will be brought in from other lands:
    people who are also looking
    for something more real, more lasting,
    more permanent maybe, than dying . . .
    I really ought to be looking for another job
    before the axe falls.

These thoughts I push away, I think that I am lucky
    to have a position by the big doors which open out
    to a short alley leading to the main street; console
    myself that if the worst happened I at least would have
    no great distance to carry my gear and tool-box
    off the premises.

I always like working near a door. I always look for a
    work-bench hard by — in case an earthquake
    occurs and fire breaks out, you know?

                      1964

No Ordinary Sun

Tree let your arms fall:
raise them not sharply in supplication
to the bright enhaloed cloud.
Let your arms lack toughness and
resilience for this is no mere axe
to blunt, nor fire to smother.

Your sap shall not rise again
to the moon's pull.
No more incline a deferential head
to the wind's talk, or stir
to the tickle of coursing rain.

Your former shagginess shall not be
wreathed with the delightful flight
of birds nor shield
nor cool the ardour of unheeding
lovers from the monstrous sun.

Tree let your naked arms fall
nor extend vain entreaties to the radiant ball.
This is no gallant monsoon's flash,
no dashing trade wind's blast.
The fading green of your magic
emanations shall not make pure again
these polluted skies... for this
is no ordinary sun.

O tree
in the shadowless mountains
the white plains and
the drab sea floor
your end at last is written.

1964

The Old Place

No one comes
by way of the doughy track
through straggly tea tree bush
and gorse, past the hidden spring
and bitter cress.

Under the chill moon's light
no one cares to look upon
the drunken fence-posts
and the gate white with moss.

No one except the wind
saw the old place
make her final curtsy
to the sky and earth:

and in no protesting sense
did iron and barbed wire
ease to the rust's invasion
nor twang more tautly
to the wind's slap and scream.

On the cream-lorry
or morning paper van no one comes,
for no one will ever leave
the golden city on the fussy train;
and there will be no more waiting
on the hill beside the quiet tree
where the old place falters
because no one comes any more

no one.

1964

Friend

Do you remember
that wild stretch of land
with the lone tree guarding the point
from the sharp-tongued sea?

The fort we build out of branches
wrenched from the tree is dead wood now.
The air that was thick with the whirr of
toetoe spears succumbs at last to the grey gull's wheel.

Oyster-studded roots
of the mangrove yield no finer feast
of silver-bellied eels, and sea-snails
cooked in a rusty can.

Allow me to mend the broken ends
of shared days:
but I wanted to say
that the tree we climbed
that gave food and drink
to youthful dreams, is no more.
Pursed to the lips her fine-edged
leaves made whistle — now stamp
no silken tracery on the cracked clay floor.

Friend,
in this drear
dreamless time I clasp
your hand if only to reassure
that all our jewelled fantasies were
real and wore splendid rags.

Perhaps the tree
will strike fresh roots again:
give soothing shade to a hurt and
troubled world.

1964

The Girl in the Park

The girl in the park
    saw a nonchalant sky
    shrug into a blue-dark
    denim coat.
    The girl in the park
    did not reach up to touch
    the cold steel buttons.

The girl in the park
    saw the moon glide into a dead tree's arms
    and felt the vast night
    pressing.
    How huge it seems,
    and the trees are big, she said.
    The stars heard her
    and swooped down perching
    on treetop and branch
    owl-like and unblinking.

The grave trees,
    as muscular as her lover
    leaned darkly down to catch
    the moonrise and madness
    in her eyes:
    the moon is big, it is very big,

she said, with velvet in her throat.
An owl hooted.
The trees scraped and nudged
each other and the stars
carried the helpless
one-ribbed moon away . . .

The girl in the park
does not care: her body swaying
to the dark-edged chant
of storms.

1964

Tangi

I did not meet her
on the bordered path
nor detect her fragrance
in the frolic of violets
and carnations.

She did not stroll riverward
to sun-splash and shadows
to willows trailing garlands
of green pathos.

Death was not hiding in the cold rags
of a broken dirge:
nor could I find her
in the cruel laughter of children,
the curdled whimper of a dog.

But I heard her with the wind
crooning in the hung wires
and caught her beauty by the coffin
muted to a softer pain —
in the calm vigil of hands
in the green-leaved anguish
of the bowed heads
of old women.

1964

Haiku (1)

Stop
your snivelling
creek-bed:

come rain hail
and flood-water

laugh again

1970

Rain

I can hear you
making small holes
in the silence
rain

If I were deaf
the pores of my skin
would open to you
and shut

And I
should know you
by the lick of you
if I were blind

the something
special smell of you
when the sun cakes
the ground

the steady
drum-roll sound
you make
when the wind drops

But if I
should not hear
smell or feel or see
you

you would still
define me
disperse me
wash over me
rain

1970

Who Tests Today?

Something stirs in the night
a cat? A fish? A rat?
How strange. Am I dreaming?
Rain-pimples on glass: are they real?
Is the door unhinged?

It is not a cat. It is not a fish
Neither rat door-bang nor trickle
of rain on the windows

It is the void: the stillness in the void
emptied of all sound. There is no human cry
glad or sad: cat-spit fish-burp rat-squeal

The door you see has quite effaced itself
and is at one with the molten glass
and hinge
The houses are as powder sweet smelling
talcum-dust: there is nothing

And the stillness? Ah yes
The stillness may I say is Absolute
The ascension is complete: and the people
long gone to Christ knows where
with a whopping great hallelujah shout: this

is no dream
Something stirs in the night
A cat-fish-rat? A door slammed shut?
And the rain? What of the rain?

It is silent. It is insidious
It falls; there is no comment

1970

To a Maori Figure Cast in Bronze Outside the Chief Post Office, Auckland

I hate being stuck up here, glaciated, hard all over
and with my guts removed: my old lady is not going
to like it

I've seen more efficient scarecrows in seedbed
nurseries. Hell, I can't even shoo the pigeons off

Me: all hollow inside with longing for the marae on
the cliff at Kohimarama, where you can watch the ships
come in curling their white moustaches

Why didn't they stick me next to Mickey Savage?
'Now then,' he was a good bloke
Maybe it was a Tory City Council that put me here

They never consulted me about naming the square
It's a wonder they never called it: Hori-in-the-gorge-at-
bottom-of-hill. Because it is like that: a gorge,
with the sun blocked out, the wind whistling around
your balls (your balls mate) And at night, how I
feel for the beatle-girls with their long-haired
boyfriends licking their frozen finger-chippy lips
hopefully. And me again beetling

my tent eyebrows forever, like a brass monkey with
real worries: I mean, how the hell can you welcome
the Overseas Dollar, if you can't open your mouth
to poke your tongue out, eh?

If I could only move from this bloody pedestal I'd
show the long-hairs how to knock out a tune on the
souped-up guitar, my mere quivering, my taiaha held
at the high port. And I'd fix the ripe kotiro too
with their mini-piupiu-ed bums twinkling: yeah!

Somebody give me a drink: I can't stand it

1972

A Fall of Rain at Mitimiti: Hokianga

Drifting on the wind, and through
the broken window of the long house
where you lie, incantatory chant
of surf breaking, and the Mass
and the mountain talking.

At your feet two candles puff the
stained faces of the whanau, the vigil
of the bright madonna. See, sand-whipped
the toy church does not flinch.

E moe, e te whaea: wahine rangimarie

Mountain, why do you loom over us like
that, hands on massive hips? Simply
by hooking your finger to the sea,
rain-squalls swoop like a hawk, suddenly.
Illumined speeches darken, fade to metallic
drum-taps on the roof.

Anei nga roimata o Rangipapa.

Flat, incomprehensible faces: lips moving
only to oratorical rhythms of the rain:

quiet please, I can't hear the words.
And the rain steadying: black sky leaning
against the long house. Sand, wind-sifted
eddying lazily across the beach.

And to a dark song lulling: *e te whaea, sleep.*

1974

A Death at Sea

He died when the sun found a steamy slot
in the sea

He died when the wind's mouth slackened
in sleep

He was dead when the sea came up rough
again, nudging the small boat in; held now

between black fangs of rock, the body bottomed,
feet and lower parts awash in water, and no

sign ever of rowlocks oars or bailer. *Three days
out, sea: hold, bring him in again.*

Stand away: get back. Let's have a gawp at our
bonnie prince. Remarkable. Eye-sockets picked

clean: mouth and ears pulsing with maggots.
Tomorrow sun and wind will prance and scrape:

and bring back my bonnie to me, to me...
the sea intones, drunkenly.

1974

Heemi

for James K. Baxter

No point now my friend in telling
you my lady's name.
She wished us well, offered wheels
which spun my son and me like
comets through the lonely night.
You would have called her Aroha.

And when we picked up three young
people who'd hitched their way
from the Ninety Mile Beach to be
with you, I thought: yes
your mana holds, Heemi. Your mana
is love. And suddenly the night
didn't seem lonely anymore.

The car never played up at all.
And after we'd given it a second
gargle at the all-night bowser
it just zoomed on on gulping
easily into the gear changes
up or down.

Because you've been over this road
many times before Heemi, you'd
know about the steady climb ahead
of us still. But once in the tricky
light, Tongariro lumbered briefly
out of the clouds to give us the old
'up you' sign. Which was real friendly.

When we levelled off a bit at the top
of the plateau, the engine heat couldn't
keep the cold from coming in, the fog
swamping thick and slushy, and pressing
whitely against tired eyeballs.

Finally, when we'd eased ourselves
over a couple of humps and down down
the winding metalled road to the river

and Jerusalem, I knew things would be
all right. Glad that others from the
Mainland were arrowing toward the dawn
like us.

Joy for the brother sun chesting over
the brim of the land, and for the three
young blokes flaked out in the back seat
who would make it now, knowing that they
were not called on to witness
some mysterious phenomenon of birth on
a dung-littered floor of a stable

but come simply to call
on a tired old mate in a tent
laid out in a box
with no money in the pocket
no fancy halo, no thump left in the old
ticker.

1974

Papa-tu-a-nuku (Earth Mother)

We are stroking, caressing the spine
    of the land.

We are massaging the ricked
    back of the land

with our sore but ever-loving feet:
    hell, she loves it!

Squirming, the land wriggles
    in delight.
      We love her.

1978

Sun o (2)

Gissa smile Sun, giss yr best
good mawnin' one, fresh 'n cool like

yore still comin' — still
half in an' half outa the lan'scape?

An' wen yore clear of that eastern rim
of hills an' tha whole length of tha

valley begins to flood wit yr light, well
that's wen I could just reach out 'n stroke

tha pitted pock-marked pores of yr shiny
skin an' peel ya — just like a orange, right

down to yr white under-skin, but I wouldn't
bite ya — well, not until the lunch-bell goes

at noon wen I can feel ya hot an' outa reach
an' balanced right there — above my head.

C'mon, gissa smile Sun.

1978

The River Is an Island

You are river. This way and that
and all the way to sea two escorts
shove and pull you. Two escorts
in contention.

Left bank or right bank, how can
you be a river without either?

Thus are U-bends made. Thus are
S-bends made. Your direction
is assured and sometimes running
perfectly and quite straight.

A low bank on your left holds your
laughing stitches in. On your right
side skips another hushing your
loud protests.

You are river. Joy leaping down
a greenstone stairway: anger cradled
in a bed of stones.

You're a harbour; a lake; an island
only when your banks lock lathered
arms in battle to confine you: slow-release you.

Go river, go. To ocean seek your
certain end. Rise again to cloud;
to a mountain — to a mountain
drinking from a tiny cup.
Ah, river

you are ocean: you are island

1982

A Talk with My Cousin, Alone

And afterwards, after the shedding of mucus, the droll
    speeches and the hongi for my cousin in the box,
    we were called to meal at the long tables.
    But I hadn't come for that.

I could hear the Tasman combers shredding themselves
    nearby, wishing then for a cawing beak of sound
    to help me reassemble myself. Taking my shoes off,
    I trudge a steep dune; sand, a cool silken lisp
    spilling through my toes.

Bottomed on a hill of sand, I wondered wry dry leaves
whether the Pakeha marine authorities would sell
us back ephemeral Maori land (now exposed to bird,
bleached crab and shrimp) lying somewhere between
low-water mark and high.

A pounding gavel is the sun today — a brassy auctioneer:
the sea, his first assistant. Of this, no instant
favour offered me in stint. I cushion my elbows
deeper in sand. I'm the only bidder.
For this beautiful piece of land/seascape, I will
start the bidding at twenty falling axes per square
centimetre, said the sun looking hard at me for an
earlobe twitch, or, other sign.
Get stuffed, I reply, holding my middle finger
straight up — turning it. Slowly.

Idly I think, that after the eleven o'clock prayers
tomorrow (and before lunch) my cousin will have
gone to ground.
'They may ban tangi-hanga in the future,' I say
to him. 'Right now you're doing your job. This
moment is forever as the splayed fingers of the hand
drawn together, like a fist.' I look up at the sun
and blink. The sun is beside itself, dancing. There are
two of them.

1982

We, Who Live in Darkness

It had been a long long time of it
wriggling and squirming in the swamp of night.
And what was time, anyway? Black intensities
of black on black on black feeding on itself?
Something immense? Immeasureless?

No more.
There just had to be a beginning somehow.
For on reaching the top of a slow rise suddenly
eyes I never knew I possessed were stung by it
forcing me to hide my face in the earth.

It was light, my brothers. Light.
A most beautiful sight infiltered past
the armpit hairs of the father. Why, I could
even see to count all the fingers of my hands
held out to it; see the stain — the clutch of
good earth on them.

But then he moved.
And darkness came down even more oppressively
it seemed and I drew back tense; angry.

Brothers, let us kill him — push him off.

1987

Dear Cousin

Some day soon old friend, before either
of us can throw our hand in, I'll say
to you: come.

Then, I'd roll out my threadbare whaariki
— to help you remember to take your boots
off — spread an old newspaper on the floor

and on it place a steaming pot of puha,
kamokamo, riwai, brisket-on-the-bone and
dumplings what we call: doughboys.

For sweeteners, I'll produce another pot
of boiled fish-heads with onions, cracking
open the heads afterwards for the succulent

eyes and the brains: that will be a special
treat, because we're both brainy buggers.
Then — because I know that you are also

a devout man — deeper than any prayer can
grab you — I will simply say: go for it.
And we'd crack a bottle or three together

you and me, swap lies and sing: happy days
are here again.
We would never hurt ourselves because we

wouldn't have far to bump our heads sitting
on the floor where only a small effort
is needed to roll over, rise on one knee

stand up — go out and wring your best friend's
neck. What do you reckon, Cous?

1987

Deep River Talk

It's cold: it's golden; a magnificent
orange disc playing peek-a-boo
from the far-side of straggly
strings of leafless rastafarian willows
growing on the other side of the river.
The river's wide here: it's

undecided: it's steeling itself
never to turn and go back uphill.
Steam's rising from it and it's
not the early morning sun that's
doin' it; I can't raise heat
from the sun yet.

The veins of the river are swollen.
They're bending to the tide's
up-swing: tempers are like sails

shredding in a gale.

There's talk of a merger. A know-all
insect on stilts has just walked out
on top of the waters to supervise
the talks; I suppose pretending
to be Jesus.

In the sunlight mullet are jumpin'
and making lovin' archways of silver
for the migratory ocean-seeking eels
eeling their way down down; down
to the river-mouth and away.

The river's pushy, 'Back off! Thus far
and NO further —'

I'll see YOU outside, mate,' says
the sea, turning. A swish, a tiny
whip and swirl of water —

Snap!

Daddy-long-legs has joined his
ancestors by way of a hungry trout's
stomach & stomach-ejector.

Happens to people too, nowadays — with
sharks hangin' around a lot.

1993

C. K. STEAD

*Born in Auckland in 1932, C. K. Stead was educated at the University of Auckland
and the University of Bristol. A critic, editor and novelist, he took early retirement in
1986 from the University of Auckland, where he was Professor of English. Since then
he has devoted most of his time to writing novels, criticism, and poetry.*

from Pictures in a Gallery Undersea

i

Binnorie, O Binnorie

In Ladbroke Square the light on waxen branches —
The orange light through two veined leaves
Tenacious in frost.
                    Upstairs, she lit the gas,
And drew bright curtains on the whitened eaves,
And said (her hand above the slowly turning disc)
'I shall never go back'.
                    Mozart in the delicate air
Slid from her glass, beat vainly against the cushions,
Then took off gladly across the deserted Square.
'You too must stay' (loosening her sun-bleached hair)

'You more than I — you will defeat their fashions.'

Invisible fins guided her to my chair.

Pictures in a gallery undersea
Were turned facing the wall, and the corridors were endless;
But in the marine distance, floating always beyond me,
A girl played Mozart on her sun-bleached hair.

So that wherever I walked on that long haul, midnight to dawn,
Stones of a sunken city woke, and passed the word,
And slept behind me; but the notes were gone,
Vanished like bubbles up through the watery air
Of London, nor would again be heard.

v

I dreamt tonight that I did feast with Caesar

Wilde had been lynched. His head, grown larger, grinned
        from the Tower of London,
Swung by its hair under the Marble Arch,
And looked out from the point of a spear down Constitution Hill.
South of the River they were roasting him slowly on a spit,
And in Knightsbridge several of the best families dined
        delicately on his battered parts.
He, in Reading, enjoyed the debauch by proxy,
Bored at last with the rented corpse of Art
Whose delicate lusts had never been near to his heart.

Snow fell — fell where Hueffer ascended
From Great Russell Street to meet the eyes of Garnett,
And heard the scholar's voice: 'Now it is all ended, —
England shall breed no poet for fifty years.'

Yeats not a mile from where they stood.
                                        And Yeats
Drew down the dim blind of Olivia's hair
And dreamed of a great bird. Then woke
Calling 'Maud. Maud.' But the room was empty.
Across the narrow alley he drank coffee,
Bought his paper from me at the corner
(I only a few feet tall, in cloth cap and boots
Three sizes too large. He the toff of the buildings.)

And as he went a man approached me, shouting
'This paper you sold me, there's nothing in it'
(Waving the packed pages and snatching back his money).

And the toff, a hundred yards along the street,
And Ezra in billiard-cloth trousers across the street
Wearing an ear-ring of aquamarine,
And old Possum hackneying past in a bowler to his funeral at
        the bank,
Turned
        turned, and watching, faded from sight.

vi

Now it was time for the drawing of curtains.
The smoke climbed, hand over hand, its difficult way,
Rested, or sank back in the thick air.
The River swans nor sang for the dead day
Nor proudly departed; but each hooked
One leg across its back, displaying a dirty web,
And (strong beak poised on graceful neck) poked
The rubbish drifting at the water's edge.

vii

Chanterez-vous quand vous serez vapoureuse?

And as the last orange of the sun was crushed
The River accepted its lights, from Kew to Battersea
On, winding, to the Tower.
                              It was winter, the year '58,
And many were dead. But into the same heart and out
Through channels of stone and light, the blood still pulsed —
Carried me with it down New Oxford Street
Through Soho to the whirling clock of the Circus,
Then down, on to the bridge. The snow was freezing.
A train stood middle-poised beside the footpath
Above the water. And in a corner, hunched,
An old man's unsheathed fingers struggled to revive
The dead years on a battered violin.

                                     1964

from Walking Westward

October she phoned to say
for her at last it was   over
                              forgotten
                              irrelevant
3 nails meant for the heart

might have made use of the new maths
that has a cold beauty
like the beauty of a fiction

as for example that a survey of 19 love affairs showed
    17 were over
    7 were forgotten
    and 13 irrelevant
    but only 2 were all three

9 were over and irrelevant but not forgotten
5 were over and forgotten but not irrelevant

how many that were over were neither irrelevant nor forgotten?

to which a Venn diagram
viz:

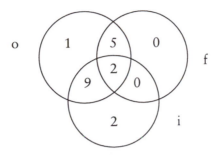

returns the answer 1
(rendered poetically: one only)
    irrefutable
as to say in the language of another dimension
he had explored with her
the caves of generation and the terraces of the stars

1979

from Twenty Two Sonnets

Spring 1974

1

(1 September 1974)

Maurice, I dreamed of you last night. You wore
A black track-suit, red-striped. Saying goodbye

We fought back tears. I woke thinking you dead.
Here in the North manuka is flecked with flowers,

Willows bent in stream-beds are edged with green,
But the tall-striding poplars seem no more

Than ghostly sketches of their summer glory.
Beyond the dunes blue of the sky out-reaches

The blue of ocean where the spirits of our dead
Stream northward to their home. Under flame-trees

By Ahipara golf-course someone's transistor tells me
The news again, and down on the hard sand

In letters large enough to match the man
The children have scrawled it: BIG NORM IS DEAD.

8

To Maurice and to Maurice and to Maurice
Duggan, Shadbolt, Gee, how they load us down with fictions

And all our yesterdays maybe have lighted fools
The way to Dostoyevski. How many years ago was it

That Curnow's bantams roosted in his macrocarpas
And he and I one midnight crept under the moon

And swung on the branches bringing those feathered half-wits
Down around our heads with a flapping and a squawking

That echoed over Big Shoal Bay? Do good poets
Make bad professors? Do many Maurices

Make light work, as one Sargeson made a summer?
How many K.S.'s could the North Shore harbour

Before the Fall? I tell you my lord fool
Out of these nettle prophets we still pluck our safety-pins.

16

Xuan Loc fallen, Danang fallen, we wait for the fall of Saigon.
Nobody weeps or cheers, nobody puts on sack-cloth

For the thousand thousand lives we took or broke
To get our own sweet way. We didn't get it.

Does Lyndon Johnnie underground sleep sound
Dreaming light at the end of a tunnel? Holyoake hasn't been told.

Harold Holt went swimming, and all those airy ministers
Of canister bombs and body counts took jobs

With the World Bank, UNESCO, the Ford Foundation.
Washington, Wellington, leather chairs, inflatable arses

'Peace with Honour' — and last night, walking home,
I saw in a darkened house a fish tank glowing

With purple lights. There's no God. We don't answer for
Our violences, nor even for our sense of beauty.

20

(Tauranga)

Five children and a shag are fishing from the wharf.
Across the estuary autumn has taken away

From willows and poplars their definitive shapes.
Yellow-brown, slate-grey, hazy, smudged,

They fade into green fields and blue-green hills.
An empty sky is immense and fills the frame.

I count 41 launches, 72 parked cars.
How can a faraway world be made to seem

Less unreal than its image? If the cars were people
And people cars the sky might fill with bombers

Trying to decide their future. Into the picture
Come four young Maoris with flax kits and their granny

Who clutches a thermos. They row away in a dinghy.
If life goes on without thought, is it right to complain?

                                                    1975–1983

from The Clodian Songbook

           Air New Zealand
                          old friend of Catullus
        you offer a quick hike
                          to Disneyland
                          the South Pole
         Hong Kong's hotspots
            to ease jealous ache.

           Thanks brother
                          but I'd rather
        you flew downcountry a message to Clodia.
        Tell her she's known to her 300 loveless lovers
           as the scrum machine.
                          Tell her
           Catullus loves her
         as the lone lawn daisy
                          loves
                          the Masport mower.

        *   *   *   *

Death, you clever bugger
              who would have credited you
with such finesse!
              Your shadow passed over me
and took instead
Clodia's white pigeon
              that used to peck her fingers
              and warble obscure reflections
among her vines.

There he lies
dried out
feet up
              weightless in summer grass.

           And look at her tears!

Venus and Cupid
are moved to join her in weeping.

Congratulations Death —

you're an artist.
You know just how to strike
and where.

Had I been the one
called down your dark road
no such flood
would have followed me into the night.

          *   *   *   *

'Young man,' she used to say
          'you stay away from old Furius.
His hedge is a disgrace to the suburb.'

I tried to excuse it:
'You should see the vegetables he grows
behind that hedge.'

'That may be so'
she said
          'but they say he doesn't have a
          washing machine.'
          'He always looks clean'
I said.
'He's a great cook
and he lets me borrow his books.'

She wanted to know
why he didn't cut his hedge.
          'He's a writer'
I told her.
          'He's very busy and famous.
His books are published in England.'

'What's the good of that'
she asked
'if he doesn't have a washing machine
          and his hedge
is falling over the pavement?'

          *   *   *   *

Remember, poor ghost of Furius
          those Eliot lines
          we used to quote
          with ghostly relish:
'What is that noise?
   "The wind under the door."'

Auster blew from the south
Boreas from the north
          Favonius from the west
          Apheliotes from the east

                    but that overdraft of yours
£1250
                                    it blew
up through the floorboards
                making the scrim billow
and the roof-iron groan.

            *   *   *   *

'It may not be God exactly'
                            Clodia tells me
                lying back among sheets
                in an unwonted moment
of unwanton wonder
                'but *there's something up there*'
— and why not?
                but if there must be a Big One
            I choose for myself that goddess
daughter of Latona
born under an olive
                            among Delian hills
who sees to crops and hunting
                    — or in her darker moments
when wars threaten and the rocks
                        shake underfoot
let her be that one
                who turned over in sleep
closing her legs
on Maui's trespass
                and laid him to rest for ever.

            *   *   *   *

Today there's something in the winter sky
                    signalling spring
something to do with light —
and the hand of the wind on our cheeks
is less rough than it was.
                But my bags are packed —
I'm flying north
into the last of that hemisphere's summer.
                    Goodbye Clodia
        I don't ask you to be faithful
but keep safe
remember my birthday
and never doubt I love you.
                    Travel is my vice.
Already it's as if I can see
            the first brown leaves
falling into the Thames.

My heart is an anchor
    my head a dinghy on the running tide.

                            1982–1988

After The Wedding

1

After the wedding comparing notes with
Cousin Elspeth and Cousin Caroline
about our childhood bareback riding
on the Kaiwaka farm —

      How, fallen with your
10-year legs did you get back up
even supposing he stood for you?

Cousin E remembered vaulting from the back
of her pet pig.
                I used the ruts worn deep
by the cream sledge — stood him in the hollow
and leapt from its edge.
                  Elspeth
and her sister, blond babies
under the trees I climbed —

      wooden verandah
hot dry garden sheltered by macrocarpa
dogs panting in shade
                my face black
from the summer burn-off.

2

In sleep I still trace those tracks
below gum trees
            skirting the swamp
through bush to that pool of pools
where the small brown fish suspend themselves
in shafts of light.
        My feet sink
midstream in heaped silt
clouding the flow.

      Water had cut its way
through black rock greened with moss
down to that glassy stillness overhung
with trees.

      In the rock cleft
a deep hole water-worn and cold and dark —

I caught the eel that lived there
        its sinuous spirit.

3

In recollection summer is forever
renewing itself even in the thickest
leafmould shade.
                     It draws a life
from heat in the ploughed field
where I gathered fossil gum
                     or in the hayfield
or in sunlight above the flame
above the dam.

        Cousin Elspeth, Cousin Caroline
cantered bareback
                               fell
(years after me) from the same horse.

4

Weddings are full of God and the word of God
and the word God. I wonder what they mean.
To be one with your body, your body one with the world —
more than a marriage, it's a consummation
bracken and oil-flame like red cellophane
flapping on the hill-slope.
                     Eden
won't ask you back, you must make your way
in dreams, by moonlight, or by the broad light of day.

5

There was another stream, a creek
on the far side of the road
where the old house had been.
        It ran through reeds
silent.

The moons repeat themselves
the moreporks retort
the eel and its sibilants
are fluent
        an old chimney stands.

6

It's not what the landscape says
but the way it's said which is a
richness of saying, even of the thing
said —

        that finely articulated slope
a few words at the water
the breathy manuka and the precise

pernickity ti tree

      a long last sentence of cloud
struck out by the dark.

After the wedding
I lie in darkness
I see something that might be myself
      step out for a moment.

It makes the moon
look at itself in water
      it makes the stars
gaze.
   It hears a nightbird and something
      that rustles
in reeds.

It sees itself called
  to light up a silent
vast
    beautiful
        indifferent
waste —

mirror to the mystery
mirrored.

7

Break it
  (the mirror)

the Supreme Intelligence
is always silent
      and death will come
in the guise of just this stillness
or another
    but that was always the case.

8

'Marriages are made in Heaven'
        — not so.

We marry to be nearer the earth
cousins of the fur and stalk
        talking together

that brown water reflecting
those green hills.

      1988

At the Grave of Governor Hobson

You started it all. Here for you it ended.
Here it goes on. A bridge over Grafton Gully
casts morning shadow. A motorway shaves the graveyard
and crops it back. Through oaks and undergrowth
the interrupted light on broken gravestones
writes and erases itself. Further down
was once a stream. Sometimes a former someone,
drunk, derelict, or dead by misadventure,
was found there. It was our forest in the city
with paths and dangers — most of it now cut down.

Immemorial aunts, great uncles, cousins
I'm told are here. A still decipherable headstone
remembers my forebear who walked behind your coffin
and five years later joined you under the oaks.
Your children went back to England. We remained
to inherit your city, and that distrusted Treaty
you made as instructed by those who would later call it
'little more than a legal fiction'. Your dearest Liz
took home her title to two hundred Auckland acres,
prospered, a widow in Plymouth, and didn't remarry.

Shadow pickets fall on the raised white slab
that marks your grave. A Caribbean pirate
once put a noose to your neck, then changed his mind
and set you adrift without sail. You lived to die
at a desk in a dream of Auckland, clouded by
headaches that came from the south. A riderless horse
was led behind the coffin eight sailors carried.
All day the tribes lamented. 'Send us no boy,'
a Chief wrote to the Queen, 'nor one puffed up,
but a man good as this Governor who has died.'

'Remote,' they called it; 'lacking natural advantage.'
That you chose the Waitemata, that your choice attracted
artisans from the south, that from this site
you asserted your right to govern — these were facts
the Wakefields wouldn't forgive. 'It is not my purpose,'
you wrote, 'that I should disparage Port Nicholson,
but only, against deceptions to say that I find
here a more genial climate, more fertile soil.'
No people chooses its history. Doubting our own,
we can say at least in this we know you were right.

Our chopper-cops go over, eyeing Auckland.
From a car radio a voice I'm sure belongs
to Kiri te Kanawa skies itself through the branches
with 'Let the Bright Seraphim'. Under the bridge
Maori street-kids have tuned their ghetto-blaster
to Bobby Brown. A boy sniffs glue from a bag
beneath his jacket. Messages on the arch
in well-schooled spray-can read 'King Cobras Rule'

and 'The Treaty is a Fraud'. Governor, all about you
for better and worse, your memorial goes on growing.

Last night, yellow as butter, an outsize moon
sailed over the ridge of Parnell. In Emily Place
it picked the obelisk out that marks the place
where you laid the first stone for the first St Paul's;
it gilded the six-lane highway, once a track,
where you used to lead your Lila and her schoolfriend
Harriet Preece, and lift them over the ditch;
it laid a lily of light on 'this beautiful plot
on the slope of a wooded valley looking to the sea',
once yours and, given to the city, yours again.

Let today be all the days we've lived in New Zealand:
stench of whale-meat, a rat cooked on a spit,
morning boots frozen hard, the southern Maori
ravaged by measles, rum, Te Rauparaha;
wars in the north, gumfields, forests falling
to ruminant grassland, cities climbing like trees;
and everywhere this language both subtle and strong.
You didn't start it, Governor. As we do, you fashioned
what time, and the times that live in us, required.
It doesn't finish. These verses have no end.

1990

PETER BLAND

Born in 1934 in Yorkshire, Peter Bland emigrated to New Zealand aged 20. A found-ing member of Downstage Theatre, he has worked for many years, both here and abroad, as an actor as well as a writer.

Kumara God

Three days and still the slow fogged rain
Drifts inland: all along the valley
Light melts to clusters of steamed-up panes.
All's formlessness. A sharpened will
Won't chip us free of it. It's
A melting back, an elemental drift
Beyond time or season . . .
                  And so I bring
The little stone cramped kumara god
In from the garden, take down the clock
And set him there, upon the mantelpiece,
To be my curled-in self, grown
Old in embryo, slightly sardonic . . .
Feeling around me this slow retreat
Of lives gone underground, of sleep turned solid.

1964

The Happy Army

The child has a vision of the happy army. He
has carefully sketched in my appointment book
the smiles, the fingers, the boots and guns
his happy army wave like rattles. No
one is dying, no one's bad or good,
and even the one at the back has a medal
while the generals beam pure love. The sun
has rolled to the ground, has been caught up
in a growing air of excitement that runs
riot, filling the sky with faces, arms, legs
and bits of old tanks. It is natural
that everyone, everywhere, faces the front,
not out of discipline or to scare the enemy
but in frank expectancy of applause. And
of course this is why this particular army
is happy, why no one dies, why the sun
shares in the happy army's happiness
and rolls down to earth. It is why I run
towards the boots and guns, why I come
as far as I dare to the edge of the paper
to stare . . . to stare and to cheer them on.

1972

Letters Home — New Zealand 1885

for Allen Curnow

1

Flocks sway, packed tight against the rails.
We boil them down for soap. Each
ewe's worth fourpence for her fat alone:
twice what we'd get by shipping them back home.
(How patiently they wait, heads bowed
like girls at Sunday School.) I try
to catch up on my notes
describing specimens of plant and stone
picked up on my walks. We hacked
cross-sections from live kauri trunks
before we burned the slopes. I hope
to show them at Kew that decent work's being done
out here in the colonies. The smell
of blood and melting bones
fouls the verandah where I smoke.
(My notes on fault-lines are especially good.)
The lake's almost dried up. It's been
like Africa this year. The black
swans die in hundreds, eating
their own yolk. Eels
glut the crimson mud for scraps

tipped from the vats. I've seen
them crawl across the lawn
to grab a live sheep's foot. At night
I read the psalms . . . *The Lord's*
my Shepherd. It's most apt. Two
years here now. It almost feels like home.

2

Dear *friend* (there's no one here
called that) I intend
to write a natural history
of these hills. (Most plants
are primitive, some unique. My wife
says we are Adam and Eve.)
My mind's escaped old ways of seeing,
strict categories of breeding, station, class:
it roams, almost unprincipled, between
these tremendous horizons
and the new small print
used in the bibles that you've sent.
Much thanks. I wish
you could see my lake. I've made
a local version of our Oxford punt.

3

At Sunday School my dear wife reads
The Song of Solomon to a Maori chief.
He likes the *old* testament (those simple tales
of bygone kings and queens). He'll
listen for hours. His moko gleams
like blue blood on his cheeks. Once,
at a wedding feast, he ate the heart
of a living lamb — holding it up
still beating to the sun. It was
a sort of Grace — *For what we are . . .*
but that's perhaps difficult to understand
back in New Brighton. Suffice to say
he's *not* a violent man. He asks
why Jesus did not marry? *The Son*
of God should father sons himself.
A tribe of Gods! That's what he wants.
We need a priest. My poor wife does her best.

4

Our lake's one island — a sunken raft —
was once the home of cannibals:
blood-soaked it's taken root — become
a Pavilion, a Chinese glade
of willows and bamboo. Swans
crowd there in their thousands. Some

hang themselves in their haste to breed
(long necks caught on willow forks
breasts spiked by green bamboo).
Their skeletons, so fine and white,
are delicate harps for the wind's tune.

*

At night I go down to the lake alone
haunted by the swans' cold song
(that hollow aboriginal throb). Black
swans, black eels, are all that live
in that still pond. For company
I recite to myself *The Lady of Shalott*
and see her white limbs floating past
my growing tin-roofed Camelot.
My wife's gone back. I cannot keep
her soft hands tied to this hard land.
God called her home to Camberley.
(She begs me to sell up.) I like
my lonely midnight strolls . . . eels
splashing . . . dark wings flying off.
I feel new silences. I hear Noah's doves.
I see the first hills loom above
these slow black waters fleeced in fog.

5

My wife's last letter with a pressed rose
arrived with the first snow. (How I ache
to hold her!) I've arranged my notes
in evolutionary order — according
to Lyell and Spencer. Strange
how the well-established species
show signs of regression. They 'give up'.
These acres obviously need new blood.
(Did she prick her finger? There's a stain
on the petals.) I couldn't live
without these hills, this
sense of space that goes on and on
inside my head as well as
all around me. I remember once
she said *Our pohutukawa blossoms
have the scent of salt and oranges*. That's what
this rose smells of — not Surrey
but her that summer on an Auckland beach
swimming with chestnut hair piled up
like one of Millais' women. The lake
has frozen over. Another week
and it will hold my weight. I'll
skate out all alone to my island
(half-a-mile!) and count the unhatched eggs.
The swans have long gone north. Some ewes
are already lambing. In birth and death

(and love) the world goes mad.
There are no rules for our inmost feelings.
I must question Lyell and Spencer about that.

6

I'm working hard. (Six months
since I wrote you?) Lambs
to the slaughter and these endless notes!
My room is barely habitable . . .
roots, rocks, unopened bills. My drover
says that I'm being eaten up
by this 'great cannibal land.'
He's a hard worker, fresh from Yorkshire,
but a secretive and venal man.
(Some talk of crude high-country habits
and weekends at the Pa.) I've finally
got my index going. So many entries!
Where to end or begin? I've
consulted Darwin, always the best on sources,
but God still goes back further than we think.

7

Her chestnut hair and white limbs floating . . .
My bedroom mirror's cracked. I shave
two faces . . . or I did . . . my beard's
as thick as gorse and mad with ticks.
I've sent the first proofs off (not
happy with my quotes). The drover's left.
The front door's hanging on torn hinges.
Sheep are dying on the library steps.
The shearers are late this year. I'm lonely.
My head hurts and the blackberry patch
whimpers all night with tangled flesh.
No one comes near me. I'll leave this letter
under an ammonite. The lake keeps calling.
I'd like to lie down where the black swans nest.

                                    1985

A Last Note from Menton

i.m. Louis Johnson 1924–1988

'Displacement,' you wrote, 'is a kind
of freedom . . . Let's count ourselves lucky
we don't belong!' Some mention then
of how Lawrence died
in sunny Venice, with freezing legs,
while back in New Mexico his allotment bloomed
with English beans. You enjoyed a sense
of ironies on the move. They
scissored at the truth. 'In the end,'

you said, 'it's always a passing love.'

Back home, you feared we were 'digging in'
. . . that old Kiwi regressive thing
disguised as growing roots. You
fought all your life for a local voice
but knew — to misquote — that it often grew
'out of the mouths of foreign mums.'

Again and again you mention Mansfield's
'broad light of day' — that glare
she turned away from when
it pinned her to this land. That view
has still to be faced, across
tin roofs and tidal mud. Is it
a place where only prophets thrive,
never coming down from the hills
to do the washing up? You
turned away from that well-worn path
to look an exile in the eye,
living the question Katherine asked:
can one stay and keep an open heart,
discard the sackcloth, let the spirit dance?

Today I almost gave myself over
to your 'friendly enemy' Colin McCahon.
Well, what's a little puritan thunder
when it gives you the shape
and feel of the land? But you'd
have none of him. In Mansfield's study
a print of *The Virgin as a Jug of Water
and the Infant Jesus compared to a Lamp*
made you hopping mad. 'It's
Kiwi Kindergarten stuff . . . Mum
knows best . . . the bullying voice of God!'
You slammed the door and drove to Cannes
hungry for Matisse, writing back
that 'life's too short to be preached at! Oh
these golden nudes with tits like melons
and flowers growing out of their bums!'
A kid's vernacular, poking its tongue
at stern big Daddy and know-all Mum.

We never finished our last chat
about Ashbery, that New York voice,
always refusing to bore us with
'old anecdotes'. Unfair, I know,
but I had to laugh at your sudden roar
of disapproval when his language shifts
from 'the merely provisional'
to the fashionably chic. In Lambland, I guess
we're inclined to take our egos home
bruised but intact, slapping them down
like raw steak on the page. It's as if
we *need* something 'seen-and-known,'

even 'roundly human,' with which to face
the local bully on his own home-ground.

Which brings us to the question of place . . .
not always the same as feeling
we belong. 'We'll take *that*
from anywhere we can get it;
a kiss or the rim of a glass!'
You shunned a tribal embrace, that sense
of a race apart. What
mattered wasn't raising flags
but keeping love afloat. You liked
a busy harbour, boats bustling in
from London, New York, Camelot.

I think of you in a room not a landscape,
at home among 'domestic gifts' —
wife, children, friends, twin terrapins,
and that happy exile, your Australian cat
(always one up on the local mice).
A world within arm's reach . . .
the antithesis of that childhood house
with its 30's furniture rigidly arranged
like 'a row of cold old ladies
eaten by life and work.' That place
haunted you all your life, and made
a religion for you out of hospitality:
as if your own love could erase the pain
of a prim parental parlour
reserved for guests who never arrived.
I sensed your hatred for illusions of grandeur,
your distrust of 'the new men with no qualities'
who push the vernacular aside. 'The beach
at the end of the world,' was how
you described a life-long sense
of being born marooned. What
earthed you was your love of light. (Those
huge horizons beached outside.) Each
day arrived like a guest at your door . . .

You died where you felt alive . . . in 'old Europe,'
that charnel-house of human love
where you cut through the crap of class and privilege
with such an equalising laugh. Blair
Peach died there, his skull caved in
by a bunch of *Specials* as he tried to stop
some Fascist bully-boys from playing god.
Increasingly I'm talking to the dead . . .
Jim, Renato, Stefan, yourself;
post-war émigrés and local bit-players
who belted it out, taking their bows
with more than a dash of self-conscious sweat.

Detail . . . detail . . . garlic and lemons
in a blue bowl, the moon near full,
your poems spilt like milk on the table,
the cat in the sand-box, poised like a sphinx.
I describe these things
'as they are,' as you'd find them
if you were sitting here, looking out
at Rangitoto — a tent under starlight —
with a Russian cruise-ship looming by
like that moment in Fellini's *Roma*
when the little boy looks up to find
a skyscraper silently sailing past.
Our generation's almost gone:
a handful of hermits and refugees
who loosened local speech, but rarely
shaped the language with a conscious grace.
You wrote that you 'couldn't will our history
to include those qualities we lack ourselves.'
What a relief! All that heavy ancestry
now left to others. Your poems adrift
like paper boats or messages-in-bottles,
careless of landfall, happy to be themselves.

1991

FLEUR ADCOCK

Born in New Zealand in 1934, Fleur Adcock spent the war years in England, return-
ing to Wellington in 1947. After reading Classics at Victoria University, she moved to
London in 1963, working as a librarian until 1979 when she became a full-time
writer.

Note on Propertius

Among the Roman love-poets, possession
Is a rare theme. The locked and flower-hung door,
The shivering lover, are allowed. To more
Buoyant moods, the canons of expression
Gave grudging sanction. Do we, then, assume,
Finding Propertius tear-sodden and jealous,
That Cynthia was inexorably callous?
Plenty of moonlight entered that high room
Whose doors had met his Alexandrine battles;
And she, so gay a lutanist, was known
To stitch and doze a night away, alone,
Until the poet tumbled in with apples
For penitence and for her head his wreath,
Brought from a party, of wine-scented roses —
(The garland's aptness lying, one supposes,
Less in the flowers than in the thorns beneath:
Her waking could, he knew, provide his verses
With less idyllic themes.) On to her bed

He rolled the round fruit, and adorned her head;
Then gently roused her sleeping mouth to curses.
Here the conventions reassert their power:
The apples fall and bruise, the roses wither,
Touched by a sallowed moon. But there were other
Luminous nights — (even the cactus flower
Glows briefly golden, fed by spiny flesh) —
And once, as he acknowledged, all was singing:
The moonlight musical, the darkness clinging,
And she compliant to his every wish.

                                        1964

Unexpected Visit

I have nothing to say about this garden.
I do not want to be here, I can't explain
What happened. I merely opened a usual door
And found this. The rain

Has just stopped, and the gravel paths are trickling
With water. Stone lions, on each side,
Gleam like wet seals, and the green birds
Are stiff with dripping pride.

Not my kind of country. The gracious vistas,
The rose-gardens and terraces, are all wrong —
As comfortless as the weather. But here I am.
I cannot tell how long

I have stood gazing at grass too wet to sit on,
Under a sky so dull I cannot read
The sundial, staring along the curving walks
And wondering where they lead;

Not really hoping, though, to be enlightened.
It must be morning, I think, but there is no
Horizon behind the trees, no sun as clock
Or compass. I shall go

And find, somewhere among the formal hedges
Or hidden behind a trellis, a toolshed. There
I can sit on a box and wait. Whatever happens
May happen anywhere,

And better, perhaps, among the rakes and flowerpots
And sacks of bulbs than under this pallid sky:
Having chosen nothing else, I can at least
Choose to be warm and dry.

                                        1964

Incident

When you were lying on the white sand,
A rock under your head, and smiling,
(Circled by dead shells), I came to you

And you said, reaching to take my hand,
'Lie down.' So for a time we lay
Warm on the sand, talking and smoking,
Easy; while the grovelling sea behind
Sucked at the rocks and measured the day.
Lightly I fell asleep then, and fell
Into a cavernous dream of falling.
It was all the cave-myths, it was all
The myths of tunnel or tower or well —
Alice's rabbit-hole into the ground,
Or the path of Orpheus: a spiral staircase
To hell, furnished with danger and doubt.
Stumbling, I suddenly woke; and found
Water about me. My hair was wet,
And you were sitting on the grey sand,
Waiting for the lapping tide to take me:
Watching, and lighting a cigarette.

1964

Wife to Husband

From anger into the pit of sleep
You go with a sudden skid. On me
Stillness falls gradually, a soft
Snowfall, a light cover to keep
Numb for a time the twitching nerves.

Your head on the pillow is turned away;
My face is hidden. But under snow
Shoots uncurl, the green thread curves
Instinctively upwards. Do not doubt
That sense of purpose in mindless flesh:
Between our bodies a warmth grows;
Under the blankets hands move out,
Your back touches my breast, our thighs
Turn to find their accustomed place.

Your mouth is moving over my face:
Do we dare, now, to open our eyes?

1964

For a Five-Year-Old

A snail is climbing up the window-sill
Into your room, after a night of rain.
You call me in to see, and I explain
That it would be unkind to leave it there:
It might crawl to the floor; we must take care
That no one squashes it. You understand,
And carry it outside, with careful hand,
To eat a daffodil.

I see, then, that a kind of faith prevails:
Your gentleness is moulded still by words

From me, who have trapped mice and shot wild birds,
From me, who drowned your kittens, who betrayed
Your closest relatives, and who purveyed
The harshest kind of truth to many another.
But that is how things are: I am your mother,
And we are kind to snails.

1964

Advice to a Discarded Lover

Think, now: if you have found a dead bird,
Not only dead, not only fallen,
But full of maggots: what do you feel —
More pity or more revulsion?

Pity is for the moment of death,
And the moments after. It changes
When decay comes, with the creeping stench
And the wriggling, munching scavengers.

Returning later, though, you will see
A shape of clean bone, a few feathers,
An inoffensive symbol of what
Once lived. Nothing to make you shudder.

It is clear then. But perhaps you find
The analogy I have chosen
For our dead affair rather gruesome —
Too unpleasant a comparison.

It is not accidental. In you
I see maggots close to the surface.
You are eaten up by self-pity,
Crawling with unlovable pathos.

If I were to touch you I should feel
Against my fingers fat, moist worm-skin.
Do not ask me for charity now:
Go away until your bones are clean.

1967

A Surprise in the Peninsula

When I came in that night I found
the skin of a dog stretched flat and
nailed upon my wall between the
two windows. It seemed freshly killed —
there was blood at the edges. Not
my dog: I have never owned one,
I rather dislike them. (Perhaps
whoever did it knew that.) It
was a light brown dog, with smooth hair;
no head, but the tail still remained.
On the flat surface of the pelt
was branded the outline of the

peninsula, singed in thick black
strokes into the fur: a coarse map.
The position of the town was
marked by a bullet-hole; it went
right through the wall. I placed my eye
to it, and could see the dark trees
outside the house, flecked with moonlight.
I locked the door then, and sat up
all night, drinking small cups of the
bitter local coffee. A dog
would have been useful, I thought, for
protection. But perhaps the one
I had been given performed that
function; for no one came that night,
nor for three more. On the fourth day
it was time to leave. The dog-skin
still hung on the wall, stiff and dry
by now, the flies and the smell gone.
Could it, I wondered, have been meant
not as a warning, but a gift?
And, scarcely shuddering, I drew
the nails out and took it with me.

1971

Against Coupling

I write in praise of the solitary act:
of not feeling a trespassing tongue
forced into one's mouth, one's breath
smothered, nipples crushed against the
ribcage, and that metallic tingling
in the chin set off by a certain odd nerve:

unpleasure. Just to avoid those eyes would help —
such eyes as a young girl draws life from,
listening to the vegetal
rustle within her, as his gaze
stirs polypal fronds in the obscure
sea-bed of her body, and her own eyes blur.

There is much to be said for abandoning
this no longer novel exericise —
for not 'participating in
a total experience' — when
one feels like the lady in Leeds who
had seen *The Sound of Music* eighty-six times;

or more, perhaps, like the school drama mistress
producing *A Midsummer Night's Dream*
for the seventh year running, with
yet another cast from 5B.
Pyramus and Thisbe are dead, but
the hole in the wall can still be troublesome.

I advise you, then, to embrace it without
encumbrance. No need to set the scene,
dress up (or undress), make speeches.
Five minutes of solitude are
enough — in the bath, or to fill
that gap between the Sunday papers and lunch.

                                              1971

Kilpeck

We are dried and brittle this morning,
fragile with continence, quiet.
You have brought me to see a church.
I stare at a Norman arch in red sandstone
carved like a Mayan temple-gate;
at serpents writhing up the doorposts
and squat saints with South-American features
who stare back over our heads
from a panel of beasts and fishes.
The gargoyles jutting from under the eaves
are the colour of newborn children.

Last night you asked me
if poetry was the most important thing.

We walk on around the building
craning our heads back to look up
at lions, griffins, fat-faced bears.
The Victorians broke some of these figures
as being too obscene for a church;
but they missed the Whore of Kilpeck.
She leans out under the roof
holding her pink stony cleft agape
with her ancient little hands.
There was always witchcraft here, you say.

The sheep-track up to the fragments
of castle-wall is fringed with bright bushes.
We clamber awkwardly, separate.
Hawthorn and dog-rose offer hips and haws,
orange and crimson capsules, pretending
harvest. I taste a blackberry.
The soil here is coloured like brick-dust,
like the warm sandstone. A fruitful county.
We regard it uneasily.

There is little left to say
after all the talk we had last night
instead of going to bed —
fearful for our originality,
avoiding the sweet obvious act
as if it were the only kind of indulgence.

Silly perhaps.
              We have our reward.
We are languorous now, heavy
with whatever we were conserving,
carrying each a delicate burden
of choices made or about to be made.
Words whisper hopefully in our heads.

Slithering down the track we hold hands
to keep a necessary balance.
The gargoyles extend their feral faces,
rosy, less lined than ours.
We are wearing out our identities.

                      1974

The Soho Hospital for Women

1

Strange room, from this angle:
white door open before me,
strange bed, mechanical hum, white lights.
There will be stranger rooms to come.

As I almost slept I saw the deep flower opening
and leaned over into it, gratefully.
It swimmingly closed in my face. I was not ready.
It was not death, it was acceptance.

*

Our thin patient cat died purring,
her small triangular head tilted back,
the nurse's fingers caressing her throat,
my hand on her shrunken spine; the quick needle.

That was the second death by cancer.
The first is not for me to speak of.
It was telephone calls and brave letters
and a friend's hand bleeding under the coffin.

*

Doctor, I am not afraid of a word.
But neither do I wish to embrace that visitor,
to engulf it as Hine-Nui-te-Po
engulfed Maui; that would be the way of it.

And she was the winner there: her womb crushed him.
Goddesses can do these things.
But I have admitted the gloved hands and the speculum
and must part my ordinary legs to the surgeon's knife.

2

Nellie has only one breast
ample enough to make several.
Her quilted dressing-gown softens
to semi-doubtful this imbalance
and there's no starched vanity
in our abundant ward-mother:
her silvery hair's in braids, her slippers
loll, her weathered smile holds true.
When she dresses up in her black
with her glittering marcasite brooch on
to go for the weekly radium treatment
she's the bright star of the taxi-party —
whatever may be growing under her ribs.

*

Doris hardly smokes in the ward —
and hardly eats more than a dreamy spoonful —
but the corridors and bathrooms
reek of her Players Number 10,
and the drug-trolley pauses
for long minutes by her bed.
Each week for the taxi-outing
she puts on her skirt again
and has to pin the slack waistband
more tightly over her scarlet sweater.
Her face, a white shadow through smoked glass,
lets Soho display itself unregarded.

*

Third in the car is Mrs Golding
who never smiles. And why should she?

3

The senior consultant on his rounds
murmurs in so subdued a voice
to the students marshalled behind
that they gather in, forming a cell,
a cluster, a rosette around him
as he stands at the foot of my bed
going through my notes with them,
half-audibly instructive, grave.

The slight ache as I strain forward
to listen still seems imagined.

Then he turns his practised smile on me:
'How are you this morning?' 'Fine,
very well, thank you.' I smile too.
And possibly all that murmurs within me
is the slow dissolving of stitches.

4

I am out in the supermarket choosing —
this very afternoon, this day —
picking up tomatoes, cheese, bread,

things I want and shall be using
to make myself a meal, while they
eat their stodgy suppers in bed:

Janet with her big freckled breasts,
her prim Scots voice, her one friend,
and never in hospital before,

who came in to have a few tests
and now can't see where they'll end;
and Coral in the bed by the door

who whimpered and gasped behind a screen
with nurses to and fro all night
and far too much of the day;

pallid, bewildered, nineteen.
And Mary, who will be all right
but gradually. And Alice, who may.

Whereas I stand almost intact,
giddy with freedom, not with pain.
I lift my light basket, observing

how little I needed in fact;
and move to the checkout, to the rain,
to the lights and the long street curving.

1979

Below Loughrigg

The power speaks only out of sleep and blackness
no use looking for the sun
what is not present cannot be illumined

Katherine's lungs, remember, eaten by disease
but Mary's fingers too
devoured and she goes on writing

The water speaks from the rocks, the cavern speaks,
where water halloos through it
this happens also in darkness

A steep bit here, up from the valley
to the terraces, the path eroded by water
Now listen for the voice

These things wane with the vital forces
he said, little having waned in him
except faith, and anger had replaced it

One force can be as good as another
we may not think so; but channelled

in ways it has eaten out; issuing

into neither a pool nor the sea
but a shapely lake afloat with wooded islands
a real water and multiplied on maps

which can be read in the sunlight; for the sun
will not be stopped from visiting
and the lake exists and the wind sings over it.

                                        1979

Crab

Late at night we wrench open a crab;
flesh bursts out of its cup

in pastel colours. The dark fronds attract me:
Poison, you say, Dead Men's Fingers —

don't put them in your mouth, stop!
They brush over my tongue, limp and mossy,

until you snatch them from me, as you snatch
yourself, gently, if I come too close.

Here are the permitted parts of the crab,
wholesome on their nests of lettuce

and we are safe again in words.
All day the kitchen will smell of sea.

                                        1983

Icon

In the interests of economy
I am not going to tell you
what happened between the time
when they checked into the hotel

with its acres of tiled bathrooms
(but the bidet in theirs was cracked)
and the morning two days later
when he awoke to find her gone.

After he had read her note
and done the brief things he could do
he found himself crossing the square
to the Orthodox Cathedral.

The dark icon by the door
was patched with lumpy silver islands
nailed to the Virgin's robes; they looked
like flattened-out Monopoly tokens,

he thought: a boot, and something like
a heart, and a pair of wings, and something

oblong. They were hard to see
in the brown light, but he peered at them

for several minutes, leaning over
the scarved head of an old woman
on her knees there, blocking his view,
who prayed and prayed and wouldn't move.

1986

KEVIN IRELAND

Born in Auckland in 1933, Kevin Ireland lived for many years in London and Ireland before returning to New Zealand in 'the year of the comet', 1986. In recent years, he has written a novel, short stories and a collection of poems, Skinning a Fish.

Thorn and Wind

on the spring day
that love was born
the wind whipped
the budding thorn

on the winter's day
that love was dead
the thorn ripped
and the wind bled

1967

Striking a Pose

we'll stock up books
and wine and pie
then stop the clocks
and never die

we'll nail the windows
brick up the door
and live on a mattress
on the floor

if death still comes
we'll strike a pose
and hold our breath
until he goes

1967

A Kuala Lumpur Notebook

for Bob Jago

monkeys dive and splash through jungle trees
before the balcony

swifts skim the whirlpools of the air

from a book of birds I label warbler munia
fantail woodpecker sunbird
and learn last evening's chonk chonk chonk

was a nightjar — so tropical so eastern
so exotic —
how shall I think it's only as it ought to be?

the sudden darkness swirls across the lawn
surges through the trees
and rises to submerge the hills

then gongs and drums play swing and rock
in the temple down the road
the midnight sound of parties in Parnell

the clouds the skies bruise purple-black
the fireflies are on
in the Auckland zoo monkeys huddle for the night

a gecko licks an insect from a wall
its jaws fold up a butterfly
like the pleats of a schoolgirl's skirt

the rare the dazzling and the everyday now coincide
Bob comes from the refrigerator
in his enchanted hands the bottles go chonk chonk chonk

1984

Expedition to a Mountain Lake

for Neil Perrett

standing almost to the waist at evening in a mountain lake
the rod unflexing the line curling away — the action
like knocking in a nail

thinking how we have come so far yet brought it all along
nothing forgotten nothing left behind
such odd remembrances as

picturing how I used to check my fire exits
when climbing stairs — and when I slept above ground level
I'd sometimes keep rope coiled by the bed

the line curves out again — I recollect some years ago
visiting a man who kept a silver ladder on an upstairs wall
my cure was this credential of dementia

the chill of the lake is like sleeping with legs dangling
from the blankets — ripples fan from the fly's jolt
the symmetry of dream

I can see him now telling me how he'd do survival drill
leaping from bed sometimes in the middle of the night
then — counting steps —

he'd unhitch the ladder swing it to the ceiling
mount it fling the skylight open scramble out
and escape over the roof

but the flame that gutted him was a slow carcinoma
no sprint from sleep and out — I remember the months
he lingered and smouldered

an eye fixed on the one last impossible dash and vault
a cold combustion in the blood
a body burnt to clinker

the fly has the body of sunset — a twist of silver
a flare of orange and red — another cast unwinds
a shiver on the lake

and three times the tinfoil flash of the trout's rise
means eye betrayed and all that drilled response
becomes an error of dementia

then I know again the briefness of her lips — that searing
that splash of muscle leaping
silver orange red

her arm trembling her breath fanning ripples on my skin —
what makes me now remember exactly how she asked me
why I could not escape?

a setting sun — then at last the strike — a fish skittering
across the skin of the lake
a man now dead

the cold and darkness trembling out from the shore
the earth tilting away from daylight
lovers untangling and turning

memory is a rusty nail banged into an invisible wall —
the hammer-action of the rod the line uncoiling and dropping
the demented lunge

I rip the hook from the trout's eyeball — the whole weight
the madness the hurricane of its fight for life
snagged in a frozen look

a long wade through the shallows to the land
a night breeze braiding an outsize silver ladder
down the middle of the lake

the rungs of the moon hurtling by — darkness leaping
through the window of the sky — a day burnt out
memories escaping

1984

Intimations of Mortality

being dead
means only a game
to the young
a terror

to boot about
and toy with
in the head

being old
means making a meal
of death
we gnaw
the problem
like a bone
as the lean meat
grows cold

1984

from The Year of the Comet

3

Perhaps I never left
A dream. Time passes. Eyes open. Still here?

How confusing was the voyage.
A comet clocks the seven-and-a-half decades

a lucky, Western health-freak might expect to last,
skipping wars, car-crashes or a late-night assignation

with a casual virus. Yet, clutching at a wisp
of heavenly fluff, we fizz past worlds colliding,

showers of meteorites like champagne diamonds,
the bursting puffballs of stellar clusters,

nebulae spilling hundreds and thousands,
a popping, swirling, dazzling, tinsel dust —

that's all. A planet implodes in a poem. A cosmic
exclamation mark. A huge hunk of black ice. Nothing.

21

While the Comet plods
across a cocktail-party sky

of gods and demi-gods —
a cosmic gatecrasher-in-tails slowly elbowing by

heavenly bodies and clusters of starlets —
a vine growing just outside my window

spurts a green and scarlet
track as it rockets through the shadows.

Forty centimetres every day
it powers up the crust of concrete firmament —

up walls of flocculus and sills
of lunar grey —

hurtling past the moon, made almost permanent,
and Comet Halley, roughly standing still.

24

'Now — imagine a voice from memory
across a half-forgotten bay

on a summer's moonlit night . . . '
It seems impossible to escape the inaccuracies

of the heart. I resurvey
the old, true outlines of the past and sight

nostalgia where the reefs of pain
jutted like needles from the surf.

All those years away, yet the habit remains —
I can actually hear the voice begin to laugh . . .

Between the curtains see the light like silica
track across the lawn to the beach . . .

A night distorted. Out of reach.
And the pathway of a falling star.

1986

Pinnacle Ridge, Mt Ruapehu

in memory of Colin Hill

The last rock at the top that for a time
caps the rocks below is where we stand,
also for a time. The summit of the ridge.

Pebble, boulder and stone slab arrange
a precedence. A backbone and a skull.
Sooner or later, wind-worn, flaked by ice,

or kicked to bits by a boot, the line alters.
The next rock along becomes the new summit.
We search for the safe way down. The fall

comes years later, in a bed or an armchair,
a seat in a café, a patch of shade on the lawn
where you lean your back against a tree.

The view across the peaks always ends
at the wall of the sky, a bedroom door,
a prospect across a street and no farther,

a garden hedge. Calcium, phosphorus —
a ridge of minerals rising to a bone summit
where the eyes squint for the least perilous

descent, an outlook across a valley rattling
with pebbles and boulders. Your death rearranges
the view. Sitting safely beyond that place,

that time, suddenly you are flung into the sky.
I remember you as the shape of an eyelash.
A curved shadow of stone dislodged on the climb.

(1989)

GORDON CHALLIS

Born in Wales in 1932, Gordon Challis emigrated to New Zealand in 1953 and studied at Victoria University. He worked variously as a journalist and social worker both here and abroad. He now lives in Nelson.

The Postman

This cargo of confessions, messages,
demands to pay, seems none of my concern;
you could say I'm a sort of go-between
for abstract agents trusting wheels will turn,
for censored voices stilled in space and time.

Some people stop me for a special letter;
one or two will tell me, if it's fine, that I
have picked the right job for this kind of weather.
A boy who understands life somewhat better
asks where postmen live — if not our office, why?

The work is quite routine but kindnesses
and awkward problems crop up now and then:
one old lady sometimes startles passers-by
claiming she is blameless as she hisses
at people present in her reminiscent ken;

she startled me as well the other day,
gave me a glass of lemonade, and slipped
me a letter to deliver — 'Don't you say
a word to anyone, it's no concern
of theirs, or yours.' Nor no more it was, except

here was this letter plainly marked 'To God'
and therefore insufficiently addressed.
I cannot stamp it now 'Return to sender'
for addressee and sender may be One. The best
thing is burn it, to a black rose He'll remember.

1963

The Thermostatic Man

The world could fall to pieces any moment now;
with luck it won't,

mainly because it hasn't yet. Though cracks appear,
I'll merely count
them leeway spaces left so masses may expand
to meet and don't.

But I, who used to walk bolt upright, this day bow
as meek as wheat:
how can I be sure I shall not always fear
to face fierce heat,
to face the sun, not watch my shadow lagging back behind,
and feel complete?

From strips of many metals am I made. I grow
beneath the sun
unevenly. I cannot cry lest the least tear
should cool down one
soft element and strain the others. I am bland,
bend to become

the thermostat which keeps my spirit burning low.
One day I shall
perhaps be tried by a more humble, human fire
which, blending all
my elements in one alloy, will let me stand
upright, ready to fall.

1963

After Shock Treatment

Now that the stopgap lightning has, for the meantime,
hamstrung death's dark horses, drowning those
heartfelt hoofbeats in its general thunder,
I do not care to catch up on the latest news
of a world I never bargained for, was never
that much sold on anyway. I'll not amuse

myself with whether the soul exists at birth
or after death. I do not greatly care
if human fate is worked out all beforehand
and taken so for graphlike granted, writ so clear
that, knowing the coefficients, all could read:
such issues, which once troubled me, are no affair

of mine these days. I do not wish to fathom
the human heart and mind, our purpose here, our lot
of happiness or anything so trivial.
I only want to know one thing — the spot
where the first pedestrian crossing is in Willis Street,
whether it's at the corner with Lambton Quay . . . or not.

1963

The Asbestos-Suited Man In Hell

(A homily for saints)

I can indeed afford a pause of peace,
a brief abode in shade beneath my cloak
for those, inscription-blind or heedless,
who hope that love still functions, does not choke

like sulphur in the lungs. I cannot say:
'But blow you Jack,' knowing well how far
from fireproof I am. Even this five-ply
cone of woven wet asbestos cannot bar

out heat completely. Nor in this torment
can I claim: 'I know just how you feel'
unless I am to throw away my garment
which, once parted, would not even conceal

a single sufferer beyond the grasp
of flame's bright blind yet finding fingers.
Thus, one by one, my brothers come and clasp
my calves, like children. Each soul lingers

as long as possible but finds small aid
that I should come to hell — and suffer
at my leisure, seeing meantime others wade
in pain — simply to make myself tougher.

And it is easy for me to preach salvation:
'Bring all your burning world and let me hide
you for a little while.' This insulation
shields me from all mortal sins save only pride.

1963

Thin Partition

Someone next door is moving things about —
dusting the shelves which don't need dusting
making changes simply for the sake of change
or hoping that new order in the room will rout
those evil demons who resent what's new and strange.

Someone next door is singing as she moves —
maybe this tune will mark the turning,
work the trick for years-old resolutions
really to come true; but then she leaves
a word amiss and spoils the spell's relations.

Someone next door is thinking what to do —
wondering what meat to buy for Sunday
or shall she go back home and try again
to hide the fact that there she feels more lonely
and knows the reason yet cannot explain.

Someone is talking to us in her way —
her shadow gestures windlike through the scrim;
my wife and I are hurried, we are going out;
someone next door is asking us to stay
someone next door is moving things about.

1963

The Iceman

What happened to the iceman after all?
Amazing how we waited for his call
and ran across to pick up chips of light
as the iceman's hook would beak-like bite
deep into ice, which he shouldered on a sack
and carried to our verandah at the back,
invisible the winter halo round his head.

We have other means of freezing now instead
of ice; it only lasted half a day
unwinding summer's waterclock away,
filling the tank, falling on zinc
under the icebox.
            Nowadays I think
the nameless birds outside have hauled
some massive block of silence called
the morning to my door; with beaks well-ground
have started chipping splinters made of sound,
have sung me almost unaware how sick
I felt one childhood day, the embryonic
pain of seeing yolk and shell all splashed
together yellow where a bird's egg smashed;
yet pain evolves, perception grows more keen
as fits the many-coloured bird that might have been.

What happened to the iceman after all?
Amazing, how we waited for his call.

1963

MAURICE DUGGAN

One of New Zealand's most innovative and technically adroit short story writers, Maurice Duggan (1922–1974) was born in Auckland, where he lived for most of his life, working some of the time in advertising. Around the time of his death, two small selections of his poetry were published in Islands.

Ponsonby Circa 1930

We were clean children
and the school was bitterly neat
but in the dungeon kitchen
in the leap of Lincoln Street
dark grandma picked for nits
with the palping slums of her fingers.

Salt from Shelly Beach baths
might rime our local skulls
supple spokes of octopus leave trace
on teasing hands by tidefall rock
embrace our kiddy wrists
in that dawdle of peccavi days

But grandma's eager headholds
knew no translation from the bogside Gael.
How we hated the black enactment
of her implacable memory but loved
the floury scones with skidding pats of cream.
God bless you go slowly stupid loves.

(1974)

Take a Peck at Papa Pupa

Lines in memoriam Robert Harbron Duggan

A life small tidy and insignificant
long enough for him who lived it, even too long by far,
but short by anyone else's measure and an irritating
buzzing little boring little thing
best forgotten as quickly as might be possible
by them who observed it, suffered its midge-like stings,
but in no way wished, and were in no way invited, to share it.
So that his nameplate carries name and dates
and it would have puzzled anyone or everyone to add
one word more. Some hand might however have inscribed:
He was not loved, he did not love; in a way he lived, and died.

Weeds moss lichen probably will obliterate his place of rest.
The whole thing was a steal, its total unimportance terrible, really.
You see, expecting no assistance he received none;
detecting no expectation in others he assumed all pupated,
dolls and guys, until the undertaker came to box death away;
and no grain's blowing was marked or could be
in the desert of undifferentiation, neither presence
nor absence notable and the sands infinite, infinite.
Born lace Mountmellick 1886: buried lawn Makara 1971. Man.

How sad upon a stick this plain bird singing.

(1974)

Winter Solstice

These are not the latitudes
of that long wind, not yet the days
to start anew the long haul, dedication
to the coral task of quotidian accretion.

Under a gentle blanket of dead fur —
hours of passing and escaping time,
moments of the clemency of needles —
accept the even weather of the ward.

Birds observed through winter window
whirr like triggered clockwork toys
in the rain-filled birdbath to suggest
their analogues of ice and shock.

We wash less urgently our fewer feathers
and yet with luck and lavings hope to find
gift as simple and as sourceless
as this thrown crust on that green lawn.

(1974)

In the Territory

Expecting this turning, this ascent
to open a clear vista to the coast
he confronts another range, more bush
across a valley of unpromising aspect:
the map is vague beyond this point.
The immediate problem is less the going
than the blisters and the pack-rash,
the usual trouble with constipation
and the absence of any clear horizon.

The momentum of his eager departure
pushes him forward through the lichened trees.
There is no direction but forward:
from here on his ordinary skills
assume proportions of an absolute routine
whose goal is this night's fire this night's sleep.
The magnitude of any day is now reduced
to one mile of scree, two cups of brackish tea
and the certainty of knowing no way back.

Nothing so grand or challenging as Terra Incognita,
no legend reading Here be Dragons,
just this unfriendly skim of river water,
tape of steel light, impassable canyon there,
and the grey incessant veils of persisting rain.
The map dribbles possibilities eastwards.
From this morning's doused and comfortless fire
to tonight's tongues of flame and steam of socks —
measure and description enough of this explorer's day.

(1975)

W. H. OLIVER

Born in Feilding in 1925 and educated at Victoria and Oxford Universities, W. H. Oliver was founding editor of the quarterly Comment. *He has published widely in the field of history and was General Editor of the* Dictionary of New Zealand Biography.

Silent Revolution

Try it out with a bird or a fish. Though a woman would do.
They are well used to handling such weighty matters.
Like all the lesser creatures they have been
serious-minded since the first daub made them symbols.
Suppose, suppose, the bird took flight from the lectern
and swept through the nave wingtip to either wall,
or out of the font rose, huge, Leviathan
and it was all quite suddenly submarine?
Suppose, to bring it closer home, the mirror
you looked in every morning was removed
and there your image stood quite unsupported
by any frame, and subtly changed in ways
that changed the more you looked, would you
be able, even, to wonder who was there?

1980

Counter-revolution

Did it go wrong just about a hundred
years ago? A ramshackle self-appointed
cast-off elite of first comers,
promoters, bent lawyers and sham doctors
set it up for themselves, a gentry of sorts,
saw it collapse and crept away with slim gains.
The cities grew, married men left home,
children were tall and wild, women restless.
Something had to be done. Seddon the burly
village policeman, a pattern for the future,
rose like a cork, admonishing finger aloft,
ponderously sly, licking his stub of a pencil,
selecting and rejecting, always with good humour,
not harsh in the least, but in the end obscene.

1980

Parihaka

The province has set up shrines
to its martyrs and heroes Te
Rangi Hiroa to the north
where his vikings landed von
Tempsky well to the south
at the scene of his last encounter

with the spirit of '48
the Richmond cottage with two
volumes of the *Evangelical
Magazine* (but Harry
Atkinson out with the militia
read Mill *On Liberty*
a year after publication)
colonial gothic St Mary's
with neat rows in the graveyard
soldiers sailors settlers
killed by the rebel natives
regimental hatchments
one for the Friendly Maoris
a 20th century second
thought in bright blond wood
to remember all who died
a patch on a war scarred face
no sign for Parihaka
a broken road a set
of ruinous foundations
charred remains of timber
a '38 Chevrolet
under the cloudy mountain.

1980

PAUL HENDERSON
[RUTH FRANCE]

Ruth France (1913–1968) lived most of her life in Canterbury, publishing poetry under the pen-name Paul Henderson. She also published fiction under her own name.

Return Journey

Wellington again slaps the face with wind
So well remembered; and now the mind
Leaps; all sea, all tossed hills, all white-
Edged air poured in tides over the tight
Town. Bleached bones of houses are hard
To distinguish, at some distance, from a graveyard.

But do not consider death; we have tucked
Too snugly into the valleys; we have mucked
With the rake of time over the tamed
Foreshore. Battering trams; Lambton, lamed
With concrete, has only a hint of ghost waters
On the Quay stranded among elevators.

There is no need to remember swamp-grass,
Or how the first women (let the rain pass,
They had prayed) wept when the hills reared up
Through the mist, and they were trapped

Between sea and cliffed forest. No ship could be
More prisoning than the grey beach at Petone.

No need to consider (here where we have shut
The tiger tight behind iron and concrete)
How we might yet drown deep under the wind;
And the wind die too; and an insect find
(Columbus of his day) the little graveyard town
Set in a still landscape like porcelain.

1955

Elegy

1

Morning after death on the bar was calm;
There was no difficulty in looking for the boy's body.
The boat had been found in the dark, overturned,
And at dawn the men went out again
To search the beaches and sweep, in the boats, offshore.
The mountains to the north stood up like sepulchres
Rising white-boned out of a black sea.
The flat hymnal of light lay asleep in the sky
And sang morning in a minor key
To wake the wheeling flights of birds
That, curious, mark down all drifting wrack
And disabled drowned bodies.

2

He should not have attempted the bar, of course;
The tide was ebbing but he was making for home.
On the wide sea with night falling,
Only the open, small yacht to uplift him,
He must have felt, well, try it.

Moments make miniature green globes in the mind;
Light flaring on dark from house windows
As the lifeboat slid out on the ways;
Searchlight like an awed moon at sea
Probing the black night and white breakers,
A drawn will of the anxious, twining a tight knot
In the shadows of Shag Rock; car lights
A stereoscopic, too brutal revelation of tears.

The shocked boy saying that his friend was gone;
That they'd found the boat, turned turtle,
But that Jack was lost, they couldn't find him.
O weep all night for this drowned youth,
Waiting in the rock's black arms for the foreseen time
Of lifeboat returning, lonely, in the small hours;
Of certainty frozen in the immutable shape of hands;

Of a boy's boat is no bond, nor even a safe coffin.

Get some sleep, if you can; by now he's dead,
The water is too cold, it is almost winter.

3

Yet at dawn they were searching the beaches.
In the immense dawn distances the groups of men
Walked like little pins over the sandspits
And the morning light broke bitterly like snowflakes

On the sun-dazed self-conscious sea
That tight-lipped along the beaches hides
Its dreadful truths, its doused, its double-drowned boys
Lying like Jonahs in a beast's belly.

The sun rose on a silver-lidded sea that lapped
Over the sandbanks like turning shillings,
Making enormous shadows which, when reached,
Were nothing at all. In such confusion
Of light and lazing sand-pipers and lumps of seaweed
How find in this vast soul of silver and of sand
All that is left of one boy?

Yet at noon the beast opened its lips,
Or perhaps it was just that, with the sun higher,
The light was no longer tricky, but anyway
The boy was spewed up, and the body was seen
Floating face down, in a life-jacket, beyond the surf.

So is the sea-god fed, and one more sacrifice
Strewn on the waves. No fairer limbs
Are demanded, their separate toll will delay
Disaster in the mind's millennial time and kiss
The countless bare noons where there are no shadows.

It was easy enough then to go out on surf-skis,
Into the light that by afternoon would be blue,
And bring in the boy's body, for a calmer burial.

1961

MARY STANLEY

Born in Christchurch, Mary Stanley (1919–1980) was educated at the University of Auckland. Her ground-breaking collection Starveling Year *was published by the Pegasus Press in 1953 and reissued in an expanded edition in 1994.*

To B—

Here or hereafter there is no escape
From me. My guardian spirit is gone out
Into the far shadowy paths where rest now

Your feet. I hide amongst the olive boughs,
The slender wreathing tendrils of the grape
Are my wild hair. Look up and see my face
Amongst the ice-bright peaks. Though sharp spears hem
You in they cannot build a wall too high
To shut me out. I am sweet water, ease
After pain, the shadow in the burning place.

And should this harsh storm shatter your belov'd
And gentle head, the thunder burst your ears,
The swift decisive steel bite your dear flesh
And dark lost ways of death's strange kingdom claims
Your naked soul, you still have not removed
My love's light harness shaken off my flying
Feet. Through heaven's far valleys I shall still
Pursue and hunt you down amongst the stars
And dim blue aisles of air. I shall awake
Hell's fiery deeps with echoes of my crying.

And if beyond this life only the grey
Waters of oblivion lie, and all that once
You were goes down into that waste of silence,
I still shall rest in that same earth that shelters
Your dead hands and sightless eyes. Day
And night spin round us both. The wind and clear
Rains dissolve and fuse our final dust
As once our bodies were when strong waves,
Lifting, drowned us. Blind and breathless we lay
At the world's heart, O my very dear.

1943

Sestina

The body of my love is a familiar country
read at the fingertip, as all children learn
their first landscape. This is the accepted face
secure of harm, in whose eye I am at home
and put on beauty as the thorn in autumn wears
its bright berry, the sky its haycock summer of cloud.

And here in a miracle season no storms cloud
our halcyon day nor prophet stains a green country
with wry mouth twisted to what vision wears
his own griefs. Music is struck off rocks, we learn
the sun ripening behind walls of flesh, the bird called home
pilgrim tracing with sure wing a world's face.

He whom I love is more near than this one face
shaped for me at my beginning, dispersed like cloud
in death's careless weather. At the end we come home
to the same bed, fallen like stones or stars in a country
no one travels. Only the mindless winds learn
our history, yet for us each man his mourning wears.

We are what we have been. The living creature wears
like trees his grain of good and evil years. The face
is schooled by daily argument of pain to learn
disguises for the private wound. None knows what country
lies under the shut skull, or dazzling beacon of cloud
beckons the always outcast through stubborn exile home.

This dear shell, this curve my hand follows, is home
also to the stranger I may not meet, who wears
deeper than tears his secret need. He walks a country
I cannot touch or reach, where the remembered face
burns under brittle glass of winter, and every cloud
holds in its core of ice the dream I may not learn.

Or is he Orpheus, leaving my daylight kingdom to learn
Eurydice for whom he enters the dark god's home?
Hermes, show him this woman, in her cerecloth cloud
of sleep! She is not prey to the subtle worm which wears
already at my cheek. No word unlocks her face
or voice answers him out of that silent country.

Yet always we ride out winter and the face
of famine. We return, and O then morning wears
mountains, our signal joy climbing a cloud.

1953

Per Diem et per Noctem

Birds in their oratory of leaves
clamour at morning over my love.
All waters praise him, the sea harbours
from harm, all islands are his neighbour
and rain at daybreak feathers his peace
softer than pillows or my kiss.

O may his lucky hand at noon
pluck down the sun, all day his keen
eye be darkened by no cloud.
Sky-walker, the lonely hawk, applaud
his purpose, the equipoise among
cliff and rock, his difficult song.

O never may night confound or send
him lost into that hinterland
far from my coasts. Where is your moon,
Endymion, trimming her thin
flame to light my love? The world
lifts its shoulder to shelter him curled
in the lap of sleep. By falling star
I wish all his tomorrows fair.

1953

Night Piece

Turning from sleep I seek the final word
of love, the world that weighs my lids and binds
my tongue to silence, while the darkness winds
its spool of hours and in my side the sword
peels off the flesh, lays bare the bone. We heard
a voice over the northern sea, and hinds
in the enchanted wood. The fable blinds
the beggar prince, cages his golden bird.
Not here, in any angel, lyre or rose
I find the touchstone phrase but in the kiss
that knocks along the blood and, wordless, knows
its way of tears and holds dumb hands to bless.

1953

The Wife Speaks

Being a woman, I am
not more than man nor less
but answer imperatives
of shape and growth. The bone
attests the girl with dolls,
grown up to know the moon
unwind her tides to chafe
the heart. A house designs
my day an artifact
of care to set the hands
of clocks, and hours are round
with asking eyes. Night puts
an ear on silence where
a child may cry. I close
my books and know events
are people, and all roads
everywhere walk home
women and men, to take
history under their roofs.
I see Icarus fall
out of the sky, beside
my door, not beautiful,
envy of angels, but feathered
for a bloody death.

1953

Love by Candlelight

Lift up your brown arms
   And let fall your heavy hair.
Here no one may enter
None climb this stair.

Bend down your ripe mouth.
    Love's fire-bright silence, this
Half-painful, shadow haunted
So-much-longed-for kiss.

Open your green eyes.
    Pin-points of candleshine
In caverns of coolness gleam
Here, close to mine.

Rest your dear head night-long
    In its accustomed place.
I seek no other heav'n
Beyond your mortal face.

1994

Morepork

Morning will never come nor light return;
But in the dark and drift of time this tree
Is night, a tent for the uneasy sleep
Of strangers. In his high pulpit the owl
Broods on a congregation of thieves,
Their honour threadbare in the pinching cold.
With the holy fire of his eye he keeps the door
Of each separate dream and in the secret ear
He'll preach a sermon of despair. Forewarned
One sleeper knows for the least moment
That last when the heart stops; puts out a hand
To brush away the covetous soft worm.
Prophet or soothsayer, terrible bird in a tower
Of leaves, crying repentance to the wind,
What is the antique rite you celebrate?
What strange gods wait in the black branches?
We have forgotten their names and attributes,
And they are angry, making our thin skin sweat.
Hearing your voice out of the great tree
In a long night full of claws and eyes,
We crouch at the first fire and are afraid.

1994

Question Without Answer

What shall I ask the rising tide?
To be midsummer fire, this burning tree?
Or shall I rest content one day, worn thin
By the rub of events as this frail
Opaline shell I crush under my nail?
Escape like a gull in the straight sharp well
Of the sky, let the uncaring wind
Support me, weightless, in its hand?

How shall I answer the grieving sea?
Remember the gilded day gone down

In shadow on the cooling sand,
My barefoot children lingering home
In a long dusk to bed? Or climb
The last hill in hope, to find
The taste and smell of brightness fail,
The tongue with too much sweet grown stale?

1994

KEITH SINCLAIR

Best known for his A History of New Zealand, *Sir Keith Sinclair (1922–1993) was a major historian as well as a poet.*

Memorial to a Missionary
Thomas Kendall, 1778–1832, first resident missionary in New Zealand, author of The New Zealander's First Book (1815), *grandfather of the Australian poet, H. C. Kendall.*

Instructed to speak of God with emphasis
On sin and its consequence, to cannibals
Of the evil of sin, he came from father's farm,
The virtuous home, the comfortable chapel,
The village school, so inadequately armed,
His mail of morals tested in drawing-rooms,
Not war, to teach his obscure and pitied pupils.

There were cheers in Clapham, prayers in Lincolnshire,
Psalms on the beaches, praise, O hope above.
Angels sang as he built the south's first school,
For Augustine had landed with the love
Of God at the Bay; he would speak for his aims were full
Of Cranmer, Calvin; would teach for he brought the world
Of wisdom, dreamed of the countless souls to save.

But though he cried with a voice of bells none heard,
For who was to find salvation in the sounds
Of English words? The scurrilous sailors spoke
More clearly with rum and lusting, so he turned
To the native vowels for symbols, sought to make
The Word of God anew, in the tribes' first book
Laying in Christ's advance a path of nouns.

Seeking the Maori name for sin, for hell,
Teacher turned scholar he sat at Hongi's feet
And guns were the coin he paid for revelation.
To the south men died when Hongi spent his fees.
Wrestling with meanings that defied translation,
Christian in seeking truth found sorcery,
Pilgrim encountered sex in philosophy.

A dreaming hour he spent at the mast of a tree,
And apple of his eye his mother withheld was that love,
The night of feeling, was pure and mooned for man,
Woman was made of earth and earth for wife.

In following their minds he found the men
And reached for a vision past his mother-land,
Converted by heathen he had come to save.

He drank the waters of the underworld
Lying all day in the unconverted flesh,
Entangled in old time, before Christ's birth,
Beyond redemption, found what a nest of bliss,
A hot and mushroom love lay fair in the fern
To suck from his soul the lineaments of desire,
And leave despair, O damned undreamed of pleasures.

To cure the sick at soul the little doctor
Sought out an ardent tonic far too hot,
Though not forbidden, for his infirmity.
With the south on his tongue and sweet he had forgotten
His mission, thirsted for infinities
Of the secret cider and its thick voice in the throat,
Bringing the sun all a-blossom to his blood.

But as sudden and in between such dawns his conscience
Sharpened his sins to prick his heart like nails.
The hell the Christian fears to name was heaven
To his fierce remorse and heaven and hell
Were the day and night in his life and wasted him
With their swift circling passions, until he cursed
In prayers but hated the flush of his concupiscence.

Did he fall through pride of spirit, through arrogance
Or through humility, not scorning the prayers
Of savages and their intricate pantheon?
He lacked the confident pity of his brethren.
To understand he had to sympathize.
Then felt, and feeling, fell, one man a breath
In the human gale of a culture's thousand years.

The unfaithful shepherd was sent from the farm of souls
To live, a disgraceful name in the Christian's ear,
A breathing sin among the more tolerant chiefs.
An outcaste there, or preaching where he fled
To Valparaiso from devils and reproof,
Or coasting logs round Sydney, still he strove
To find the life in the words his past had said.

Drowning off Jervis Bay, O the pain,
For death is a virgin rich in maidenheads
And memories, trees two hundred feet and tall.
The sea is a savage maiden, in her legs
Sharp pangs no missionary drank before,
And the immortality that Maui sought.
O move to Hawaiki, to the shadow of Io's breath.

No man had died such a death of dreams and storms,
For drowning with memories came that expected devil.
He was racked on the waves and spirit wrecked he wept
For his living sins, each tear-drop swimming with evil.

O soul be chang'd into little water drops
And fall into the ocean, ne'er be found!
Dying he shrank from that chief who would seize him forever.

But there no tohunga met him, angels flew
To draw his frightened soul quivering to heaven,
Bright there, bright in the open life of light.
Trying to speak known words that the unbelievers
Might know what was said and bring their ears to Christ,
He had sung with the spirit, prayed with the understanding,
Thus saved the soul he had paid to save the heathen.

His was the plough, he turned the sacred soil
Where others reaped, a pioneer in Christ's
New clearing, strove with unswerving will
Amidst the roots, the rotting stumps and compost
Of the mind to make a bed where the gospel
Might lie down in the breeding sun and grow
A crucifix of leaves, O flowers of crosses.

Immortal in our mouths, and known in heaven,
Yet as we praise we wish him greater — left
On our fractured limb of time, not yet possessed,
Where north will not meet south, of the south's lost gift.
Taught of the sinful flesh he never sensed
That to reach for truth was to reach for God, nor found
God immanent in the cannibals' beliefs.

Father he left us a legacy of guilt,
Half that time owed us, who came from the north, was given:
We know St Paul, but what in that dreaming hour,
In that night when the ends of time were tied — and severed
Again and so ever — did he learn from the south?
He could not turn to teach his countrymen,
And lost, (our sorrow), lost our birthright forever.

1952

from Te Kaminara

2

we placed our loving gently in a hollow
and did not look toward the sea again
or at the hills or sky,
yet in our farthest happiness,
lying all day together in the grass,
we made the land more lovingly our own.
all day our faces burnt into our eyes,
etching images upon our brains
for all the time of flesh,
your pulse's rhythm lent to mine

new music for my blood to dance
down hills, down waves, down skies.
down, round and down the staircase of your mind
my heart went leaping, singing,
round and down, my night, my dreams, my sea,
while I inhabit you,
and all your life is living in my bones,
we are our own New Zealand;
while our minds
breed futures from the touch and breath of love
we are our own safe island,
and hold our world of cliffs and towns
and bush and farms all whole,
alive and integrated in our arms,
granting a little life from every kiss
to impregnate this rock, and know
our island virtues are all outside storms
and any death will knock in vain.

1954

The Bomb Is Made

The bomb is made will drop on Rangitoto.
Be kind to one another, kiss a little
And let love-making imperceptibly
Grow inwards from a kiss. I've done with soldiering,
Though every day my leave-pass may expire.

The bomb is made will drop on Rangitoto.
The cell of death is formed that multiplied
Will occupy the lung, exclude the air
Be kind to one another, kiss a little —
The first goodbye might each day last forever.

The bomb is made will drop on Rangitoto;
The hand is born that gropes to press the button.
The prodigal grey generals conspire
To dissipate the birth-right of the Asians.
Be kind to one another, kiss a little.

The bomb is made will drop on Rangitoto.
The plane that takes off persons in a hurry
Is only metaphorically leaving town,
So if we linger we will be on time.
Be kind to one another, kiss a little.

The bomb is made will drop on Rangitoto.
I do not want to see that sun-burned harbour,
Islandless as moon, red-skied again
Its tide unblossomed, sifting wastes of ash.
Be kind to one another, kiss a little,
Our only weapon is this gentleness.

1963

M. K. JOSEPH

Born in England, M. K. Joseph (1914–1981) was educated at Auckland and Oxford universities. An accomplished novelist and critic, he taught English at the University of Auckland until just before his death.

Off Cape Leeuwin

Leviathan the ocean, spiked and mailed,
    Scalloped with imbricated scales,
With clots of granite clawed and tailed
    (His parasites are wandering whales)

Hails in Behemoth the ship
    A creature of the self-same mould
Nonchalantly in iron grip
    Bearing its passengers embowelled.

Leviathan's somnolent shoulder nudges
    Behemoth's ridged and riveted flank,
Who majestically heaving, sideways budges
    Flounders and skids like a mudded tank,

Poises straddling, wavers and heels,
    Peers at the moon with squinted face,
Then hip and shoulder to Leviathan reels,
    In a solemn brotherly drunken embrace.

Above them in sky's spinning dome
    Stars bloom to meteors at each roll —
These tipsy monsters reeling home
    Between Australia and the Pole.

                1950

Secular Litany

That we may never lack two Sundays in a week
One to rest and one to play
That we may worship in the liturgical drone
Of the race-commentator and the radio raconteur
That we may avoid distinction and exception
Worship the mean, cultivate the mediocre
Live in a state house, raise forcibly-educated children
Receive family benefits, and standard wages and a pension
And rest in peace in a state crematorium
    Saint Allblack
    Saint Monday Raceday
    Saint Stabilisation
        Pray for us.

From all foreigners, with their unintelligible cooking
From the vicious habit of public enjoyment
From kermesse and carnival, high day and festival

From pubs cafés bullfights and barbecues
From Virgil and vintages, fountains and fresco-painting
From afterthought and apperception
From tragedy, from comedy
And from the arrow of God
   Saint Anniversaryday
   Saint Arborday
   Saint Labourday
     Defend us.

When the bottles are empty
And the keg runs sour
And the cinema is shut and darkened
And the radio gone up in smoke
And the sports-ground flooded
When the tote goes broke
And the favourite scratches
And the brass bands are silenced
And the car is rusted by the roadside
   Saint Fathersday
   Saint Mothersday
   Saint Happybirthday
     Have mercy on us.

And for your petitioner, poor little Jim,
   Saint Hocus
   Saint Focus
   Saint Bogus
   And Saint Billy Bungstarter
     Have mercy on him.

              1950

Mercury Bay Eclogue

(for Rachel and David)

I

The child's castle crumbles; hot air shimmers
Like water working over empty sand.
Summer noon is long and the brown swimmers
For fear of outward currents, lie on land.
With tumbleweed and seashells in its hand
The wind walks, a vigorous noonday ghost
Bearing gifts for an expected guest.

Hull down on horizon, island and yacht
Vanish into blue leaving no trace;
Above my head the nebulae retreat
Dizzily sliding round the bend of space
Winking a last red signal of distress.
Each galaxy or archipelago
Plunges away into the sky or sea.

In the dry noon are all things whirling away?
They are whirling away, but look — the gull's flight,
Stonefall towards the rainbows of the spray
Skim swim and glide on wing up to the light
And in this airy gesture of delight
See wind and sky transformed to bless and warn,
The dance, the transfiguration, the return.

The turning wheels swing the star to harbour
And rock the homing yacht in a deep lull,
Bring children to their tea beneath the arbour,
Domesticate the wind's ghost and pull
Islands to anchor, softly drop the gull
Into his nest of burnished stones and lead
The yachtsmen and the swimmers to their bed.

II

A shepherd on a bicycle
Breaks the pose of pastoral
        But will suffice to keep
        The innocence of sheep.

Ringing his bell he drives the flock
From sleepy field and wind-scarred rock
        To where the creaming seas
        Wash shoreward like a fleece.

The farmer and his wife emerge
All golden from the ocean-surge
        Their limbs and children speak
        The legend of the Greek.

The shadowy tents beneath the pines
The surfboards and the fishing-lines
        Tell that our life might be
        One of simplicity.

The wind strums aeolian lyres
Inshore among the telephone wires
        Linking each to each
        The city and the beach.

For sunburnt sleepers would not come
If inland factories did not hum
        And this Arcadian state
        Is built on butterfat.

So children burn the seastained wood
And tell the present as a good
        Knowing that bonfires are
        Important as a star.

And on his gibbet the swordfish raised
With bloody beak and eye glazed

Glares down into the tide
Astonishment and pride.

Machine once muscled with delight
He merges now in primitive night;
   The mild and wondering crowd
   Admire the dying god
   Where Kupe and where Cook have trod.

III

Over the sea lie Europe and Asia
   The dead moulded in snow
The persecution of nuns and intellectuals
   The clever and the gentle
The political trials and punishment camps
   The perversion of children
Men withering away with fear of the end.

Fifteen years of a bad conscience
   Over Spain and Poland
Vienna Berlin Israel Korea
   Orphans and prostitutes
Unburied the dead and homeless living
   We looked on ruined cities
Saying, These are our people.

We sat in the sun enduring good luck
   Like the stain of original sin
Trying to be as God, to shoulder
   The world's great sorrow
Too shaken to see that we hadn't the talent
   That the clenching heart is a fist
And a man's grasp the reach of his arm.

Be still and know: the passionate intellect
   Prepares great labours
Building of bridges, practice of medicine.
   Still there are cows to be milked
Students to teach, traffic direction
   Ships unloading at wharves
And the composition of symphonies.

IV

The poets standing on the shelf
Excavate the buried self
Freud's injunction they obey
Where id was, let ego be.

Yeats who from his tower sees
The interlocking vortices
Of the present and the past,
Shall find the centre hold at last.

Eliot whose early taste
Was for the cenobitic waste
Now finds the promise of a pardon
Through children's laughter in the locked garden.

Pound in his barbed-wire cage
Prodded into stuttering rage
Still earns reverence from each
Because he purified our speech.

Cavalier or toreador
Is Campbell expert to explore
The truthful moment when we face
The black bull in the arid place.

And Auden who has seen too much
Of the wound weeping for the healer's touch
A surgeon in his rubber gloves
Now cauterizes where he loves.

The summer landscape understood
The morning news, the poet's mood,
By their imperatives are defined
Converging patterns in the mind.

V

Come fleet Mercury, messenger of gods and men
Skim with your winged sandal the resounding surf
Quickly come bearing to all things human
Celestial medicine for their tongueless grief.
Heaven's thief and merchant, here is your port
Lave with your gifts of healing and of speech
All mortals who shall ever print with foot
These silent hills and this forsaken beach.

Come sweet Venus, mother of men and beasts
While meteors fall across the yellow moon
Above the hills herded like sleeping beasts,
Gently come lady, and with hand serene
Plant fruits of peace where by this mariner's mark
The torrents of your sea-begetting roar
And trouble in their dreams of glowing dark
These sleeping hills and this forbidden shore.

Come swift ship and welcome navigators
Link and line with your instruments this earth
To heaven under the propitious stars,
Show forth the joined and fortune-bearing birth
And set this fallen stone a meteorite
Where Mercury and Venus hand in hand
Walk on the waters this auspicious night
And touch to swift love this forgotten strand.

1959

The Nurses' Song of the Earth

Warm was our youth under the milky stars and the buttersoft
sun lads and girls in the little green fields and under the shadows
of the pointed woods girls and dancing lads
all shining pink and brown skins stuffed full
of jolly flesh as sound as sausages and as sharp
as honey the men strongchested like their horses
between the handles of the plough the women going sweetly
as the cows who stood kneedeep in the mirrors of the lake
the scythemen moving like planets among the cornbeards
and the women binding the sheaves the seed in the womb
of the fields the flowers fat with fruit bee
at the flower's lip and apples dropping ripe
in the long grass blossom blown and buxom unto fruit
full baskets cracking granaries wine boiling in the vats

on an evening it was the moon waxripe and yellow
laughter from the open windows over the orchards
full of sleeping bees and the fields
submitted to the plough and on a morning
it was babies sprawling in the sun drunk with milk
from the dug the husband who laboured and cropped
the land and the wife at the byre and the churn and the oven
their children prodigally savouring milk and baked bread
the thyme from the hill the hawthorn in the hedge the sound of
swallows and the tale of clouds and the smell of the fatherly sun

afternoons rang down through clouds through leaves
through windows handing the sun to the earth like a bridegroom
the seed to the turned field man to woman
the whole land fat as wax in the dust
in the dusk in the dew of rams and boars
bred out of thick grass roosters crowing like cool
water men strong as trees in whose shade
sat the woman to spin and the tumbling child for praise
and service and splendour and love one of another

strength fell from the sun into our shoulders
and our loins till our sweat dripped on the rich crumb
of earth clouds staved like colliding casks
all soused in streams in flows in floods
down into earth all simmering in the sun till
rose the steam in which we walked golden as grain
in a mist of milk and out of the earth and into
man and woman and child and up to the
sky and into the sun poured strength

in cool weathers came the town and the wheels
of oxcarts groaning among the tall bells
voices in hall and arbour and crying of fresh
fish cherries and gingerbread jugglers ropedancers
swordswallowers tumblers and fire-eaters stalls

heaped with figs melons grapes hams
brawns dressed capons and coneys chitterlings
flapjacks eggs cheeses and skins of resinous wine

and the comings and goings in service to master and lady
fetch and carry upstairs and down wooden
trencher silver ewer cup and spoon
beds of cool linen mistress and master butler
and groom child in cradle horse in stable
fingers nimbling to sew mend bake
scrub dust and lay all things on hobs
on tables in presses all things in their places because
what are lords for if not for lordship

plain day high day fast on saltfish or the
suckingpigs of celebration loving and labouring in a round
that I a heavybodied woman who had borne
my children and buried my man could yet sit in the sun
fingers able at the linen watching the green lads
and golden girls buds burst corn sprang children
capered in the shade and ran to mothers and men
came home from the field the fold the forge the mill
so that my heart cried out under trees and the round
bells calling over the rooftops ringing their flocks
to the priest who in his hands raises
the blessed bread above the cup of wine

the chapmen have gone away the children are abed
doors bolted and fires covered and cupboards
closed and the light burns down yet still
my dry dugs remember the lips of the little bubbing child
and the soles of my feet remember the steps of the old dance
and my bent bones resume the fulness of sap
    under the green sun
    under the gay leaves
    under the flesh of soil

1959

A L I S T A I R   T E   A R I K I
C A M P B E L L

Born in Rarotonga in 1925, Alistair Te Ariki Campbell moved to New Zealand on the death of his parents in 1933. He has published a trilogy of novels and an autobiography, and his Pocket Collected Poems *appeared in 1996. A full-time writer, he lives at Pukerua Bay, just north of Wellington.*

At a Fishing Settlement

October, and a rain-blurred face,
And all the anguish of that bitter place.
It was a bare sea-battered town,
With its one street leading down
On to a shingly beach. Sea winds

Had long picked the dark hills clean
Of everything but tussock and stones
And pines that dropped small brittle cones
On to a soured soil. And old houses flanking
The street hung poised like driftwood planking
Blown together and could not outlast
The next window-shuddering blast
From the storm-whitened sea.
It was bitterly cold; I could see
Where muffled against gusty spray
She walked the clinking shingle; a stray
Dog whimpered and pushed a small
Wet nose into my hand — that is all.
Yet I am haunted by that face,
That dog, and that bare bitter place.

1950

from Elegy

In memoriam

Roy M. Dickson,
killed in the Alps
1 January 1947, aged 20

I

The Hollyford Valley

Storm. Storm in the trees;
Everywhere the hidden sound
Of water, like hives of bees
Up-tilted deep underground.

The shattered cliff's sheer
Face spurts myriads
Of waterfalls, like tears
From some deep-bowed head

Whose colossal grief is stone.
Great trees rooted fast
In ice nightlong moan
Down the gleaming pass.

VII

The Laid-Out Body

Now grace, strength and pride
Have flown like the hawk;
The mind like the spring tide,

Beautiful and calm; the talk;
The brilliance of eye and hand;

The feet that no longer walk.

All is new, and all strange —
Terrible as a dusty gorge
Where a great river sang.

1950

The Return

And again I see the long pouring headland,
And smoking coast with the sea high on the rocks,
The gulls flung from the sea, the dark wooded hills
Swarming with mist, and mist low on the sea.

And on the surf-loud beach the long spent hulks,
The mats and splintered masts, the fires kindled
On the wet sand, and men moving between the fires,
Standing or crouching with backs to the sea.

Their heads finely shrunken to a skull, small
And delicate, with small black rounded beaks;
Their antique bird-like chatter bringing to mind
Wild locusts, bees, and trees filled with wild honey—

And, sweet as incense-clouds, the smoke rising, the fire
Spitting with rain, and mist low with rain —
Their great eyes glowing, their rain-jewelled, leaf-green
Bodies leaning and talking with the sea behind them:

Plant gods, tree gods, gods of the middle world ... Face down-
    ward
And in a small creek mouth all unperceived,
The drowned Dionysus, sand in his eyes and mouth,
In the dim tide lolling — beautiful, and with the last harsh

Glare of divinity from lip and broad brow ebbing ...
The long-awaited! And the gulls passing over with shrill cries;
And the fires going out on the thundering sand;
And the mist, and the mist moving over the land.

1950

from Sanctuary of Spirits

IX *Against Te Rauparaha*

Kei hea koutou kia toa — Be brave that you may live.
                                        Hongi Hika

        The records all agree
you were a violent, a pitiless man,
        treacherous as an avalanche
poised above a sleeping village.
        Small, hook-nosed as a Roman,
haughty, with an eagle's glance,
        Caligula and Commodus
            were of your kin.

Kapiti floats before me,
and the shadows round the island
prickle
like the hairs of my scalp.
Shadows of war canoes
splinter the bright sea.
And I hear on the cliff below
the low cry of a chief:
'*Ka aue te mamae!* —
Alas! the pain.'

Ironical to think your island pa,
once drenched with the blood
of men and whales,
has since become a sanctuary for birds.
Would this make sense to you, I wonder.
That life is holy would seem
a dubious proposition to you,
old murderer —
most laughable.

Pathetic ghost!
Sometimes you hoot despairingly
across the valley,
and my small daughter sobs in her sleep,
convinced an engine is pursuing her.
Black as anthracite,
issuing in steam
out of the bowels of the hill,
yours is a passable imitation, I'll allow.
But where is the rage that terrorised the coast?
the towering pride not to be withstood?
Imperial violence . . . !
Imperial poppycock!
I saw you slink away in the moonlight —
a most solitary, attenuated ghost
reduced to scaring little girls.
The worst that you can do is raise a storm,
and try to tear my roof off . . .

But why deceive myself?
I know you as the subtlest tormentor,
able to assume at will
the features of the most intimate terrors.

Remember Tama, who betrayed his friends,
guests on his *marae*,
to the murderous vengeance of Hakitara —
Pehi and forty others,
all great chiefs,
impiously butchered in their sleep!
How, spider-clever, you again escaped
to spin a web and snare him.

And how Te Hiko, Pehi's son,
glared at him for fully half an hour,
lifted Tama's upper lip
with a forefinger,
and tapped the wolfish teeth,
crying wildly:
'These teeth ate my father!'

Tamaiharanui
who strangled in the night
his beautiful daughter
that she might not be a slave.
But afterwards,
plump goose for a widow's oven,
plucked of his honour,
what remained of Tama
but a victim for a ritual vengeance?

Tama and Hiko too were of your kin,
and vengeful Hakitara — violent men,
crazed with the lust for blood!
Who would have guessed that they were also
dutiful sons, affectionate fathers?
or that, decorous on the *marae*,
they entertained their guests
with courtly ease?

Scarer of children, drinker of small girls,
your malicious eye stares down
out of the midday sun,
blasting the seed in the pod,
choking the well with dust.

These teeth ate my father —
ate the heart of the bright day!

Insidious enmity!
I know you by these signs:
the walls crack without cause,
heads show pointed teeth,
leer and fall away,
the dog barks at nothing,
whimpers and hides his head,
and something wild
darts into the night
from under my window . . .
YOU — Te Rauparaha!

The wind rises,
      lifts the lid off my brain —

Madman, leave me alone!

1963

Bitter Harvest

The big farm girl with the dumb prophetic body
And shoulders plump and white as a skinned peach
Goes singing through the propped-up apple boughs.

Behind her steps an ancient Jersey cow
With bones like tent-poles and udder swinging.

And last a hairy boy who with a fishing-pole
Drives youth and age before him, flanked by boulders
More yielding than his love. O bitter harvest

When drought affirms and plenitude denies!
Well, let them pass. Assuredly the boy
Will drop his worm into a dusty hole

And fish up ... death, and the ancient cow
On which so much depends will clear the moon.

1964

Bon Voyage

to Meg

Crossing the straits is easy
As sleeping with you, my sweet:
The waves just keep slipping away
Like the bedclothes from our feet.

A salt moon leans to the mast,
White as your head on my arm —
I'm afraid of the lights on the sea,
I'm afraid of the calm.

A gull falls away in the dark,
Like your lost hand under a sheet
When hunger is deep as the ocean
And there's no advance or retreat.

Drowning is easy, my darling,
As when foundering lip to lip
Horizons topple and vanish
And into your breathing I slip.

1964

Green

Dressed in green she came
   and like a tulip
leaned her head against the door
   and looked at me.
Her hand lay cool as a stone
   against her dress
     and her sandalled feet
showed white as a pair of doves
    on grass.
   She did not stir
but wanted me to speak to her.
   Her words
were lilies on a green stem
   the small wind shakes.

1972

from The Dark Lord of Savaiki

I *Under the Tamanu Tree*

Who, who and who?
Who is the dark Lord of Savaiki?
   Crab castings,
      convulsions under the house
where the landcrabs
   tell their grievances
to the roots of the *tamanu* tree.
Agitation of the leaves,
   the palm trees clash
     their fronds,
and the wind hurries past
   clutching in its fingers
the leaf-wrapped souls
    of children torn
     from the eyelids
of despairing mothers.
    Hung
on spiderwebs for safekeeping,
   they will dangle there,
until the spirits come
    and eat them.

III *Teu*

Mother, you were there
   at the passage
     when our ship arrived.
The sea, heavy as oil,
   heaved unbroken
     on the reef,

the stars
    lay in clusters
        on the water,
and you wept
    when you laid
        the Southern Cross
upon our eyes.

IV *At Nahe*

At Nahe, attended by a sandshark,
    I waded in the shallows
that seemed as white and pure
        as happiness,
    or the shark itself.
I was happy being a child again,
    and, careless as a child
        in a treasure house,
I ripped up chunks of coral
    to take home.
        Horrid amputation!
The living creatures seemed
        to shriek,
and bled a kind of ichor.

VI *Tapu*

The sea gnaws at Paroa's bones
    where he lies at Nahe,
but Paetou,
    beloved of Maringikura,
sleeps secure at Hanoa
under an untidy heap of stones.

VIII *Omoka*

It will be like this one day
    when I sail home to die —
the boat crunching up on to the sand,
then wading through warm water
    to the beach,
the friendly voices
    round me in the darkness,
the sky dying out
    behind the trees of Omoka,
        and reaching out of hands.

IX *Trade Winds*

You were just a girl,
    one of two wild sisters,
when he came to Tongareva,
        a gloomy trader,
    his soul eaten away

by five years
              in the trenches.
     You followed him
from island to island,
              bore his children
only to see your dreams
              break up
on the hidden reef
     of Savaiki.
              Mother,
your footsteps falter
              outside my window,
where you have waited
              fifty years
for your children
              to return.

The moon comes out,
              lovely
as a mother's face
     over a sleeping child.
The trade winds
     are your fingers
on my eyelids.

                                        1980

from Soul Traps

I A Stranger from Rakahanga

A stranger has arrived from Rakahanga.
     Nobody knows how he came:
          no strange canoe has been reported —
none could survive in such a sea.
     Our villages are awash, and our dead groan
          as they sit up to the chin in water.
Such a stranger, you would think, would be
     so singular, so arresting,
          once seen, nobody could forget him.
Nobody remembers a single thing —
     the look on his face (if he has a face),
          his size, or if he is young or old.
He arrived, some say, a few hours ago,
     others claim it is more than a week,
          since he was first seen at Omoka.
On one thing, though, all are agreed:
     he is a traveller from Rakahanga —
          but why Rakahanga, they can't say.
They stand around in silent groups, expecting
     the worst — but not a thing happens.
          No deaths or accidents are reported.
They will turn soon to urgent tasks, repair
     the storm damage, but strangely empty
          as if nursing a disappointment.

II Sina

You were a tender girl, Sina,
 fragrant as the *komuko*
  of the young coconut tree.
Throughout our adolescence
 our entire universe
  was the floor of a canoe
where we lay together
 drifting among the *motu*.
  Every night I would pluck
for your breasts and hair
 the flowers of the sky.
  And then one night
we drifted far from shore
 through the scented darkness,
  oblivious of the reef
until too late — *aue!*
 Now you are a woman
  lovelier even than the girl
I lay with long ago,
 and another suitor
  drinks from your calabash . . .
Ru the fisherman
 knows all the secret places
  in the ocean floor.
His spear is probing
 for an answer.
  I watch and wait.

VIII Maui's Whare

Maui hauled it up from the sea.
 His fish-hook caught it
  by a window-frame,
and when he landed it
 the structure was askew.
  But the strange thing was
an old man and his wife
 and daughters were still
  in residence: four pairs
of eyes stared out at him,
 utterly astonished,
  but not as much as he.
He scowled, took up the *whare*
 and shook it angrily
  until the old man and
his family fell screaming
 through the doorway
  and smashed their brains out
on the rocks of Kura Passage
 fifty feet below.
  Thereupon, with infinite care,
the mischief-maker

took up the broken bodies
    and tried to breathe life
into their gaping mouths,
    but their spirits had already
        fled to Te Po,
squeaking with indignation.
    Then Maui put the *whare* down
        tried to straighten it,
failed and went away.

XI *Parire*

Parire, lover of sunlight,
    Tuturi and Kekeso,
        Kiki and Kaka too,
are dead, all dead —
    swept off the reef
        at Takuua Passage
in the big wind
    that struck our island
        the Sunday
after you died.
    I dreamed one night
        a crab had
stolen your eyes,
    one in each claw,
        and that the sea
closed over them,
    but could not extinguish
        the light within.
And now, on certain nights,
    a strange glow
        surfaces and spreads
across the lagoon . . .
    Parire, is it you?

XIV *Solomona*

To die is simply to walk
    away from the body
        without regret or pain,
and with no thought of
    turning back, for there is
        nothing to turn back to,
except the empty shell
    that relatives weep over.
        I have often left
my body here at Te Tautua,
    crossed the lagoon and
        walked among my sleeping
kinsfolk at Omoka to see
    if all was well.

My family know my door
must be kept open
    if I am to rejoin my body,
      but sometimes through
carelessness they have
    almost shut me out.
      Now it is time to go,
to walk the steep track
    to Savaiki alone. I have
      enjoined my dear ones
to close my door firmly
    after me, when I leave
      on my last visit to Omoka.
They weep, but will obey.

           1985

RUTH GILBERT

Born in 1917, Ruth Gilbert was educated at Hamilton High School and the Otago School of Physiotherapy, from which she graduated in 1938. Her first book was Lazarus and Other Poems *(1949). She now lives in Motueka.*

from Lazarus

1. *Betrothed to Lazarus*

Music there was, but not of flute or bird,
And rain, but not from cloud,
And for those things which he has felt and heard
He mourns, but not aloud.

Light too there was, but not the light of day,
And through our alien noon
He walks aggrieved, as one that, gone away,
Is summoned back too soon.

Our truths to him are strangely fraught with lies,
Our spring-times chill with frost,
He looks on earth with unfamiliar eyes,
A Lazarus home, yet lost.

But what befell in that half-land of sleep
To change the mountain eagle to the dove
I cannot tell. I only know I weep,
For this is not my love.

           1949

2. *The Sisters of Lazarus*

They say he walked by Lethe unaware,
And through its waters trailed rash finger-tips,

They say some feckless angel touched his lips
With coals of heaven, and left a madness there.

They say he looks askance on flower and girl,
As if in some far, visionary place
He knew a brighter bloom, a fairer face —
They call him dreamer, idiot, and churl.

Some say he did not die, but only slept
The simple, happy slumber of a child,
But grief is not so easily beguiled —
We saw the stone, we know the tears we wept.

And if he speaks in words that are not plain,
If, dull of wit, we cannot understand,
Enough for us that we can touch his hand,
And see his face, and know him home again.

1949

3. Lazarus Speaks

I looked on that whereon no man should look,
I heard the song not sung for mortal ear,
And for His voice who called me I forsook
The paths of light to walk the darkness here.

I saw the glory, and I felt the power,
Amazement leapt within me like a flame,
And peace was mine that unforgotten hour,
Then stricken, lost, I heard him call my name.

And all was changed; the friends that once I had
Decried as dreams the revelation given,
Proclaimed me witless, moon-bewitched, and mad,
But he is sane whose feet have walked in heaven.

They will not heed the wisdom I would teach,
Their laughter mocks the truest word I say,
The star of knowledge gleams beyond their reach,
And from its shining they have turned away.

Yet what of this? but when each day I see
My love's dark eyes estranged and bright with pain
I cry to Him whose mercy wakened me
To speak once more, and bid me sleep again.

1949

from Leah

Jacob

Laban, I curse you for this trick you played!
What have I done that you should use me so?
Your herded cattle fatten in the shade,
Their harvest in, your wine-vats overflow.

Only my corn is blighted in the ear,
Only my grapes tread vinegar for wine,
Have I not served you well this seven year?
By law and love the guerdon claimed was mine.

From that first hour I saw her at the well
Leaning her pitcher and her beauty down,
Her red mouth laughing as the bright drops fell
Like truant rain from brim to flowing gown

My heart was Rachel's — and the longest day
But brief, could it be ended at her knees,
Her hands enticing weariness away,
Her voice a music in the olive trees.

What shall requite her for this mischief done?
And what undo his infinite despair
Who clasped the moon, believing it the sun,
And crying 'Rachel' drowned in Leah's hair.

1949

RUTH DALLAS

Born in Invercargill in 1919, Ruth Dallas has spent most of her life in Dunedin. The
University of Otago Press published her Collected Poems in 1987 and her autobiography in 1991.

Deep in the Hills

Once I thought the land I had loved and known
Lay curled in my inmost self; musing alone
In the quiet room I unfolded the folded sea,
Unlocked the forest and the lonely tree,
Hill and mountain valley beach and stone,
All these, I said, are here and exist in me.

But now I know it is I who exist in the land;
My inmost self is blown like a grain of sand
Along the windy beach, and is only free
To wander among the mountains, enter the tree,
To turn again a sea-worn stone in the hand,
Because these things exist outside of me.

O far from the quiet room my spirit fills
The familiar valleys, is folded deep in the hills.

1953

Wild Plum

The fruit is gathered and gone,
    Strawberry, greengage, pear,
        Raspberry, apricot;
    If the late apples lean
Still on their props and crutches

And the mulberries wait
    Their hour draws near.

But to the wild plum,
    Bird-sown in the hedges,
       The pickers will not come;
    Purple, dusky as a grape,
Its fruit may drop or hang,
    Like all things sour, sharp,
       Or bitter on the tongue.

            1966

Rainy Sunday

The branches of the autumn trees
Are black with rain;
Saffron leaves
Like lanterns
Hang
    In the grieving sky.
Someone with a red umbrella
Goes
Through the rain
And the trees,
    Hurrying by.

            1968

Shadow Show

Watch, now.
From this black paper,
If I cut a silhouette,
Hands blown sideways by unceasing winds,
Shoulders bowed under a burden,
Knees bent,
A birdsclaw foothold on the earth,
You could say that I made a tree,
Storm twisted.

Or a woman, or a man.

           1966

A Girl's Song

When love came
    glancing
        down our street
Scarlet leaves
    flew
       round our feet,
     sang the girl, sewing.

He told me
    he would
        come again
Before
    the avenue
        turned green,
    sang the girl, sewing.

How could I know,
    or guess,
        till now
The sadness
    of a
        summer bough,
    sang the girl, sewing.

1968

In Central Otago

Seek foliage and find
Among cracked boulders
Scab of lichen, thyme.

Seek a burgeoning tree
Discover
Upended witches' brooms.

Seek grass and tread
Stiff sheet of ice drawn
Over the land dead.

Moon country.
No one could live here,
In the houses squat on shingle.

Fields scorched,
Snow gripping the mountains;
Nothing could recover

From such desolation,
Jack Frost's sheep-run,
Mirror of the bleak mind.

But come back in a month —
See blanketing the slits
And sockets of the land's skeleton

Square eiderdowns of peach-bloom,
Old crone, Plum, unpick
A feather mattress from a bald stone.

1976

Kyeburn Diggings

Someone has been looking under the stones
For gold,
Has lifted every stone and knocked it clean,
Brown mountain stones,
White river stones,
A stock of cannon balls
Pitched into hills for the frost to crack,
Sun to bake,
Deck for the lizard to roast his back.
Whether gold was found or no,
The stones are scrubbed sterile as snow,
Too hot, too cold for grass to grow.

The desert thorn now tries her skill
To shift or anchor at her will.

1976

Pickers Wanted

Through a hamlet remembered
For a goldbag robbery
A boy rides a bicycle
First thing at sun-up,

Skirting the river-flats
Dandelion-yellow,
That in winter were iron-
bound, fast as a bankbox;

His hat of white towelling's
For the sweat of mid-day
(Don't you know?) when he's out
Boysenberry-picking,

Never doubting his bike
Dropped against a post
Will wait all day in the straws
Of the dry ditch untouched.

That old robbery,
That's history and bullsh,
The stuff they teach you at school,
Or you see in Westerns on TV.

It's nothing to do
With biking in hot sun
Out to the berryfarms,
Eating ripe apricots,

Waiting for the applecrop,
And for the big gales from the gorge
That will shake down twelve sacks
Of walnuts from a single tree.

1976

Living with a Cabbage-tree

A cabbage-palm is not an interesting tree.
Its single trunk resembles a telegraph-pole.
Botanists say it is not a tree at all,
But a lily, grown exceptionally rampant.
This, I think, could happen only in New Zealand,
Where birds have left us skeletons as big as horses'.

I did not want a cabbage-tree in the garden.
There's plenty of room on the Canterbury plains
Where a tree of any kind relieves the eye.
Its life began as a little harmless flax-bush,
I thought a pot-plant — ornamental leaves
Someone had planted out for variety of foliage.
I had hardly turned my back when it soared up
Into a shape like a coconut-palm in a strait-jacket.

The flax-bush-part is elevated now, say fifteen feet,
And casts the smallest patch of shadow and the fastest
In the garden. It's enough to cover your head;
But if you take a chair outside you must be prepared
To shift from west to east more quickly
Than you have ever chased the shelter of a tree.

I like the way the shadow of its bole
Moves like the finger of a giant sun-dial
Over the concrete; that's rather romantic;
Reminding us that time is passing, passing;
And cats declare it without peer for sharpening claws.
But it's a dull tree, inclined to fancy itself
As a musical instrument, when the wind blows,
Sometimes tuning up like an orchestra.
You listen expectantly. But nothing happens.
The wind drops and it falls silent.

1976

The Lamp

In youth it is the body's line,
    A curve, a lift of the head,
The bloom of apples on the flesh,
    That fastens us
        Whether we will or no,
            On love's
                Tight leash.

Older, with power to stay or go,
    We know the line will fail,
And would no more choose by the skin
    Than choose a lamp
        By form,
            And not by the flame
                Within.

1976

The Weather Clock

When Joan came swinging out the sun would shine;
But boot-and-mackintoshed Darby prophesied rain.

Sun buttering a patch on the kitchen floor
Told Joan it was right she had left her narrow door;

Rain in cataracts descending fast
Confirmed old Darby's gloomy forecast.

Sun plus rain? The most mixed-up weather
The ill-matched couple were never seen out together.

At most they would stand aloof, each at a door,
Like neighbours who were not speaking any more.

But when the household children lay asleep,
Did they still their polar distance keep?

I tell you this! says Joan. *I tell you that!*
Says Darby. Perhaps they fought like dog and cat?

Or with all differences reconciled
Sat together by their fire, and smiled

To think how little other people knew
Of what went on when they were out of view.

Soon the house would wake; the frost flowers fade;
And the children rise and inspect their strict parade.

1976

On Reading Love Poems

Gentle reader, do not
Spit, I pray, the pip
Of Love's deep fruit,
The indigestible
Eyes that were her pearls,
Or let your ear be lulled
With all a triumphant tale.

Observe
Between the lines of Jack
In your own street
Not every Darby has his Joan.
At times recall
The basement room
Where Jill lives on.

1976

Photographs of Pioneer Women

You can see from their faces
Life was not funny,

The streets, when there were streets,
Tugging at axles,
The settlement ramshackle as a stack of cards.
And where there were no streets, and no houses,
Save their own roof of calico or thatch,
The cows coming morning and afternoon
From the end-of-world swamp,
Udders cemented with mud.

There is nothing to equal pioneering labour
For wrenching a woman out of shape,
Like an old willow, uprooted, thickening.
See their strong arms, their shoulders broadened
By the rhythmical swing of the axe, or humped
Under loads they donkeyed on their backs.
Some of them found time to be photographed,
With bearded husband, and twelve or thirteen children,
Looking shocked, but relentless,
After first starching the frills in their caps.

                                    1976

Pioneer Woman with Ferrets

Preserved in film,
As under glass,
Her waist nipped in,
Skirt and sleeves
To ankle, wrist,
Voluminous
In the wind,
Hat to protect
Her Victorian complexion,
Large in the tussock
She looms,
Startling as a moa.
Unfocussed,
Her children
Fasten wire-netting
Round close-set warrens,
And savage grasses
That bristle in a beard
From the rabbit-bitten hills.
She is monumental
In the treeless landscape.
Nonchalantly she swings
In her left hand
A rabbit,
Bloodynose down.
In her right hand a club.

                    1976

The Falling House

The sea has smashed
The clay bank
And its retaining wall,
Undermined the garden,
The house we pulled
For safety
To its utmost boundary,
The house itself
Falls now into the sea;
To lie with the roads
That are only to be found
In dusty maps on shelves
Of Lands & Survey offices,
Paper roads, butt
For the waves' laughter.
The house itself
Falls now,
Its roots, its leaves,
Hands
That set the trees
In their selected places
The roads
The hands
The trees —
The house is falling,
Licked by the slippery
Tongues of the sea.

1976

A New Dress

I don't want a new dress, I said.
My mother plucked from her mouth ninetynine pins.
I suppose there are plenty, she said, *girls of ten
Who would be glad to have a new dress.*

Snip-snip. Snip-snip. The cold scissors
Ate quickly as my white rabbit round my arm.

She won't speak to me if I have a new dress !
My feet rattled on the kitchen floor.

How can I fit you if you won't stand still ?

My tears made a map of Australia
On the sofa cushion; from the hot centre
My friend's eyes flashed, fierce as embers.
She would not speak to me, perhaps never again.
She would paralyse me with one piercing look.

I'd rather have my friend than a new dress!

My mother wouldn't understand, my grownup mother
Whose grasshopper thimble winked at the sun,
And whose laughter was made by small waves
Re-arranging seashells on Australia's shore.

1979

The Leopard

How beautiful the leopard in his spots,
With rhythms in his blood like the dappled
Shadows of leaves on desert earth,
Or the blowing undulations of the plain.

He unfolds himself like a freckled lily,
Yawns widely in the sun, and if we met
Would strike his teeth into my skull.
He, too, will pass, his bone, my bone,

Becoming mild marigolds and forgetmenots
Gleaming a moment in the light from stars.

1979

Girl with Pitcher

The lion and his shadow the lioness
Stalk the terraces above the river.
I balance my pitcher and must pass them.
Terror sticks from my back like an arrow.

I slip with the move-
     ment of air through the sedges.

The river is not evaporated, as I feared.
I paddle in its shining verge,
Then dip my pitcher full of clear water.
I listen for the sound of the lion's shadow.

1979

Jenny's Song

Once I loved a tall man
   Cold as mountain snow,
Fair as a golden poplar
   When spring winds blow,
     Who knew no more of joy or pain
     Than a callous mountain crow.
      Come fine or windy.

Once I loved a warm man
   Whose heart stood in his eyes,
Who told me he loved me truly,

And a thousand pleasant lies,
    But proved as light-winged as a bee
    That over the sweet earth flies.
      Come fine or windy.

Now I am off, I am off, hey!
    I'll not be bound again,
Let all the larks rise singing
    That once would wake old pain,
      Leave the chameleon sea to mirror
      The moods of sun and rain.
        Come fine or windy.

1979

KENDRICK SMITHYMAN

Born in Te Kopuru, near Dargaville, Kendrick Smithyman (1922–1995) worked as a primary school teacher before taking a position at the University of Auckland. He published 11 collections of poetry, including a Selected Poems *(1989), and a study of New Zealand poetry,* A Way of Saying *(1965).*

Hint for the Incomplete Angler

Not too far north from where I write set dawn
Before your bow precisely. Out there, cast
The kingfish from his feeding while you prey.

Smug blue worms will peck at your neat craft's side.
Show due respect then while you steal the tide.

There was a fisherman once who did things right.

For more than forty years he pulled fish out.
By line, net or pot God's plenty hauled to pout
And puff on the bottomboards, to smack
Themselves silly and die, else were tossed back
Until they swelled a right size for the pan
He kept on the wall by his sink. That man
Had long outgrown the truth of simple tales
Which said if he stroked his arm he showered scales,
That said for years he nourished an old mermaid
All to himself in his bach. Friend, he was staid,
Ordinary, and (it may be) none too bright,
But who could come godlike home with that high light
Morning on morning, to be sane as we
Would claim we are? Yet he did fittingly
More than we'd dream, and with more dignity.

For when he couldn't heave any more at the net,
When the old man snapper clung too hard, he set
His nose to the sea away out east of the Head
To give what was due from good years to the tide.

Watch for the worms as you go, at your dinghy's side.

1968

Blackleg

Careering on a downslope from the bail,
it was myself, in part it was myself
committed to the pothole, steep
sickening rumbledumble with a fly's
rude concert at the end. Such a close
to round one only summer, and be dung
or even less than dung: a dissolution
of the parts corporal, their incorporeal arts.

In the holding yard where the calves guzzled
tippling skim milk, pattering, I bawled
that he was found the missing one,
him offered to arbitrary summer
where one by one or squadrons at a whim
thistles discharged their flights.
Gauze in a fine wearing, but the yard
unhallowed; he must have been lying
all through the day near the trough
coarsening — you know how the eyes are,
looking past seeing and not looking,
his near forequarter swollen blackly.
Or the tongue, although it is not
detail which quickens remembering,
the masculine pouch prematurely
unrealised, the not-meditative horns.

While wood pigeons grossly fed on
karaka berries, exulting appetite,
I looped a chain about the hindlegs,
the Thing in his unbecoming I dragged
downhill to a pothole which had
been abandoned by the Forest stream,
there resigned him
to be forgotten. And washed my hands
where a pool blinks with native trout.

It was February in nineteen thirty-nine.
I was old enough and too young to know
that exceptions breed like flies,
but what is to be imported
in a commonplace? The younger bulls
in their simplicity sported the paddock.

1968

An Ordinary Day Beyond Kaitaia

1

Cabbage tree heads, they nod,
profoundly confirmed,
towards a church's new white paint.

About midmorning an elementary
summer breeze arrives from the coast
too late to alter. The township has
already dedicated this day, to usage.
An old disorder yields, to wise men
who come from the south. Where was a stable,
they made the Tourist Inn; for shepherds,
a public convenience of concrete blocks,
the kind that's called hollowstone.

Fused with, confused as, memories,
assumed a means of tree pollens
or a shifty heat off the church's
dazzling corrugated roof,
inconstant air implicates farmlands
in a conspiracy of nation, utility,
populist myth. You must change
your life, Rilke's archaic Apollo urged.
They have done so. They have put by.
Between a sea and an ocean
the farmlands lie low
without a hill to comfort them.

A peasant people won hard
from waste, teaching their weird flats
a novel language, an old belief.
Saint Cyril and Saint Methodius
they pray for, but at the bridge
to the dairy factory at midmorning
those echoes which coil remember
a coast not broken or so far displaced,
just accommodated. You breathe
a last of ozone, of kelp iodine.
Like the popping of kelp on a drift
fire, you hear pods closer.

Between the soil, the sand, swamp
and sea, is an understanding.
To change your life you must understand
how your life goes, and where.

2

Like so many huntsmen
they move intently.
They have an assignation
with a wildfowl, garishly feathered,
a fowl of unearthly voice.
You have not seen her like.

Dear object, lulled in myth,
you may yet be splendid
as the firebird, birdwoman,

the snowbird, woman of white
fire
   though here the quarry, much
harried, burns away through heavy
scent down to the burning clay
under an overburden of flowers.

The wreaths are already wilting
and they are not yet out of town.
Today a myth dies a little more,
a little less than kind.
We are aliens.

3

And the kin: tanned, earnest
Slavic Polynesian faces,
all the men wearing dark
suits. Perhaps they are going
to a wedding beyond
the dairy factory.

Do not think so.
You must change your life.
As of now, you marry conflicting wishes.
You also will progress
towards the sunbaked slope,
being contracted. Hedged about
with hakea, you go. Bitterns nest
in a raupo swamp beside, harriers
stiffly tread its edge.
Archaic Apollo, your people,
they taught the vine to grow
wild along their roads. Clay
like talc, mica-sharp grits dust
the grapes' tight premature testicular
clusters. If the fruits will seed,
who will pick them over? They go
earth-borne. Hard, to discover
when they ripen. Hard to know,
the end due of their season.

On the west course to Tasman's sea
pine stumps, insignis, broken teeth.
Alien forests, made quick
to accommodate, sicken.
Go slowly, carefully, like those
who pick a path among stumps,
like the funeral cars in high
day, headlamps teasing on low beam.
My wife's dark glasses reflected
cars, lights, unreconciled twin suns.

4

They have put by

an earliest type washing-machine
several lawnmowers (hand and powered)
tables   deckchairs   beds

a 1911 Montgomery Ward mailorder catalogue
wirestrainers spanners crosscut saws
shark-repellents surfcasting rods
lifebuoys and a mae west (with whistle)
an almost complete household physician

they have put by in a colonial junkshop

ships' riding lamps,
verdigrised brass
horseless carriage lanterns,
bullseyes, hurricanes with bent
wires and no glass, their wicks
shrivelled, smoke blanked.

Fires banked, they see perpetually
nothing. Illustrate nothing.
Shelve them beside
fossil eggs by whale vertebrae
windwashed, seablown, beyond
whiteness hardly temporised
by the mere dust which they breed
or dust which is imported from their road
tending eastward to the Pacific

past garage, past creek
where fishermen compare. Turbid
weed congregates in the gut.

Changing, their lives' style.

5

Their river decayed,
but their soil learned new tricks
of speech, for winds of hay paddocks,
a dialect fitting herds,
a stress and accent of flocks and crops.

Why, if intensely assured
by confident highlights every
where present to trouble exposure,
should I sourly dawdle,
doodling mementoes, cryptically
muttering
        I go, thou goest, he/she/or it,
and one (impersonally) goes

If we live,
we go. You go. They, a common gender, go.

I am a stranger. Too facile, to say
we are all strangers. The land is made
to our liking. Not far north
they are going, to offer.

To Hine, whose likeness still the swamp.
To Hine-nui, whose tumultuous hair the chattering
   idiot cabbage trees mimic,
Hine-nui-te-Po, She who is darkness,
at the heart speaking of the land,
along the wind's edge, at the sea line.
You cannot put by. I write in her dust
on the bonnet of our station wagon
M A T E. That will do, for a time.

If we live, we stand in language.
You must change your words.

1972

Colville

That sort of place where you stop
long enough to fill the tank, buy plums,
   perhaps, and an icecream thing on a stick
while somebody local comes
   in, leans on the counter, takes a good look
     but does not like what he sees of you,

intangible as menace,
a monotone with a name, as place
   it is an aspect of human spirit
(by which shaped), mean, wind-worn. Face
   outwards, over the saltings: with what merit
     the bay, wise as contrition, shallow

as their hold on small repute
good for dragging nets which men are doing
   through channels, disproportioned in the blaze
of hot afternoon's down-going
   to a far fire-hard tide's rise
     upon the vague where time is distance?

It could be plainly simple
pleasure, but these have another tone
   or quality, something aboriginal,
reductive as soil itself — bone
   must get close here, final
     yet unrefined at all. They endure.

A school, a War Memorial
Hall, the store, neighbourhood of salt
   and hills. The road goes through to somewhere else.
Not a geologic fault
   line only scars textures of experience.
     Defined, plotted; which maps do not speak.

1972

Waitomo

Guides ask for silence, and have
no difficulty in getting their parties
to go quiet. At a dollar a head, nations
file underground. All shapes of age bow
their heads, step carefully after.
Go deep, go down to silence.

Bridal Chamber, and Cathedral,
play of fancy which wants to discover
limestone making metaphors, shadow likenesses
and shadow play. Here is Dog, there is
Camel. We call this the Modern Art
gallery, but go down
further, one more, a couple more flights.
A boat at a landing stage idles,
another will carry us, silently
animated through the grotto
where cannibal worms hunt, breed, age,
consume their partners, are consumed.

How this would have pleased Coleridge,
riding a verbless river, the dome,
darkness, glowworm haven
generously imitating, freely outdoing, stars.

I have been here before, without words.
After their climax of love people lie thus,
as though drifting dark waters, caverned.
If you speak, all the lights will go out.
Say nothing. She reaches for his hand,
he presses her finger. The boat slides
curving back to its landing.

A guide at the stage sweeps his lamp
over a pool. What is he looking for?

1985

from Reading the Maps An Academic Exercise

All grid co-ordinates on this sheet are in terms of
false origin

Today when I was leaving you were gone
to the Library, hunting. So I couldn't say
what I wanted to say. No matter.
At nine I phoned about the mice and rats
which infest us, and departmental cats.
Are they procurable or not? No matter.

On the wall in front of my table are four
map sheets of Hokianga. One weakly faded,
the main part of a research scheme gone

mainly down the drain. Even when bought
it did not tell the truth (if truth I sought)
about that district. Some roads were gone

already, some were petered out to tracks,
some only projected. I quibble. It was truth
I pressed after to the blazing four
dusty points of the local compass, ground
by ground hunting for Mahimai and found
how legend bred him still, not one but four,

five or more versions of his Life and Times
in their ways different but yet held true for some
around those parts. They've not roads, mere tracks
in scrub or scruffy bush, beaten, halfway lost,
uncertain where they go, or stay. What cost
to follow them? What gains? Tracks are just tracks.

Or legends of them, getting nowhere much;
otherwise, fictions of any parish's mild dreams
mounted towards a future where times
would not work out of joint. Those sad dreams ailed
materially, the vision in them failed,
sailed off like so much junk caught up in Time's

hard-driving westerlies or blustering tides,
dumped among mangroves, slumped like driftwood on water
frontages. 'The tourist will find much
to interest him, from … ' From here to there,
hunting or haunted. Finding, found out where
roads disappear or don't amount to much.

Like schemes which I may think of, truth to tell,
No matter—no, that isn't true. Dusty, bitter
our ways work out, crudely move like tides,
nonetheless turn; comes turnabout in flow
and ebb, they matter. Down at the Head glow
finely the dunes. Promise still rides the tides.

. . . .

Leave the highway just past a store
almost opposite this shortcut through the gorge.
You want to bear west beyond the store,
back of the district high school. As you go
you raise an abandoned church (which is here)
with a small marae. Shortly, the river.
Follow its bank for a bit, until
a farmer's yard, between the cowbail and pigpens.
So drive slowly. You'll need to.
The map says the road ends there. Not true.

You are now right under a stone face.
See the quarry sign? Drive
into the quarry, keeping to the hill side
(because of a fall on the other hand to the river).
You skirt a shoulder. Look for an unformed road

lifting suddenly, steep. But get over the crest,
you're on top of packed sand.
Carry on to the Head. You cross
the old tramway which used to go up to
the Harbour, remains of the one time main road
to gumfields (south of the river and this next
river) out from the edge of the Forest. It went on
down the coast, then climbed inland on the line
of a Maori trail. Of course, the map doesn't
say anything about that. Maps can

tell you about what is supposedly present.
They know little about what's past and only
so much about outcomes. They work within
tacit limits. They're not good at predicting.
If everything is anywhere in flux
perhaps we may not read the same map twice.

. . . .

We may not read the same map twice,
especially where sands are on the move.

I speak loosely because thinking
not of a map's ineptitude but of
some shiftless nature which is prior.
Maps merely feign to represent the case.
Shiftless? A shifty case, more like,
unsure in its election as well as
in its origin, in its ground
of being as well as in its becoming—
neither works any way too well
for this instance. Are we not assuming
that what one has here to purport
to use as an example will survive
scrutiny? Somehow, has survived?

You follow me: I talk of what we have
and have not, of a sandhill lake
which comes and goes. Or maybe, came and went
since when I was last probing there
forestry men and engineers intent
on reform were then debating
how best to right an aberrant nature.

Their maps could not properly cope
with it. It was offence to natural
justice, natural right, and law.

It came and went. Worse, it was essential
when not existent. Boundaries
tentatively it had, often flouted.
It had? Check my legal fiction.
Rather, they had. Sometimes three lakes flaunted
themselves, sometimes two, or only

one, or none. Not only sands were on the move,
the lake dissolved, moved, reappeared,
will dwindle, again quicken. In remove
a presence, in presence a fact
substantial, insubstantial form
no less? This play with arid words,
dry as lake beds where cloudy midges swarm
until extinguished, the dunes made
to conform to rational order and
rabid, but useful, their surgent pines
established turn to increase wayward sand.

Something we know lost, gained by that.
Then how, best right aberrant nature?
Terms of reference not precise,
you guess, we may not read the same map twice.

. . . .

SYMBOLS

I cannot see our land clearly.
It comes and goes because covered with symbols.
Isn't this symptom of a psychotic state?

Take England now. In England I was given
to hold in my hand a necessary guide to
SYMBOLS USED ON THE MAPS, to hold as I was driven.
'O take fast hold'—that's Sidney, in *CS 32.*

Eleven different sections of symbols on one sheet,
twenty of them in one section. Here's from
another:
> *Castle or house with interesting interior*
> *Abbey, priory or other ecclesiastical*
> *   building (usually in ruins)*
> *Parish church*
> *Castle or house in ruins*
> *Archaeological monument*
> *Garden (usually attached to private house)*
> *Botanical gardens*
> * Zoological gardens*

but no *Interesting church*. Interesting churches are
in Symbols Used on Town Plans, another section.

Another section, of another life.
Here I am told how to find a *Frontier post.*
I shall go down to the river which may be

demented. I shall go on hoping to cross over.
Perhaps this is a frontier. We have crossed
frontiers before this.

Here is a sheet of paper. Write on it for me.
Go on, write on it. Why do you write *No.?*

What number do you mean?

. . . .

A QUESTION OF SCALE

To bring it all to scale, the given
    is 1:63360, 1 inch to 1 mile,
       and is outmoded.

That, given. Also false origin
    is given as base from which we work, almost capable
       until outmoded.

To bring it to scale I was driven
    or drove headlong, taking whatever a telltale dial
       on an outmoded

dashboard said was nearly true of *Then*
    and *There*, the literal. Metaphor too, and parable
       long since outmoded.

                       1985

Stories About Wooden Keyboards

That notable Pole, their pianist,
supremely their patriot, their first President
his countrymen's darling, darling of
highest society's *belle époque*,
he travelled the world with a wooden keyboard,
his practised toy. In an Atlantic liner's suite,
a stateroom on the Union Pacific,
at hotel windows commanding some boulevard
stippled with Monegasque vowels like flower baskets,
hour after hour he sat, his hands working,
working. After he went out — to Wigmore Hall,
Salle Pleyel, Carnegie, the Opera House.
There he put his hands to work. Acclaimed,
he made them legends. Everyone heard them,
knew them by heart. The heart was his, in them.
He stepped into his carriage and drew away.

Where pick up a story about a man in prison,
more likely a prisoner of war camp?
He got hold of a slab of wood,
something as ordinary as a bit of six by one, say.
Scratched on it with (suppose) a nail.
He etched a keyboard.

A notable Pole, he stopped being President.
He travelled the world on like Atlantic liners,
growing older. When asked would he play
he might agree, only if salon lights were turned down
so nobody saw his fingers arthritic knots,
the mistakes they were making.
Everyone pretended. He still had red hair?

That man in the *Stalag*. I know about him.
He played upon silence. That was what he had.
In the inner ear, by heart he got, a soprano
musicking *Hate! I loathe you. You're driving
me out of my mind . . . you want to commit me.*
He sweated it out at his keyboard. Silence was
just about all he had to play on. He didn't have to like it.

People who shared the hut with him pretended
not to hear. He sat for hours working his hands.
He might look through the mesh window,
through the camp's perimeter wire. Sometimes
in fields beyond he saw peasant women.
Perhaps one like you, as far apart.

1985

Deconstructing

I'm not going to try describing that run
from down by the creek where it starts being
a river, up to the ridge where everything falls
away westward. For the first time again
you look out on a sea bigger, further, than remembered.
Although, you have waited for it
                              from down there
where *shabby, ramshackle, derelict* are just terms
for occupation. An abandoned railway line's last
station, scruffy general store also garage,
wornout fridges at roadside where used to be
old milkcans for meat and mail; after,
that place where the post office was and the school
then, and then where the school before that was.
It's all sheep now.
                      God, how many years of it
passing through, passing by. I was transported,
have driven, drive. Going from here to there,
that's a text. And another text, and one more, rewritten.
The seeing part, and saying part:

I said to one wife, replied.
I said to another wife, replied.
Each, another text, another saying, another seeing.
Neither did the one see or other say but yet
what one saw another has or has not said,
while I am telling one what I am thinking/said
to other ("Around this bend used to be
a hell of a big pothole—*whang!* Still is")
as if it were always true. We live by
what's past made over 'As if', so many milkcans,
so many projects for the future

You can't step twice into the same river.
What you first dipped toe in was only as if, truly.
But when you get up on the top, and the sea

is there, the remembering of it as well
from before first perhaps, that's another
part of a text and feels like
                      the same again.
Heraclitus was only talking about rivers,
or about when a shallow creek running over stone
begins to think that it's a river.

                                        1985

Carp

Without trailing any words like bubbles
a jade carp swims only a few metres above

parti-coloured houses across our street,
an ordinary street in our ordinary suburb.

There are no strings attached to this deal.
The carp swims steadily, rising over a pine —

a Norfolk pine — which you might have thought
was in the way, but no. It's no problem.

Now the fish steers towards the bush gully
where heron are nesting, and disappears.

Mr Whippy comes down the slope in low gear
sadly crying *to you Happy birthday to you*

and stops to confide, 'It's not every day
you see something like that,' and we agree.

We too are sad. Where has all the magic gone?
Is it, back underground where this carp came from?

Grandson Bernard stepped out of the car, opened
his arms, and the fish flew away without even
    saying Goodbye.

                                      1992

LOUIS JOHNSON

Louis Johnson (1924–88) published his first collection, Stanza and Scene: Poems, *in 1945. A journalist, editor and teacher, Johnson founded the* New Zealand Poetry Yearbook. *After spending much of the 1970s in Australia, he returned to Wellington in 1980. His* Last Poems *were published posthumously in 1990.*

Magpie and Pines

That dandy black-and-white gentleman doodling notes
on fragrant pinetops over the breakfast morning,
has been known to drop through mists of bacon-fat,
with a gleaming eye, to the road where a child stood, screaming.

And in the dark park — the secretive trees — have boys
harboured their ghosts, built huts, and buried treasure,
and lovers made from metallic kisses alloys

more precious, and driven the dark from pleasure.

A child was told that bird as his guardian angel
reported daily on actions contrived to displease;
stands petrified in the sound of wings, a strangle
of screams knotting his throat beneath the winter leaves.

Look back and laugh on the lovers whose white mating
made magpie of dark; whose doodling fingers swore
various fidelities and fates. They found the world waiting,
and broke the silence. A raven croaks 'Nevermore'

to their progenitive midnight. The guardian is aloof
on his roof of the small world, composing against morning
a new, ironic ballad. The lover has found small truth
in the broken silence, in faith, or the fate-bird moaning.

1952

Here Together Met

I praise Saint Everyman, his house and home
   In every paint-bright gardened suburb shining
With all the age's verities and welcome
   Medalled upon him in contentment dining:
      And toast with gin and bitters
      The Muse of baby-sitters.

I sing Dame Everyone's whose milky breast
   Suckles the neighbourhood with pins and plans
Adding new rooms to their eternal rest,
   The next night's meat already in the pan:
      And toast with whisky and ice,
      The Goddess who keeps things nice.

I honour Maid Anybody's whose dreams are shaping
   Lusts in her heart down the teasing garden-path
Where she stops in time as she must at the gaping
   Graveyard of Hell and rescues her girlish laugh:
      And toast in rum and cloves
      The course of balanced love.

I drink to Son Mostpeople's whose honourable pride
   In things being what they are will not let him run,
But who keeps things going even after he has died
   In a distant desert clutching an empty gun:
      And toast in brandy and lime
      The defenders of our great good time.

1957

Bread and a Pension

It was not our duty to question but to guard,
maintaining order; see that none escaped
who may be required for questioning by the State.
The price was bread and a pension and not a hard

life on the whole. Some even scraped
enough on the side to build up a fairish estate

for the day of retirement. I never could
understand the complaints of the restless ones
who found the hours long, time dragging;
it always does. The old hands knew how good
the guardroom fire could be, the guns
gleaming against the wall and the nagging

wind like a wife — outside. There were cards
for such occasions and good companions
who truly were more than home since they shared
one's working life without difference or hard words,
aimed at much the same thing, and shared opinions
on news they read. If they cared

much it was for the quiet life. You cannot hold
that against them, since it's roundly human
and any decent man would want it the same.
For these were decent: did as they were told,
fed prisoners, buried the dead, and, on occasion
loaded the deathcart with those who were sent to the flames.

1964

Song in the Hutt Valley

Cirrus, stratus, cumulus,
Gentle or giant winds
Invoke the trees and cabbages;
The rising jet-trail finds
Space out of sight of valleys
Where the muddy rivers run
Past houses, groves and alleys
In the residential sun.

The placid eaves of evening
Purpled by homing sun
Pay little heed to reckoning
Broadcast by weathermen.
Houses still grow, the children
Like cabbages are seen;
Grandfather's thoughts are hidden
Upon the bowling green.

The sky's as much ambition
As anyone could eye,
Forecasts of nimbus, aeroplane
Pass over and pass by;
Tucked up at home, the passive
Who own their plot of ground
Sleep though the radio-active
Have a new formation found.

While history happens elsewhere
And few of us get hurt

Why should Grandad wish for hair
To line his sporting shirt?
His heart's at one with the children,
He can be overlooked
And left to play in the garden,
His place in heaven's booked.

The weather is established;
It will be wet — or fine —
The houses all are furnished —
In the styles of 'forty-nine.
No need to worry, hurry;
The questionmarks will keep;
The clouds and airmen marry
And the boisterous children sleep.

1965

Death of the Bosun's Mate

I, the bosun's mate, John Reading,
this morning, in rum-reeking bedding,
departed this life while full as a tick:
in a sheet I roll in Endeavour's wake.

I had been at the wine, then was given rum,
which oiled my entry to Kingdom Come;
what better way to meet one's maker
than full of Madeira and black Jamaica?

I lived a full life — kept full as I could,
sustained by foods that came casked in wood;
now I must suck at the mermaid's nipple,
the salt Pacific my only tipple.

None can ask more than to die as he lived,
so with these words I'd be engraved:
Content as the groom on his night of wedding,
lies the bosun's mate, John Reading.

1975

The Perfect Symbol

I remember reading as a boy, Giotto,
Asked for a picture fit for a Pope's wall,
Picked up a brush, painted a perfect circle,
And offered this as prize to the puzzled pontiff
Whose shocked reaction was a dark reproof.
'No, sir,' the painter answered, 'Nothing less
Than this would be apt gift for your great grace.
This line is endless and begins nowhere.
It contains all the truth a man might know
And is a barrier excluding dross.
Or, it's a world, and outside it, the heavens
And every aspiration worthy of him.
I made it with one stroke: you cannot tell

Where I began it, only that, through grace,
Patience, the pain of all my craft,
I made what Nature does not make — the circle,
The thing enclosed, entire, perfection's symbol.'

Humbled, his master gave it pride of place
Upon the palace wall, and no doubt gave
Much thought, as well, to what might burn within
A peasant breast that beat beyond itself
In realms of contemplation learning strove for
Without, always, the same degrees of insight.
Then let Giotto's circle stand for those
Who see beyond the lines and shapes of things,
The orders, and the orderings of men's lives,
And all the passing show, to what might be
Ultimate truths contained in a simple act,
The maker's hand unveiling what is hidden
From understanding by what's understood,
And what is real surprisingly revealed,
Hard, simple, whole, something to stand forever.

                                                    1975

The Seventies

These days you keep on meeting,
stooped and desiccated, those
who laugh sadly, describe themselves
as 'the oldest living hippie', or
'the first bikie': looking back over a shoulder
uncertain how they got here so unprepared
for the ongoing, familiar, habitual world crisis.

They're a little out of tune
with the new music and cannot do
much about the falling birthrate.
Perhaps the world will not become
as young as it seemed to be getting
when they were. And if the roads are better
they are not leading anywhere now so soon.

A little less inclined to believe
what they read on placards, and more
amiable about opposing forces,
they see their strength had to be tested —
that even the new was not to be totally trusted —
and power still corrupts. In high places
they recognise no gods; sense father's many faces.

And the pulse of the big machines
still revvs between odd-jobs and going
to funerals. Change has indeed come,
they console themselves, between one suburb
of the global village and others. The road-houses
serve blander plastic steaks: their sons
commute to bread in the dying days of Ford.

                                                    1982

Uneasy Resident

You could say I came home to the hooley,
met up with the Maoritanga and found
everything up the booai. It hasn't
been easy to learn to relive the language.

Or to rethink the position, or any one
of the sixty-nine that used to add up to love:
something sickens in the social stewpot:
the prices are up and everyone has to pay.

Outside the electric fences a few talk barter,
know there is wind, trees, but that there was never
much evidence of active nature — a thriving
animal life — nothing larger than vermin, drab birds.

Not a country for people. Everyone here is
a migrant spat from another climate of failure
to feed on roots or look for them. To make
clearings in the undergrowth, proselytize innocence.

All of these factors seem to tell us something
of a rough message like an ad-man's jingle:
A great place to raise children — but we cannot
easily let them grow to full stature, laugh, fart,

stand. Lately we have begun to tear more of it
down to rebuild. We erect the age of plastic
towers and the glassy stare. A new law shaping
intends the roads shall be safer for heavy traffic.

Wherever you go you take yourself. Returning,
I sense the drift is not movement so much
as a running-on-the spot as in those younger dreams:
you were always running away but never moving

while the hot breath of pursuit pounded behind
nearer and nearer with a tongue like a stopwatch.

1984

JOHN MALE

Born in 1913, John Male served with the New Zealand Forces in the North African and Italian campaigns. Later he served for 18 years on the staff of the United Nations before retiring to New Zealand and co-founding the New Zealand Foundation for Peace Studies. He lives in Mahurangi Heads, Warkworth. His poems were composed circa 1944.

Political Footnote

Over the town of Sant' Eusanio del Sangro the cold
   inaccessible snows of Maiella. Peasants
   looked to them for weather
   when the Romans were here.

Now the town is silent:
    two days ago the Germans, strong
    alpine soldiers, laid
    high-explosive under buildings; before they left
    machine-gunned Luigi Consalvo
    who had barred them entry . . .

Tear down, discreetly, the portrait of Mussolini
    from the wall of the carbinieri office;
    take away the symbols from the Casa del Fascio;
    obliterate the salutations to Duce, Duce, Duce.

But who will rebuild, from this rubble,
    homes for two thousand seven hundred and fifty people,
    and who will comfort the widow
    of Luigi Consalvo,
    and whose portrait shall we substitute
    in the carabinieri office?

De Giacomo admitted he had been a fascist
    (but I had to be, or I didn't eat,
    nor would my children eat;
    we peasants knew nothing of politics).

O.K. signore. Maybe you didn't
    see which way the corporate state was heading,
    and sure your children had to eat;
    but meantime you'd better set about
    rebuilding the town of Sant Eusanio del Sangro,
    and comforting the widow of Luigi Consalvo.

                                                    1989

from Four Italian Seasons

2. *Filignano, April 1944*

In this village the people
    are tired of politics. Politics is the size
    of the flour ration, the lifting of mines
    from the fields of the commune. Home
    is where an old woman makes bean soup
    over a twig fire. Home
    is a troubled sleep on flagstones
    under one blanket.

They are tired of politics, and love
    died last year when the enemy
    took labourers by force; love
    died, and the leaves fell, and
    all winter the boughs were black
    and bare, shell-splintered.

But already on the trees, green leaves,
    and in the vineyard
    promise of next year's red wine.

                                                    1989

Girl with Her Hair Cut Short

Bencini Paolo, partisan, having fought
   against tedeschi and republican fascists
   six months, having lost home and wife and all
   I hoped to be, now declare, I the undersigned:

That Adriana, the daughter of Pavolini Giulio, he deceased,
   went to bed with the tedeschi, offered
   herself for pleasure, not gain,
   because they pleased her, she for her part
   pleasing them for the moment.

She also it was who betrayed three of us,
   three partisan fighters, telling
   in passionate whispers where they lay hiding
   in the woods behind Montespertoli.

So two nights ago we took her quickly
   and cut short her black hair with scissors
   and shaved her head.

This is a sign to wantons . . .
   let those others whom the enemy pleased, take warning
   from the bald white head of Adriana,
   and may her shame and her humiliation
   and her fierce hate against us
   smoulder a life-time.

          1989

Not All of Us

Not all of us are articulate
   but is it necessary to tell everything?

Easy to record minutely the tortured
   second between whine and shell burst,
   the road bracketed, the Military Policeman at the corner
   staggering concussed to the ambulance;
   easy to record afterwards the mock heroics
   about numbers on high-explosive shells.

These things are with us continually;
   day after day; and we are careless and dull, finally,
   from too much experience.

Who wants to be articulate? These
   are years we have lost; love a memory;
   excuse us if we are silent
   as the dead are.

          1989

JAMES K. BAXTER

Born in Dunedin, James K. Baxter (1926–1972) was schooled in England and New Zealand before attending the University of Otago. A prolific poet, playwright, critic, amateur theologian and social commentator, Baxter became a prominent figure in the late 1960s counter-culture and established a community at Jerusalem on the Whanganui River.

High Country Weather

Alone we are born
   And die alone;
Yet see the red-gold cirrus
   Over snow-mountain shine.

Upon the upland road
   Ride easy, stranger:
Surrender to the sky
   Your heart of anger.

1948

The Bay

On the road to the bay was a lake of rushes
Where we bathed at times and changed in the bamboos.
Now it is rather to stand and say:
How many roads we take that lead to Nowhere,
The alley overgrown, no meaning now but loss:
Not that veritable garden where everything comes easy.

And by the bay itself were cliffs with carved names
And a hut on the shore beside the Maori ovens.
We raced boats from the banks of the pumice creek
Or swam in those autumnal shallows
Growing cold in amber water, riding the logs
Upstream, and waiting for the taniwha.

So now I remember the bay and the little spiders
On driftwood, so poisonous and quick.
The carved cliffs and the great outcrying surf
With currents round the rocks and the birds rising.
A thousand times an hour is torn across
And burned for the sake of going on living.
But I remember the bay that never was
And stand like stone, and cannot turn away.

1948

Blow, wind of fruitfulness

Blow, wind of fruitfulness
   Blow from the buried sun:
Blow from the buried kingdom
   Where heart and mind are one.

Blow, wind of fruitfulness,
   The murmuring leaves remember;
For deep in doorless rock
   Awaits their green September.

Blow from the wells of night:
   The blind flower breathes thy coming
Birds that are silent now
   And buds of barren springing.

Blow from beyond our day.
   The hill-born streams complain;
Hear from their stony courses
   The great sea rise again.

Blow on the mouth of morning
   Renew the single eye:
And from remembered darkness
   Our immortality.

             1948

The Cave

In a hollow of the fields, where one would least expect it,
Stark and suddenly this limestone buttress:
A tree whose roots are bound about the stones,
Broad-leaved, hides well that crevice at the base
That leads, one guesses, to the sunless kingdom
Where souls endure the ache of Proserpine.

Entering where no man it seemed
Had come before, I found a rivulet
Beyond the rock door running in the dark.
Where it sprang from in the heart of the hill
No one could tell: alone
It ran like Time there in the dank silence.

I spoke once and my voice resounded
Among the many pillars. Further in
Were bones of sheep that strayed and died
In nether darkness, brown and water-worn.
The smell of earth was like a secret language
That dead men speak and we have long forgotten.

The whole weight of the hill hung over me.
Gladly I would have stayed there and been hidden
From every beast that moves beneath the sun,
From age's enmity and love's contagion:
But turned and climbed back to the barrier,
Pressed through and came to dazzling daylight out.

             1948

Wild Bees

Often in summer, on a tarred bridge plank standing,
Or downstream between willows, a safe Ophelia drifting

In a rented boat — I had seen them come and go,
Those wild bees swift as tigers, their gauze wings a-glitter
In passionless industry, clustering black at the crevice
Of a rotten cabbage tree, where their hive was hidden low.

But never strolled too near. Till one half-cloudy evening
Of ripe January, my friends and I
Came, gloved and masked to the eyes like plundering desperadoes,
To smoke them out. Quiet beside the stagnant river
We trod wet grasses down, hearing the crickets chitter
And waiting for light to drain from the wounded sky.

Before we reached the hive their sentries saw us
And sprang invisible through the darkening air,
Stabbed, and died in stinging. The hive woke. Poisonous fuming
Of sulphur filled the hollow trunk, and crawling
Blue flame sputtered — yet still their suicidal
Live raiders dived and clung to our hands and hair.

O it was Carthage under the Roman torches,
Or loud with flames and falling timber, Troy!
A job well botched. Half of the honey melted
And half the rest young grubs. Through earth-black smouldering
    ashes
And maimed bees groaning, we drew out our plunder.
Little enough their gold, and slight our joy.

Fallen then the city of instinctive wisdom.
Tragedy is written distinct and small:
A hive burned on a cool night in summer.
But loss is a precious stone to me, a nectar
Distilled in time, preaching the truth of winter
To the fallen heart that does not cease to fall.

                                                      1953

Poem in the Matukituki Valley

Some few yards from the hut the standing beeches
Let fall their dead limbs, overgrown
With feathered moss and filigree of bracken.
The rotted wood splits clean and hard
Close-grained to the driven axe, with sound of water
Sibilant falling and high nested birds.

In winter blind with snow; but in full summer
The forest blanket sheds its cloudy pollen
And cloaks a range in undevouring fire.
Remote the land's heart. Though the wild scrub cattle
Acclimatized, may learn
Shreds of her purpose, or the taloned kea.

For those who come as I do, half-aware,
Wading the swollen
Matukituki waist-high in snow water,
And stumbling where the mountains throw their dice
Of boulders huge as houses, or the smoking

Cataract flings its arrows on our path —

For us the land is matrix and destroyer,
Resentful, darkly known
By sunset omens, low words heard in branches;
Or where the red deer lift their innocent heads
Snuffing the wind for danger,
And from our footfall's menace bound in terror.

Three emblems of the heart I carry folded
As charms against flood water, sliding shale:
Pale gentian, lily, and bush orchid.
The peaks too have names to suit their whiteness,
Stargazer and Moonraker,
A sailor's language and a mountaineer's.

And those who sleep in close bags fitfully
Besieged by wind in a snowline bivouac —
The carrion parrot with red underwing
Clangs on the roof by night, and daybreak brings
Raincloud on purple ranges, light reflected
Stainless from crumbling glacier, dazzling snow,

Do they not, clay in that unearthly furnace,
Endure the hermit's peace
And mindless ecstasy? Blue-lipped crevasse
And smooth rock chimney straddling — a communion
With what eludes our net — Leviathan
Stirring to ocean birth our inland waters?

Sky's purity; the altar cloth of snow
On deathly summits laid; or avalanche
That shakes the rough moraine with giant laughter;
Snowplume and whirlwind — what are these
But His flawed mirror who gave the mountain strength
And dwells in holy calm, undying freshness?

Therefore we turn, hiding our souls' dullness
From that too blinding glass: turn to the gentle
Dark of the human daydream, child and wife,
Patience of stone and soil, the lawful city
Where man may live, and no wild trespass
Of what's eternal shake his grave of time.

1953

Lament for Barney Flanagan

Licensee of the Hesperus Hotel

Flanagan got up on a Saturday morning,
Pulled on his pants while the coffee was warming;
He didn't remember the doctor's warning,
    'Your heart's too big, Mr Flanagan.'

Barney Flanagan, sprung like a frog
From a wet root in an Irish bog —

May his soul escape from the tooth of the dog!
    God have mercy on Flanagan.

Barney Flanagan R.I.P.
Rode to his grave on Hennessy's
Like a bottle-cork boat in the Irish Sea.
    The bell-boy rings for Flanagan.

Barney Flanagan, ripe for a coffin,
Eighteen stone and brandy-rotten,
Patted the housemaid's velvet bottom —
    'Oh, is it you, Mr Flanagan?'

The sky was bright as a new milk token.
Bill the Bookie and Shellshock Hogan
Waited outside for the pub to open —
    'Good day, Mr Flanagan.'

At noon he was drinking in the lounge bar corner
With a sergeant of police and a racehorse owner
When the Angel of Death looked over his shoulder —
    'Could you spare a moment, Flanagan?'

Oh the deck was cut; the bets were laid;
But the very last card that Barney played
Was the Deadman's Trump, the bullet of Spades —
    'Would you like more air, Mr Flanagan?'

The priest came running but the priest came late
For Barney was banging at the Pearly Gate.
St Peter said, 'Quiet! You'll have to wait
    For a hundred masses, Flanagan.'

The regular boys and the loud accountants
Left their nips and their seven-ounces
As chickens fly when the buzzard pounces —
    'Have you heard about old Flanagan?'

Cold in the parlour Flanagan lay
Like a bride at the end of her marriage day.
The Waterside Workers' Band will play
    A brass goodbye to Flanagan.

While publicans drink their profits still,
While lawyers flock to be in at the kill,
While Aussie barmen milk the till
    We will remember Flanagan.

For Barney had a send-off and no mistake.
He died like a man for his country's sake;
And the Governor-General came to his wake.
    Drink again to Flanagan!

Despise not, O Lord, the work of Thine own hands
And let light perpetual shine upon him.

1954

Crossing Cook Strait

The night was clear, sea calm; I came on deck
To stretch my legs, find perhaps
Gossip, a girl in green slacks at the rail
Or just the logline feathering a dumb wake.

The ship swung in the elbow of the Strait.
'Dolphins!' I cried — 'let the true sad Venus
Rise riding her shoals, teach me as once to wonder
And wander at ease, be glad and never regret.'

But night increased under the signal stars.
In the dark bows, facing the flat sea,
Stood one I had not expected, yet knew without surprise
As the Janus made formidable by loveless years.

His coat military; his gesture mild —
'Well met,' he said, 'on the terrestrial journey
From chaos into light — what light it is
Contains our peril and purpose, history has not revealed.'

'Sir —', I began. He spoke with words of steel —
'I am Seddon and Savage, the socialist father.
You have known me only in my mask of Dionysus
Amputated in bar rooms, dismembered among wheels.

'I woke in my civil tomb hearing a shout
For bread and justice. It was not here.
That sound came thinly over the waves from China;
Stones piled on my grave had all but shut it out.

'I walked forth gladly to find the angry poor
Who are my nation; discovered instead
The glutton seagulls squabbling over crusts
And policies made and broken behind locked doors.

'I have watched the poets also at their trade.
I have seen them burning with a wormwood brilliance.
Love was the one thing lacking on their page,
The crushed herb of grief at another's pain.

'Your civil calm breeds inward poverty
That chafes for change. The ghost of Adam
Gibbering demoniac in drawing-rooms
Will drink down hemlock with his sugared tea.

'You feed your paupers concrete. They work well,
Ask for no second meal, vote, pay tribute
Of silence on Anzac Day in the pub urinal;
Expose death only by a mushroom smell.

'My counsel was naïve. Anger is bread
To the poor, their guns more accurate than justice,
Because their love has not decayed to a wintry fungus
And hope to the wish for power among the dead.

'In Kaitangata the miner's falling sweat
Wakes in the coal seam fossil flowers.
The clerk puts down his pen and takes his coat;
He will not be back today or the next day either.'

With an ambiguous salute he left me.
The ship moved into a stronger sea,
Bludgeoned alive by the rough mystery
Of love in the running straits of history.

1958

My love late walking

My love late walking in the rain's white aisles
I break words for, though many tongues
Of night deride and the moon's boneyard smile

Cuts to the quick our newborn sprig of song.
See and believe, my love, the late yield
Of bright grain, the sparks of harvest wrung

From difficult joy. My heart is an open field.
There you may stray wide or stand at home
Nor dread the giant's bone and broken shield

Or any tendril locked on a thunder stone,
Nor fear, in the forked grain, my hawk who flies
Down to your feathered sleep alone

Striding blood coloured on a wind of sighs.
Let him at the heart of your true dream move,
My love, in the lairs of hope behind your eyes.

I sing, to the rain's harp, of light renewed,
The black tares broken, fresh the phoenix light
I lost among time's rags and burning tombs.

My love walks long in harvest aisles tonight.

1958

Ballad of Calvary Street

On Calvary Street are trellises
Where bright as blood the roses bloom,
And gnomes like pagan fetishes
Hang their hats on an empty tomb
Where two old souls go slowly mad,
National Mum and Labour Dad.

Each Saturday when full of smiles
The children come to pay their due,
Mum takes down the family files
And cover to cover she thumbs them through,
Poor Len before he went away
And Mabel on her wedding day.

The meal-brown scones display her knack,
Her polished oven spits with rage,
While in Grunt Grotto at the back
Dad sits and reads the Sporting Page,
Then ambles out in boots of lead
To weed around the parsnip bed.

A giant parsnip sparks his eye,
Majestic as the Tree of Life;
He washes it and rubs it dry
And takes it in to his old wife —
'Look Laura, would that be a fit?
The bastard has a flange on it!'

When both were young she would have laughed,
A goddess in her tartan skirt,
But wisdom, age and mothercraft
Have rubbed it home that men like dirt:
Five children and a fallen womb,
A golden crown beyond the tomb.

Nearer the bone, sin is sin,
And women bear the cross of woe,
And that affair with Mrs Flynn
(It happened thirty years ago)
Though never mentioned, means that he
Will get no sugar in his tea.

The afternoon goes by, goes by,
The angels harp above a cloud;
A son-in-law with spotted tie
And daughter Alice fat and loud
Discuss the virtues of insurance
And stuff their tripes with trained endurance.

Flood-waters hurl upon the dyke
And Dad himself can go to town,
For little Charlie on his trike
Has ploughed another iris down.
His parents rise to chain the beast,
Brush off the last crumbs of their lovefeast.

And so these two old fools are left,
A rosy pair in evening light,
To question Heaven's dubious gift,
To hag and grumble, growl and fight:
The love they kill won't let them rest,
Two birds that peck in one fouled nest.

Why hammer nails? Why give no change?
Habit, habit clogs them dumb.
The Sacred Heart above the range
Will bleed and burn till Kingdom Come,
But Yin and Yang won't ever meet
In Calvary Street, in Calvary Street.

1960

On the Death of her Body

It is a thought breaking the granite heart
Time has given me, that my one treasure,
Your limbs, those passion-vines, that bamboo body

Should age and slacken, rot
Some day in a ghastly clay-stopped hole.
They led me to the mountains beyond pleasure

Where each is not gross body or blank soul
But a strong harp the wind of genesis
Makes music in, such resonant music

That I was Adam, loosened by your kiss
From time's hard bond, and you,
My love, in the world's first summer stood

Plucking the flowers of the abyss.

1961

At Taieri Mouth

Flax-pods unload their pollen
Above the steel-bright cauldron

Of Taieri, the old water-dragon
Sliding out from a stone gullet

Below the Maori-ground. Scrub horses
Come down at night to smash the fences

Of the whaler's children. Trypots have rusted
Leaving the oil of anger in the blood

Of those who live in two-roomed houses
Mending nets or watching from a window

The great south sky fill up with curdled snow.
Their cows eat kelp along the beaches.

The purple sailor drowned in thighboots
Drifting where the currents go

Cannot see the flame some girl has lighted
In a glass chimney, but in five days' time

With bladder-weed around his throat
Will ride the drunken breakers in.

1966

A Takapuna Business Man Considers his Son's Death in Korea

Your sailboat yawns for you in the spidery shed
Among the mangrove trunks; I watched you build it
Before they hid you under stones in a pit
In North Korean ice. Your mother's head,

High cheekbones, hard black eyes! At Cherry Farm
She waits for God, a tube-fed schizophrene
With the unwrinkled forehead of eighteen.
The harbour's death-mask sweats in summer calm.

In my wall safe I keep the fir tree cone
You gave me once. You liked your whisky-mad
Iron-gutted killjoy of a Dad;
Too well perhaps. Why did I let you groan

That rugged year, when you reached out to me
For help, down South? I thought, 'The lion's whelp
Must learn to fight the jackals without help' —
And you became a prefect. Sodomy

Is what they teach. I heard that little slut,
Your stepmother, after she'd piled me drunk
Under a blanket in my dogbox bunk,
Creep out to join you in the garden hut;

I never whispered of it. Muskets blazed
From the hunched snipers of pohutukawa
The day you stole my wallet and my car
And drove to Puhoi. Now I fumble dazed

Outside the door. O Absalom, the beast
Of anger, time and age will grind my skull
To powder! Spiders web your sailboat's hull.
The sword of Joab rages in the East.

1966

from Pig Island Letters

(to Maurice Shadbolt)

1

The gap you speak of — yes, I find it so,
The menopause of the mind. I think of it
As a little death, practising for the greater,
For the undertaker who won't have read
Your stories or my verse —
Or that a self had died
Who handled ideas like bombs,

In that bare southern town
At a party on a cold night
Men seen as ghosts, women like trees walking,
Seen from the floor, a forest of legs and bums
For the climbing boy, the book-bred one.

And this, the moment of art, can never stay.
Wives in the kitchen cease to smile as we go
Into the gap itself, the solid night
Where poor drunks fear the icy firmament:
Man is a walking grave,

That is where I start from. Though often
Where the Leith Stream wandered down
Its culvert, crinkled labia of blossom
On the trees beside the weir
Captured and held the fugitive
From time, from self, from the iron pyramid,

These were diversions. Give my love
To Vic. He is aware of
The albatross. In the Otago storms
Carrying spray to salt the landward farms
The wind is a drunkard. Whoever can listen
Long enough will write again.

2

From an old house shaded with macrocarpas
Rises my malady.
Love is not valued much in Pig Island
Though we admire its walking parody,

That brisk gaunt woman in the kitchen
Feeding the coal range, sullen
To all strangers, lest one should be
Her antique horn-red Satan.

Her man, much baffled, grousing in the pub,
Discusses sales
Of yearling lambs, the timber in a tree
Thrown down by autumn gales,

Her daughter, reading in her room
A catalogue of dresses,
Can drive a tractor, goes to Training College,
Will vote on the side of the Bosses,

Her son is moodier, has seen
An angel with a sword
Standing above the clump of old man manuka
Just waiting for the word

To overturn the cities and the rivers
And split the house like a rotten totara log.
Quite unconcerned he sets his traps for 'possums
And whistles to his dog.

The man who talks to the masters of Pig Island
About the love they dread
Plaits ropes of sand, yet I was born among them
And will lie some day with their dead.

9

Look at the simple caption of success,
The poet as family man,
Head between thumbs at mass, nailing a trolley,

Letting the tomcat in:
Then turn the hourglass over, find the other
Convict self, incorrigible, scarred
With what the bottle and the sex games taught,
The black triangle, the whips of sin.
The first gets all his meat from the skull-faced twin
Sharpening a dagger out of a spoon,
Struggling to speak through the gags of a poem:
When both can make a third my work is done.

Nor will the obituary ever indicate
How much we needed friends,
Like Fitz at the National
Speaking of his hydatid cyst,
A football underneath the lung,
Or Lowry in Auckland: all who held the door
And gave us space for art,
Time for the re-shaping of the heart:
Those whom the arrow-makers honour least,
Companions to the manbeast,
One man in many, touching the flayed hide gently,
A brother to the artist and a nurse.

The trees rustle as October comes
And fantails batter on the glass,
Season when the day nurse tuts and hums
Laying out pills and orange juice
For one who walks the bridge of dread
As oedema sets in,
While through the bogs and gullies of Pig Island
Bellies are beaten like skin drums
In pup tents, under flax or lupin shade,

As if the sun were a keg. And this man
On the postman's round will meditate
The horns of Jacob withered at the root
Or quirks of weather. None
Grows old easily. The poem is
A plank laid over the lion's den.

1966

A Small Ode on Mixed Flatting

*Elicited by the decision of the
Otago University authorities to
forbid this practice among students*

Dunedin nights are often cold
(I notice it as I grow old);
The south wind scourging from the Pole
Drives every rat to his own hole,
Lashing the drunks who wear thin shirts
And little girls in mini-skirts.
Leander, that Greek lad, was bold
To swim the Hellespont raging cold

To visit Hero in her tower
Just for an amorous half-hour,
and lay his wet brine-tangled head
Upon her pillow — Hush! The dead
Can get good housing — Thomas Bracken,
Smellie, McLeod, McColl, McCracken,
A thousand founding fathers lie
Well roofed against the howling sky
In mixed accommodation — Hush!
It is the living make us blush
Because the young have wicked hearts
And blood to swell their private parts.
To think of corpses pleases me;
They keep such perfect chastity.
O Dr Williams, you were right
To shove the lovers out of sight;
Now they can wander half the night
Through coffee house and street and park
And fidget in the dripping dark,
While we play Mozart and applaud
The angel with the flaming sword!
King Calvin in his grave will smile
To know we know that man is vile;
But Robert Burns, that sad old rip
From whom I got my Fellowship
Will grunt upon his rain-washed stone
Above the empty Octagon,
And say — 'O that I had the strength
To slip yon lassie half a length!
Apollo! Venus! Bless my ballocks!
Where are the games, the hugs, the frolics?
Are all you bastards melancholics?
Have you forgotten that your city
Was founded well in bastardry
And half your elders (God be thankit)
Were born the wrong side of the blanket?
You scholars, throw away your books
And learn your songs from lasses' looks
As I did once —' Ah, well; it's grim;
But I will have to censor him.
He liked to call a spade a spade
And toss among the glum and staid
A poem like a hand grenade —
And I remember clearly how
(Truth is the only poet's vow)
When my spare tyre was half this size,
With drumming veins and bloodshot eyes
I blundered through the rain and sleet
To dip my wick in Castle Street,
Not on the footpath — no, in a flat,
With a sofa where I often sat,
Smoked, drank, cursed, in the company
Of a female student who unwisely

Did not mind but would pull the curtain
Over the window — And did a certain
Act occur? It did. It did.
As Byron wrote of Sennacherib —
'The Assyrian came down like a wolf on the fold
And his cohorts were gleaming in purple and gold' —
But now, at nearly forty-two,
An inmate of the social zoo,
Married, baptized, well heeled, well shod,
Almost on speaking terms with God,
I intend to save my moral bacon
By fencing the young from fornication!
Ah, Dr Williams, I agree
We need more walls at the Varsity;
The students who go double-flatting
With their she-catting and tom-catting
Won't ever get a pass in Latin;
The moral mainstay of the nation
Is careful, private masturbation;
A vaseline jar or a candle
Will drive away the stink of scandal!
The Golden Age will come again —
Those tall asthenic bird-like men
With spectacles and lecture notes,
Those girls with wool around their throats
Studying till their eyes are yellow
A new corrupt text of *Othello*,
Vaguely agnostic, rationalist,
A green banana in each fist
To signify the purity
Of educational esctasy —
And, if they marry, they will live
By the Clinical Imperative:
A car, a fridge, a radiogram,
A clean well-fitted diaphragm,
Two-and-a-half children per
Family; to keep out thunder
Insurance policies for each;
A sad glad fortnight at the beach
Each year, when Mum and Dad will bitch
From some old half-forgotten itch —
Turn on the lights! — or else the gas!
If I kneel down like a stone at Mass
And wake my good wife with bad dreams,
And scribble verse on sordid themes,
At least I know man was not made
On the style of a slot-machine arcade —
Almost, it seems, the other day,
When Francis threw his coat away
And stood under the palace light
Naked in the Bishop's sight
To marry Lady Poverty
In folly and virginity,

The angels laughed — do they then weep
Tears of blood if two should sleep
Together and keep the cradle warm?
Each night of earth, though the wind storm,
Black land behind, white sea in front,
Leander swims the Hellespont;
To Hero's bed he enters cold;
And he will drown; and she grow old —
But what they tell each other there
You'll not find in a book anywhere.

1967

from Jerusalem Sonnets

(Poems for Colin Durning)

1

The small grey cloudy louse that nests in my beard
Is not, as some have called it, 'a pearl of God' —

No, it is a fiery tormentor
Waking me at two a.m.

Or thereabouts, when the lights are still on
In the houses in the pa, to go across thick grass

Wet with rain, feet cold, to kneel
For an hour or two in front of the red flickering

Tabernacle light — what He sees inside
My meandering mind I can only guess —

A madman, a nobody, a raconteur
Whom He can joke with — 'Lord,' I ask Him,

'Do You or don't You expect me to put up with lice?'
His silent laugh still shakes the hills at dawn.

2

The bees that have been hiving above the church porch
Are some of them killed by the rain —

I see their dark bodies on the step
As I go in — but later on I hear

Plenty of them singing with what seems a virile joy
In the apple tree whose reddish blossoms fall

At the centre of the paddock — there's an old springcart,
Or at least two wheels and the shafts, upended

Below the tree — Elijah's chariot it could be, Colin,
Because my mind takes fire a little there

Thinking of the woman who is like a tree
Whom I need not name — clumsily gripping my beads,

While the bees drum overhead and the bouncing calves look at
A leather-jacketed madman set on fire by the wind.

10

Dark night — or rather, only the stars
Somebody called 'those watchfires in the sky' —

Too cold for me the thoughts of God — I crossed
The paddock on another errand,

And the cows were slow to move outside the gate
Where they sleep at night — nevertheless I came

As it were by accident into the church
And knelt again in front of the tabernacle,

His fortress — man, His thoughts are not cold!
I dare not say what fire burned then, burns now

Under my breastbone — but He came back with me
To my own house, and let this madman eat,

And shared my stupid prayer, and carried me up
As the mother eagle lifts her fluttering young with her wings.

14

I had lain down for sleep, man, when He called me
To go across the wet paddock

And burgle the dark church — you see, Colin, the nuns
Bolt the side door and I unbolt it

Like a timid thief — red light, moonlight
Mix together; steps from nowhere

Thud in the porch; a bee wakes up and buzzes;
The whole empty pa and the Maori dead

Are present — there I lie down cruciform
On the cold linoleum, a violator

Of God's decorum — and what has He to tell me?
'More stupid than a stone, what do you know

'Of love? Can you carry the weight of my Passion,
You old crab farmer?' I go back home in peace.

18

Yesterday I planted garlic,
Today, sunflowers — 'the non-essentials first'

Is a good motto — but these I planted in honour of
The Archangel Michael and my earthly friend,

Illingworth, Michael also, who gave me the seeds —
And they will turn their wild pure golden discs

Outside my bedroom, following Te Ra
Who carries fire for us in His terrible wings

(Heresy, man!) — and if He wanted only
For me to live and die in this old cottage,

It would be enough, for the angels who keep
The very stars in place resemble most

These green brides of the sun, hopelessly in love with
Their Master and Maker, drunkards of the sky.

27

Three dark buds for the Trinity
On one twig I found in the lining of my coat

Forgotten since I broke them from the tree
That grows opposite the RSA building

At the top of Vulcan Lane — there I would lay down my parka
On the grass and meditate, cross-legged; there was a girl

Who sat beside me there;
She would hold a blue flower at the centre of the bullring

While the twigs on the tree became black
And then slowly green again — she was young — if I had said,

'Have my coat; have my money' —
She would have gone away; but because I gave her nothing

She came again and again to share that nothing
Like a bird that nests in the open hand.

37

Colin, you can tell my words are crippled now;
The bright coat of art He has taken away from me

And like the snail I crushed at the church door
My song is my stupidity;

The words of a homely man I cannot speak,
Home and bed He has taken away from me;

Like an old horse turned to grass I lift my head
Biting at the blossoms of the thorn tree;

Prayer of priest or nun I cannot use,
The songs of his House He has taken away from me;

As blind men meet and touch each other's faces
So He is kind to my infirmity;

As the cross is lifted and the day goes dark
Rule over myself He has taken away from me.

1970

The Ikons

Hard, heavy, slow, dark,
Or so I find them, the hands of Te Whaea

Teaching me to die. Some lightness will come later
When the heart has lost its unjust hope

For special treatment. Today I go with a bucket
Over the paddocks of young grass,

So delicate like fronds of maidenhair,
Looking for mushrooms. I find twelve of them,

Most of them little, and some eaten by maggots,
But they'll do to add to the soup. It's a long time now

Since the great ikons fell down,
God, Mary, home, sex, poetry,

Whatever one uses as a bridge
To cross the river that only has one beach,

And even one's name is a way of saying —
'This gap inside a coat' — the darkness I call God,

The darkness I call Te Whaea, how can they translate
The blue calm evening sky that a plane tunnels through

Like a little wasp, or the bucket in my hand,
Into something else? I go on looking

For mushrooms in the field, and the fist of longing
Punches my heart, until it is too dark to see.

                                        1971

He Waiata mo Te Kare

1

Up here at the wharepuni
That star at the kitchen window
Mentions your name to me.

Clear and bright like running water
It glitters above the rim of the range,
You in Wellington,
I at Jerusalem,

Woman, it is my wish
Our bodies should be buried in the same grave.

2

To others my love is a plaited kono
Full or empty,
With chunks of riwai,
Meat that stuck to the stones.

To you my love is a pendant
Of inanga greenstone,
Too hard to bite,
Cut from a boulder underground.

You can put it in a box
Or wear it over your heart.

One day it will grow warm,
One day it will tremble like a bed of rushes
And say to you with a man's tongue,
'Taku ngakau ki a koe!'

3

I have seen at evening
Two ducks fly down
To a pond together.

The whirring of their wings
Reminded me of you.

4

At the end of our lives
Te Atua will take pity
On the two whom he divided.

To the tribe he will give
Much talking, te pia and a loaded hangi.

To you and me he will give
A whare by the seashore
Where you can look for crabs and kina
And I can watch the waves
And from time to time see your face
With no sadness,
Te Kare o Nga Wai.

5

No rafter paintings,
No grass-stalk panels,
No Maori mass,

Christ and his Mother
Are lively Italians
Leaning forward to bless,

No taniko band on her head,
No feather cloak on his shoulder,

No stairway to heaven,
No tears of the albatross.

Here at Jerusalem
After ninety years

Of bungled opportunities,
I prefer not to invite you
Into the pakeha church.

6

Waves wash on the beaches.
They leave a mark for only a minute.
Each grey hair in my beard
Is there because of a sin,

The mirror shows me
An old tuatara,
He porangi, he tutua,
Standing in his dusty coat.

I do not think you wanted
Some other man.

I have walked barefoot from the tail of the fish to the nose
To say these words.

7

Hilltop behind hilltop,
A mile of green pungas
In the grey afternoon
Bow their heads to the slanting spears of rain.

In the middle room of the wharepuni
Kat is playing the guitar, —
'Let it be! Let it be!'

Don brings home a goat draped round his shoulders.
Tonight we'll eat roasted liver.

One day it is possible,
Hoani and Hilary might join me here,
Tired of the merry-go-round.

E hine, the door is open,
There's a space beside me.

8

Those we knew when we were young,
None of them have stayed together,
All their marriages battered down like trees
By the winds of a terrible century.

I was a gloomy drunk.
You were a troubled woman.
Nobody would have given tuppence for our chances,
Yet our love did not turn to hate.

If you could fly this way, my bird,
One day before we both die,

I think you might find a branch to rest on.

I chose to live in a different way.

Today I cut the grass from the paths
With a new sickle,
Working till my hands were blistered.

I never wanted another wife.

9

Now I see you conquer age
As the prow of a canoe beats down
The plumes of Tangaroa.

You, straight-backed, a girl,
Your dark hair on your shoulders,
Lifting up our grandchild,

How you put them to shame,
All the flouncing girls!

Your face wears the marks of age
As a warrior his moko,
Double the beauty,
A soul like the great albatross

Who only nests in mid ocean
Under the eye of Te Ra.

You have broken the back of age.
I tremble to see it.

10

Taraiwa has sent us up a parcel of smoked eels
With skins like fine leather.
We steam them in the colander.
He tells us the heads are not for eating.

So I cut off two heads
And throw them out to Archibald,
The old tomcat. He growls as he eats
Simply because he's timid.

Earlier today I cut thistles
Under the trees in the graveyard,
And washed my hands afterwards,
Sprinkling the sickle with water.

That's the life I lead,
Simple as a stone,
And all that makes it less than good, Te Kare,
Is that you are not beside me.

1972

from Autumn Testament

1

As I come down the hill from Toro Poutini's house
My feet are sore, being bare, on the sharp stones

And that is a suitable penance. The dust of the pa road
Is cool, though, and I can see

The axe of the moon shift down behind the trees
Very slowly. The red light from the windows

Of the church has a ghostly look, and in
This place ghosts are real. The bees are humming loudly

In moonlight in their old hive above the church door
Where I go in to kneel, and come out to make my way

Uphill past a startled horse who plunges in the paddock
Above the nunnery. Now there are one or two

Of the tribe back in the big house — What would you have me do,
King Jesus? Your games with me have turned me into a boulder.

2

Wahi Ngaro, the void from which all life comes,
Has given us these woven spider-cages

That tie together the high heads of grass,
A civilization in each. A stick can rip the white silk,

But that is not what I will do, having learnt
With manhood mercy, if no other good,

Two thousand perhaps in the tribe of nga mokai
Scattered like seeds now in the bins and the jails

Or occupied at their various occasions
Inside the spider-cage of a common dream,

Drugs, work, money. Siân, Kat,
Don and Francie, here with me at home

In the wharepuni — One great white flower
Shakes in the wind, turning a blind head towards our veranda.

6

The darkness of oneself returns
Now that the house is empty,

A sense of danger in the room half dark,
Half lighted, seen through a squarish doorway,

Sticky rings left by cups on the table,
Darkness, the flutter of a moth,

A table spread in a tomb for the dead to eat at, —
That's it, the Dead! — 'Why did you pay

'A visit to Toro at night? Night is the time for the morepork,'
Wehe told me today, as we sat down to

Fried Maori bread, meat and pickle,
We who will certainly each of us one day return

To our mother the grave. The darkness of oneself
Comes from knowing nothing can be possessed.

7

To wake up with a back sore from the hard mattress
In a borrowed sleeping bag

Lent me by Anne — it was her way, I think
Of giving at the same time a daughter's

And a mother's embrace — friend, daughter, mother —
These kids have heart enough to nourish the dead world

Like David in his bed — to wake up and see
The sun, if not the light from behind the sun,

Glittering on the leaves beside the graveyard
Where some of them cleared the bramble and placed on the
        bare slab

A jam jar full of flowers — to wake is to lift up
Again on one's shoulder this curious world

Whose secret cannot be known by any of us
Until we enter Te Whiro's kingdom.

27

When I stayed those three months at Macdonald Crescent
In the house of Lazarus, three tribes were living

In each of the storeys — on the ground floor, the drunks
Who came there when the White Lodge burnt down;

Above them, the boobheads; and scattered between the first
And second storey, the students who hoped to crack

The rock of education. The drunks are my own tribe.
One Sunday, the pubs being shut, they held a parliament

In the big front room — Lofty with his walking stick,
Phil the weeper, Taffy who never spoke much,

And one or two others — in conclave they sat, like granite
        columns
Their necks, like Tritons their faces,

Like tree-roots their bodies. Sober as Rhadamanthus
They judged the town and found it had already been judged.

29

I think the Lord on his axe-chopped cross
Is laughing as usual at my poems,

My solemn metaphors, my ladder-climbing dreams,
For he himself is incurably domestic,

A family man who never lifted a sword,
An only son with a difficult mother,

If you understand my thought. He has saddled me again
With the cares of a household, and no doubt

Has kept me away from Otaki
Because I'd spout nonsense, and wear my poverty

As a coat of vanity. Down at the Mass
Today, as Francie told me to, I took Communion

For her (and Siân as well) cursing gently
The Joker who won't let me shuffle my own pack.

39

The centre of our dreaming is the cave
That the world translates as brothel. Margaret told me once

A dream she had, about a house
In a meadow by the sea, old and full of passages,

Upstair and downstair rooms where the tribe were sleeping,
And three great waves came out of the sea

And washed around the house and left it standing,
Though for a while they had hidden the sun and the moon.

There has to be, I think, some shelter,
A home, an all-but-God, an all-but-mother

In time and place, not just the abstract void
Of I looking for me. Around these walls

They dipped their hands in paint and left their handprints
As on the walls of caves the Magdalenian hunters.

42

The rata blooms explode, the bow-legged tomcat
Follows me up the track, nipping at my ankle,

The clematis spreads her trumpet, the grassheads rattle
Ripely, drily, and all this

In fidelity to death. Today when Father Te Awhitu
Put on the black gown with the silver cross,

It was the same story. The hard rind of the ego
Won't ever crack except to the teeth of Te Whiro,

That thin man who'll eat the stars. I can't say
It pleases me. In the corner I can hear now

The high whining of a mason fly
Who carries the spiders home to his house

As refrigerated meat. 'You bugger off,' he tells me,
'Your Christianity won't put an end to death.'

48

The spider crouching on the ledge above the sink
Resembles the tantric goddess,

At least as the Stone Age people saw her
And carved her on their dolmens. Therefore I don't kill her,

Though indeed there is a simpler reason,
Because she is small. Kehua, vampire, eight-eyed watcher

At the gate of the dead, little Arachne, I love you,
Though you hang your cobwebs up like dirty silk in the hall

And scuttle under the mattress. Remember I spared your children
In their cage of white cloth you made as an aerial castle,

And you yourself, today, on the window ledge.
Fear is the only enemy. Therefore when I die,

And you wait for my soul, you hefty as a king crab
At the door of the underworld, let me pass in peace.

1972

CHARLES BRASCH

Born in Dunedin, Charles Brasch (1909–1973) worked as an archaeologist in Egypt, then as a teacher and civil servant in England. On his return to New Zealand, he founded the quarterly Landfall, *which he edited until 1966.*

Forerunners

Not by us was the unrecorded stillness
Broken, and in their monumental dawn
The rocks, the leaves unveiled;
Those who were before us trod first the soil

And named the bays and mountains; while round them spread
The indefinable currents of the human,
That still about their chosen places
Trouble the poignant air.

But their touch was light; warm in their hearts holding
The land's image, they had no need to impress themselves
Like conquerors, scarring it with vain memorials.
They had no fear of being forgotten.

In the face of our different coming they retreated,
But without panic, not disturbing the imprint
Of their living upon the air, which continued
To speak of them to the rocks and the sombre, guarded lakes.

The earth holds them
As the mountains hold the shadows by day
In their powerful repose, only betrayed by a lingering
Twilight in the hooded ravines.

Behind our quickness, our shallow occupation of the easier
Landscape, their unprotesting memory
Mildly hovers, surrounding us with perspective,
Offering soil for our rootless behaviour.

1948

A View of Rangitoto

Harshness of gorse darkens the yellow cliff-edge,
And scarlet-flowered trees lean out to drop
Their shadows on the bay below, searching

The water for an image always broken
Between the inward and returning swells.
Farther, beyond the rocks, cuffed by pert waves

Launches tug at their moorings; and in the channel
Yachts that sprint elegantly down the breeze
And earnest liners driving for the north.

Finally, holding all eyes, the long-limbed mountain
Dark on the waves, sunk in a stone composure;
From each far cape the easy flanks lift

In slow unison, purposeful all their rising length,
To meet and lock together faultlessly,
Clasping the notched, worn crater-cone between them.

That cup of fire, drooped like an ageing head,
Is fed with dew now and a paler brightness;
For the rushing anger sank down ages past,

Sank far beneath the sea-bed, leaving only
A useless throat that time gradually stopped
And sealed at last with smoky lichen-skin.

But the mountain still lives out that fiercer life
Beneath its husk of darkness; blind to the age
Scuttling by it over shiftless waters,

The cold beams that wake upon its headlands
To usher night-dazed ships. For it belongs to
A world of fire before the rocks and waters.

1948

Great Sea

Kona Coast, Hawaii

Speak for us, great sea.

Speak in the night, compelling
The frozen heart to hear,
The memoried to forget.
O speak, until your voice
Possess the night, and bless
The separate and fearful;
Under folded darkness
All the lost unite —
Each to each discovered,
Vowed and wrought by your voice
And in your life, that holds
And penetrates our life:
You from whom we rose,
In whom our power lives on.

All night, all night till dawn
Speak for us, great sea.
                    August 1939
                              1948

from The Islands

2

Always, in these islands, meeting and parting
Shake us, making tremulous the salt-rimmed air;
Divided, many-tongued, the sea is waiting,
Bird and fish visit us and come no more.
Remindingly beside the quays the white
Ships lie smoking; and from their haunted bay
The godwits vanish towards another summer.
Everywhere in light and calm the murmuring
Shadow of departure; distance looks our way;
And none knows where he will lie down at night.
                                        1948

Oreti Beach

To Ruth Dallas

Thunder of waves out of the dying west,
Thunder of time that overtakes our day;
Evening islands founder, gold sand turns grey
In ocean darkness where we walk possessed.

What does it mean, this clamorous fall of night
Upon the heart's stillness? What pledge can they give,
These passionate powers of the world, that we might live
More surely than by the soul's solitary light?
                                        1957

from The Estate

To T. H. Scott

. . . haben die Sterblichen denn
kein Eignes nirgendswo?
Hölderlin

iv

Dreaming that I am far from home, I come at dawn
To a white gate under a macrocarpa, giant-grown
Over its shaded paddock of worn and cropped grass
That swelling and curving outward dips, falls into space —
Bare scroll of sky, bare sea, that end-of-the-world sea
Nuzzling our rocks, the rocks of earth. And it is day,
Look, the white gate opens on crystal, on crests of fire
That glow, that hover; and in the stillness I can hear
(As light invokes hillside and town and river-bed
And models boulder and tree out of anonymous shade)
A new wind far off waking in tussock and bed of thorns,
And magpie's water-music among the parched stones.

ix

An afternoon of summer, and white curtains —
Sunlit curtains hung to the floor and pulsing
Calmly in and out through wide french windows
In warm and drowsy light; from the lawn beyond them
Cool undertone of leaves lifted and fretted
On wandering airs, and that of all sounds peaceful
The happiest — the engrossed, ecstatic murmur
Of bees and sunbeam flies endlessly intoning
Their mass of life: and in that joyous intoning
All summer swam and all our years were wafted
Through life and death breathed in the pulsing curtains.

xi

What are we then that speak and turn to silence
When the oracular heart answers our question
With its dark saying echoed in every silence?

Side by side we listened to one another
As trees in wind listen, rooted dumbly
Although their branches signal from one to another.

We drank life from life as the spring wind mounted
And carried us through a strange masque of seasons
Far into landscapes of being no word had mounted,

Where we have been borne apart, yet speak over ocean
Silence, and answer question with echoing question
That haunts the hollow waste of the heart's ocean.

xii

Noon. In the campanile's narrowed shadow,
Before our eyes the dazzle of the laguna
And in the air its murmuring obbligato,
We lay and rested, gazing outward, upward,
And speaking fell into silence. High above us
In that white calm that breathed from all things living
The campanile soared in motionless bird-flight
Far beyond day, disclosing fathomless heavens,
Abysses of warm sky deeper than darkness,
Clearer than light, that seemed a vaster ocean
Where foundering time had cast its woeful treasure
As the ripe centuries sank in quiet, purged of
Their bitterness, an ocean free for entry,
Its trembling threshold limned in lightest outline
At the arrow's mark of the campanile, visible
Or hidden as lucent vapours flowed and parted
Admitting me or excluding, intent watcher
Lost to myself, lost even to Torcello's
Millennial stones and waters waiting on me
With all their past now in my meagre present
And drawing all my life into their stillness.
So for a moment under the wheeling tower
I dreamed, or woke; and bear that waking with me
Across the years, as then I bore these islands
Sleeping, and you unthought of, and all the future,
And those I shall meet for the first time tomorrow.

xxiv

What have you seen on the summits, the peaks that plunge their
Icy heads into space? What draws you trembling
To blind altars of rock where man cannot linger
Even in death, where body grows light, and vision
Ranging those uninhabitable stations
Dazzled and emulous among the range of summoning
Shadows and clouds, may lead you in an instant
Out from all footing? What thread of music, what word in
That frozen silence that drowns the noise of our living?

What is life, you answer,
But to extend life, press its limits farther
Into the uncolonized nothing we must prey on
For every hard-won thought, all new creation
Of stone bronze music words; only at life's limit
Can man reach through necessity and custom
And move self by self into the province
Of that unrealized nature that awaits him,
His own to enter. But there are none to guide him
Across the threshold, interpret the saying of perilous
Music or word struck from that quivering climate,
Whose white inquisitors in close attendance
Are pain and madness and annihilation.

1957

from In Your Presence

IV

In the dark of dawn
Your going lies before me like a death.

*

The rabbit on the fence
Swings in his last dance
As the rattling wind
Takes his hand
And they grin
Under a ghost moon
Wraith to skeleton.

We too shall skip so
Never caring who
Mocks at us
Through the death house,
In our last revel
Surrendering all
That soul hides from soul.

*

You are the last signpost;
Looking back from death
I see your white pointing arm
And the lamplight of your eyes,
Night and day of established love.

World, my world, how shall I learn to forget you?
How sleep
With your face blinding my darkness,
The bell of your voice ringing —
Ringing in my heart's blood?

I lie down in your arms,
My light goes out in your light
To the burden of your voice
Sounding deep in a shell cavern
That holds the ocean of life.

*

In dying love
I take this talisman your hand, rehearse
For ever and for ever.

In dying love
I memorize your face over and over,
Map for a long journey.

In dying love
I trace it to the edge of infinity

And burn up my last life

Still, still to see
You my one world and covenanted day
Of dying love.

*

Death is a house where your voice cannot reach me.
O love, in the stillness nightly
I practise the deaf-mute I must play there.

1964

Signals

No two bodies taste alike or smell alike.
Your cat will tell you so sooner than I can,
But not more certainly.

You are not what you were before we knew each other;
I cannot explain the difference, but
All my antennae report it.

Nor can I put my finger on the difference in myself
Now we have learned to answer signals
We did not receive once.

Your skin tastes and smells of tropics where I walked
Barefoot, nostrils wide and fingers
Winged over waves,

Where shadows drew me in through their like leafiness
That is yours now, leafy, woodier to taste
And salt with the salt we share insatiably,

Yours, mine, still distinguishable though mingled
As limbs are, as breathing is,
As tongues that taste each other.

1969

Down Ferry Road

Holding herself carefully
As a precious vase
Or a coal red-hot
She steps down young from the bus
Into a new day
Of faces, wishes.

Not far off
In fields beyond the houses
Naked fires
Sway and flicker
Edged with black smoke
Thinning into air.

1969

Shoriken

1

Feel the edge of the knife
Cautiously —
Ice-keen
It lies against your cheek
Your heart
Will pierce at once if you should stir
Yet offers
A pillow loving to your head
A sword to cross the malevolent sea.

2

The wood of the world harbours
Lamb and lion, hawk and dove.
A world of lions alone
Or a world of doves — would it
Capture our headstrong devotion
Harness the wolf-pack of energies
That unsparing we spendthrift
Earning our lives till death?
Where in its white or black would be work for love?

3

The merciless strike with swords
With words
With silences
They have as many faces as the clouds
As many ruses as the heart
The fountains of their mercy never run dry.

4

In a world of prisoners
Who dare call himself free?

5

Every mark on your body
Is a sign of my love.
Inscribed by the years, you tell
Unwittingly
How we travelled together
Parted and met again
Fell out sometimes, then made peace.
Crowsfoot, scar, tremulous eyelid
Are not matters for shame
But passages of the book
We have been writing together.

6

Giver, you strip me of your gifts
That I may love them better.

7

To remember yesterday and the day before
To look for tomorrow
To walk the invisible bridge of the world
As a tightrope, a sword edge.

8

What wages are due to you
Unprofitable servant?
You come asking for wages?
Fifty years long you have breathed
My air, drunk my sweet waters
And have not been cut down.
Is it not a boon, living?
Do not your easy days mark
The huge forbearance of earth?

9

The bluntest stones on the road will be singing
If you listen closely
Like lilies or larks
Those that may stone you to death after.

10

Rising and setting stars
Burn with the same intensity
But one glows for the world's dark
One whitens into tedious day.

11

All yours that you made mine
Is made yours again.

12

To speak in your own words in your own voice —
How easy it sounds and how hard it is
When nothing that is yours is yours alone

To walk singly yourself who are thousands
Through all that made and makes you day by day
To be and to be nothing, not to own

Not owned, but lightly on the sword edge keep
A dancer's figure — that is the wind's art
With you who are blood and water, wind and stone.

13

One place is not better than another
Only more familiar
Dearer or more hateful
No better, only nearer.

14

He is earth, dying to earth.
The charge of life spends itself
Wears, wears out.
His sole enemy is the self
That cannot do otherwise
Than live itself to death
    death
The desert sand
That dries all tears
    death
Our rest and end.

15

Selfless, you sign
Your words mine.

16

To cross the sea is to submit to the sea
Once venture out and you belong to it
All you know is the sea
All you are the sea
And that sword edge itself a wave-crest of the sea.

1974

from Home Ground

xxiii

It is years now since I left the house
Where you keep looking for me still.
Day by day I change my custom,
Seldom sleep twice in the same bed.
Where I shall be tomorrow
And what face wearing
You might as well ask the wind.
You will find me only in yourself.

xxiv

Wind: displacement of air: liquefaction of forms.
The letters of the earth's book melted down
And every self dissolved to dust —
Dust that witnesses dissolution.

And then the air settles.

Leaves and houses reassume their bodies.

The alphabet is distilled out again.

1974

LEN LYE

*Born in Christchurch, Len Lye (1901–1980) moved to London in the late 1920s
before settling in New York, where he lived from 1944 until the end of his life. A
major international figure as both kinetic sculptor and experimental film maker, Lye
published his first book in 1930 under the auspices of Laura Riding and Robert
Graves. Figures of Motion, a selection of his writings appeared in 1984 and included
the following prose poems, which were originally published in 1938.*

Dazing Daylight

Out of the dim paleface past a continual daylight mind has given
us an alibi for reality. The age old eye check double check on
surroundings to ease our doubts. So now reality you don't bogey
us we bogey you with a ten out of ten tag everytime. All's set in
the world with a visual chamber in broad dazing daylight.

(1938)

Chair in Your Hair

Painting painting where is thy mind sting: there there under the
chair: not *under* the chair says poppa Cézanne in the legs of the
chair says poppa Cézanne: that old chair? Chair in your hair
Cézanne Cézanne. A chair in the mind is worth none in the bush.
A chair is a chair so leave it there.

(1938)

The Beautiful Weather a Lovely Moll

When you're in the weather of it don't forget the middlet bit. For
instance don't trouble time trouble mind: till trouble troubles find:
till troubles trouble mind: till trouble trouble time — is trouble-
trouble mind. That's a round-a-bout saying for trouble and no
trouble mind. No trouble mind is act of living grace: trouble mind
is act of time face without facet. No trouble wild flowers on the
bank of the beautiful river: lovely weather afterglow we're having
isn't it. Health and gingerbread wealth and early to rise what a
constitution livin' makes a numb thumblin' thing happy and wood
pappy all worldly wise. Yes indeed a lovely sunset. The horizon is
the pink of it. Very climatic this time of the rheumatic pine of the

blue ridged year isn't it. I'd rather smoke a reefer and or sit on a
reef than commune with the lovely weather of it: in converse.
Raining? Spaining? Really? Goodbye. Goodbye.

(1938)

from Passing the Buck to the Brontës

If that's the case I prefer the melons of summer to the last parsley
clothes of what I wear in winter to try to keep warm. Personal
blood thinosity in my winter conch shell: but still wind-drifts and
heart-aches they say have their esoteric compensations. Did not
the Brontës know the exodus of matter in an english manner. It's
up once again to you to accept or not such a buck. One may
always pass the buck as well as the torch if one does not wish to
retain it. Does one. One never knows does one. Thank goodness
there are always freshets: fresh bucks: and buckets. A page or two
more of this and a pretty fine stew pickle or cold December isn't it.
One knows sometimes doesn't one: or does one never know. You
take the buck eddie: breeze you never know.

(1938)

D E N I S   G L O V E R

---

*Born in Dunedin and educated at the University of Canterbury, Denis Glover
(1912–1980) founded the Caxton Press before serving, during the Second World War,
in the Royal Navy. An inspired typographer and book designer, Glover was an important literary figure from the 1930s onwards.*

Home Thoughts

I do not dream of Sussex downs
or quaint old England's
quaint old towns —
I think of what may yet be seen
in Johnsonville or Geraldine.

1981
(first published in 1936 in a longer version)

The Road Builders

Rolling along far roads on holiday wheels
now wonder at their construction, the infinite skill
that balanced the road to the gradient of the hill,
the precision, the planning, the labour it all reveals.

An unremembered legion of labourers did this,
scarring the stubborn clay, fighting the tangled bush,
blasting the adamant, stemming the unbridled rush
of torrent in flood, bridging each dark abyss.

Their tools were pitiful beside the obdurate strength of the
    land:

crosswire of the theodolite, pick-point, curved shovel,
small tremor of a touched-off charge; but above all
the skill and strength, admirable in patience, of the hand.

These men we should honour above the managers of banks.
They pitted their flesh and their cunning against odds
unimagined by those who turn wordily the first sods.
And on the payroll their labour stands unadorned by thanks.

Who they are, or where, we do not know. Anonymous they die
or drift away; some start the job again; some in a country pub
recount old epic deeds amid that unheeding hubbub,
telling of pitiless hills, wet mountain roads where rusting barrows lie.

1939

The Magpies

When Tom and Elizabeth took the farm
The bracken made their bed,
And *Quardle oodle ardle wardle doodle*
The magpies said.

Tom's hand was strong to the plough
Elizabeth's lips were red,
And *Quardle oodle ardle wardle doodle*
The magpies said.

Year in year out they worked
While the pines grew overhead,
And *Quardle oodle ardle wardle doodle*
The magpies said.

But all the beautiful crops soon went
To the mortgage-man instead,
And *Quardle oodle ardle wardle doodle*
The magpies said.

Elizabeth is dead now (it's years ago);
Old Tom went light in the head;
And *Quardle oodle ardle wardle doodle*
The magpies said.

The farm's still there. Mortgage corporations
Couldn't give it away.
And *Quardle oodle ardle wardle doodle*
The magpies say.

1941

Threnody

In Plimmerton, in Plimmerton,
The little penguins play,
And one dead albatross was found
At Karehana Bay.

In Plimmerton, in Plimmerton,
The seabirds haunt the cave,
And often in the summertime
The penguins ride the wave.

In Plimmerton, in Plimmerton,
The penguins live, they say,
But one dead albatross they found
At Karehana Bay.

1945

Centennial

In the year of centennial splendours
There were fireworks and decorated cars
And pungas drooping from the verandas
   — But no one remembered our failures.

The politicians like bubbles from a marsh
Rose to the platform, hanging in every place
Their comfortable platitudes like plush
   — Without one word of our failures.

1945

Sings Harry

Songs

I

These songs will not stand —
The wind and the sand will smother.

Not I but another
Will make songs worth the bother:
    The rimu or kauri he,
    I'm but the cabbage tree,
        Sings Harry to an old guitar.

II

If everywhere in the street
Is the indifferent, the accustomed eye
Nothing can elate,
It's nothing to do with me,
        Sings Harry in the wind-break.

To the north are islands like stars
In the blue water
And south, in that crystal air,
The ice-floes grind and mutter,
        Sings Harry in the wind-break.

At one flank old Tasman, the boar,
Slashes and tears,
And the other Pacific's sheer
Mountainous anger devours,
 Sings Harry in the wind-break.

From the cliff-top a boy
Felt that great motion,
And pupil to the horizon's eye
Grew wide with vision,
 Sings Harry in the wind-break.

But grew to own fences barbed
Like the words of a quarrel;
And the sea never disturbed
Him fat as a barrel,
 Sings Harry in the wind-break.

Who once would gather all Pacific
In a net wide as his heart
Soon is content to watch the traffic
Or lake waves breaking short,
 Sings Harry in the wind-break.

III

When I am old
 Sings Harry
Will my thoughts grow cold?
Will I find
 Sings Harry
For my sunset mind
Girls on bicycles
Turning into the wind?

Or will my old eyes feast
Upon some private movie of the past?
 Sings Harry.

Fool's Song

All of a beautiful world has gone
— Then heigh ho for a biscuit,
And a buttered scone.
For a dog likes his biscuit
And a man his buttered scone,
 Sings Harry.

I Remember

I remember paddocks opening green
On mountains tussock-brown,
And the rim of fire on the hills,
And the river running down;

And the smoke of the burning scrub,
And my two uncles tall,
And the smell of earth new-ploughed,
And the antlers in the hall,
        Sings Harry.

Then Uncle Jim was off to the wars
With a carbine at his saddle
And was killed in the Transvaal
— I forget in just what battle.

And Uncle Simon left the farm
After some wild quarrel,
Rolled his blanket and rode off
Whistling on his sorrel.

My father held to the land
Running good cattle there,
And I grew up like a shaggy steer
And as swift as a hare
While the river ran down.

But that was long ago
When the hawk hovered over the hill
And the deer lifted their heads
And a boy lay still
By the river running down,
        Sings Harry.

Once the Days

Once the days were clear
Like mountains in water,
The mountains were always there
And the mountain water;

And I was a fool leaving
Good land to moulder,
Leaving the fences sagging
And the old man older
To follow my wild thoughts
Away over the hill,
Where there is only the world
And the world's ill,
        Sings Harry.

Lake, Mountain, Tree

Water brimmed against the shore
Oozing among the reeds,
And looking into the lake I saw
Myself and mountains and weeds.

From the crystal uttermost ridge
Dwarfed was the river's course;

Cloud-shouting, to the world's edge
I rode a whole island for my horse.

Forlorn at the last tree,
Grey shingle bruised our bones;
But there holding tenaciously
Were roots among stones.

Knowing less now, and alone,
These things make for me
A gauge to measure the unknown
— Lake, mountain, tree,
    Sings Harry.

The Casual Man

Come, mint me up the golden gorse,
Mine me the yellow clay
— There's no money in my purse
For a rainy day,
    Sings Harry.

My father left me his old coat,
Nothing more than that;
And will my head take hurt
In an old hat?
    Sings Harry.

They all concern themselves too much
With what a clock shows.
But does the casual man care
How the world goes?
    Sings Harry.

A little here, a little there —
Why should a man worry?
Let the world hurry by,
I'll not hurry,
    Sings Harry.

Thistledown

Once I followed horses
And once I followed whores
And marched once with a banner
For some great cause,
    Sings Harry.
But that was thistledown planted on the wind.

And once I met a woman
All in her heart's spring,
But I was a headstrong fool
Heedless of everything
    Sings Harry.
— I was thistledown planted on the wind.

Mustering is the life:
Freed of fears and hopes
I watch the sheep like a pestilence
Pouring over the slopes,
 Sings Harry.
And the past is thistledown planted on the wind.

Dream and doubt and the deed
Dissolve like a cloud
On the hills of time.
Be a man never so proud,
 Sings Harry.
He is only thistledown planted on the wind.

The Park

The river slower moved
And the birds were still.

Leaf and tree in silence hung
Breathless on the plunging sun.

Now came still evening on,
And suddenly the park was full of pedals,
 Sings Harry.

Mountain Clearing

It was a friendly and a private place
 Sings Harry.
Where a moss-grown track beside the stream
Led to the clearing in the birches. The face
Of the dark hill above was darkling green.

And in the morning came the sound of the axe
 Sings Harry.
Or the bush-buried shot at mountain deer;
The river talked to the stones and swamp-smothered flax,
And the hut smoke rose clear.

That was a good place to be camping in
 Sings Harry.
Where we unsaddled and hobbled the horses,
Heading over Honeycomb Pass and Mount Thin
For sheep and heat and dust and a hundred
 water-courses.

The Flowers of the Sea

Once my strength was an avalanche
 Now it follows the fold of the hill
And my love was a flowering branch
 Now withered and still.

Once it was all fighting and folly
And a girl who followed me ;
Who plucked at me plucked holly,
But I pluck the flowers of the sea,
Sings Harry
For the tide comes
And the tide goes
And the wind blows.

Themes

What shall we sing? sings Harry.

Sing truthful men? Where shall we find
The man who cares to speak his mind;
Truth's out of uniform, sings Harry,
That's her offence
Where lunacy parades as commonsense.

Of lovers then? A sorry myth
To tickle tradesmen's palates with.
Production falls, wise men can prove,
When factory girls dream dreams of love.

Sing of our leaders? Like a pall
Proficiency descends on all
Pontific nobodies who make
Some high pronouncement every week.

Of poets then? How rarely they
Are more than summer shadow-play.
Like canvassers from door to door
The poets go, and gain no ear.

Sing of the fighters? Brave-of-Heart
Soon learns to play the coward's part
And calls it, breaking solemn pacts,
Fair Compromise or Facing Facts.

Where all around us ancient ills
Devour like blackberry the hills
On every product of the time
Let fall a poisoned rain of rhyme,
Sings Harry,
But praise St Francis feeding crumbs
Into the empty mouths of guns.

What shall we sing? sings Harry.

Sing all things sweet or harsh upon
These islands in the Pacific sun,
The mountains whitened endlessly
And the white horses of the winter sea,
Sings Harry.

On the Headland

Wrapped in the sea's wet shroud
The land is a dream, is a cloud.
The mist and the sun
Have made it their own,
        Sang Harry,
And hand on hips
Watched the departing ships.

                                                1951

from Arawata Bill

The Scene

Mountains nuzzle mountains
White-bearded rock-fronted
In perpetual drizzle.

Rivers swell and twist
Like a torturer's fist
Where the maidenhair
Falls of the waterfall
Sail through the air.

The mountains send below
Their cold tribute of snow
And the birch makes brown
The rivulets running down.

Rock, air and water meet
Where crags debate
The dividing cloud.

In the dominion of the thorn
The delicate cloud is born,
And golden nuggets bloom
In the womb of the storm.

The River Crossing

The river was announcing
An ominous crossing
With the boulders knocking.
'You can do it and make a fight of it,
Always taking the hard way
For the hell and delight of it.

But there comes the day
When you watch the spate of it,
And camp till the moon's down
— Then find the easy way
Across in the dawn,

Waiting till that swollen vein
Of a river subsides again.'

And Bill set up his camp and watched
His young self, river-cold and scratched,
Struggling across, and up the wrong ridge,
And turning back, temper on edge.

Camp Site

Earth and sky black,
And an old fire's sodden ashes
Were puddled in porridge clay
On that bleak day.
An old coat lay
Like a burst bag, worn
Out in a tussle with thorn.
Water ran
Through a hole in the rusted can.

The pass was wrapped
In a blanket of mist,
And the rain came again,
And the wind whipped.

The climbers had been there camping
Watching the sky
With a weatherwise eye.
And Paradise Pete
Scrabbling a hole in the sleet
When the cloud smote and waters roared
Had scrawled on a piece of board
RIVERS TOO DEEP.

Wata Bill stuck his shovel there
And hung his hat on the handle,
Cutting scrub for a shelter,
Lighting wet wood with a candle.

To the Coast

I

There's no horse this time,
Going's too rough.
It's a man with an eighty-pound pack,
And that's more than enough.

> *Always the colour, in quartz or the river,*
> *Never the nuggets as large as a liver.*

Five years ago I tried this route
Taking the left branch. Now try the right.
It'll mean tramping half the night
Before the weather breaks, turning

Tarns into lakes.

The colour is elusive, like streaks
Of wind-cloud. Gold dust must
Come from somewhere. But where?

Neither river nor mountain speaks.

II

The divide should make a decision here,
Parting the melting trickle of snow
As a woman parts her hair.

And finding a way through this muddle
Of snow and rock on the saddle
My intention is to crawl
Down the far side's precipitous wall
To more of the colour.

What metal lies
Between those granite thighs,
What parturition of earth
Yields the golden miraculous birth?

Bee carries golden pollen
Mountain and mist breed schist,
And the swollen river runs sullen
With the dust I have missed.

III

Jacksons Bay on the Tasman, the end
Of many a search round many a bend.

Does the terminus of the sea
Contain my mystery,
Throwing back on the beach
Grains of gold
I have followed from sea to sea
Thirty times and again
Since I was thirty years old?

A seaboot full of gold, tempest tossed,
They hid somewhere on the coast
When their ship was lost.

But back to the mountains!
I know
The fire of gold
Lies under that cold snow.

The Crystallised Waves

Snow is frozen cloud
Tumbled to the ravine,
The mist and the mountain-top
Lying between.

The cloud turns to snow or mist,
The mist to the stream,
The stream seeks out the ocean
All in a geographer's dream.

What are the mountains on high
But the crystallised waves of the sea,
And what is the white-topped wave
But a mountain that liquidly weaves?

The water belongs to the mountain.
Belongs to the deep;
The mountain beneath the water
Suckles oceans in sleep.

How are the tops in the dawn?

The Little Sisters

The Little Sisters of the Poor
Take me in without demur.
Good meals and a clean bed
And a pillow to my head.
Do they, curing my body's ills,
Know I must go back to the hills?

It sets me dreaming
To watch their gowns as black as birch
And their white wimples gleaming.

The End

It got you at last, Bill,
The razor-edge that cut you down
Not in the gullies, nor on the pass
But in a bed in town.

R.I.P. where no gold lies
But in your own questing soul
Rich in faith and a wild surmise.

You should have been told
Only in you was the gold:
Mountains and rivers paid you no fee,
Mountain melting to the river,
River to the sea.

1953

Here Is the News

When the BBC announced
The end of the world,
It was done without haste,

It was neutrally, gentlemanly done,
It was untinged with distaste,
It was almost as if the BBC had won.

1968

Brightness

I am bright with the wonder of you
And the faint perfume of your air

I am bright with the wonder of you
You being far away or near

I am bright with the wonder of you
Warmed by your eyes' blue fire

I am bright with the wonder of you
And your mind's open store

I am bright with the wonder of you
Despite the dark waiting I endure

I am bright with the wonder of you.

1970

GLORIA RAWLINSON

Gloria Rawlinson (1918–1995) was born in Tonga and came to New Zealand in 1924. Her first collection, Gloria's Book, was published when she was 15. She has written fiction and lived most of her life in Auckland.

The Islands Where I Was Born

I

Fragrances that like a wind disturb
The child's pacific dry in suburban shell
And send it murmuring through time's bony curb
Have caught me in the glassbright thoroughfare:
Pineapples oranges limes, their island smell
A catspaw rocking heart to hoist and dare
The long remembrance. Heart, if you would mime
Journeys to where a child blinked half the truth
Let points of origin be fixed where time
May be measured for a meaningful azimuth;
Your flowery isles are masked in Medusa's blood
And the sapphiry elements wear a darker hood.

II

There was no Pacific then, reef-broken spray
Flared on extremities of childish vision,
Under the mango tree's dim acre, at play
In sunflower groves I lived my changeless season.

When insular hours with morning steps unfurled
Chickens and coconuts, bronze fisherboy,
And old deaf Ka Ngutu's wagon howled
Past the tree of flying foxes it seemed that joy

Was born like my shadow in the sun's presence
With fuming orange in hand and the everywhere
Odour steaming from copra's oily crescents
Soothed and smoothed the least rebellious air.

Then foster speech of my Friendly Islands tongue
Could wag its music, the Ofa Atu sworn
With a white smile and all sweet change sung
For trade or gift or guile where I was born.

And I didn't believe in that realm of banished fairies
The Graveyard of Disobedient Children and hushed
Sleepers who once ran hatless, ate tapu'd berries
Or cut their feet on coral and never confessed.

For then I thought we lived on the only route,
In the apple of a heavenly eye, the fond
Providence of flowery oils and fruit,
Kingdom of Joy and Enjoy to the farthest frond.

It was out of all reckoning one last Steamer Day
When I saw the Pacific skyward beyond our coral;
Farewells fluttered . . . palm-trees turned away
And cool on my cheeks the wind from a new littoral.

III

The key was your clear maternal voice
In stories drolled like a deepsea shell
Except they smacked of human salt
And fancy that your witty mind
Spun from the long-fetched tale,
But colour was counted less than fault
Since truth was nearest to be found
In the swift light of your humorous eyes.

Friends at our fireside listened and laughed.
I blazed with private wonder.
You spoke of places I knew when small
But Oh how far may living stretch?
How many fathoms does heart fall under?
And mind grows — how many mountains tall?
The world's wild wisdom sang out of reach
Till one had learned its tortuous craft.

IV

They were our legends, we flagged them on our lives;
Though tattered with telling I wouldn't haul them down!
Sometimes you remembered the two days journey
' — in a boat rigged with twine, leaking at every seam.

When a tall sea rushed upon us
Thrust the roaring tongue-tip of its swell
Under the boozing timbers, how they groaned, staggered
    down!
One small rusty tin was our bailer
And this I scooped in the settling weight of our death
While the Tongan crew prayed and sang for mercy of our
    lives.
And how we survived, by craft or prayer or bailer
Seems crazy now, and the last thing to be dreamed
That land's relief humped on the reddening west.'
    'Jiali was the girl from Nukualofa
Swam forty miles from where a boat went down.
Through the sun-beaten, shark-schooled waters
Armed with a high heart swam the long day home;
When her hair snatched on coral, the foaming breakers
Shelved her torn and screaming on the reef,
    She said a spirit wouldn't let her drown.'
    'Hunting one brilliant midnight by calm lagoon
And burning copra to range the wild pigs near,
No grunting, no scuffle we heard, no sound
But where our horses pulled on their tethered reins
And the inward step by step of mounting fear.
Then smashing mirrored light with gulching waves
Lunged to the shoregrass out of the lagoon
A huge sea-beast, ball-eyed, long-necked, frill-maned.
Leaping to horse we saw with twisted glance
That image, unforgettable, reared at the moon.'
    'Once on an island voyage
A mating of whales, the thing most rarely seen;
How she, pale belly up, lay still on the moving blue,
And was the centre of the circling bull;
How whorling out to the rim of the sky he turned
And shirring a leaguelong wake flashed for his centre.
And they at the clash stood up like two enormous columns,
Fell with splashing thunder, rolled over and under,
Down through the sealight's fathoms, into the ocean's
    night.'
    'Eua Iki! Quite lacking in mementoes
And I never thought to bring back seeds and cuttings.
Rips, foam-fierce, guarded the narrow entry,
Bucking between the reefs you were cannoned ashore.
They were silks of sand one stepped on, warm and shining
As the island's phantasy. No one would believe . . .
Flowers, but I can't name them,
Stemmed perhaps from that oldest and richest of gardens.
    We skipped on ropes of orchids
In moist rock-hollows hung with trumpeting vines;
    Roamed little valleys
Where grass like green mice meadowed tiny ponies;
    Bathed in crystal —
Clear sweet fathoms, watching jewels of fish in the coral-
    trees —
(They matched I thought the giant butterflies in the sun's
    gleam.)

     Slept at last to the island's
Soft Ariel untragic sigh of a futureless dream.
Sometimes I wonder was it really so.'
Years later you remembered
'Eua Iki lies on the edge of the Tongan Deep.'

V

The stars that sing for recollective sails
With no iron pulling at the point of pleasure
Are child and dreamer exulting in fabled isles
That Maui fished out of the dolphined azure.

'The goldless age where gold disturbs no dreams',
so Byron burning for a south could sigh
With lovesweet oil of his romantic themes
Drawn from the leaves of Mariner and Bligh.

Perhaps that goldless age is the fruit-full sense
Of the islands where I was born, when servitor
Of earthly wishes the sun spreads an immense
Glitter over the Deep's unfathomable sore.

The Tongan Deep! Like death's gut or time's cleft
One grinding yard for dug-out galleon schooner,
Husking bones and bells to pelagic drift,
Repelling our brightest reason, the quick lunar

Tides of our laughter and grief with a quietest mouth.
Thereover we blue-weather-wise would sail
Leaving the wounded day unturned for truth
But mind hears soundings, haulnets a dragon's scale

And must pursue beyond the serving sun
Its utter depth; as Oh, wild-fire-west hurled
To the cod of the track its vast hurricane
Of gilded dreams across the nescient world.

But old as man the island ghosts that rise
From sacrificial stones, purgations of history,
Rinse with undying rains our turnaway eyes
Till the coiled mountain sombres the sapphire sea.

Fear we to know these things? The changing wind
Itself must halt before the Royal Tombs,
Old Lord Tortoise wanders battered and blind
Who shielded his sleep against a thousand dooms;

So in the metropolis panged by the day's alarms
Sail for that strength of witness you recall
By heart to the Friendly Kingdom, its crooked palms
Shall say what pacific hand environs all.

VI

Who is the dancer
Sways at her anchorage

By the salt grave?
The palmtree our sister
Of Adam's red clay;
Slantset by hurricane
Stripped to bone courage
She claps like a scaredevil
Through the moon's and sun's day.

Who are the singers
With time beat and palmclap
Shake the green grave?
Brown lass, brown lad,
Of sweet banqueting heart:
Earth's night is long
But laughing they clip
Hibiscus and jasmine
In their hair, in their song.

                                        1955

The Hare in the Snow

Afraid and trackless between storm and storm
Runs the mountain hare blinded with snow,
Digs in its dazzle her last desperate form
But seeks a refuge not a death below.

What shall our utmost clarity unlock?

Where she had rooted for her darkened hope
Time, immense, unhumbled, turns with the sun
Stripping snows down to adamantine rock:
All that's left of grief on the bright slope
Discover now — a small crouched skeleton.

                                        1963

Ms and the Cat-Child

Paradise withered much the way
his bones yellowed in Tobruk sands
while the war hurtled backwards.
She tries, but cannot remember else
than that she lay with and loved a shadow
in an empty section; later he plucked
grasses and biddy-bids off her coat
so the family wouldn't know.
That much remained after centuries
in the garment factory, the needle
whirring up and down, from birthday
to birthday; after centuries
of part living, part a bellyful of snow.

    The garden is her man. She grows
lettuce, beans, tomatoes; a bed of zinnias
            for one small vase.

But every day, in those five minutes
when the cat-child hungers at her feet
with affectionate tail, green-eyed plea,
Ms rushes into feeling more like
old mother Eve with open arms:
then, if the world came, and she knew how,
she would receive, give, give and give.

(1979)

ALLEN CURNOW

Born in Timaru in 1911, Allen Curnow studied for the Anglican ministry but turned instead to journalism for a livelihood, first in Christchurch and for a time in London. From 1951 to 1976 he taught English at the University of Auckland. An influential editor, he compiled A Book of New Zealand Verse *(1945, 1950) and* The Penguin Book of New Zealand Verse *(1960). He lives and writes in Parnell, Auckland, and at his beach house at Karekare.*

Wild Iron

Sea go dark, dark with wind,
Feet go heavy, heavy with sand,
Thoughts go wild, wild with the sound
Of iron on the old shed swinging, clanging:
Go dark, go heavy, go wild, go round,
    Dark with the wind,
    Heavy with the sand,
Wild with the iron that tears at the nail
And the foundering shriek of the gale.

1941

House and Land

Wasn't this the site, asked the historian,
Of the original homestead?
Couldn't tell you, said the cowman;
I just live here, he said,
Working for old Miss Wilson
Since the old man's been dead.

Moping under the bluegums
The dog trailed his chain
From the privy as far as the fowlhouse
And back to the privy again,
Feeling the stagnant afternoon
Quicken with the smell of rain.

There sat old Miss Wilson,
With her pictures on the wall,
The baronet uncle, mother's side,
And one she called The Hall;

Taking tea from a silver pot
For fear the house might fall.

People in the *colonies*, she said,
Can't quite understand . . .
Why, from Waiau to the mountains
It was all father's land.

She's all of eighty said the cowman,
Down at the milking-shed.
I'm leaving here next winter.
Too bloody quiet, he said.

The spirit of exile, wrote the historian,
Is strong in the people still.

He reminds me rather, said Miss Wilson,
Of Harriet's youngest, Will.

The cowman, home from the shed, went drinking
With the rabbiter home from the hill.

The sensitive nor'west afternoon
Collapsed, and the rain came;
The dog crept into his barrel
Looking lost and lame.
But you can't attribute to either
Awareness of what great gloom
Stands in a land of settlers
With never a soul at home.

                                                    1941

The Unhistoric Story

Whaling for continents coveted deep in the south
The Dutchman envied the unknown, drew bold
Images of market-place, populous river-mouth,
The Land of Beach ignorant of the value of gold:
      Morning in Murderers' Bay,
      Blood drifted away.
      It was something different, something
      Nobody counted on.

Spider, clever and fragile, Cook showed how
To spring a trap for islands, turning from planets
His measuring mission, showed what the musket could do,
Made his Christmas goose of the wild gannets.
      Still as the collier steered
      No continent appeared;
      It was something different, something
      Nobody counted on.

The roving tentacles touched, rested, clutched
Substantial earth, that is, accustomed haven
For the hungry whaler. Some inland, some hutched

Rudely in bays, the shaggy foreshore shaven,
  Lusted, preached as they knew;
  But as the children grew
  It was something different, something
  Nobody counted on.

Green slashed with flags, pipeclay and boots in the bush,
Christ in canoes and the musketed Maori boast;
All a rubble-rattle at Time's glacial push:
Vogel and Seddon howling empire from an empty coast
  A vast ocean laughter
  Echoed unheard, and after
  All it was different, something
  Nobody counted on.

The pilgrim dream pricked by a cold dawn died
Among the chemical farmers, the fresh towns; among
Miners, not husbandmen, who piercing the side
Let the land's life, found like all who had so long
  Bloodily or tenderly striven
  To rearrange the given,
  It was something different, something
  Nobody counted on.

After all re-ordering of old elements
Time trips up all but the humblest of heart
Stumbling after the fire, not in the smoke of events;
For many are called, but many are left at the start,
  And whatever islands may be
  Under or over the sea,
  It is something different, something
  Nobody counted on.

                                        1941

The Skeleton of the Great Moa in the Canterbury Museum, Christchurch

The skeleton of the moa on iron crutches
Broods over no great waste; a private swamp
Was where this tree grew feathers once, that hatches
Its dusty clutch, and guards them from the damp.

Interesting failure to adapt on islands,
Taller but not more fallen than I, who come
Bone to his bone, peculiarly New Zealand's.
The eyes of children flicker round this tomb

Under the skylights, wonder at the huge egg
Found in a thousand pieces, pieced together
But with less patience than the bones that dug
In time deep shelter against ocean weather:

Not I, some child, born in a marvellous year,
Will learn the trick of standing upright here.

                                        1943

Landfall in Unknown Seas

The 300th Anniversary of the Discovery of New Zealand
by Abel Tasman, 13 December 1642

I

Simply by sailing in a new direction
You could enlarge the world.
                            You picked your captain,
Keen on discoveries, tough enough to make them,
Whatever vessels could be spared from other
More urgent service for a year's adventure;
Took stock of the more probable conjectures
About the Unknown to be traversed, all
Guesses at golden coasts and tales of monsters
To be digested into plain instructions
For likely and unlikely situations.

All this resolved and done, you launched the whole
On a fine morning, the best time of year,
Skies widening and the oceanic furies
Subdued by summer illumination; time
To go and to be gazed at going
On a fine morning, in the Name of God
Into the nameless waters of the world.

O you had estimated all the chances
Of business in those waters, the world's waters
Yet unexploited.
                    But more than the sea-empire's
Cannon, the dogs of bronze and iron barking
From Timor to the Straits, backed up the challenge.
Between you and the South an older enmity
Lodged in the searching mind, that would not tolerate
So huge a hegemony of ignorance.
There, where your Indies had already sprinkled
Their tribes like ocean rains, you aimed your voyage;
Like them invoked your God, gave seas to history
And islands to new hazardous tomorrows.

II

Suddenly exhilaration
Went off like a gun, the whole
Horizon, the long chase done,
Hove to. There was the seascape
Crammed with coast, surprising
As new lands will, the sailor
Moving on the face of the waters,
Watching the earth take shape
Round the unearthly summits, brighter
Than its emerging colour.

Yet this, no far fool's errand,
Was less than the heart desired,
In its old Indian dream
The glittering gulfs ascending
Past palaces and mountains
Making one architecture.
Here the uplifted structure,
Peak and pillar of cloud—
O splendour of desolation—reared
Tall from the pit of the swell,
With a shadow, a finger of wind, forbade
Hopes of a lucky landing.

Always to islanders danger
Is what comes over the sea;
Over the yellow sands and the clear
Shallows, the dull filament
Flickers, the blood of strangers:
Death discovered the Sailor
O in a flash, in a flat calm,
A clash of boats in the bay
And the day marred with murder.
The dead required no further
Warning to keep their distance;
The rest, noting the failure,
Pushed on with a reconnaissance
To the north; and sailed away.

III

Well, home is the Sailor, and that is a chapter
In a schoolbook, a relevant yesterday
We thought we knew all about, being much apter
    To profit, sure of our ground,
No murderers mooring in our Golden Bay.

But now there are no more islands to be found
And the eye scans risky horizons of its own
In unsettled weather, and murmurs of the drowned
    Haunt their familiar beaches—
Who navigates us towards what unknown

But not improbable provinces? Who reaches
A future down for us from the high shelf
Of spiritual daring? Not those speeches
    Pinning on the Past like a decoration
For merit that congratulates itself,

O not the self-important celebration
Or most painstaking history, can release
The current of a discoverer's elation
    And silence the voices saying,
'Here is the world's end where wonders cease.'

Only by a more faithful memory, laying
On him the half-light of a diffident glory,
The Sailor lives, and stands beside us, paying
    Out into our time's wave
The stain of blood that writes an island story.

1943

Spectacular Blossom

Mock up again, summer, the sooty altars
Between the sweltering tides and the tin gardens,
All the colours of the stained bow windows.
Quick, she'll be dead on time, the single
Actress shuffling red petals to this music,
Percussive light! So many suns she harbours
And keeps them jigging, her puppet suns,
All over the dead hot calm impure
Blood noon tide of the breathless bay.

Are the victims always so beautiful?

Pearls pluck at her, she has tossed her girls
Breast-flowers for keepsakes now she is going
For ever and astray. I see her feet
Slip into the perfect fit the shallows make her
Purposefully, sure as she is the sea
Levels its lucent ruins underfoot
That were sharp dead white shells, that will.be sands.
The shallows kiss like knives.

Always for this
They are chosen for their beauty.

Wristiest slaughterman December smooths
The temple bones and parts the grey-blown brows
With humid fingers. It is an ageless wind
That loves with knives, it knows our need, it flows
Justly, simply as water greets the blood,
And woody tumours burst in scarlet spray.
An old man's blood spills bright as a girl's
On beaches where the knees of light crash down.
These dying ejaculate their bloom.

Can anyone choose
And call it beauty? — The victims
Are always beautiful.

1957

He Cracked a Word

He cracked a word to get at the inside
Of the inside, then the whole paper bag full
The man said were ripe and good.

The shrunken kernels
Like black tongues in dead mouths derided
The sillinesses of song and wagging wisdom.
These made a small dumb pile, the hopping shells
Froze to the floor, and those made patterns
Half-witted cameras glared at, finding as usual
Huge meteorites in mouseland.
What barefaced robbery!
He sat, sat, sat mechanically adding
To the small dumb pile, to the patterns on the floor,
Conscious of nothing but memories, wishes,
And a faint but unmistakable pricking of the thumbs,
The beginnings of his joy.

1957

A Small Room with Large Windows

i

What it would look like if really there were only
One point of the compass not known illusory,
All other quarters proving nothing but quaint
Obsolete expressions of true north (would it be?),
And seeds, birds, children, loves and thoughts bore down
The unwinding abiding beam from birth
To death! What a plan!
                    Or parabola.
You describe yours, I mine, simple as that,
With a pop and a puff of nonchalant stars up top,
Then down, dutiful dead stick, down
(True north all the way nevertheless).

One way to save space and a world of trouble.

A word on arrival, a word on departure.
A passage of proud verse, rightly construed.
An unerring pen to edit the ensuing silences
(That's more like it).

ii

                    Seven ageing pine trees hide
Their heads in air but, planted on bare knees,
Supplicate wind and tide. See if you can
See it (if this is it), half earth, half heaven,
Half land, half water, what you call a view
Strung out between the windows and the tree trunks;
Below sills a world moist with new making where
The mangrove race number their cheated floods.
Now in a field azure rapidly folding
Swells a cloud sable, a bad bitching squall
Thrashes the old pines, has them twitching
Root and branch, rumouring a Götterdämmerung.

Foreknowledge infects them to the heart.

Comfortable
To creak in tune, comfortable to damn
Slime-suckled mangrove for its muddy truckling
With time and tide, knotted to the vein it leeches.

iii

In the interim, how the children should be educated,
Pending a decision, a question much debated
In our island realms. It being, as it is,
Out of the question merely to recognize
The whole three hundred and sixty degrees,
Which prudence if not propriety forbids,
It is necessary to avail oneself of aids
Like the Bible, or no Bible, free swimming tuition,
Art, sex, no sex and so on. Not to direct
So much as to normalize personality, protect
From all hazards of climate, parentage, diet,
Whatever it is exists. While, on the quiet,
It is understood there is a judgment preparing
Which finds the compass totally without bearing
And the present course correct beyond a doubt,
There being two points precisely, one in, one out.

iv

A kingfisher's naked arc alight
Upon a dead stick in the mud
A scarlet geranium wild on a wet bank
A man stepping it out in the near distance
With a dog and a bag
                          on a spit of shell
On a wire in a mist
                          a gannet impacting
Explode a dozen diverse dullnesses
Like a burst of accurate fire.

                              1962

from Trees, Effigies, Moving Objects

I *Lone Kauri Road*

The first time I looked seaward, westward,
it was looking back yellowly,
a dulling incandescence of the eye of day.
It was looking back over its raised hand.
Everything was backing away.

Read for a bit. It squinted between the lines.
Pages were backing away.
Print was busy with what print does,
trees with what trees do that time of day,

sun with what sun does, the sea
with one voice only, its own,
spoke no other language than that one.

There wasn't any track from which to hang
the black transparency that was travelling
south-away to the cold pole. It was cloud
browed over the yellow cornea which I called
an eyeball for want of another notion,
cloud above an ocean. It leaked.

Baldachin, black umbrella, bucket with a hole,
drizzled horizon, sleazy drape,
it hardly mattered which, or as much
what cometing bitchcraft, rocketed shitbags,
charred cherubim pocked and pitted the iceface
of space in time, the black traveller.
Everything was backing away.

The next time I looked seaward,
it was looking sooted red, a bloodshot cornea
browed with a shade that could be simulated
if the paint were thick enough, and audible,
to blow the coned noses of the young kauri,
the kettle spout sweating,
the hound snoring at my feet,
the taste of tobacco, the tacky fingers
on the pen, the paper from whose plane
the last time I looked seaward
would it be a mile, as the dust flies,
down the dulling valley, westward?
everything was backing away.

VIII *The Kitchen Cupboard*

Sun, moon, and tides.
With the compliments of the *New Zealand Herald*
and Donaghy's Industries Limited makers
of the finest cordage since 1876.
Look on the inside of the cupboard door,
the middle one, on the left of the sink-bench.

All the bays are empty, a quick-drying wind
from the south-west browns the grey silt
the ebb-tide printed sexily, opulently,
making Nature's *art nouveau*, little as it matters
to mudlarking crabs and the morning's blue heron.

Olive, olive-budded, mangroves wait for the turn,
little as it means, to call that waiting.

A green car follows a blue car passing a brown car
on the Shore Road beyond the mangroves which wait
no more than the tide does because nothing waits.
Everything happens at once. It is enough.

That is not to say there is nothing to cry about,
only that the poetry of tears is a dead cuckoo.

The middle one, on the left of the sink-bench.
I stuck it on with sellotape. Not quite straight.

IX *A Dead Lamb*

Never turn your back on the sea.
The mumble of the fall of time is continuous.

A billion billion broken waves deliver
a coloured glass globe at your feet, intact.

You say it is a Japanese fisherman's float.
It is a Japanese fisherman's float.

A king tide, a five o'clock low, is perfect
for picking mussels, picking at your ankle-bones.

The wind snaps at the yellow-scummed sea-froth,
so that an evanescence of irised bubbles occurs.

Simply, silverly the waves walk towards you.
A ship has changed position on the horizon.

The dog lifts a leg against a grass-clump
on a dune, for the count of three, wetting the sand.

There is standing room and much to be thankful for
in the present. Look, a dead lamb on the beach.

X *A Framed Photograph*

The renaissance was six months old.
All the Kennedys were living at that time.
Jackie was hanging pictures in the White House.
I figured he could use the experience, Jack hornered,
when he starts in legal practice, naming Bobby
for Attorney-General.

Act one, scene one,
of the bloody melodrama. Everyone listened
while everyone read his poems. BANG! BANG!
and we cried all the way to My Lai.

To be silverly framed,
stood on the Bechstein, dusted daily
by the Jamaican girl whose eyes refuse them,
seeing alien Friendship one prolonged avenue
infinitely dusted, is a destiny which simply,
silverly they walk towards, towards my chair,
what jaunty pair
smiling the air
that flutters their trousers on Capitol Hill?
Why, Hiroshima Harry and the dandy Dean,
dust free. Heavenly muse!
Fresh up your drink and sing.

What, exactly,
did he do at the Pentagon? He guessed he was
a deputy assistant secretary of defence,
a political appointment, modestly confided.
Hospitably home at cocktail time he took
one careful gin and tonic, excused himself
to mind State papers.

Dust the Bechstein, Anna.
Dust the megagothic national cathedral.
Dust destiny.

Fresh up. There is plenty of ice.

Receptacle, receive me.

XIII *A Four Letter Word*

i

A wood god bothering cantor
rolls out his call. He names

tanekaha, kaiwaka, taraire.
Mispronounced, any of these

can strike dead and dumb. Well spoken,
they are a noise neither of the writhing root

nor glabrous leaf nor staring flower,
all that can unspeakably supervene.

ii

Tane mahuta is a very big tree,
because of the signboards at the roadside.

Tired trunk, punky at the heart,
disyllabic Tane is too venerable

for words. True, that at a given sign
they stop their cars and walk no distance

to have seen, to have found themselves,
as advertised, in the absence of the god,

to have decently exposed some inches of film
in honour of his great girth.

Strike him with lightning!
the old arboreal bore.

Cut him up for signboards. Just look at that,
such longevity, such bulk, such value in board feet.

iii

Titans were titanic in the old days
before the defoliant Thunderer.

The children had no fathers then, as now.
No nativity ode for Tane. At his namegiving

nobody had the time, having time only
short of an unspeakable supervention

to blurt him, Logos begotten of log,
the disyllable, as he came.

iv

In the technologies nothing can be done
without a divine sub-contract:

this one for the felling, the hollowing,
prone canoe, erected post;

Tane demiurgos,
lord of an obsolete skill:

not to keep an old man ticking
with a dead boy's heart

(cut while warm, after the crash,
pray for this tissue not to be rejected);

an instance now, look at it like that,
of what can unspeakably supervene,

ever since like cats in the dead of night
the first heaven and the first earth

coupled and begot,
and the theogonies littered the place

with the lordliest imaginable
stumps. That's life. That's fear

of this unspeakable that smashed the mouth
open, stamped on the balls and

ripped from the tongue's root, womb syllabled,
Tane, Tane mahuta.

XVI *There Is a Pleasure in the Pathless Woods*

When the green grenade explodes, does the kauri
experience an orgasm of the spent cone?
What is the king fern doing with its hairy knuckles?
Wildling and epiphyte, do they have problems too?
There's a reason for the spastic elbow of this taraire.
Look hard at nature. It is in the nature

of things to look, and look back, harder.
Botany is panic of another description.

XVII *Lone Kauri Road*

Too many splashes, too many gashes,
too big and too many holes in the west wall:
one by one the rectangles blazed and blacked where the
sun fell out of its frame, the time of the day
hung round at a loose end, lopsided.

It was getting desperate, even a fool could see,
it was feverish work, impossible to plug them all.
Even a fool, seeing the first mountain fall
out not into the sea or the smoking west but into
the places where these had been, could see the spider
brushed up, dusted, shovelled into the stove, and
how fast his legs moved, without the least surprise.

A tui clucked, shat, whistled thrice.
My gaze was directed where the branch had been.
An engine fell mute into the shadow of the valley
where the shadow had been.

XVIII *Any Time Now*

Extraordinary things happen every day
in our street only this morning
the ground opened at my feet
without warning
unless it was a cloud in the south
balled like a swelling in the mouth.

And the air was fresh, being winter
time when the ground broke
disclosing a billion bodies burning
under a thin smoke.
Was it then that I saw in my walk
an eggshell, a capsicum stalk?

Such details are always so terribly
(if that is the word) distinct
as grit under the eyelid, like today
when the ground blinked,
disclosing what never should be seen.
Walking is a pleasure, I mean.

Fortunately there was not very much
traffic and no kiddies playing,
couldn't have picked a better day for it
I was just saying
when the ground closed over the sky
hollow as the cloud was high.

1972

Moro Assassinato

I

The Traveller

All the seas are one sea,
the blood one blood
and the hands one hand.

Ever is always today.
Time and again, the Tasman's
wrestler's shoulders

throw me on Karekare
beach, the obliterations
are one obliteration

of last year's Adriatic,
yesterday's Pacific,
the eyes are all one eye.

Paratohi rock, the bell-tower
of San Giorgio recompose
the mixture's moment;

the tales are all one tale
dead men tell, the minor
characters the living.

Nice and all as it was
and is, the dog-trotting sun
of early April nosing

the 'proud towers', to sit
at Nico's tables
on Zattere, and to watch

the Greek and the Russian ships
dead-slowing up the Giudecca
towards mainland Mestre's

raffineria, red-guttering
lanky steel candlestick:
nice and all the Chioggia

car-ferry making the long
wave wheelspoke from the bows,
slap-slop to the feet of the old

angler who trolls
past the Gesuati church, the pizzeria,
the house Ruskin lived in,

and to sit, deciphering
the morning's *Corriere*:
the lengthening anguish of

Eleonora, la Signora Moro,
now her fifth week begins
of unwidowed widowhood,

here and not here, to sit
by the sea which is all one,
where Paratohi is neither

steel stalk nor bell-tower
and either is Paratohi,
deciphering *Corriere*.

The tears of Eleonora
splash black, dry on the page,
the weather map, the fifth week

'after' the bloody abduction.
Ever remains today,
and the hands one hand.

II

An Urban Guerilla

*The real stress came from life in the group . . . we were
caught up in a game that to the present day I still don't fully
see through.* — MICHAEL BAUMANN, 'MOST SOUGHT AFTER'
GERMAN TERRORIST

It was a feather of paint
in a corner of the window,
a thread hanging from the hem
of the curtain, it was
the transistor standing on the corner
of the fridge, the switches
on the transistor, the way they were placed
in a dead design, it was where
the table stood, it was the label
Grappa Julia on the bottle
not quite half empty,

the faces that came and went,
the seven of us comrades
like the days of the week repeating
themselves, themselves,
it was cleaning your gun ten times
a day, taking time
washing your cock, no love
lost, aimlessly fondling
the things that think faster than fingers,
trigger friggers, gunsuckers.
People said, Andreas Baader

'had an almost sexual relationship
with pistols', his favourite fuck

was a Heckler & Koch. Not that sex
wasn't free for all and in all
possible styles, but not all of us
or any of us all of the time —
while agreeing, in principle,
that any combination of abcdefg
encoded orgasm, X being any
given number — got our sums right.

Dust thickened on the mirror,
the once gay playmate,
on the dildo in the drawer,
dust on the file of newspapers;
silence as dusty as death
on the radio, nobody can hear
the police dragging their feet;
sometimes we squabbled, once
could have shot one another
in the dusty time, we had to be
terrible news, or die.

III

Lampoon

Nobody less than the biggest
    would do, and who was that?
Five times Prime Minister, the top
    Christian Democrat.
Two hours on his feet that day,
    talking the Catholics round
to live with the Communists' power
    in the parliament of the land:
President next of the butcher State,
    or the next to die
the death of an old crook, come at last
    to the reckoning day.

IV

16 March 1978

Normality was this car's
warm vinyl under the buttocks,
and the driver's nape,
the knuckles of his hand on the wheel,
the knowledge of exactly where
I was going, and why, and how,
point by point of my discourse,
A could be coaxed and B persuaded
and the State saved again.

Normality was the guns
worn close to the body of each
of the guards, good friends, composing
my escort sitting beside me,
and behind me the second car
completing the squad provided
by the Ministry of the Interior:
cheap at the price, when you think
of the Titians in the Borghese.

Normality was the moment's
mixture, moment by moment
improvising myself,
ideas, sensations, among them
the lacquered acridities
of ducted air in the car,
accelerations, decelerations,
nothing to be trusted further
than the mixture's moment.

Normality was no less
what it had to be, the ambush,
the crashed cars and the guards
gunned down dead in the street;
and the car that carried me next
here, to the dark classroom
of the Prison of the People.
Normality is, do you follow?
a condition very like mine.

The child I was would have known
better than the man I am,

when they tripped him, trapped him,
ripped his shirt, emptied his bag,

caught him, laughed him to tears,
rubbed cowshit into his hair,

the irreversible justice
of the wrong once done, the victim's

yes to the crime. Who knows
he had to be punished knows

how the women who wipe away
the tears and the shit

heal no hurt but their own.
Tell the bullet to climb

back up the barrel and close
the wound behind it. They carried me,

carrying the child who could teach me
my case was not so special.

V

The Prison of the People

Our household consisted
of, at a guess, half a dozen
comrades, both sexes, and a few
more, coming and going,

never forgetting one
supremely important person
for killing when the time came,
worth something alive

but how much, and for how long?
Understand, it was not a spacious
apartment, our elderly prisoner
had his own room;

the Prison of the People
was a tight squeeze, how long
would it take to squeeze the brain
till the fuses blew?

Not that we gave it a thought,
wasn't the State on the block
and the front page yelling rape,
and the cameras in at the fuck

and the dirtied pants scared off
the arses of the Bourses,
when we took him alive and we left
five dead in the street?

Not a thought. We slipped out for the papers,
read them ten times. We photographed
him, his shirt open, an unsmiling smile

on his lips, hung behind him the Red
Star banner and the words Brigate Rosse.
Christ! They printed it all. Next thing

we sentenced him to death. They printed this.
He wrote letters, we willingly accepted them
for delivery, Fanfani, Zaccagnini, Andreotti,

Cossiga, Dell'Andro, Eleonora his wife.
Did we seriously expect these would procure
the political deal, the exchange for our comrades

gaoled by the State, their liberty for his life?
'An episode in a war', terror for terror,
an honourable swap. So his letters argued.

He knew us better than they, adduced Palestinian
precedent, humane principle, the party interest,
all that shit. What did he, or we, expect?

Jesus wrote no letters to Judas or Caiaphas.
It was he or Barabbas, and that was another Rome.
Not known at this address. Try Simon Peter.

Silence in Jesus Square, his Demo-Christians
denied him by protocol, *il vero Moro è morto*
il 16 Marzo, ultimo suo giorno di libertà.

Consenting silence in the house of the Left,
Christ's communist other woman, three in a bed
with Rome, last word of his long clever speeches,

grosso orchestratore. And among themselves
read in his letters forgery, torture, drugs,
practices in the Prison of the People

which 30,000 police, etc., could never locate.
Dead, by the party line, a just man we once knew,
of whose visible blood we shall be innocent.

See ye to it.

Can the same w.c.
receive the faeces of judge, executioner
and condemned man for 54 days,

in hearing of each other for 54 days
(and he, at an age to be father and grandfather,
with Jesuit's mastery of his Marx and his Mao,

knew us better than we knew ourselves)
and nobody be changed? 54 days
were the count-down, the Prison of the People

shrank like the ass's skin every time
the w.c. flushed, and we cleaned our guns,
and the newspapers yellowed, the execution

wouldn't wait, the silence outside
and the nothing more inside were the only orgasm
now, out of the barrel of a gun.

VI

The Letters

His letters. How can we know
who it is that speaks?
Covertly delivered by terrorist *postino*
to the press, *Messaggero, Vita, La Repubblica,*
from the Prison of the People,
so-called, an address unknown,
by what light were they written?
Under what drug? It is one
who writes with his hand, his signature,
la grafia sembra autentica.

True, I am a prisoner
and not in the best of spirits,
nevertheless believe me
this handwriting is mine,
so is the style.
Believe, do not speculate
about the effect of drugs,
my mind is clear, what I write I write
of my own will, uncoerced.

Get me out of this.

But I am, you would say,
not I but another who is not to be
taken seriously, not one word
in reply to my arguments.

My darling Noretta, After a little optimism,
fleeting and false, as it turns out, something
they said, I misunderstood, I see that the time
has come . . . no time to think
how incredible it is, this punishment
for my mildness and moderation . . . I have been wrong
all my life, meaning well, of course . . .
too late to change, nothing to do but admit
you were always right. What more can I say?
Only, could not some other way have been found to punish
us and our little ones? . . . I want one thing
to be clear, the entire responsibility
of the Demo-Christian Party by its absurd,
unbelievable conduct. Friends have done too little,
fearing for themselves perhaps . . . It has come
while hope hung by a thin thread, suddenly
and incomprehensibly, the order
for my execution . . . sweetest Noretta,
I am in God's hands and yours. Pray for me.
Remember me tenderly, take our dear children
in your arms. God keep you all. I kiss you all.

(and writes) Monday, 24 April 1978,
newspaper *Vita* to Benigno Zaccagnini,
leader in extremis to party secretary.
I repeat, I do not accept
the unjust, ungrateful judgment of the party.
I absolve, I excuse nobody.
My cry is the cry of my family, wounded to death.
I request that at my funeral, nobody
representing the State, nor men of the Party,
take part, I ask to be followed by the few
who have truly wished me well and are therefore worthy
to go with me in their prayers, and in their love.

VII

The Executioners

Christ set it going and ascended,
leaving the engine running.

The R4 is a small popular car,
but a man could hunch himself

through the hatchback, the prisoner did,
as the guns instructed.

He looked his best that day,
thanks to the girl comrade

who washed and ironed the shirt
(by Ninarelli of Bologna, initialled A.M.),

the singlet and the long johns.
He took a shower, dressed himself,

knotted the blue necktie.
Only at the last moment I noticed

the socks were wrong-side out,
but the cars were ready by then.

A gesture with guns. Get in.
Silence was the last dignity possible

to the doubled-up foetus he made
in the baggage end of the R4.

We shot him there and then,
the first of eleven bullets

clipped off the thumbnail of the left
hand raised by a stupid reflex

of the giant foetus in a dark blue
suit with cuffed trousers.

It squirmed, shrank, squirted red
and Gesù! he saw them

coming, the rods in our hands,
at one metre's range

the Beretta 7.65s
had to hit the left hunch-breast

eleven times, the grey head
whiplashed, nodding to the shots

yes yes yes yes
                    yes yes yes
yes yes yes yes.

VIII

9 May 1978

Circumvesuviano is the railway
to Ercolano, Pompeii,
Torre Greco and other incubations
of Neapolitan poverty.
If you want ghosts for your money,
dig for yourself.

They are all dead as nineteen hundred
years or the moment after.
They do not live in memory or imagination
or history, or any other
of death's entertainment. Poems
don't work any more.

Back from a day among the ruins
to Piazza Garibaldi,
the Alfas, Fiats, Lancias, *tutto klaxon;*
the stone bonneted Liberator
rides nowhere any more and what's in a statue
but rocking-horse shit?

It is five in the afternoon.
Il Mattino, page one, X-nine columns,
Edizione Straordinaria,
MORO ASSASSINATO.
You're a guest, in a stricken house,
eavesdropper, easy tourist.

One of Rome's mediaeval gutters
is Via Caetani, near Jesus Square.
They parked the R4 with its riddled man.
You will visit the spot, there will be
mourners and flowers, many weeks,
both withered and fresh.

IX

The Poor

The poor publish their grief
on doors and doorways,

the black bar printed above
and below the name of the dead,

or needing no name,
per mio marito, mia moglie,

mio fratello, the scrap of newsprint
20 by 10 centimetres

pasted to the joinery in the masonry
centuries have nibbled,

the day's news, *Death was here.*
Dreamlessly nonna nods

into her ninetieth year,
where she sits, catching the sun

at the dark doorway;
over her, in black and white

run off at the *tipografia*
round the corner, which is always busy,

Per Aldo Moro

---

strikes off one more.

1979

An Incorrigible Music

It ought to be impossible to be mistaken
about these herons, to begin with
you can count them, it's been done successfully
with swans daffodils blind mice, any number
of dead heroes and heavenly bodies.

Eleven herons are not baked in porcelain,
helpless to hatch the credulities of art
or to change places, e.g. number seven
counting from the left with number five,
or augment themselves by number twelve arriving
over the mangroves. Thirteen, fourteen, fifteen,
punctually the picture completes itself
and is never complete.
                              The air
and the water being identically still,
each heron is four herons,
one right-side-up in the air,
one up-side-down in the tide,
and these two doubled by looking at.

The mudbacked mirrors in your head
multiply the possibilities of human
error, but what's the alternative?
The small wind instruments in the herons' throats

play an incorrigible music on a scale
incommensurate with hautboys and baroque wigs.

There's only one book in the world, and that's the one
everyone accurately misquotes.

A big one! A big one!

1979

You Will Know When You Get There

Nobody comes up from the sea as late as this
in the day and the season, and nobody else goes down

the last steep kilometre, wet-metalled where
a shower passed shredding the light which keeps

pouring out of its tank in the sky, through summits,
trees, vapours thickening and thinning. Too

credibly by half celestial, the dammed
reservoir up there keeps emptying while the light lasts

over the sea, where it 'gathers the gold against
it'. The light is bits of crushed rock randomly

glinting underfoot, wetted by the short
shower, and down you go and so in its way does

the sun which gets there first. Boys, two of them,
turn campfirelit faces, a hesitancy to speak

is a hesitancy of the earth rolling back and away
behind this man going down to the sea with a bag

to pick mussels, having an arrangement with the tide,
the ocean to be shallowed three point seven metres,

one hour's light to be left and there's the excrescent
moon sponging off the last of it. A door

slams, a heavy wave, a door, the sea-floor shudders.
Down you go alone, so late, into the surge-black fissure.

1982

A Passion for Travel

Absently the proof-reader corrects
the typesetter. According to copy
the word is exotic. He cancels
the literal r and writes an x.

A word replaces a word. Discrepant
signs, absurd similitudes
touch one another, couple promiscuously.
He doesn't need Schopenhauer

to tell him only exceptional intellects
at exceptional moments ever get any
nearer than that, and when they do
it gives them one hell of a fright.

He's exercised, minding his exes and ars.
If Eros laughs, as the other philosopher
says, and if either word's a world
'offering plentiful material for humour',

that's not in copy. After dark,
that's when the fun starts, there's a room
thick with globes, testers, bell-pulls
rare fruits, painted and woven pictures,

pakeha thistles in the wrong forest,
at Palermo the palm lily *ti australis*
in the Botanical Gardens, Vincento
in white shorts trimming the red canoe

pulled the octopus inside out
like a sock, *Calamari!* The tall German
blonde wading beside, pudenda awash,
exquisitely shocked by a man's hands

doing so much so quickly,
Calamari! Those 'crystalline'
aeolian shallows lap the anemone
which puckers the bikini, her delicacy.

Short of an exceptional moment, if only
just! In his make-do world a word
replaces a white vapour, the sky
heightens by a stroke of the pen.

1982

The Parakeets at Karekare

The feathers and the colours cry
on a high note which ricochets
off the monologue of the morning sun
the long winded sea, off Paratohi posturing
on a scene waiting to be painted.

Scarlet is a squawk, the green
yelps, yellow is the tightest cord
near snapping, the one high note, a sweet-sour
music not for listening. The end is
less than a step and a wink

away as the parakeet flies.
Darkness and a kind of silence under
the cliff cuts the performance,
a moment's mixture. Can scavenging
memory help itself?

What do I imagine coloured words
are for, and simple grammatical
realities like, 'I am walking to the beach'
and 'I have no idea what the sky can mean
'by a twist of windy cloud'?

What's the distance between us all
as the rosella cries its tricolour

ricochet, the tacit cliff, Paratohi
Rock in bullbacked seas, my walking eye
and a twist of windy cloud?

1982

Canto of Signs Without Wonders

I look where I'm going, it's the way
    yesterday's and the day before's clouds
    depict themselves over and over

an affluently planted skyline:
    the clouds lay the whitenesses on thick
    over the bluenesses. The impasto

is unsigned, there's a kind of an impression
    of lettering rapidly rubbed out
    before I can read, pasted over again

and rewritten, the name of a famous
    product, the thing that's everything,
    the sky being prime space, anyway

the most public part of this universe.
    Speculative thunder is noises,
    contused vapours, colours into which

my eyes walk: high-flown language, logo and
    sign of a brand of which 'the authors
    are in eternity', at least some

country we never trade with. My eyes
    walk a tight wire made fast to a cloud,
    securest anchorage, the weather

man's promise of 'settled conditions'.
    Underfoot, the pavement keeps falling
    away step by step where I'm about

to pass the pianist's open door
    some *chant sans paroles* escapes: his patched
    iron roof leaked, he spread a tarpaulin

over the Steinway: two of his cats
    stare from the shade of the hydrangea.
    The pavement is still falling, my eyes

walk not precisely stepping high across
    craters and cones, 'best parts' of our city:
    volcanic pustules green a thousand

years, and for a couple of lifetimes
    these people, yesterday's and the day
    before's people, as far as the bluest

dilations of clouds and seas and names
  to call islands by. Less and less time
  remains, they purify their private

pools, uncapping the vials which protect
  from viral enemies: the prudent
  set aside sums for depreciation,

each year sell off a wasting asset,
  c'est la vie. The painter is freshing
  up yesterday's clouds by interior

light, he cleans his brushes, drinks a mug
  of instant coffee. The rusted VW
  meditates 'my other car is a Rolls'.

And as they walk, those two, side by side,
  his hand fondles the blueness of her
  jeans, her thready rondure and the stitched

name of Levi Strauss, below the patch
  seeking. She takes the hand. The sign is
  what the maker means. Much more than that

calls for an impossible presence
  of mind, I look where I'm going and
  that way they depict themselves, yes

that's all for today, my eyes wired
  to a system there, feet falling in turn
  on the pavement which is falling away,

unsigned whitenesses, unsigned bluenesses.

1986

The Loop in Lone Kauri Road

By the same road to the same
sea, in the same two minds,
to run the last mile blind or
save it for later. These
are not alternatives.

So difficult to concentrate! a powerful
breath to blow the sea back
and a powerful hand to haul it
in, without overbalancing.
Scolded for inattention,

depending on the wind, I know
a *rimu* from a *rewarewa*
by the leaf not 'coarsely serrate',
observant of the road roping
seaward in the rain forest.

A studied performance, the way
I direct my eyes, position

my head, 'look interested'.
Fine crystal, the man said,
you can tell by the weight,

the colour, the texture. The dog
steadies, places a healthy turd
on the exact spot. We like it
in the sun, it keeps our backs
warm, the watertables

dribble down the raw red cutting
the road binds, injured natures are
perfect in themselves. We liked it
at the movies when they nuked the city,
and suspended our disbelief

in doomsday, helping out the movie.
NEW YORK STATE jogs past me,
ribcage under the t-shirt stacked
with software, heart-muscle programmed
for the once round trip,

crosses my mind, by the bridge
at the bottom, the road over which
and the stream underneath are thoughts
quickly dismissed, as we double
back, pacing ourselves.

Concentrate! the hawk lifts off
heavily with an offal of silence.
Forget that, and how the helicopter
clapper-clawed the sea, fire-bucketing
the forest, the nested flame.

1986

A .   R .   D .   F A I R B U R N

Born in Auckland, where he worked variously as a journalist, script-writer, union secretary, and tutor in the English Department at the University, A. R. D. Fairburn (1904–1957) was also a controversial social commentator. A notable painter and fabric designer, he taught at the Elam School of Fine Arts, University of Auckland, for the last 11 years of his life.

Rhyme of the Dead Self

Tonight I have taken all that I was
and strangled him that pale lily-white lad
I have choked him with these my hands these claws
catching him as he lay a-dreaming in his bed.

Then chuckling I dragged out his foolish brains
that were full of pretty love-tales heighho the holly
and emptied them holus bolus to the drains
those dreams of love oh what ruinous folly.

He is dead pale youth and he shall not rise
on the third day or any other day
sloughed like a snakeskin there he lies
and he shall not trouble me again for aye.

1930

from Dominion

for Jocelyn

Utopia

I

The house of the governors, guarded by eunuchs,
and over the arch of the gate
these words engraved:
HE WHO IMPUGNS THE USERERS IMPERILS THE STATE.

Within the gates the retinue of evil,
the instruments of the governors:
scabs picked from the body of the enslaved,
well-paid captains and corporals
in the army of privilege
taking the bread of tyranny, wearing
the livery of extortion; and those who keep
the records of decay,
statisticians and archivists,
turning the leaves with cold hands, computing
our ruin on scented cuffs.

For the enslaved, the treadmill;
the office and adoration
of the grindstone god;
the apotheosis of the means,
the defiling of the end;
the debasement of the host
of the living; the celebration
of the black mass that casts
the shadow of a red mass.

Backblock camps for the outcast, the superfluous,
reading back-date magazines, rolling cheap cigarettes,
not mated;
witnesses to the constriction of life essential
to the maintenance of the rate of profit
as distinct from the gross increment of wealth.

II

In vicarage and manse
love is loose-lipped and flaps its feathers,
its talk is full of ifs and whethers,
spume of futility blown

from raging seas of sin
that lift and heave in the gales of chance,
beautified Nature, unhindered circumstance.
The Church Hesitant seeks for balm
in sunlit studies, a chatter of talk,
dead prayers and spurious calm:
and the dog-days claim for their own
the theological bone
the cracked and bitten shin
that can crawl but cannot walk.

III

In the suburbs the spirit of man
walks on the garden path,
walks on the well-groomed lawn, dwells
among the manicured shrubs.
The variegated hedge encircles life.
In the countryside, in shire and county,
the abode of wind and sun, where clouds trample the sky
and hills are stretched like arms heaped up with bounty,
in the countryside the land is
the space between the barbed-wire fences,
mortgaged in bitterness, measured in sweated butterfat.

IV

In this air the idea dies;
or spreads like plague; emotion runs
undamned, its limits vague,
its flush disastrous as the rolling floods,
the swollen river's rush; or dries
to a thin trickle, lies
in flat pools where swarms of flies
clouding the stagnant brim
breed from thick water, clustered slime.

V

Gross greed, mated with fear,
that feeds on the bread
of children, buying reprieve
with philanthropic pence, making profession
of charity: the pitiful cunning of the depraved.

Small greed, the starveling weed
that grows in desperate soil
in the hearts of the enslaved,
hugging a bitten crust
with the closeness of a trust
clinging to an oil concession.

VI

The press: slow dripping of water on mud;
thought's daily bagwash, ironing out opinion,
scarifying the edges of ideas.
And the hirelings; caught young;
the bough bent and twisted
to the shape of evil; tending the oaf
who by accident of birth has property
in the public conscience, a 'moulder of opinion';
turning misshapen vessels, and jars for subtle poisons;
blinde mouthes;
insulated against discontent
born dumb and tractable, swift to disremember
the waif, and the hurt eyes of the passing stranger,
and the statisitics of those who killed themselves
or were confined in asylums for the insane.

And the proletarian animal,
product of perversion and source of profit,
with a net paid circulation of a million,
and many unsold, or lying about the streets
bearing the marks of boot-protectors;

a crucified ape, preached by Darwinian bishops,
guarded by traitorous pens, handed the vinegar
of a 'belief in the essential goodness of human nature'.

VII

The army of the unliving, the cells of the cancer:
small sleek men rubbing their hands in vestibules,
re-lighting cigar-butts, changing their religions;
dabblers in expertise, licensed to experiment
on the vile body of the State; promoters of companies;
efficiency experts (unearned excrement
of older lands, oranges sucked dry),
scourges of a kindly and credulous race;
economists, masters of dead language;
sorners, bureausites; titled upstarts; men
with dry palms and a sense of humour; hagglers, hucksters,
buyers and sellers, retchings
of commerce, spawn of greed; holders of mortgages
on slum farms where children milk
with chilblained fingers; dwellers
in warm, rich flats, forced growth of luscious weed;
old wealthy women, buyers of etchings, fondlers
of dogs, holders of stocks
in sweatshops where the young virgins,
the daughters of the poor,
housed with machines endure the hands of clocks;

councillors and legislators,
toads in plush;
octogenarians who have forgotten

the heat of their youth, giving the sadic twist
to laws of marriage and divorcement, obtruding
the rancour of a swollen prostate,
the jealousy of a withered scrotum,
upon the affairs of springtime;

and those who embrace their misery
in small closed rooms,
sucking carious teeth, sniffing
the odour of themselves, gentlemen's relish:
'You must not confiscate our sufferings,
they are private poetry.'

VIII

Above the city's heap, life's bones
licked clean, void of desire,
white clouds like images of fear
move in the barren blue; the sun's cold fire
shines in the infinite crystal
the ghastly clear
frozen emptiness of air
and formless being above the walls,
beyond the concrete edges of despair.
A death has been arranged and will take place
none knows where or when, none cares
how soon the wind will whisper 'Soon, soon,'
shaking the dead leaves in the city square
at noon, in darkening air.

IX

This is our paper city, built
on the rock of debt, held fast
against all winds by the paperweight of debt.
The crowds file slowly past, or stop and stare,
and here and there, dull-eyed, the idle stand
in clusters in the mouths of gramophone shops
in a blare of music that fills the crumpled air
with paper flowers and artificial scents
and painless passion in a heaven
of fancied love.
                        The women come
from the bargain shops and basements
at dusk, as gazelles from drinking;
the men buy evening papers, scan them
for news of doomsday, light their pipes:
and the night sky, closing over, covers like a hand
the barbaric yawn of a young and wrinkled land.

X

Men and women, hands and faces; a nation established
by statute-makers, geographers, census-takers;

living like fleas in surface dust;
begetting children,
grist for the system, multiplying souls
in the jaws of chaos.
The living saddled with debt. A load of debt for the fœtus.
A load laid by for the moment of delight
hidden in the future, yet to be made flesh,
trapped in the net of statistical laws, caught
in the calculations of the actuaries.

And over all the hand of the usurer,
bland angel of darkness,
mild and triumphant and much looked up to.

Album Leaves

Imperial

In the first days, in the forgotten calendars,
came the seeds of the race, the forerunners:
offshoots, outcasts, entrepreneurs,
architects of Empire, romantic adventurers;
and the famished, the multitude of the poor;
crossed parallels of boredom, tropics
of hope and fear, losing the pole-star, suffering
world of water, chaos of wind and sunlight,
and the formless image in the mind;
sailed under Capricorn to see for ever
the arc of the sun to northward.

They shouted at the floating leaf,
laughed with joy at the promise of life,
hope becoming belief, springing
alive, alight, gulls at the masthead crying,
the crag splitting the sky, slowly
towering out of the sea, taking
colour and shape, and the land
swelling beyond; noises
of water among rocks, voices singing.

Haven of hunger; landfall of hope;
goal of ambition, greed and despair.

In tangled forests under the gloom
of leaves in the green twilight,
among the habitations of the older gods
they walked, with Christ beside them,
and an old enemy at hand, one whose creed
flourished in virgin earth. They divided the land;
some for their need, and some
for aimless, customary greed
that hardened with the years, grew taut
and knotted like a fist. Flower and weed
scattered upon the breeze
their indiscriminate seed; on every hillside fought
God's love against the old antagonist.

They change the sky but not their hearts who cross the seas.

These islands;
the remnant peaks of a lost continent,
roof of an old world, molten droppings
from earth's bowels, gone cold;
ribbed with rock, resisting the sea's corrosion
for an age, and an age to come. Of three races
the home: two passing in conquest
or sitting under the leaves, or on shady doorsteps
with quiet hands, in old age, childless.
And we, the latest: their blood on our hands: scions
of men who scaled ambition's
tottering slopes, whose desires
encompassed earth and heaven: we have prospered greatly,
we, the destined race, rulers of conquered isles,
sprouting like bulbs in warm darkness, putting out
white shoots under the wet sack of Empire.

Back Street

A girl comes out of a doorway in the morning
with hair uncombed, treading with care
on the damp bricks, picks up the milk,
stares skyward with sleepy eyes;
returns to the dewy step; leaves
with the closing of the door
silence under narrow eaves
the tragic scent of violets on the morning air
and jonquils thrust through bare earth here and there.

At ten o'clock a woman comes out
and leans against the wall
beside the fig-tree hung with washing; listens
for the postman's whistle. Soon he passes,
leaves no letter.
She turns a shirt upon the barren tree
and pads back to the house as ghost to tomb.
No children since the first. The room
papered in 'Stars', with Jubilee pictures
pasted over the mantel, spattered with fat.

Up the street
the taxi-drivers lounging in a knot
beside the rank of shining cars
discuss the speed of horses
as mariners the stars in their courses.

. . . .

Wedding Group

After the benediction and the confetti,
the photographer's parlour, the cakes and lemonade,

the bridegroom, 33, Christ's age crucified,
clerk in a bank
standing beside the bride and her best friend
discussing the beauty of the ceremony
with nervous voices, words packed in politeness
of sawdust, glumly awaiting
the nuptial taxi:

married so late they should have had many dreams,
midnight illusion, habitual fantasy: waking
not from the beauty and torpor of a dream in spring
to halcyon dawn, soft warmth of living blood,
love's aftermath in the hollow of a shoulder,
but from the excited nightmare of the self-cheated.
She, the friend, member of a literary circle,
sniggers and spreads her claws: At what hotel
do you intend to Stope for your honeymoon, te-he?
He, tapping his cigarette: No children for us
until the Budget is balanced. God save the King.

. . . .

The Possessor

On my land grew a green tree
that gave shade to the weary,
peace to my children, rest to the travel-stained;
and the waters ran beneath, the river of life.
My people drank of the waters after their labour,
had comfort of the tree in the heat of noon,
lying in summer grass ringed round with milk-white flowers,
gathering strength, giving their bodies
to the motion of the earth.

I cut down the tree, and made posts
and fenced my land,
I banished my people and turned away the traveller;
and now I share my land with sparrows that trespass
upon my rood of air. The earth
is barren, the stream is dry; the sun has blackened
grass that was green and springing, flowers that were fair.

Conversation in the Bush

'Observe the young and tender frond
'of this punga: shaped and curved
'like the scroll of a fiddle: fit instrument
'to play archaic tunes.'
                              'I see
        'the shape of a coiled spring.'

Elements

I

In the summer we rode in the clay country,
the road before us trembling in the heat
and on the warm wind the scent of tea-tree,
grey and wind-bitten in winter, odorous under summer noon,
with spurts of dust under the hoofs
and a crackle of gorse on the wayside farms.
At dusk the sun fell down in violet hills
and evening came and we turned our horses
homeward through dewy air.

In autumn, kindness of earth, covering life,
mirrored stillness,
peace of mind, and time to think;
good fishing, and burdened orchards. Winter come,
headlands loomed in mist,
hills were hailswept, flowers were few;
and when we rode on the mountains in frosty weather
the distant ranges ran like blue veins through the land.
In spring we thrust our way through the bush,
through the ferns in the deep shadow angled with sunbeams,
roamed by streams in the bush, by the scarred stones
and the smooth stones water-worn, our shoulders wet
with rain from the shaken leaves.

O lovely time! when bliss was taken
as the bird takes nectar from the flower.
Happy the sunlit hour, the frost and the heat.
Hearts poised at a star's height
moved in a cloudless world
like gulls afloat above islands.

Smoke out of Europe, death blown
on the wind, and a cloak of darkness for the spirit.

II

Land of mountains and running water
rocks and flowers
and the leafy evergreen, O natal earth,
the atoms of your children
are bonded to you for ever:
though the images of your beauty lie in shadow,
time nor treachery, nor the regnant evil,
shall efface from the hearts of your children
from their eyes and from their fingertips
the remembrance of good.
Treading your hills, drinking your waters,
touching your greenness, they are content, finding

peace at the heart of strife
and a core of stillness in the whirlwind.
Absent, estranged from you, they are unhappy,
crying for you continually
in the night of their exile.

III

To prosper in a strange land
taking cocktails at twilight behind the hotel curtains,
buying cheap and selling dear, acquiring customs,
is to bob up and down like a fisherman's gaudy float
in a swift river.

He who comes back returns
to no ruin of gold nor riot of buds,
moan of doves in falling woods
nor wind of spring shaking the hedgerows,
heartsache, strangling sweetness: pictures
of change, extremes of time and growth,
making razor-sharp the tenses,
waking remembrance, torturing sense;

home-coming, returns only
to the dull green, hider of bones,
changeless, save in the slight spring
when the bush is peopled with flowers,
sparse clusters of white and yellow
on the dull green, like laughter in court;
and in summer when the coasts
bear crimson bloom, sprinkled like blood
on the lintel of the land.

IV

Fairest earth,
fount of life, giver of bodies,
deep well of our delight, breath of desire,
let us come to you
barefoot, as befits love,
as the boy to the trembling girl,
as the child to the mother;
seeking before all things the honesty of substance,
touch of soil and wind and rock,
frost and flower and water,
the honey of the senses, the food
of love's imagining; and the most intimate
touch of love, that turns to being;
deriving wisdom, and the knowledge of necessity;
building thereon, stone by stone,
the rational architecture of truth, to house
the holy flame, that is neither reason nor unreason
but the thing given,

the flame that burns blue in the stillness, hovering
between the green wood of the flesh and the smoke of death.

Fair earth, we have broken our idols:
and after the days of fire we shall come to you
for the stones of a new temple.

. . . .

1938

Full Fathom Five

He was such a curious lover of shells
and the hallucinations of water
that he could never return out of the sea
without first having to settle a mermaid's bill.

Groping along the sea-bottom of the age
he discovered many particulars he did not care to speak about
even in the company of water-diviners
things sad and unspeakable
moss-covered skulls with bodies fluttering inside
with the unreality of specks moving before the eyes of a
    photograph
trumpets tossed from the decks of ocean-going liners
eccentric starfish fallen from impossible heavens
fretting on uncharted rocks
still continents with trees and houses like a child's drawing
and in every cupboard of the ocean
weary dolphins trapped in honey-coloured cobwebs
murmuring to the revolution Will you be long.

He was happy down there under the frothing ship-lanes
because nobody ever bothered him with statistics
or talk of yet another dimension of the mind.

And eventually and tragically finding he could not drown
he submitted himself to the judgment of the desert
and was devoured by man-eating ants
with a rainbow of silence branching from his lips.

1941

Tapu

To stave off disaster, or bring the devil to heel,
    or to fight against fear, some carry a ring or a locket,
but I, who have nothing to lose by the turn of the wheel,
    and nothing to gain, I carry the world in my pocket.

For all I have gained, and have lost, is locked up in this thing,
    this cup of cracked bone from the skull of a fellow long dead,
with a hank of thin yellowish hair fastened in with a ring.
    For a symbol of death and desire these tokens are wed.

The one I picked out of a cave in a windy cliff-face
    where the old Maoris slept, with a curse on the stranger
       who moved,
in despite of tapu, but a splinter of bone from that place.
    The other I cut from the head of the woman I loved.

1943

The Cave

From the cliff-top it appeared a place of defeat,
the nest of an extinct bird, or the hole where the sea hoards its
    bones,
a pocket of night in the sun-faced rock,
sole emblem of mystery and death in that enormous noon.

We climbed down, and crossed over the sand,
and there were islands floating in the wind-whipped blue,
and clouds and islands trembling in your eyes,
and every footstep and every glance
was a fatality felt and unspoken, our way
rigid and glorious as the sun's path,
unbroken as the genealogy of man.

And when we had passed beyond
into the secret place and were clasped
by the titanic shadows of the earth,
all was transfigured, all was redeemed,
so that we escaped from the days
that had hunted us like wolves, and from ourselves,
in the brief eternity of the flesh.

There should be the shapes of leaves and flowers
printed on the rock, and a blackening of the walls
from the flame on your mouth,
to be found by the lovers straying
from the picnic two worlds hence, to be found and known,
because the form of the dream is always the same,
and whatever dies or changes this will persist and recur,
will compel the means and the end, find consummation,
whether it be
silent in swansdown and darkness, or in grass moonshadow-
    mottled,
or in a murmuring cave of the sea.

We left, and returned to our lives:

the act entombed, its essence caught
for ever in the wind, and in the noise of waves,
for ever mixed
with lovers' breaths who by salt-water coasts
in the sea's beauty dwell.

1943

A Farewell

What is there left to be said?
There is nothing we can say,
nothing at all to be done
to undo the time of day;
no words to make the sun
roll east, or raise the dead.

I loved you as I love life:
the hand I stretched out to you
returning like Noah's dove
brought a new earth to view,
till I was quick with love;
but Time sharpens his knife,

Time smiles and whets his knife,
and something has got to come out
quickly, and be buried deep,
not spoken or thought about
or remembered even in sleep.
You must live, get on with your life.

1943

Winter Night

The candles gutter and burn out,
    and warm and snug we take our ease,
and faintly comes the wind's great shout
    as he assails the frozen trees.

The vague walls of this little room
    contract and close upon the soul;
deep silence hangs amid the gloom;
    no sound but the small voice of the coal.

Here in this sheltered firelit place
    we know not wind nor shivering tree;
we two alone inhabit space,
    locked in our small infinity.

This is our world, where love enfolds
    all images of joy, all strife
resolves in peace: this moment holds
    within its span the sum of life.

For Time's a ghost: these reddening coals
    were forest once ere he'd begun,
and now from dark and timeless boles
    we take the harvest of the sun;

and still the flower-lit solitudes
    are radiant with the springs he stole
where violets in those buried woods
    wake little blue flames in the coal.

Great stars may shine above this thatch;
   beyond these walls perchance are men
with laws and dreams: but our thin latch
   holds all such things beyond our ken.

The fire now lights our cloudy walls,
   now fails beneath the singing pot,
and as the last flame leaps and falls
   the far wall is and then is not.

Now lovelier than firelight is the gleam
   of dying embers, and your face
shines through the pathways of my dream
   like young leaves in a forest place.

1943

The Estuary

The wind has died, no motion now
in the summer's sleepy breath. Silver the sea-grass,
the shells and the driftwood, fixed in the moon's vast crystal.
Think: long after, when the walls of the small house
have collapsed upon us, each alone,
far gone the earth's invasion
the slow earth bedding and filling the bone,
this water will still be crawling up the estuary,
fingering its way among the channels, licking the stones;
and the floating shells, minute argosies
under the giant moon, still shoreward glide
among the mangroves on the creeping tide.

The noise of gulls comes through the shining darkness
over the dunes and the sea. Now the clouded moon
is warm in her nest of light. The world's a shell
where distant waves are murmuring of a time
beyond this time. *Give me the ghost of your hand:*
unreal, unreal the dunes,
the sea, the mangroves, and the moon's white light,
unreal, beneath our naked feet, the sand.

1952

I'm Older Than You, Please Listen

To the young man I would say:
Get out! Look sharp, my boy,
before the roots are down,
before the equations are struck,
before a face or a landscape
has power to shape or destroy.
This land is a lump without leaven,
a body that has no nerves.
Don't be content to live in
a sort of second-grade heaven
with first-grade butter, fresh air,

and paper in every toilet;
becoming a butt for the malice
of those who have stayed and soured,
staying in turn to sour,
to smile, and savage the young.
If you're enterprising and able,
smuggle your talents away,
hawk them in livelier markets
where people are willing to pay.
If you have no stomach for roughage,
if patience isn't your religion,
if you must have sherry with your bitters,
if money and fame are your pigeon,
if you feel that you need success
and long for a good address,
don't anchor here in the desert—
the fishing isn't so good:
take a ticket for Megalopolis,
don't stay in this neighbourhood!

1952

ROBIN HYDE

Robin Hyde was the pen-name of Iris Guiver Wilkinson (1906–1939). Born in Cape Town, she was a prolific journalist, novelist and poet. She is best remembered for her novels such as The Godwits Fly *and* Check to Your King.

Chrysanthemum

See that dishevelled head,
Its bronze curls all undone?
I am that one,
The stubborn slattern of your garden bed;
No sweetness for you here, but bittersweet
Admission that my hour must needs be fleet;
A frosty tang of wit, an autumn face,
Perchance the memory of some sharper grace,
That shone beneath the imperial yellow tiles
Nor needed stoop for princely sulks or smiles;
Tatterdemalion courage here, a ghost
To captain some obscure, defeated host. . . .
Many the springtime maidens, crisp as snow. . . .
Yet, hapless sir, we know
Your fate . . . to love me most.

1937

White Irises

But when it came to holding fast
All my heaped days as water went,
Breast-high in swirling dreams I stood,

With vain hands clutched the slipping past
Of straws and faces on the flood.
Till single among stones I saw
The white, the ragged irises,
Cold on a sky of petals dead,
Their young cheeks roughened in the wind,
White-surpliced boys, a pale line spread
With the deep nave of dusk behind.
Over their feet the spring tide bore
In green, impatient, uncurbed grass,
High bellows flecked with daisied foam.
I saw the wind, a swimmer, pass
From grey-girt isles of cloud, his home,
And mount the blue stockades of trees.
O then a singing on the air,
Caught and flung back and held again,
Curled in the rosy shells of rain
And pressed against earth's listening ear
Took up the triumph-strain.
Cold boys of spring, the irises
With parted lips stood chanting there,
The green flood restive to their knees,
Rain powdered on their hair.
Till a red moon dipped shoulder-high,
A lantern swinging from the pole
Of some old fisher of the sky
In starry waters of the soul.
And I who sought for heart's farewell
In dusk of spring, have brought you these—
The choir singing in a spell,
The white, the ragged irises.

1952

The Bronze Rider, Wellington

Riding wooden horses from the hot Christmas Caves,
The children came laughing out into the Quay,
With a prance at their hills, and a dash at their waves,
And the broad street between shining peaceful and free.
Cheeks nipped in the wind, and their curls sailing gold,
Rode the sons and the daughters . . . (come home, dears, come home.)
But a wind from the sea blows, a thin mist blows cold . . .
Faint down the Quay sounds the tuck of a drum.

Children, come home, and be kissed as you're told.
(Ah, but who said it? A child could grow old.)
Home when you're bid, or the length of my tongue.
(Ah, but who said it? A child could die young.)
Now the bronze Rider comes to stay awhile,
In our hilly heart, so haunted by running feet;
Turns to the dusk his young, mysterious smile,
Implacably, unanswerably sweet.
He props the sky up with his stiff young arm,

Lest down it drop on cradled cottages,
Do our poor groping ways of living harm,
Vex with a light our city, that was his.
O forfeit of this world . . . The great bronze hooves,
Soundless, yet trampling air as they aspire,
Fling shame on us, who tread the ancient grooves;
Dawn is his stirrup, and his reins are fire.

Riding painted horses from town to Island Bay,
Mouths pink as moss-roses, hair sailing free,
Past the penny-shops, awning-shops, red shops and grey,
Past the vast jars of peppermint down to the sea;
Past the Blue Platter Inn, that's been burnt seven year,
Ride the sons and the daughters. (Come home, loves, come home.)
But the sound of a bugle folds crisp on the air,
The swish of a keel cutting out in the foam.

Children, come home, will you hear your Dad shout?
(Ah, but who said it? A ship could glide out . . .)
Home to your broth and your books, as you're bid . . .
(Ah, but who cried it? Our lamps could be hid.)

Faint on the Quay sounds the throb of the drum.

1952

The Last Ones

But the last black horse of all
Stood munching the green-bud wind,
And the last of the raupo huts
Let down its light behind.
Sullen and shadow-clipped
He tugged at the evening star,
New-mown slivers swished like straw
Across the manuka.

As for the hut, it said
No word but its meagre light,
Its people slept as the dead,
Bedded in Maori night.
'And there is the world's last door,
And the last world's horse,' sang the wind,
'With little enough before,
And what you have seen behind.'

1952

The Beaches

I

Not here our sands, those salt-and-pepper sands
Mounding us to the chins: (don't you remember?
Won't the lost shake for any cry at all?)
Listen: our sands, so clean you didn't care

If fine grains hit your teeth, stuck in your hair,
Were moist against the sunburn on your knees.
Everything glowed — old tar-bubble November,
Nothing around us but the blue-bubbling air;
We liked being quiet then. To move or call
Crumpled the work of hands, his big red hands:
(It was he, our father, piled the mounds for us);
He sat and read, dreamed there against the wall,
Thinking perhaps how rocks are not quite lands,
Housing old barnacles and octopus;
How the wet gold soups back, strains into seas.

We closed our eyes: sunlight streamed through, in rays
Orange or green, but I liked violet most:
Black dog splashed past us, with the chewed-up ball:
Here it's so different. Flesh looks hurt, asprawl
These crayfish people; legs like fungoid trees
Lopped off.
You're playing safe to stay a ghost.

II

Island Bay, Orongorongo, Day's Bay, Miramar,
Evans Bay where the slips and the rust-red ships are;
You can't lie still, pretending those are dreams
Like us . . . Or watch, I'll show you: wet and clean,
Coming past the sand-dune couples, strung out far,
Purple on brown, his shadow grows between:
Bleached logs stare up: he's bringing us ice-creams.

III

An absent face, remote and sharp, as far
As fisher's boats that bob across the bay
Setting their cray-pots in the island's shadow;
Fat men are red . . . this one's a different red,
Thin-faced and fair, burnt up in scarlet sun.
Ganges and Jumna, half the parrot places
With screeching feathers, soapstone lantern faces,
Were his; but he can't talk of what he's done.
Sometimes he hits his skull against a star,
Rages, fizzles red at everyone.

Later you hear him again: 'Sorry, old girl.'
The lamp goes up, her face looks wringing wet,
The shadow stoops, to see that we're asleep.
I'd like to ask them questions then: but one
Thinks you're clean toothbrush homework neatly done;
One dreams, says 'A penny for a curl.'
They love you, but their thoughts tide back so deep:
Both are so very certain you'll forget.

IV

Sands, sands of my father's town,
Of my father's triple sea,
(Once for the eyes and twice for dream,
Thrice for memory):
Quilled in the dusk here, grey and brown,
Cool where the silvers gleam,
Hush your singing and let me down;
We shall hear the low-voiced sea.

What is it quickens the blood?
Smell of the sun-soaked, salt-white wood.
What is the tameless thing?
Gull's shafted wing.
What is it lads deserve?
White boat's arrowy glimpsing curve.
What is silk to my foot?
Tide on the turn, when spongy trees uproot.
What makes the sweethearts quarrel?
Third mouth, pink as coral.
What shall a maiden do,
Stay true or be untrue?
What says the Mother Sea?
On a glittering day, go free, go free.
What do fishermen keep in their pot?
Cod, garlic and crab they've got.
What makes the wanton's bed?
Sand while she's living, deep sea dead.
How about her that's nice?
Granite shone smooth as ice.
What must I do, my sea?
(With empty hands, quiet heart, little else, O Sea) . . .
Still be my child — my child to me.

Sands, sands of my mother's town,
Of my mother's secret sea.
(For the head borne high, for the lagging heart,
At last for memory,)
Feathered in dusk here, grey and black,
White where the moon's on foam,
Hush your singing and hand me back
For a bed and a lamp at home.
'White bed,'
    Sea said,
        rocking,
'White bed,
    but not
        a home.'

V

This is my secret, this is the chord most perfectly strung:
There lay the dunes: I cleared them in one white stride,
Feet flying, arms flying, seagull-swift, hair and heart flying,

Smiting my feet on sand, I was into the tide:
Catching, striking, and streaming the harp-chords: for I was young.

This in a sea-cleft bony with old spars staring out
From the rocks and the swaying livid anemones:
But the tide broke in, and with one magnificent shout
Caught me, carried me, balanced me, held by the knees:
Curled to me, high by the wrecked and foaming trees.

But the sparkling Sabine love three moments over
Ran I and laughed, from the greenbeards' following wrath:
Whirling in winds and taunted, my hollow retreating lover
Snarled at the cliffs, as his spray-drenched hands reached forth:
And in many a sucking cavern, the convex eyes peered forth.

Turned I, and shaken, a child and a woman, blindly
Shook off the weed from my breasts, and knelt upon stone:
And climbed in the yellow steeps of a hill that held me kindly,
And lay in the yellow flowers: and lay alone:
I parted the yellow flowers and lay alone.

VI

Close under here, I watched two lovers once,
Which should have been a sin, from what you say:
I'd come to look for prawns, small pale-green ghosts,
Sea-coloured bodies tickling round the pool.
But tide was out then; so I strolled away
And climbed the dunes, to lie here warm, face down,
Watching the swimmers by the jetty-posts
And wrinkling like the bright blue wrinkling bay.
It wasn't long before they came; a fool
Could see they had to kiss; but your pet dunce
Didn't quite know men count on more than that;
And so just lay, patterning the sand.
                    And they
Were pale thin people, not often clear of town;
Elastic snapped, when he jerked off her hat;
I heard her arguing, 'Dick, my frock!' But he
Thought she was bread.
I wished her legs were brown,
And mostly, then, stared at the dawdling sea.
Hoping Perry would row me some day in his boat.

Not all the time; and when they'd gone, I went
Down to the hollow place where they had been,
Trickling bed through fingers. But I never meant
To tell the rest, or you, what I had seen;
Though that night, when I came in late for tea,
I hoped you'd see the sandgrains on my coat.

VII

Cool and certain, their oars will be lifted in dusk, light-feathered
As wings of terns, that dip into dream, coming back blue; but the
    motionless gull
With his bold head, hooked beak, black-slit humped harsh back
Freezing in icy air gleams crystal and beautiful.
No longer the dark corks, bobbing bay-wide, are seen:
Dogs bark, mothers hail back their children from ripple's danger:
People dipped in the dusk-vats smile back, each stranger
Than time; each has a face of crystal and blue.
    In the jettisoned boat, the child who peered at her book
Cannot lift her glance from the running silk of the creek:
It is time to return to her mother, to call and look . . .
The sea-pulse beats in her wrists: she will not speak.
But the boats, in salt tide and smarting sunrise weathered,
Swing by an island's shadow: silver trickles and wets
The widening branch of their wake; the swart Italian faces,
Fisherman's silver fingers, fumbling the nets:
And the island lies behind them, lifting its glassy cone
In one strange motionless gesture, light on stone:
Only the gulls, the guards of the water-lapping places,
Scream at the fisherman lifting the water-lifting nets.

Far and away, the shore people hear a singing:
Love-toned Italian voices fondle the night: the hue
Of the quietly waiting people is velvet blue.

                                                    1952

The Houses

I

Old nursery chair; its legs, cut down, are broken:
Old timepiece, out-of-date, forlorn and slow:
Slow creaking shadow; somebody unawoken.
Trumpet: don't touch it, soldier, it won't blow.

II

On the asphalt a gas light pools: a child looks out
Swinging against the slotted fence and grey,
And eats the three nasturtium seeds: all day
She kept them in her pocket, for the doubt
They might be poison, as her sisters say.
But now their delicate, dubious taste can sting
Her tongue curled: snail's horns curl: they drop and cling
On round nasturtium leaves, green-saucered here.

Now she has evening all her own; the hot
Cream scent of cabbage palms, trying to flood out
Like man's love, or the Blessed Sacrament:

Sunset peaks over her, a copper tent,
Wind like God's breath goes past her in a shout:
Behind this street shine houses that are not,
Playmates she loves, or loved: but then forgot.

III

Adolicus; that's a creeper rug, its small
Pink-and-white piecemeal flowers swarm down a fence:
So little, no scent to be by; show, pretence —
Nothing to do, but hide the rotting wall.
Three slats were broken: but the street-boys eyes
Can't climb in here like ants and frighten us.
Stare if they like: we've the adolicus.

IV

Hares on their forms at dusk, were not so still
Nor those soft stones, their eyes, so warily bright
As yours, held captive by my story's will:
Candle-flame pricked between us: night
Lapped like grey water over the sill.

Why did you listen? Little enough to learn . . .
Scraps from a baked street's platter; folk we knew
Seen slantwise, through vined doorways that discern
The secret child. Did blue
Flame in my eyes so steeply burn?

Why didn't you answer back? Perhaps the wind
Was I; you the deep earth, that wouldn't care
(So dreaming) for the littler left behind:
Flame pieces out your hair,
Your hands; never that quiet coast, your mind.

V

None of it true; for Christ's sake, spill the ink,
Tear out this charnel's darnel-root, that lingers
Sprouting words, words, words! Give me cool bluegum leaves
To rub brittle between my fingers.

I had the touch of hillside once: the ever-
So-slender cold of buttercup stems in brink:
Pebbles: great prints in mud: Oh, Lazarus, bring me
Some mountain honesty to drink!

VI

Section and brick and grass;
The boys lingering home from school,
Tall girls, their long hair in plaits,
Their print frocks summer cool;
Gates creaking, doors pushed ajar,
Narrow blue panes of glass;

The shabby dreamers that pass,
Afar and afar
Spilling into this city, the sunset vats.

Oven, gas-light and sink,
The cracked plates getting hot,
The tired man's tedious return
To the house that honours him not.
Singsong of lessons; the girls
Spell out their tables; food
His own, and he knows it good:
But his dry cold senses yearn
For a friendly wine to drink,
For a laugh in his dwelling-place:
Weary his woman's face,
The bitter smoke whirls.

VII

Here the caged voice in the wood
Flown tame to hand
Told more, hinted at more
Than we understand:
Slave to the stubborn-fingered
Melted down to lullaby,
It urged more, stumbled and lingered
The advice, would not die.
Something had these to say —
Wood, string, ivory:
A prophecy out of the soul
Or out of the tree:
The singing bough was nailed
To masthead: young Argonaut
Half-hearted, shivered and failed:
Laughed, half-forgot:
And leapt out sunwards, to play
With the dogs, the white sticks of his choice —
Anything, save that lamenting
Beautiful voice:
Leaving five notes on the air,
And the sunbeams, wild
As doves flicked off from his hair,
The impatient master, the child,
Knelt, making circles of chalk;
And knew how alone
String, wood and ivory
Plead on, plead on.

VIII

But another and older music
Islanded round these keys,
Sweeping them low; black birches dragged in a brook:

So old, so tattered the book,
The names of its melodies
Were the signets of ancient kings
In a fire that leapt too quick —
The names and the fire were gone:
But the child's thin fingers drew on
Like a muslin drawn through rings
All that her dream might flag upon;
(The song gat eyes and wings):
Till the chords of the wooden heart,
The low slow messenger strings,
Gave her an art, where dwelt no art,
And songs the singer sings.
Backwards forwards and back
The spider hands in their web
Ran from the white to the quaking black
And span in the airy ebb:
Till with eyes forgetful of name,
With mind forsaken of words,
She played: and brushing her eyes as they came
The green and silver birds
Shrilled with the birds of flame,
With the instruments' red birds.

Outside mounted a hill
And flowed a moon,
Milk for the gourd-like valleys to spill,
Brimming over soon:
Yet it was evening still,
And a sprinkling hose made wet
The moth — a fluttering darker than air,
Columbines' spiky hair
And the humble mignonette.
In a cleft between dark and light,
(So the child knew,)
A road wound upwards, glassily bright,
And the trampling pines went through:
And the road and its pine-trees burned
In the glitter of fleeces blue,
In a sparkle of hooves, on the highway for which she yearned:
This the child knew,
But would not turn her head.
Slowly, solemnly, stately, she thrummed them into view —
The flocks that would feed on the dead.

                                                        1952

Pihsien Road

Old men in blue: and heavily encumbered
Old shoulders held by shadowy whips in sway,
Like ox and ass, that down this road have lumbered
All day: all the bright murderous day.
More than their stumbling footprints press this clay.

And light in air, pure white, in wonder riding,
Some crazy Phaeton these have never known
Holds by a lever their last awe, deciding
How flesh shall spurt from sinews, brain from bone —
Crushing desolate grain with a harder stone.

1952

What Is It Makes the Stranger?

What is it makes the stranger? Say, oh eyes!
Because I was journeying far, sailing alone,
Changing one belt of stars for the northern belt,
Men in my country told me, 'You will be strange —
Their ways are not our ways; not like ourselves
They think, suffer and dream.'
So sat I silent, and watched the stranger, why he was strange.
But now, having come so far, shed the eight cloaks of wind,
Ridden ponies of foam, and the great stone lions of six strange
    cities.
What is it makes the stranger? Say, oh eyes!
Eyes cannot tell. They view the self-same world —
Outer eyes vacant till throughts and pictures fill them,
Inner eyes watching secret paths of the brain.
Hands? But the hands of my country knit reeds, bend wood,
Shape the pliable parts of boats and roofs.
Mend pots, paint pictures, write books
Though different books; glean harvests, if different harvests,
Not so green as young rice first shaking its spears from water.
Hands cannot say. Feet then? They say
In shoe, not sandal, or bare if a man be poor,
They thread long ways between daylight and dark,
Longer, from birth to death.
Know flint from grasses, wear soles through, hate sharp pebbles,
Oftentimes long for the lightness of birds.
Yet in my country, children, even the poor
Wear soft warm shoes, and a little foot in the dance
Warms the looks of young men, no less than here.
In my country, on summer evenings, clean as milk poured out
From old blue basins, children under the hawthorne trees
Fly kites, lacing thin strings against the sky.
Not at New Year, but at other festivals
We light up fire-crackers
In memory of old buried danger, now a ghost danger.

On a roof garden, among the red-twigged bowing of winter trees,
The small grave bowls of dwarf pines (our pines grow tall
Yet the needle-sharp hair is the same) one first star swam,
Silver in lily-root dusk. Two lovers looked up.
Hands, body, heart in my breast,
Whispered, 'These are the same. Here we are not so strange —
Here there are friends and peace.
We have known such ways, we in our country!'

Black-tiled roofs, curled like wide horns, and hiding safe
From the eyes of the stranger, all that puts faith in you.
Remember this, of an unknown woman who passed,
But who stood first high on the darkening roof garden looking
    down.
My way behind me tattered away in wind,
Before me, was spelt with strange letters.
My mind was a gourd heavy with sweet and bitter waters.
Since I could not be that young girl, who heedless of stars
Now watched the face of her lover,
I wished to be, for one day, a man selling mandarins,
A blackened tile in some hearth place; a brazier, a well, a good word,
A blackened corpse along the road to Chapei,
Of a brave man, dead for his country.
Shaking the sweet-bitter waters within my mind,
It seemed to me, all seas fuse and intermarry.
Under the seas, all lands knit fibre, interlock:
On a highway so ancient as China's
What are a few miles more to the ends of the earth?
Is another lantern too heavy to light up, showing the face
Of farers and wayfarers, stumbling the while they go,
Since the world has called them stranger?

Only two rebels cried out 'We do not understand.'
Ear said, 'China and we
Struck two far sides of a rock; music came forth,
Our music and theirs, not the one music.
Listening in street and stall I hear two words,
Their word and mine. Mine is not understood,
Therefore am I an exile here, a stranger,
Eaten up with hunger for what I understand,
and for that which understands.'
Tongue said, 'I know
The sweet flavours of mandarin or fish. But mouth and I,
Speaking here, are mocked. Looks fall on us like blows.
Mistress, we served you well, and not for cash,
But free men. Therefore, beseech you, let us go on.'

Heart, lowlier, said, 'There is a way of patience —
Let ear study the door to understanding.
Mouth, there is silence first, but fellowship
Where children laugh or weep, the grown smile or frown,
Study, perceive and learn. Let not two parts
Unwisely make an exile of the whole.'

But still the rebels bawled, and so I saw
How in a world divorced from silences
These are the thieves.
Ear, who no longer listening well, sniffs up
The first vain trash, the first argument into his sack.
Mouth, who will spew it forth, but to be heard —
Both ill-taught scholars, credulous liars,
Seizing on, flinging up fuel.
There flamed the restlessness of such sick worlds,
As cannot know their country or earth's country;

Their moment or an age's moment.
Having such brawling servants in my train
I can be neither tile nor lamp.
Only a footprint. Some boy sees it at dawn
Before his high-wheeled cart creaks over it;
Only a sped and broken arrow,
Pointing a way where men will come in peace.

1952

The Deserted Village

In the deserted village, sunken down
With a shrug of last weak old age, pulled back to earth,
All people are fled or killed. The cotton crop rots,
Not one mild house leans sideways, a man on crutches,
Not a sparrow earns from the naked floors,
Walls look, but cannot live without the folk they loved —
It would be a bad thing to awaken them.
Having broken the rice-bowl, seek not to fill it again.

The village temple, well built, with five smashed gods, ten whole
    ones,
Does not want prayers. Its last vain prayer bled up
When the women ran outside to be slain.
A temple must house its sparrows or fall asleep,
Therefore a long time, under his crown of snails,
The gilded Buddha demands to meditate.
No little flowering fires on the incense-strings
Startle Kwan-Yin, whom they dressed in satin —
Old women sewing beads like pearls in her hair.
This was a temple for the very poor ones:
Their gods were mud and lath: but artfully
Some village painter coloured them all.
Wooden dragons were carefully carved
Finding in mangled wood one smiling childish tree,
Roses and bells not one foot high,
I set it back, at the feet of Kwan-Yin.
A woman's prayer-bag,
Having within her paper prayers, paid for in copper,
Seeing it torn, I gathered it up.
I shall often think, 'The woman I did not see
Voiced here her dying wish.
But the gods dreamed on. So low her voice, so loud
The guns, all that death-night, who would stoop to hear?'

1952

MARY URSULA BETHELL

Born in England, Ursula Bethell (1874–1945) grew up in New Zealand then returned to spend her twenties and thirties in Britain and Europe before settling in Christchurch. Her Collected Poems *were published in 1950 and again in 1985.*

Response

When you wrote your letter it was April,
And you were glad that it was spring weather,
And that the sun shone out in turn with showers of rain.

I write in waning May and it is autumn,
And I am glad that my chrysanthemums
Are tied up fast to strong posts,
So that the south winds cannot beat them down.
I am glad that they are tawny coloured,
And fiery in the low west evening light.
And I am glad that one bush warbler
Still sings in the honey-scented wattle . . .

But oh, we have remembering hearts,
And we say 'How green it was in such and such an April,'
And 'Such and such an autumn was very golden,'
And 'Everything is for a very short time.'

1929

Pause

When I am very earnestly digging
I lift my head sometimes, and look at the mountains,
And muse upon them, muscles relaxing.

I think how freely the wild grasses flower there,
How grandly the storm-shaped trees are massed in their gorges
And the rain-worn rocks strewn in magnificent heaps.

Pioneer plants on those uplands find their own footing;
No vigorous growth, there, is an evil weed:
All weathers are salutary.

It is only a little while since this hillside
Lay untrammelled likewise,
Unceasingly swept by transmarine winds.

In a very little while, it may be,
When our impulsive limbs and our superior skulls
Have to the soil restored several ounces of fertiliser,

The Mother of all will take charge again,
And soon wipe away with her elements
Our small fond human enclosures.

1929

Aesthetic

Yellow daisy, yellow daisy, where have I known you?
Something comes back to me from a far distant past —
Now I remember you were painted on a mantel-piece,
A Victorian mantel-piece, on a green background,
By one called Ethel, out of Thackeray.

1929

Glory

This same evening that I write I witnessed,
Resting on a garden bench and looking westward,
Sublime splendours.

Beyond the blood-red rose-engarrisoned footpath,
And in the dun green flatlands where a few human lights
    glimmered,
Wild indigo and magenta rainstorms invested
The dark recesses of the mountain ranges.

Clouds overhead burst into cornelian flames,
Transmuting by their strange flow all the garden pigments.
Then was revealed, in a dim turquoise interstice,
A very young, remote, and slender, but outshining,
But all predominant moon.

In such an hour the soul finds an appeasement
Not justified by reasons of commonsense.
In that hour she asks of the inscrutable
No more petulant questions.

1929

Fortune

'At least we shall have roses' laughed my companion,
Looking on the bundles arrived from the nursery,
All with their labels tied up so neatly,
All with their shaven crests and roots so well developed —
'We shall always have roses here.'

'At least we shall have roses' this morning I repeated,
Looking on the summer's lustrous assemblage,
Beholding the long shoots, as once before in spring-time,
Zestfully preparing for their latter blooming —
'We shall always have roses, here.'

Others may sail away to the sea-coasts of Bohemia,
Cathay, and Coromandel, Malay, and Patagonia,
Hong Kong, and Halifax, Bombay, and Pernambuco,
Frisco and Singapore, and all the world's fine harbours —
Wistfully we may watch them loosed from our limitations, —
But for us, at least, roses, here.

1929

Old Master

Or picture, here, some *Conversazione*
With flowers, birds, grass, and purple hills beyond,
And gilding sunlight, eloquent chiaroscuro,
And noble forms augustly grouped, and still —
  Smiling and still. Initiate and aware.

And thronging on the outskirts, in the foreground,
You, and you, and you, beloved familiars,
Bearing your individual sign and coat of arms,
Surprised and still, smiling and yet expectant —
  Found. Known. Secure. And reconciled.

                                    1929

Detail

My garage is a structure of excessive plainness,
It springs from a dry bank in the back garden,
It is made of corrugated iron,
And painted all over with brick-red.

But beside it I have planted a green Bay-tree,
— A sweet Bay, an Olive, and a Turkey Fig,
— A Fig, an Olive, and a Bay.

                                    1929

Erica

Sit down with me awhile beside the heath-corner.

Here have I laboured hour on hour in winter,
Digging thick clay, breaking up clods, and draining,
Carrying away cold mud, bringing up sandy loam,
Bringing these rocks and setting them all in their places,
To be shelter from winds, shade from too burning sun.

See, now, how sweetly all these plants are springing
Green, ever green, and flowering turn by turn,
Delicate heaths, and their fragrant Australian kinsmen,
Shedding, as once unknown in New Holland, strange scents on
  the air,
And purple and white daboecia — the Irish heather —
Said in the nursery man's list to be so well suited
For small gardens, for rock gardens, and for graveyards.

                                    1929

Warning of Winter

Give over, now, red roses;
Summer-long you told us,
Urgently unfolding, death-sweet, life-red,
Tidings of love. All's said. Give over.

Summer-long you placarded
Leafy shades with heart-red
Symbols. Who knew not love at first knows now,
Who had forgot has now remembered.

Let be, let be, lance-lilies,
Alert, pard-spotted, tilting
Poised anthers, flaming; have done flaming fierce;
Hard hearts were pierced long since, and stricken.

Give to the blast your thorn-crowns
Roses; and now be torn down
All you ardent lilies, your high-holden crests,
Havocked and cast to rest on the clammy ground.

Alas, alas, to darkness
Descends the flowered pathway,
To solitary places, deserts, utter night;
To issue in what hidden dawn of light hereafter?

But one, in dead of winter,
Divine *Agape*, kindles
Morning suns, new moons, lights starry trophies;
Says to the waste: Rejoice, and bring forth roses;
To the icefields: Let here spring thick bright lilies.

1936

The Long Harbour

There are three valleys where the warm sun lingers,
gathered to a green hill girt-about anchorage,
and gently, gently, at the cobbled margin
of fire-formed, time-smoothed, ocean-moulded curvature,
a spent tide fingers the graven boulders,
the black, sea-bevelled stones.

The fugitive hours, in those sun-loved valleys,
implacable hours, their golden-wheeled chariots'
inaudible passage check, and slacken
their restless teams' perpetual galloping;
and browsing, peaceable sheep and cattle
gaze as they pause by the way.

Grass springs sweet where once thick forest
gripped vales by fire and axe freed to pasturage;
but flame and blade have spared the folding gullies,
and there, still, the shade-flitting, honey-sipping lutanists
copy the dropping of tree-cool waters
dripping from stone to stone.

White hawthorn hedge from old, remembered England,
and orchard white, and whiter bridal clematis
the bush-bequeathed, conspire to strew the valleys
in tender spring, and blackbird, happy colonist,
and blacker, sweeter-fluted tui echo
either the other's song.

From far, palm-feathery, ocean-spattered islands
there rowed hither dark and daring voyagers;
and Norseman, Gaul, the Briton and the German
sailed hither singing; all these hardy venturers
they desired a home, and have taken their rest there,
and their songs are lost on the wind.

I have walked here with my love in the early spring-time,
and under the summer-dark walnut-avenues,
and played with the children, and waited with the aged
by the quayside, and listened alone where manukas
sighing, windswept, and sea-answering pine-groves
garrison the burial-ground.

It should be very easy to lie down and sleep there
in that sequestered hillside ossuary,
underneath a billowy, sun-caressed grass-knoll,
beside those dauntless, tempest-braving ancestresses
who pillowed there so gladly, gnarled hands folded,
their tired, afore-translated bones.

It would not be a hard thing to wake up one morning
to the sound of bird-song in scarce-stirring willow-trees,
waves lapping, oars plashing, chains running slowly,
and faint voices calling across the harbour;
to embark at dawn, following the old forefathers,
to put forth at daybreak for some lovelier,
still undiscovered shore.

                                        1936

Envoy

Over and over, carefully to con
'thy tablets, Memory,'
myself accustomed, the one being gone
who prompted all; night having fallen upon
that territory
where, season by season, we had watched unfold
fugitive beauty; impotent and cold
transcriptions, yet these now shall be
thanks for felicity.

                                        1936

Autumn Roses

The roses of Autumn are less numerous
Than the accoutrement of valiant Spring,
But they are more beautiful, and far more precious,
Each several flower presents itself a perfect thing.
They are more lasting, their colour is more lustrous,
With a more intimate and insistent voice
Their pungent scent speaks . . . What is meant to us
By these perfect, departing roses? The joys
Adorning the declension of life's afternoon,

Infrequent, rarer, to be remitted soon,
Are so much the fairer, so much the dearer to us,
Declaring the ineffable vision to be nearer to us.
Their perfume is the incense of jubilee
For what the deaf shall hear soon, and the blind see.

1936

Decoration

This jar of roses and carnations on the window-sill,
Crimson upon sky-grey and snow-wrapt mountain-pallor,
(Sharp storm's asseveration of cold winter's on-coming,)
How strange their look, how lovely, rich and foreign,
The living symbol of a season put away.

A letter-sheaf, bound up by time-frayed filament,
I found; laid by; youth's flowering.
The exotic words blazed up blood-red against death's shadow,
Red upon grey. Red upon grey.

1939

Spring Snow and Tui

We said: there will surely be hawthorn out
down in the sun-holding folds of the hills by the sea;
but suddenly snow had forestalled the thorns there,
death-white and cold on their boughs hung the festival wreaths.

It is all one. The same hand scatters the blossoms
of winter and spring-time. The black-robed psalmodist,
traversing swiftly the silent landscape like Azrael,
echoed in clear repetition his well-tuned antiphon;
a waking bugle it might be, a passing bell,
of life, death, life, life telling: it is all one.

1939

Candour

Everything was white this morning.
    White mists wandered all about the river-bed,
Grey clouds, light-infused, conveyed the morning,
    Covering with whiteness the wide sky overhead.

White, past belief, the high and snowy mountains,
    Phantom-like, visionary; whiteness upon whiteness
Of frozen foam from far celestial fountains
    Suffused with soft and universal brightness.

Everything was white, this morning,
    Untroubled, luminous and tranquil pure;
Bright as an affianced bride, adorning
Herself with white upon the plighted morning;
    Past all debate, all hazard, still, and sure.

1939

Summer Afternoon

All through the sun-possessed long afternoon of midsummer
    drowsing,
the rustle of leaves has solaced my ear-sense, the green-blue,
    green-blue
exhilaration of lively leafage on sky-spaces eye-sense
amused, as the crossing of elegant segmented wreathe of wistaria
and tend of interlaced spirals wavering lightwards and woven
on skeleton lattice above has cut out the shimmering pattern
of sky, and I lie in an ice-green and sapphire diapered cavern,
cerulean radiance by verdurous trellis sevenfold intensified.

Whispering fitfully reminiscence of snow-fields, the south wind
fans to dispersal the breath of heliotrope and jasmin
out of their pleasant enclosure, and yonder the coastwise vision
between insignis branches of heavenly azured Pacific
shows where the ultimate plunge of surf on invisible sand-dunes
always resounds, as it lashes its spray in the face of the breeze and
dazzle of sun; flashing and white I descry in the farthest distance
the line of its foaming circle below the delicate amethyst hills.

The bees and the buzzing flies, the hum of scurrying motorists
beyond the musical leaves has lullabied my passivity;
what honey, what hidden rewards sought for by restless gyrators
they know; by burning sky and iridescent seclusion
boundlessly prisoned secure, I husband the intermission
from curious chase; beside me a jungle-beast, gentled,
slumbers; together cast by the slow up-surging of centuries
on actual beach, we absorb the genial effulgence of here and now.

The current sap, impulse of piston or fluttering pinion,
the way of the wind with the waves, facture of subtle aroma,
beating of ocean-tide, impregnation of planet
by potent star, heart-cries: fearful dynamics propounded,
passed by and postponed, to-day like sheep of the pasture
we lie down at ease; not we ourselves made us;
for joy and heat of the westering sun his benign incandescence
let be, let be; enough, my furry comrade, to drowse and dream
    that we are.

                                1939

Night Rain

In the dark of the night, rain;
Unlocking of water-floods;
Washing away, obliterating
All night-whisperings;
Nought but the sound of falling waters
Returning whence they came.

By the noise of the rain set apart
In a lightless cloister,
What am I, in the night,
Listening to my suppliant heart

In the play of thy forces, Genetrix,
What am I but a particle tossed
Upon vast arterial waterways,
Borne down in the dark?

In the ark of thought I abide,
Lattice-wrought of experience,
Faith-pitched for bitumen,
And apocalypse to guide,
Riding on the tide of consciousness,
On waves of pleasure, pain;
Responsive microcosm, alive
And free upon the great main,
Out of this musical enclosure,
This ringing cage of rain.

1939

14th August, 1930

Pensive, I apprehend the unending pageant
Set forth before my waking eyes this tender morning,
Veil upon veil of ocean-whispered vapour
Driven slowly westwards by the sea-sprung east wind.

Softly the drifts of mist-grey into lilac,
To purple turn, to umber, shell-rose and vermilion,
Passing on the sea-breeze slowly and dissolving
Into the periwinkle dome of noble daybreak.

And, breasting eagerly the sea-fresh current,
Seawards beat three birds, with urgent flutterings,
Lost now in wreathing dusk, and now emerging,
Till, bare-discerned black specks, far haze receives them.

The mountains stand fast in their ranks, numinous,
Imperial calm in white snow, lordly sun-gilt,
Stand fast over against the sea, and north, and westwards,
Eminent from steel-blue shadow, shining splendid;

But the impermanent clouds drift, drift to dissolution,
And the black, fluttering birds, so sharply there, now are not;
Even so we, athwart insentient largeness,
We flutter eager, a few moments, and then are not.

1950

from By the River Ashley

1

It was the river, the river. We played there,
out, out of the house, out of the garden, out under the wide sky.
The little rivers, convenient to us, they ran apart, they conjoined.
They ran clear and bright over precious stones,
purple and pale green and dark green, and the white pebbles too.

Take them home, the best colours, put them to dry in the sun —
Gone! out of the water of illusion, gone dull, all the same grey.
(Well we understood the experience of Rosamund and her
      Purple Jar!)
But there were still good shapes and good smooth feel;
find these for pockets.
So many little moss fields, red fields with harvests, green cushions,
very small white flowers there were among the big stones,
and the stones had strange ornamentations.
Always the chatter of the waters, cheerful chattering,
rippling over the pebbles, round the stones . . .

    (Over there by the bank the deep water,
    cart-wheels going down — don't look there to-day;
    grand with a shudder of fear when the two-ponied
    wagon of ours would splash in and dash up
    and our carriage rugs wet from the ford.
    A Drive! a day of excitement,
    carried away over the foothills,
    our river dwindled behind, other strange rivers beyond.)

  . . . .

18

That bridge from the city, that was Waimakariri,
Greater than our River Ashley, the playground.

The rivers, over and over again the rivers.
They hasten to you, look up them, up the riverbeds.
From the soft dark forest they come down,
Or from the snows, carving their patterns
Of tawny terraces they come hastening down
To where by archipelagos of silver,
Lizard twists of azure, tranced lagoons,
We hear the ripples and the silence sing together
With the small soft sighing of the tussock,
And flax-spears' rattle, and, might be, a seabird's call.
These were the harmonies, splashed often now
By sudden hue of alien weed, still beautiful.

    Too late we hear, too late, the undertones
    Of lamentations in all the natural songs —
    What have you done with my mountains?

    What have you done with my forests?
    What have you done to your rivers?
    Too late.

19

Alternate with the schoolroom plan
of books to scan and sums to score,
my father's powerful edict ran
at his convenience I should ride

out on my pony at his side
attentive to equestrian lore.

On a fine morning thus we rode
at foot-pace on the formal street
(observant of accepted code).
But soon upon the grassy verge
of stony road no need to urge
impatient horses' eager feet.

Then slowly towards us we perceived
a train of spring-carts coming near;
it was a procession of the bereaved.
My father checked the horses' stride,
and quickly had them side by side
to face the road, the approaching bier.

I watched his gestures — lowered eyes,
and hat held lifted, till the train
of silent ones had passed us by —
The vision of that simple rite
brought apprehension, set alight
new understanding in my brain.

No pomp of Paul's high dome, or dim
mysterious Abbey's requiem,
or shrine where echoes Latin hymn,
no act that speaks more loud than speech,
has brought more nigh the spirit's reach
the unveiling made at Bethlehem.

The cortège passed, our ride resumed,
we cantered by the river-bed.
The world its wonted face assumed.
My lathering pony to restrain
engaged my wits with seat and rein.
I thought not on the passing dead.

Happy — but ah, the fleeting years
too few such filial mornings gave.
Too soon I knew strange choking tears,
and helped with unaccustomed hands
to fashion flowery wreaths and bands
for carrying to my father's grave.

21

The hour is dark. The river comes to its end,
Comes to the embrace of the all enveloping sea.
My story comes to its end.
    Divine Picknicker by the lakeside,
    Familiar friend of the fishermen,
    Known and yet not known, lost and yet found,
    The hour is dark, come down to the riverside,

The strange river, come find me.
Bring if it might be companions
In the tissue of the Kingdom, but come thou,
Key to all mystery, opening and none shall shut again,
Innermost love of all loves, making all one,
Come.

1950

Evening Walk in Winter

Tussock burned to fine gold, and the sheep bore golden fleeces
by the sudden alchemy of wintry waning sun,
and stepping eastwards
My arrowy shadow sapphire led me on.

So airy light I seemed to climb, the earthly path so gilded,
the illumined hill appeared in that transmuted hour
olympian,
the self a quenchless effluence of fire.

But overhead marmoreal white now hung the cold moon ominous
in ashen blue of empty dome, our doom
exhibit thus
even so to frozen death we must all come.

Now lost the living orb, and all his spacious ardours
concealed behind black rocky alps in wintry grave.
Falling darkness
possessed the plain, pale streams, sad fields and groves.

Now stars rushed out to fill the void with sparkling affirmations,
their cold acumen spoke no comfort, as before,
the heavens vacant;
mirror-moon shone false from fire afar.

Darkly alone, the errant hour outspent, led downwards
by homing track, the lowly glittering chain
lit round
hearth-fastness beckoned there was warmth within.

Oh not by late-launched planets flung in heavens equivocal
may we, or making moonlight wan and wild
oracular,
be certified of life or death, of heat or cold.

The bright particular hearts mysteriously enkindled
for us — the daily love, like fire that glows and runs
half hidden
among the embers — this the warmth we live by, our unsetting sun.

What if the light go out? What if some black disaster
of total nightfall quench the vivid spark?
Oh might we hearken,
then, with night-initiate Spaniard to the Answerer
who said: I am the dark.

1950

R. A. K. MASON

Born in Auckland, R. A. K. Mason (1905–1971) published his first book The Beggar *in 1924 (he is said to have despondently dumped most of the edition into Auckland Harbour). He spent his life in Auckland, working as a teacher and trade union official, and was active in left-wing politics. For many he was the first genuinely New Zealand poet.*

Old Memories of Earth

I think I have no other home than this
    I have forgotten much remember much
    but I have never any memories such
    as these make out they have of lands of bliss.

Perhaps they have done, will again do what
    they say they have, drunk as gods on godly drink,
    but I have not communed with gods I think
    and even though I live past death shall not.

I rather am for ever bondaged fast
    to earth and have been: so much untaught I know.
    Slow like great ships often I have seen go
    ten priests ten each time round a grave long past

And I recall I think I can recall
    back even past the time I started school
    or went a-crusoeing in the corner pool
    that I was present at a city's fall

And I am positive that yesterday
    walking past One Tree Hill and quite alone
    to me there came a fellow I have known
    in some old times, but when I cannot say:

Though we must have been great friends, I and he,
    otherwise I should not remember him
    for everything of the old life seems dim
    as last year's deeds recalled by friends to me.

        1924

The Vigil

All night long I lay awake
    fearful hoping for daybreak

All night long alone I lay
    longing for some god to pray

All night long I heard bells toll
    where the cruel grey breakers roll

All night long I heard that cry
    such as men give when they die

All night long where the bleak big
   lone cliffs shelve I heard men dig

Morning came and the cock crew
   clearly, shrilly, and I knew.

1924

Body of John

Oh I have grown so shrivelled and sere
   But the body of John enlarges,
   and I can scarcely summon a tear
   but the body of John discharges

It's true my old roof is near ready to drop
   But John's boards have burst asunder
   and I am perishing cold here atop
   but his bones lie stark hereunder.

1924

Sonnet of Brotherhood

Garrisons pent up in a little fort
   with foes who do but wait on every side
   knowing the time soon comes when they shall ride
   triumphant over those trapped and make sport
   of them: when those within know very short
   is now their hour and no aid can betide:
   such men as these not quarrel and divide
   but friend and foe are friends in their hard sort

And if these things be so oh men then what
   of these beleaguered victims this our race
   betrayed alike by Fate's gigantic plot
   here in this far-pitched perilous hostile place
   this solitary hard-assaulted spot
   fixed at the friendless outer edge of space.

1924

Wayfarers

That I go out alone to them it seems
   because they see none with me in the way
   ignorant that the fabrics of my dreams
   are less intangible to me than they

Ignorant that I have heard and seen Christ break
   the bondage of his tongue-tied sightlessness
   have walked with firm-faithed Mary to the stake
   and kissed the hem of martyred Flora's dress

And I in Lichfield frequently have been
   Chatterton's accessory in suicide
   have Gaius Marius in Minturnae seen
   for many hours by Waitemata's tide

Burnt Dian's temple down at Otahuhu
   and slain Herostratus at Papatoe
   and here in Penrose brought Aeneas through
   to calm Ausonian lands from bloody Troy.

1924

The Spark's Farewell to Its Clay

I

Well clay it's strange at last we've come to it:
   after much merriment we must give up
   our ancient friendship: no more shall we sup
   in pleasant quiet places wanly-lit
   nor wander through the falling rain, sharp-smit
   and buffeted you, while I within snug-shut:
   no longer taste the mingled bitter-sweet cup
   of life the one inscrutable has thought fit

To give us: no longer know the strife
   that we from old have each with each maintained:
   now our companionship has certain end
   end without end: at last of this our life
   you surely have gained blank earth walls my friend
   and I? God only knows what I have gained.

II

There is no thought that any hope can give
   for this fine hair and these long pliant hands
   and this proud body that so firmly stands
   these eyes deep delicate and sensitive:
   vain vain for such in mind towards hope to strive.
   What if my body has at its commands
   strength beauty knowledge rule of many lands
   still is not any hope that it can live.

Perhaps I seek myself and am not whole:
   times think I in some pure place there can wait
   a far surpassing fellow for my soul
   and joy to think when I shall find that mate —
   still you good easy earth must pay earth-toll
   I recollect and so am desolate.

1924

Latter-Day Geography Lesson

This, quoth the Eskimo master
   was London in English times:
   step out a little faster
   you two young men at the last there
   the Bridge would be on our right hand
   and the Tower near where those crows stand —
   we struck it you'll recall in Gray's rhymes:
   this, quoth the Eskimo master
   was London in English times.

This, quoth the Eskimo master
   was London in English days:
   beyond that hill they called Clapham
   boys that swear Master Redtooth I slap 'em
   I dis-tinct-ly heard — you — say — Bastard
   don't argue: here boys, ere disaster
   overtook her, in splendour there lay
   a city held empires in sway
   and filled all the earth with her praise:
   this quoth the Eskimo master
   was London in English days.

She held, quoth the Eskimo master
   ten million when her prime was full
   from here once Britannia cast her
   gaze over an Empire vaster
   even than ours: look there Woking
   stood, I make out, and the Abbey
   lies here under our feet *you great babby*
   Swift-and-short do — please — kindly — stop — poking
   your thumbs through the eyes of that skull.

                               (1924)

Song of Allegiance

Shakespeare Milton Keats are dead
   Donne lies in a lowly bed

Shelley at last calm doth lie
   knowing 'whence we are and why'

Byron Wordsworth both are gone
   Coleridge Beddoes Tennyson

Housman neither knows nor cares
   how 'this heavy world' now fares

Little clinging grains enfold
   all the mighty minds of old . . .

They are gone and I am here
   stoutly bringing up the rear

Where they went with limber ease
   toil I on with bloody knees

Though my voice is cracked and harsh
   stoutly in the rear I march

Though my song have none to hear
   boldly bring I up the rear.

1925

A Fragment

By Penrose bridge where shrill winds sung
three scarlet signal-lamps were hung
like those three balls that overtop
the careless splendour of a shop
where some old Jew whose ancestors
in Sinai were wanderers
hoards white coins golden candlesticks
pale plates a pain-racked crucifix
medals that when Spain's prime was full
were struck in gold and a grey skull,
or rather two halves together set,
proclaiming how when in Tibet
an adulterous pair are ta'en
the man and woman both are slain
and the halved skulls of each the twain
are joined:
         there it is stuck up plain
for all this distant town to stare —
cold earnest that hot love will dare
all things for love's sake everywhere.

1925

On the Swag

His body doubled
   under the pack
   that sprawls untidily
   on his old back
   the cold wet dead-beat
   plods up the track.

The cook peers out:
   'oh curse that old lag —
   here again
   with his clumsy swag
   made of a dirty old
   turnip bag.'

'Bring him in cook
   from the grey level sleet
   put silk on his body
   slippers on his feet,

give him fire
and bread and meat.

Let the fruit be plucked
and the cake be iced,
the bed be snug
and the wine be spiced
in the old cove's night-cap:
for this is Christ.'

1934

Judas Iscariot

Judas Iscariot
sat in the upper
room with the others
at the last supper

And sitting there smiled
up at his master
whom he knew the morrow
would roll in disaster.

At Christ's look he guffawed —
for then as thereafter
Judas was greatly
given to laughter,

Indeed they always said
that he was the veriest
prince of good fellows
and the whitest and merriest.

All the days of his life
he lived gay as a cricket
and would sing like the thrush
that sings in the thicket

He would sing like the thrush
that sings on the thorn
oh he was the most sporting bird
that ever was born.

1934

Footnote to John ii 4

Don't throw your arms around me in that way:
    I know that what you tell me is the truth —
    yes I suppose I loved you in my youth
as boys do love their mothers, so they say,
but all that's gone from me this many a day:
    I am a merciless cactus an uncouth

wild goat a jagged old spear the grim tooth
of a lone crag . . . Woman I cannot stay.

Each one of us must do his work of doom
  and I shall do it even in despite
  of her who brought me in pain from her womb,
  whose blood made me, who used to bring the light
  and sit on the bed up in my little room
  and tell me stories and tuck me up at night.

                                        1934

Ecce Homunculus

Betrayed by friend dragged from the garden hailed
  as prophet and as lord in mockery
  hauled down where Roman Pilate sat on high
  perplexed and querulous, lustily assailed
  by every righteous Hebrew cried down railed
  against by all true zealots — still no sigh
  escaped him but he boldly went to die
  made scarcely a moan when his soft flesh was nailed.

And so he brazened it out right to the last
  still wore the gallant mask still cried 'Divine
  am I, lo for me is heaven overcast'
  though that inscrutable darkness gave no sign
  indifferent or malignant: while he was passed
  by even the worst of men at least sour wine.

                                        1934

The Young Man Thinks of Sons

Did my father curse his father for his lust I wonder
        as I do mine
and my grand-dad curse his sire for his wickedness his
    weakness his blunder
        and so on down the whole line

Well I'll stop the game break the thread end my race: I will
    not continue
        in the old bad trade;
I'll take care that for my nerveless mind weakened brain
    neglected sinew
        I alone shall have paid.

Let the evil book waste in its swathings the ill pen write not
    one iota
        the ship of doom not sail,
let the sword rot unused in its scabbard let the womb lack its
    quota:
        here let my line fail:

Let the plough rust untouched of the furrow, yea let the blind semen
> stretch vain arms for the virgin:
I'll hammer no stringed harps for gods to clash discords, or women:
> my orchard won't burgeon.

I'll take care that the lust of my loins never bring to fruition
> the seed of a son
who in his nettle-grown kingdom should curse both my sins of commission
> and what I left undone.

1934

Be Swift O Sun

Be swift o sun
> lest she fall on some evil chance:
> make haste and run
> to light up the dark fields of France.

See already the moon
> lies sea-green on our globe's eastern rim:
> speed to be with her soon:
> even now her stars grow dim.

Here your labour is null
> and water poured upon sand
> to light up the hull
> which at dawn glimmers on to the land

And here you in vain
> clothe many coming sails with gold
> if you bring not again
> those breasts where I found death of old.

Why bring you ships
> from that evil Dis of a shore
> if you bring not the lips
> I kissed once and shall kiss no more:

O sun make speed
> and delay not to send her your rays
> lest she be in need
> of light in those far alien ways.

That you may single
> my love from the rest, her eyes
> her wide eyes commingle
> all innocence with all things wise:

Raindrops at eve fall
> in your last rays no lovelier:
> her voice is the madrigal
> at your dawn when the first birds stir,

Be swift o sun
> lest she fall on some evil chance:

make haste and run
to light up the dark fields of France.

1934

Our love was a grim citadel

Our love was a grim citadel:
  no tawdry plaything for the minute
  of strong dark stone we built it well
  and based in the ever-living granite:

The urgent columns of the years
  press on, like tall rain up the valley:
  and Chaos bids ten thousand spears
  run to erase our straw-built folly.

1934

Prelude

This short straight sword
  I got in Rome
  when Gaul's new lord
  came tramping home:

It did that grim
  old rake to a T —
  if it did him,
  well, it does me.

Leave the thing of pearls
  with silken tassels
  to priests and girls
  and currish vassals:

Here's no fine cluster
  on the hilt, this drab
  blade lacks lustre —
  but it can stab.

1936

KATHERINE MANSFIELD

Katherine Mansfield (pen-name of Kathleen Beauchamp 1888–1923) was born in Wellington and educated in Wellington and London. She returned to England in 1908 and established herself as a leading international exponent of the short story form.

The Awakening River

The gulls are mad-in-love with the river
And the river unveils her face and smiles.
In her sleep-brooding eyes they mirror their shining wings.
She lies on silver pillows: the sun leans over her.

He warms and warms her, he kisses and kisses her.
There are sparks in her hair and she stirs in laughter.
Be careful, my beautiful waking one! you will catch on fire.
Wheeling and flying with the foam of the sea on their breasts
The ineffable mists of the sea clinging to their wild wings
Crying the rapture of the boundless ocean.
The gulls are mad-in-love with the river.
Wake! we are the dream thoughts flying from your heart.
Wake! we are the songs of desire flowing from your bosom.
O, I think the sun will lend her his great wings
And the river will fly away to the sea with the mad-in-love
     birds.

                                                    1923

Sanary

Her little hot room looked over the bay
Through a stiff palisade of glinting palms
And there she would lie in the heat of the day
Her dark head resting upon her arms
So quiet so still she did not seem
To think to feel or even to dream.

The shimmering blinding web of sea
Hung from the sky and the spider sun
With busy frightening cruelty
Crawled over the sky and spun and spun
She could see it still when she shut her eyes
And the little boats caught in the web like flies.

Down below at this idle hour
Nobody walked in the dusty street
A scent of dying mimosa flower
Lay on the air but sweet — too sweet.

                                                    1923

To L. H. B. (1894–1915)

Last night for the first time since you were dead
I walked with you, my brother, in a dream.
We were at home again beside the stream
Fringed with tall berry bushes, white and red.
'Don't touch them: they are poisonous,' I said.
But your hand hovered, and I saw a beam
Of strange bright laughter flying round your head
And as you stooped I saw the berries gleam —
'Don't you remember? We called them Dead Man's Bread!'
I woke and heard the wind moan and the roar
Of the dark water tumbling on the shore.
Where — where is the path of my dream for my eager feet?
By the remembered stream my brother stands
Waiting for me with berries in his hands . . .
'These are my body. Sister, take and eat.'

                                                    1923

Night Scented Stock

White, white in the milky night
The moon danced over a tree
'Wouldn't it be lovely to swim in the lake!'
Someone whispered to me.

'Oh, do-do-do!' cooed someone else
And clasped her hands to her chin.
'I should so love to see the white bodies
All the white bodies jump in!'

The big dark house hid secretly
Behind the magnolia and the spreading pear tree
But there was a sound of music — music rippled and ran
Like a lady laughing behind her fan
Laughing and mocking and running away —
Come into the garden — it's as light as day!

'I can't dance to that Hungarian stuff
The rhythm in it is not passionate enough'
Said somebody. 'I absolutely refuse . . .'
But he took off his socks and his shoes
And round he spun. 'It's like Hungarian fruit dishes
Hard and bright — a mechanical blue!'
His white feet flicked in the grass like fishes . . .
Some one cried: 'I want to dance, too!'

But one with a queer russian ballet head
Curled up on a blue wooden bench instead.
And another, shadowy — shadowy and tall
Walked in the shadow of the dark house wall,
Someone beside her. It shone in the gloom,
His round grey hat like a wet mushroom.

'Don't you think, perhaps . . .' piped someone's flute . . .
'How sweet the flowers smell!' I heard the other say —
Somebody picked a wet, wet pink
Smelled it and threw it away.

'Is the moon a virgin or is she a harlot?'
Asked somebody. Nobody would tell.
The faces and the hands moved in a pattern
As the music rose and fell.

In a dancing, mysterious, moon bright pattern
Like flowers nodding under the sea
The music stopped and there was nothing left of them
But the moon dancing over the tree.

1923

The Man with the Wooden Leg

There was a man lived quite near us
He had a wooden leg and a goldfinch in a green cage
His name was Farkey Anderson

And he'd been in a war to get his leg.
We were very sad about him
Because he had such a beautiful smile
And was such a big man to live in a very little house.
When he walked on the road his leg did not matter so much
But when he walked in his little house
It made an ugly noise.
Little Brother said his goldfinch sang the loudest of all
     birds
So that he should not hear his poor leg
And feel too sorry about it.

                                                                    1923

To Stanislaw Wyspianski

From the other side of the world,
From a little island cradled in the giant sea bosom,
From a little land with no history,
(Making its own history, slowly and clumsily
Piecing together this and that, finding the pattern, solving
     the problem,
Like a child with a box of bricks),
I, a woman, with the taint of the pioneer in my blood,
Full of a youthful strength that wars with itself and is lawless,
I sing your praises, magnificent warrior; I proclaim your
     triumphant battle.
My people have had nought to contend with;
They have worked in the broad light of day and handled the
     clay with rude fingers;
Life — a thing of blood and muscle; Death — a shovelling
     underground of waste material.
What would they know of ghosts and unseen presences,
Of shadows that blot out reality, of darkness that stultifies
     morn?
Fine and sweet the water that runs from their mountains;
How could they know of poisonous weed, of rotted and
     clogging tendrils?
And the tapestry woven from dreams of your tragic childhood
They would tear in their stupid hands,
The sad, pale light of your soul blow out with their childish
     laughter.
But the dead — the old — Oh Master, we belong to you there;
Oh Master, there we are children and awed by the strength of a
     giant;
How alive you leapt into the grave and wrestled with Death
And found in the veins of Death the red blood flowing
And raised Death up in your arms and showed him to all the
     people.
Yours a more personal labour than the Nazarene's miracles,
Yours a more forceful encounter than the Nazarene's gentle
     commands.
Stanislaw Wyspianski — Oh man with the name of a fighter,

Across these thousands of sea-shattered miles we cry and
   proclaim you;
We say 'He is lying in Poland, and Poland thinks he is dead;
But he gave the denial to Death — he is lying there, wakeful;
The blood in his giant heart pulls red through his veins.'

1938

EILEEN DUGGAN

Eileen Duggan (1894–1972) was for a time New Zealand's most internationally acclaimed poet. Her reputation, after some decades of decline, is now being reassessed. Born at Tua Marina, Marlborough, she worked for the most part as a professional writer and journalist. She was also a classical scholar and devout Roman Catholic. Her Selected Poems *were published in 1994, marking the centenary of her birth.*

Rosa Luxembourg

For some the shuttle leaping in the sun,
Laburnum leaves above the quiet door,
And song that drips like water, cool and slow,
And when the hands are still and day is done,
The swaying crib upon the firelit floor,
Ah how could you those gentle things forego?

Wild heart that beat beneath its tattered shawl,
Wild voice that broke upon its ceaseless cry
For those whose lips are dumb beneath the sky,
Whose feet beneath the stars must stumbling fall,
Whose hands must turn in toil until they die!
Which is the nobler task? God knows, not I.

For you no threaded spool, no singing time,
No young bees flying through laburnum boughs,
No little rolling head upon the breast,
But now, beyond the bourn of flower or chime,
May He who set the storm between your brows
Pity your broken bones and give them rest.

1921

And at the End

Once on a dewy morning
With the bright sky blowing apart,
Each bud broke on my eyelids,
Each bird flew through my heart.
I prayed for the faith of a starling
Under the tawny trees,
A child or a holy woman —
What could be greater than these?

But now on a heavy morning
With the dull sky blowing apart,

When no flower blesses my eyelids,
And no wing brushes my heart,
I, made surer by sorrow,
Beg what seems more to me
The faith of a willow in winter,
Or a blind hound nosing the knee.

1937

The Tides Run Up the Wairau

The tides run up the Wairau
That fights against their flow.
My heart and it together
Are running salt and snow.

For though I cannot love you,
Yet, heavy, deep, and far,
Your tide of love comes swinging,
Too swift for me to bar.

Some thought of you must linger,
A salt of pain in me,
For oh what running river
Can stand against the sea?

1937

Twilight

I was driving the cows and the frogs were soothsaying,
'Woe, land and water! All, all is lost!'
It was winter full grown and my bones were black in me.
The tussocks were brittling from dew into frost.

The earth looked at me, ears up in a stillness.
I was nine at the time and a coward by fate:
The willow-trees humped into cringing old swaggers,
And the cows lunged up unicorns, passing the gate.

A sudden wind clouted the nose of our chimney,
It rumbled and bellowsed its sparks in a spray;
I took to my heels in the terrible twilight,
For I thought that the sky was blowing away.

1937

The Bushfeller

Lord, mind your trees to-day!
My man is out there clearing.
God send the chips fly safe.
My heart is always fearing.

And let the axehead hold!
My dreams are all of felling.

He earns our bread far back.
And then there is no telling.

If he came home at nights,
We'd know, but it is only —
We might not even hear —
A man could lie there lonely.

God, let the trunks fall clear,
He did not choose his calling;
He's young and full of life —
A tree is heavy, falling.

1937

Cloudy Bay

Where the racing Wairau slows, homesick for its snowshed,
Tua Marina murmurs in the south,
Caught in a loop of sighing, saltless waters
Running intently into one great mouth.

I was born inland between the creek and river
In the heart of paddocks troubled by their stir
For in between the hills' great riven horseshoe
Land and all seemed flowing with lonely, long demur:

And the west sinking with its light so low there
Left the sunset growing in the fences' hold,
Paradisal grasses, knee-deep and molten,
In their stillness running sap of ember-gold.

Once a great aurora played to the southward —
And, fetlocks burning, foal after foal,
Clodding the icefloes as a colt the paddocks,
Rushed up, uncalkined, from the silver Pole.

Where the horseshoe opened in came the morning,
There to the eastward lay the hidden sea,
The same footloose mountains that taunted Magellan,
Massive and flying and nothing to me.

We were held fast by the glitter of a solstice,
Or by a smoulder of autumns to the land;
But in the winter the booming of its groundswell,
Thundering a shoreline back upon the sand,

Lunged in our ears and forced us to remember
What was too wild, too great for any law,
Holding us in from the tip of Reinga
To where the Bluff folds down a heavy paw.

Here the great air-currents, cloven by the alp-line,
Roll and soar above us with a salty boast;
Almost any seawind, streaming from the Tasman,
In these narrow islands blows from coast to coast.

Love is around me like that hidden ocean
And I, inland, forget I have a shore.
It needs the breakers of your anger to remind me
That I am yours and yours forevermore.

1937

Tua Marina

Though all my heart is in this windy city
With its street corners and its masts and mills,
Often I wonder have any of its dwellers
Seen the rangiora on the southern hills.

Who here has seen upon the road to Para
Five tuis swinging on a bough at noon?
Who here has heard the wind among the raupo,
As I have heard it by the old lagoon?

Who here recalls how in the wet Septembers
Snows on Mount Arnaud sent the great floods down,
Or how the men with lanterns watched the Wairau,
Wading like otters in its waters brown?

Who here would know how by the small blind river
Each sighing tussock roofs a quiet lark,
Who here would care that in Brunetti's orchard
Blithe buds are horning through the bitter bark?

No one here knows, or knowing would remember,
Nor would I remember if they let me be,
For she is dead, with northern clods upon her,
Who, in our childhood, knew these things with me.

1940

The Country

All that green calm crept in and flowed around me,
Not as a sea that crouches back and rises
But as a river-flood that slowly, slowly swelling
Upward and upward by its depth surprises.

I was afraid my heart would be lapped over
The countryside had swamped so many another
As surely as in springtime all its paddocks
The dull, deep waters of the Wairau smother.

I wanted it to flood and not be flooded,
Hearts should flow out and not be covered over
But mine to-day is hopeless for the grasses
And for the slow, upwelling lakes of clover.

Towns are as vain as a king that is doting,
Babbling to himself of laurel on laurel.
I who shirked peace know north and south of trouble.
Ah for my birthright, the green grass and sorrel!

1940

Brooding

Ah lift yourself from your own pain
And think of others' misery.
It is a swamp that sours in rain.
The good land drains into the sea.

1940

The Bushwoman

They're bidding me to town.
   They say they are ashamed
That I should live alone —
   My sons' wives will be blamed.

It's strange that sons of mine
   Should love the town the best,
When all my life's been spent
   In moving farther west.

We'd sell and pack our things,
   My oven and his axe —
If they had seen us then
   With swags upon our backs!

My hands are old and rough.
   Those women's hands are white.
They have big standing lamps.
   I had a dip at night.

I'd let the wrong things out
   And I would have no say.
I might be lonely here
   But I can have my way.

They're bidding me to town —
   But will I go? Not I!
If you root up old trees
   They bleed until they die.

1940

Night

You are the still caesura
That breaks a line in two;
A quiet leaf of darkness
Between two flowers of blue;

A little soft indrawing
Between two sighs;
A slender spit of silence
Between two seas of cries.

1951

The Answer

How can spirit flow
Through a crust of grief?
Tears freeze as they fall.
No relief!

It will come out pure
Though it filter slow,
As of old they strained
Wine through snow.

1951

Truth

Some can leave the truth unspoken.
Oh truth is light on such!
They may choose their time and season,
Nor feel it matters much.

I am not their judge, God help me!
Though I am of the crew
For whom is only truth or treason —
No choice between the two.

But pity wrestles with my fury
Till, spent and dumb and dry,
I envy bees which, barbed with reason,
Give the whole sting and die.

1951

Two Towns

Two towns in one town,
Flagged both with stones,
One full of living men,
One full of bones.

This town of live men
Keeps its streets clean;
No trailer on the stones,
No grass between.

That town of dead men
Lets its boughs blow
Lets clover urchins slouch,
Lets daisies crow.

Yet all the quick folk,
When their days pass,
Sloven of boughs will be,
Slattern of grass.

All those astir now,
Tidy and blind,
End with the blowsy rose,
Feckless and kind.

1994

Tide

Such as I am I owe all to grief,
Though from the debt I cower,
It drew my spirit into tides
That, flood or neap, have power.
A stream is slow to the moon at full;
Its waters reason like the mind;
It is the salt that stirs the sea
And the soul is of its kind.
Salt water feels. It is instinct
And by the moon is stretched apart.
Better a swell of agony
Than an untided heart.

1994

The Dead Queen

They said she had strange ways and fed the poor,
That she could read old books and cross the wise,
And that she held much speech with serf and boor,
For clog and shoe were equal in her eyes.

They said that her young robes could awe the Nine,
And set the proudest embassy to school;
Yet she would close the charters of her line
To melt in tender laughter at her fool.

They said she did not end her grace with men,
But honoured from her birth until her death
The smallest stirring thing within its den
That shared with her the magic beat of breath.

All this, and more, they said about her there,
And I — what was their murmuring to me,
Who could remember but her knot of hair,
Her eyes like Spanish shells that stoup the sea?

1994

'Had It Been You'

'Had it been you . . .' my mother said,
    And put my comfort by.
I was wept out and overspent
    To ask her why.

It's sad to see a tree in flower
    Blown over to the dust,
And mothers love a splendid thing

Because they must.

It did not even hurt me much,
    I was so strange and sore.
Ah, when the sky has rained a flood,
    What's one drop more?

It is a way they have in grief:
    Not knowing what they do,
They turn upon the nearest one,
    'Had it been you . . .'

1994

BLANCHE BAUGHAN

Born in Putney, London, Blanche Baughan (1870–1958) graduated from the University of London, majoring in Greek, before emigrating to New Zealand. She spent most of the rest of her life on Banks Peninsula, dying at Akaroa in 1958.

The Old Place

So the last day's come at last, the close of my fifteen year —
The end of the hope, an' the struggles, an' messes I've put in here.
All of the shearings over, the final mustering done, —
Eleven hundred an' fifty for the incoming man, near on.
Over five thousand I drove 'em, mob by mob, down the coast;
Eleven-fifty in fifteen year . . . it isn't much of a boast.

    Oh, it's a bad old place! Blown out o' your bed half the nights,
And in summer the grass burnt shiny an' bare as your hand, on
    the heights:
The creek dried up by November, and in May a thundering roar
That carries down toll o' your stock to salt 'em whole on the shore.
Clear'd I have, and I've clear'd an' clear'd, yet everywhere, slap in
    your face,
Briar, *tauhinu*, an' ruin! — God! it's a brute of a place.
. . . An' the house got burnt which I built, myself, with all that
    worry and pride;
Where the Missus was always homesick, and where she took fever,
    and died.

    Yes, well! I'm leaving the place. Apples look red on that bough.
I set the slips with my own hand. Well — they're the other man's now.
The breezy bluff: an' the clover that smells so over the land,
Drowning the reek o' the rubbish, that plucks the profit out o'
    your hand:
That bit o' Bush paddock I fall'd myself, an' watch'd, each year,
    come clean
(Don't it look fresh in the tawny? A scrap of Old-Country green):
This air, all healthy with sun an' salt, an' bright with purity:
An' the glossy *karakas* there, twinkling to the big blue twinkling sea:
Ay, the broad blue sea beyond, an' the gem-clear cove below,
Where the boat I'll never handle again, sits rocking to and fro:
There's the last look to it all! an' now for the last upon

This room, where Hetty was born, an' my Mary died, an' John . . .
Well! I'm leaving the poor old place, and it cuts as keen as a knife;
The place that's broken my heart — the place where I've lived my life.

1903

A Bush Section

Logs, at the door, by the fence; logs, broadcast over the paddock;
Sprawling in motionless thousands away down the green of the
    gully,
Logs, grey-black. And the opposite rampart of ridges
Bristles against the sky, all the tawny, tumultuous landscape
Is stuck, and prickled, and spiked with the standing black and grey
    splinters,
Strewn, all over its hollows and hills, with the long, prone, grey-
    black logs.

    For along the paddock, and down the gully,
    Over the multitudinous ridges,
    Through valley and spur,
    Fire has been!
Ay, the Fire went through and the Bush has departed,
The green Bush departed, green Clearing is not yet come.
    'Tis a silent, skeleton world;
    Dead, and not yet re-born,
    Made, unmade, and scarcely as yet in the making;
    Ruin'd, forlorn, and blank.

At the little raw farm on the edge of the desolate hillside,
Perch'd on the brink, overlooking the desolate valley,
To-night, now the milking is finish'd, and all the calves fed,
The kindling all split, and the dishes all wash'd after supper:
Thorold von Reden, the last of a long line of nobles,
Little 'Thor Rayden', the twice-orphan'd son of a drunkard,
Dependent on strangers, the taciturn, grave ten-year-old,
Stands and looks from the garden of cabbage and larkspur, looks
    over
The one little stump-spotted rye-patch, so gratefully green,
Out, on this desert of logs, on this dead disconsolate ocean
Of billows arrested, of currents stay'd, that never awake and flow.
Day after day,
The hills stand out on the sky,
The splinters stand on the hills,
In the paddock the logs lie prone.
The prone logs never arise,
The erect ones never grow green,
Leaves never rustle, the birds went away with the Bush, —
There is no change, nothing stirs!
And to-night there is no change;
All is mute, monotonous, stark;
In the whole wide sweep round the low little hut of the settler
No life to be seen; nothing stirs.
    Yet, see! past the cow-bails,
      Down, deep in the gully,

What glimmers? What silver
    Streaks the grey dusk?
'Tis the River, the River! Ah, gladly Thor thinks of the River,
His playmate, his comrade,
Down there all day,
All the long day, betwixt lumber and cumber,
Sparkling and singing;
Lively glancing, adventurously speeding,
Busy and bright as a needle in knitting
Running in, running out, running over and under
The logs that bridge it, the logs that block it,
The logs that helplessly trail in its waters,
The jamm'd-up jetsam, the rooted snags.
Twigs of *konini*, bronze leaf-boats of wineberry
Launch'd in the River, they also will run with it,
They cannot stop themselves, twisting and twirling
They too will keep running, away and away.
Yes; for on runs the River, it presses, it passes
On — by the fence, by the bails, by the landslip, away down the gully,
On, ever onward and on!
The hills remain, the logs and the gully remain,
Changeless as ever, and still;
But the River changes, the River passes.
Nothing else stirring about it,
It stirs, it is quick, 'tis alive!
    'What is the River, the running River?
    Where does it come from?
    Where does it go?'

    Listen! Listen! . . .
Far away, down the voiceless valley,
Thro' league-long spaces of empty air,
A sound! as of thunder.
    Look! ah, look!
    Yonder, deep in the clear dark distance,
At the foot of the shaggy, snow-hooded ranges, —
Out on the houseless and homeless country
Suddenly issuing, eddying, volleying —
Smoke, bright smoke! Not the soft blue vapour
By day, in the paddock there, wreathing and wavering,
O'er the red spark well at work in the stumps:
Not the poor little misty pale pillar
Here straggling up, close at hand, from the crazy tin chimney: —
No! but an airy river of riches,
Irrepressibly billowing, volume on volume
Rolling, unrolling, tempestuously tossing,
Ah! like the glorious hair of some else-invisible Angel
Rushing splendidly forth in the darkness —
Gold! gold on the gloom!
. . . . Floating, fleeing, flying . . . .
Thor catches his breath . . . . Ah, flown!
Gone! Yes, the torrent of glory,
The Voice and the Vision are gone —
For over the viaduct, out of the valley,

It is gone, the wonderful Train!
Gone, yet still going on: on: on! to the far-away township
(Ten miles off, down the track, and the mud of the metal-less
    roadway:
Seen, once at Christmas, and once on a fine summer Sunday:
Always a dream, with its dozens of passing people,
Its three beneficent stores) . . . .
And past the township, and on!
— The hills and the gully remain;
One day is just like another;
In the paddock the logs lie still;
But the Train is not still; every evening it sparkles out, streams by
    and goes.
       'What is the Train, that it travels?
        Where does it come from?
        Where does it go?'

It is gone. And the evening deepens.
Darker the grey air grows.
From the black of the gully, the gleam of the River is gone.
Scarcely the ridges show to the sky-line,
Now, their disconsolate fringe;
But, bright to the deepening sky,
The Stars creep silently out.
'Oh, where do you hide in the day?'
. . . . It is stiller than ever; the wind has fallen.
The moist air brings,
To mix with the spicy breath of the young break-wind
    macrocarpa,
Wafts of the acrid, familiar aroma of slowly-smouldering logs.
And hark, through the empty silence and dimness
Solemnly clear,
Comes the wistful, haunting cry of some lonely, faraway morepork,
'*Kia toa*! Be Brave!'
— Night is come.
Now the gully is hidden, the logs and the paddock all hidden.
Brightly the Stars shine out! . . . .
The sky is a wide black paddock, without any fences,
The Stars are its shining logs;
Here, sparse and single, but yonder, as logg'd-up for burning,
Close in a cluster of light.
And the thin clouds, they are the hills,
They are the spurs of the heavens,
On whose steepnesses scatter'd, the Star-logs silently lie:
Dimm'd as it were by the distance, or maybe in mists of the
    mountain
Tangled — yet still they brighten, not darken, the thick-strewn
    slopes!
But see! these hills of the sky
They waver and move! their gullies are drifting, and driving;
Their ridges, uprooted,
Break, wander and flee, they escape! casting careless behind them
Their burdens of brightness, the Stars, that rooted remain.

— No! they do not remain. No! even they cannot be steadfast.
For the curv'd Three (that yonder
So glitter and sparkle
There, over the bails),
This morning, at dawn,
At the start of the milking,
Stood pale on the brink of yon rocky-ledged hill;
And the Cross, o'er the viaduct
Now, then was slanting,
Almost to vanishing, over the snow.
So, the Stars travel, also?
The poor earthly logs, in the wan earthly paddocks,
Never can move, they must stay;
But over the heavenly pastures, the bright, live logs of the heavens
Wander at will, looking down on our paddocks and logs, and pass on.
'O friendly and beautiful Live-Ones!
Coming to us for a little,
Then travelling and passing, while here with our logs we remain,
  What are you? Where do you come from?
  Who are you? Where do you go?'

Ah, little Questioner!
Son of the Burnt Bush;
Straightly pent 'twixt its logs and ridges,
To its narrow round of monotonous labours
Strictly tether'd and tied:
And here to-night, in the holiday twilight,
Conning, counting, and clasping as treasures,
Whatsoever about your unchanging existence
Moves and changes and lives: —
One delight have you miss'd, and that one of more import than any:
More quick than the River, more fraught than the Mail-Train,
More certain to move than the Stars in their courses,
The most radiant wonder, the rarest excitement of all.
  What is it ? Oh, what can it be ?
  — It is you, little Thor! 'Tis yourself!
  Little, feeble, ignorant, destitute: —
  Wondering, questioning, conscious, alive!
A Mind that moves 'mid the motionless matter:
'Mid the logs, a developing Soul:
From the battle-field bones of a ruin'd epoch,
Life, the Unruin'd, freshly upspringing,
Life, Re-creator of life!

Yea, spark of Life!
Begotten, begetter, of changes:
Yea, morn of Man,
Creature design'd to create:
Offspring of elements all, appointed their captain and ruler:
Here dawning, here sent
To this, thy disconsolate kingdom —
What change, O Changer! wilt thou devise and decree?
Hail to thy god-ship, O Thor! Good luck to the Arm with the

    Hammer!
Good luck to that little right arm!
Green Bush to the Moa, Burnt Bush to the resolute Settler!
In strenuous years ahead,
Wilt thou wield the axe of the Fire?
Wilt thou harness the horse of the Wind?
Shall not the Sun with his strong hands serve thee, and the tender
        hands of the Rain?
Daytime and Night spring in turn to thy battle,
Time and Decay run in yoke to thy plough,
And Earth, from the sleep of her sorrow
Waked at thy will, with an eager delight rise, requicken'd, and heartily
        help thee?
— Till the charr'd logs vanish away;
Till the wounds of the land are whole:
Till the skeleton valleys and hills
With greenness and growing, with multiplied being and
        movement,
Changeful, living, rejoice!

Yea, newly-come Soul!
Here on Earth, from what region unguess'd at?
Here, to this rough and raw prospect, these back-blocks of Being,
        assign'd —
Lean, cumber'd with ruin, lonely, bristling with hardship,
A birthright that fires have been through —
What change, O Changer! creature, Creator, of Spirit!
In this, thy burden'd allotment, wilt thou command and create?
        Finite, yet infinite,
        Tool, yet Employer,
        Of Forces Almighty,
        Beyond thee, within, —
What Fires, of the Spirit, what Storms, wilt thou summon?
What Dews shall avail thee, what Sunbeams? What seed wilt thou
        sow?
Ease unto weaklings: to thews and to sinews, Achievement!
What pasture, Settler and Sovereign, shall be grazed from the soil-
        sweetening ashes?
What home be warm in the wild?
Nay, outflowing Heart! thou highway forward and back:
Thought-trains of the Mind! commercing with far-away worlds:
What up-country traffic and freight shall travel forth into the
        world?
What help will ye summon and send?
Spirit, deep in the Dark! with the light of what over-head worlds
Wilt thou in the Dark make friends?
O pioneer Soul! against Ruin here hardily pitted,
What life wilt thou make of existence?
Life! what more Life wilt thou make?

Ah, little Thor!
Here in the night, face to face
With the Burnt Bush within and without thee,
Standing, small and alone:

Bright Promise on Poverty's threshold!
    What art thou? Where hast thou come from?
    How far, how far! wilt thou go?

1908

A R N O L D   W A L L

Born in England, Arnold Wall (1869–1966) took up a position as Professor of English at Canterbury University in 1898. As well as publishing copious amounts of poetry, he was a broadcaster, botanist and mountain climber.

The City from the Hills

There lies our city folded in the mist,
Like a great meadow in an early morn
Flinging her spears of grass up through white films,
Each with its thousand thousand-tinted globes.

Above us such an air as poets dream,
The clean and vast wing-winnowed clime of Heaven.

Each of her streets is closed with shining Alps,
Like Heaven at the end of long plain lives.

1900

A Time Will Come (1915)

A time will come, a time will come,
    (Though the world will never be quite the same),
When the people sit in the summer sun,
    Watching, watching the beautiful game.

A time will come, a time will come,
    With fifteen stars in a green heaven,
Two to be batting, two to judge,
    And round about them the fair Eleven.

A time will come, a time will come,
    When the people sit with a peaceful heart,
Watching the beautiful, beautiful game,
    That is battle and service and sport and art.

A time will come, a time will come,
    When the crowds will gaze on the game and the green,
Soberly watching the beautiful game,
    Orderly, decent, calm, serene.

The easy figures go out and in,
    The click of the bat sounds clear and well,
And over the studying, critical crowds
    Cricket will cast her witching spell.

Yet a time will come, a time will come,
    Come to us all as we watch, and seem

To be heart and soul in the beautiful game,
When we shall remember and wistfully dream —

Dream of the boys who never were here,
Born in the days of evil chance,
Who never knew sport or easy days,
But played their game in the fields of France.

1922

D A V I D   M C K E E   W R I G H T

Born in the north of Ireland, David McKee Wright (1869–1928) arrived in New Zealand in 1887 and was a station worker in Otago and, for a time, a rabbiter, before training for the Congregational Ministry. After serving as a pastor in Wellington and Nelson, he moved to Sydney where he wrote for the Bulletin *and other publications.*

While the Billy Boils

The speargrass crackles under the billy and overhead is the winter sun;
There's snow on the hills, there's frost in the gully, that minds me of things that I've seen and done,
Of blokes that I knew, and mates that I've worked with, and the sprees we had in the days gone by;
And a mist comes up from my heart to my eyelids, I feel fair sick and I wonder why.

There is coves and coves! Some I liked partic'lar, and some I would sooner I never knowed;
But a bloke can't choose the chaps that he's thrown with in the harvest paddock or here on the road.
There was chaps from the other side that I shore with that I'd like to have taken along for mates,
But we said, 'So long!' and we laughed and parted for good and all at the station gates.

I mind the time when the snow was drifting and Billy and me was out for the night —
We lay in the lee of a rock, and waited, hungry and cold, for the morning light.
Then he went one way and I the other — we'd been like brothers for half a year;
He said: 'I'll see you again in town, mate, and we'll blow the froth off a pint of beer.'

He went to a job on the plain he knowed of and I went poisoning out at the back,
And I missed him somehow — for all my looking I never could knock across his track.
The same with Harry, the bloke I worked with the time I was over upon the Coast,
He went for a fly-round over to Sydney, to stay for a fortnight — a month at most!

He never came back, and he never wrote me — I wonder how
  blokes like him forget;
We had been where no one had been before us, we had starved for
  days in the cold and wet;
We had sunk a hundred holes that was duffers, till at last we came
  on a fairish patch,
And we worked in rags in the dead of winter while the ice bars
  hung from the frozen thatch.

Yes, them was two, and I can't help mind them — good mates as
  ever a joker had;
But there's plenty more as I'd like to be with, for half of the blokes
  on the road is bad.
It sets me a-thinking the world seems wider, for all we fancy it's
  middling small,
When a chap like me makes friends in plenty and they slip away
  and he loses them all.

The speargrass crackles under the billy and overhead is the winter
  sun;
There's snow on the hills, there's frost in the gully, and, Oh, the
  things that I've seen and done,
The blokes that I knowed and the mates I've worked with, and the
  sprees we had in the days gone by;
But I somehow fancy we'll all be pen-mates on the day when they
  call the Roll of the Sky.

1897

Our Cities Face the Sea

Jack came from Cornwall, and Pat from Donegal
'Arry came from London, the first place of all,
Sandy came from Aberdeen, and Tom's native-born,
But they're all mates together in the lands of the morn.
    Pulling, pulling on the one rope together,
    Bringing up the future with a golden tether,
Cousin Jack and Cockney, Irishman and Scot,
And the native is a brother to the whole blooming lot.

He worked at Gabriel's gully, he was there at the Dunstan rush,
He was first when the reefing opened and the batteries started to
  crush;
He was favourite ever with fortune, and whatever he touched
  would pay,
And his life was a song with the chorus, 'I'm going home some day.'
But he made his home on the hillside where the city faces the sea,
And he saw the houses rising and the children on his knee,
And he toiled, and laughed, and was happy, as the years went
  rolling by;
For we take our homeland with us, however we change our sky.

He thought of a far-off village, and a steeple grey with years,
The cottages white in the sunshine, and a parting day of tears;
He saw the gardens blooming with lavender around the beds,

And the doors that were bowered with roses that nodded over
    their heads;
He heard the thrushes singing, and the sparrows chirping at morn;
He saw the joy of the hay-time, and the poppies that starred the corn;
But up on the bush-covered hill-side the years went laughing by;
For we take our homeland with us, however we change our sky.

He left the windy city for the home beyond the sea, —
He would spent his age in the village beneath the old roof-tree;
He would hear again the ringing of the mellow Sunday bell,
And the folk would gather round him for the tales he had to tell,
The glamour of days long faded he would gather again anew;
He would see the happy meadows and the daisies washed in dew —
He went, and he saw, and he wearied, and ever his thoughts would fly
To another and dearer homeland under another sky.

He had learned the charm of the mountains, the breath of the
    tussocks he knew;
He had lived in a land of sunshine, under skies of cloudless blue;
And the charm of the old had faded, as the charm of the new had
    grown,
Till he hailed the windy islands with their flax and fern as his own.
Till he thought with a tender longing of lake, and mountain, and
    plain,
And the digger's camp in the gully, with its toil and its laughter again.
The old land could not hold him, its ways were sere and dry;
For we take our homeland with us in youth when we change our sky.

Our cities look to the ocean, the homeland is far away;
The ships come sailing, sailing, and anchor in the bay;
Oh, tender the ties that bind us to the land our fathers knew,
And rich the storied record of a people strong and true;
Our thoughts will linger fondly in the North-land far away,
But our own land, our homeland is where we live today.
For together in toil and laughter the years go rolling by,
And we take our homeland with us, however we change our
    sky.

Jack came from Cornwall, and Pat from Donegal
'Arry came from London, the first place of all,
Sandy came from Aberdeen, and Tom's native-born,
But they're all mates together in the lands of the morn.
    Pulling, pulling on the one rope together,
    Bringing up the future with a golden tether,
Cousin Jack and Cockney, Irishman and Scot,
And the native is a brother to the whole blooming lot.
    Pulling, pulling on the one rope strong
    Bringing up the future with a shout and a song,
But the tides rise and fall, and the steamers come to call,
And the cities face the sea, and the winds are blowing free,
And out across the ocean is our home after all.

                      (1900)

JESSIE MACKAY

Born at Rakaia Gorge, Jessie Mackay (1864–1938) grew up on Canterbury sheep stations and, prior to full-time writing, worked as a teacher.

The Charge at Parihaka

Yet a league, yet a league
    Yet a league onward,
Straight to the Maori Pah
    Marched the Twelve Hundred.
'Forward the Volunteers!
Is there a man who fears?'
Over the ferny plain
    Marched the Twelve Hundred!

'Forward!' the Colonel said;
Was there a man dismayed?
No, for the heroes knew
    There was no danger.
Theirs not to reckon why,
Theirs not to bleed or die,
Theirs but to trample by:
    Each dauntless ranger.

Pressmen to right of them,
Pressmen to left of them,
Pressmen in front of them,
    Chuckled and wondered.
Dreading their country's eyes,
Long was the search and wise,
Vain, for the pressmen five
Had, by a slight device,
    Foiled the Twelve Hundred.

Gleamed all their muskets bare,
Fright'ning the children there,
Heroes to do and dare,
Charging a village, while
    Maoridom wondered.
Plunged in potato fields,
Honour to hunger yields.
Te Whiti and Tohu
Bearing not swords or shields,
Questioned nor wondered,
Calmly before them sat;
    Faced the Twelve Hundred.

Children to right of them,
Children to left of them,
Women in front of them,
    Saw them and wondered;
Stormed at with jeer and groan,
Foiled by the five alone,
Never was trumpet blown

O'er such a deed of arms.
Back with their captives three
Taken so gallantly,
    Rode the Twelve Hundred.

When can their glory fade?
Oh! the wild charge they made.
    New Zealand wondered
Whether each doughty soul,
Paid for the pigs he stole:
    Noble Twelve Hundred!

                    1889

Rona in the Moon

Rona, Rona, sister olden, —
    Rona in the moon!
You'll never break your prison golden, —
    Never, late or soon!

Rona, for her crying daughter,
    At the dead of night
Took the gourd and went for water;
    Went without a light.

There she heard the owlets wrangle
    With an angry hoot;
Stick and stone and thorny tangle
    Wounded Rona's foot.

'Boil the moon!' she said in passion;
    'Boil your lazy head!
Hiding thus in idle fashion
    In your starry bed!'

Angry was the moon in heaven;
    Down to earth she came: —
'Stay you ever unforgiven
    For the word of shame!

Up! — you made the moon a byword —
    Up and dwell with me!'
Rona felt the drawing skyward, —
    Seized a ngaio tree.

But from earth the ngaio parted
    Like a bitten thread;
Like a comet upward darted
    Rona overhead.

In the moon is Rona sitting,
    Never to be free;
With the gourd she held in flitting,
    And the ngaio tree.

You'll never break your prison golden, —
    Never, late or soon,
Rona, Rona, sister olden, —
    Rona in the moon!

1909

The Gray Company

O the gray, gray company
    Of the pallid dawn!
O the ghostly faces,
    Ashen-like and drawn!
The Lord's lone sentinels
    Dotted down the years,
The little gray company
    Before the pioneers!

Dreaming of Utopias
    Ere the time was ripe,
They awoke to scorning,
    To jeering and to strife.
Dreaming of millenniums
    In a world of wars,
They awoke to shudder
    At a flaming Mars.

Never was a Luther
    But a Huss was first, —
A fountain unregarded
    In the primal thirst.
Never was a Newton
    Crowned and honoured well,
But first a lone Galileo
    Wasted in a cell.

In each other's faces
    Looked the pioneers; —
Drank the wine of courage
    All their battle years.
For their weary sowing
    Through the world wide,
Green they saw the harvest
    Ere the day they died.

But the gray, gray company
    Stood every man alone
In the chilly dawnlight:
    Scarcely had they known
Ere the day they perished,
    That their beacon-star
Was not glint of marshlight
    In the shadows far.

The brave white witnesses
    To the truth within
Took the dart of folly,
    Took the jeer of sin.
Crying 'Follow, follow,
    Back to Eden-gate!'
They trod the Polar desert, —
    Met the desert fate.

Be laurel to the victor,
    And roses to the fair;
And asphodel Elysian
    Let the hero wear:
But lay the maiden lilies
    Upon their narrow biers —
The lone gray company
    Before the pioneers!

1909

ELEANOR ELIZABETH MONTGOMERY

Little is known about Eleanor Elizabeth Montgomery except that her family farmed at Brunswick, near Wanganui. She worked as housekeeper for her brother William, a Palmerston North JP, around the turn of the century. She is listed as a ratepayer in 1907, but no references to her after that date can be found.

The River Song

Where the woods and waters meet,
Last night we stood together;
Through the air came, low and sweet,
Soft murmurings from the river.
Each twinkling star on Heaven's blue breast,
Smiled on my Allan's love confest!

    While the river sang softly to me,
    While the river sang softly to me,
    Give your smiles to him, give your tears to me,
    And I'll carry them down
    To the salt salt sea.

O! quickly sped the entranced hours,
All, all unwatched they passed us by:
The honeysuckle's floating showers
Of balmy fragrance drifted nigh:
Nor brighter shone those orbs above
Than those two human stars I love.

    While the river sang softly to me, &c.

Bright beamed each golden eye above,
When on my happy, happy hand,
With many a tender word of love,
My Allan placed a sacred band
Saying, 'Within this circling gold
My love, my hope, my life you hold.'

  While the river sang softly to me, &c.

WILLIAM PEMBER REEVES

After studying law, William Pember Reeves (1857–1932) became a journalist then entered parliament where he was appointed Minister of Education, Justice and Labour in the Liberal Government. He later became New Zealand's Agent-General in London and did not return to New Zealand.

A Colonist in His Garden

He reads a letter.

'Dim grows your face, and in my ears,
Filled with the tramp of hurrying years,
 Your voice dies, far apart.
Our shortening day draws in, alack!
Old friend, ere darkness falls, turn back
 To England, life and art.

'Write not that you content can be,
Pent by that drear and shipless sea
 Round lonely islands rolled:
Isles nigh as empty as their deep,
Where men but talk of gold and sheep
 And think of sheep and gold.

'A land without a past; a race
Set in the rut of commonplace;
 Where Demos overfed
Allows no gulf, permits no height,
And grace and colour, music, light,
 From sturdy scorn are fled.

'I'll draw you home. Lo! as I write
A flash — a swallow's arrow-flight!
 O'erhead the skylark's wings
Quiver with joy at winter's rout:
A gust of April from without
 Scents of the garden brings.

'The quickening turf is starred with gold;
The orchard wall, rust-red and old,
 Glows in the sunlight long.
The very yew-tree warms to-day,

As the sun-dial, mossed and grey,
   Marks with a shadow strong.

'Tired of the bold, aggressive New,
Say, will your eyes not joy to view,
   In a sedater clime,
How mellowing tones at leisure steal,
And age hath virtue scars to heal,
   And beauty weds grey Time!'

    He speaks.

Good wizard! Thus he weaves his spell.
Yet, charm he twenty times as well,
   Me shall he never spur,
To seek again the old, green land,
That seems from far to stretch a hand
   To sons who dream of her.

For is my England there? Ah, no.
Gone is my England, long ago,
   Leaving me tender joys,
Sweet, fragrant, happy-breathing names
Of wrinkled men and grey-haired dames,
   To me still girls and boys.

With these in youth let memory stray
In pleasance green, where stern to-day
   Works Fancy no mischance.
Dear pleasance — let no light invade
Revealing ravage Time hath made
   Amid thy dim romance!

Here am I rooted. Firm and fast
We men take root who face the blast,
   When, to the desert come,
We stand where none before have stood
And braving tempest, drought and flood,
   Fight Nature for a home.

Now, when the fight is o'er, what man,
What wrestler, who in manhood's span
   Hath won so stern a fall,
Who, matched against the desert's power,
Hath made the wilderness to flower,
   Can turn, forsaking all?

Yet that my heart to England cleaves
This garden tells with blooms and leaves
   In old familiar throng,
And smells, sweet English every one,
And English turf to tread upon,
   And English blackbird's song.

'No art?' Who serve an art more great
Than we, rough architects of State

With the old Earth at strife?
'No colour!' On the silent waste,
In pigments not to be effaced,
   We paint the hues of life.

'A land without a past?' Nay, nay.
I saw it, forty years this day.
   — Nor man, nor beast, nor tree:
Wide, empty plains where shadows pass
Blown by the wind o'er whispering grass
   Whose sigh crept after me.

Now when at midnight round my doors
The gale through sheltering branches roars,
   What is it to the might
Of the mad gorge-wind that o'erthrew
My camp — the first I pitched — and blew
   Our tents into the night?

Mine is the vista where the blue
And white-capped mountains close the view.
   Each tapering cypress there
At planting in these hands was borne,
Small, shivering seedlings and forlorn,
   When all the plain was bare!

Skies without music, mute through time,
Now hear the skylark's rippling climb
   Challenge their loftier dome.
And hark! A song of garden floats,
Rills, gushes clear, — the self-same notes
   Your thrushes flute at Home.

See, I have poured o'er plain and hill
Gold open-handed, wealth that will
   Win children's children's smiles,
— Autumnal glories, glowing leaves,
And aureate flowers, and warmth of sheaves,
   'Mid weary pastoral miles.

Yonder my poplars, burning gold,
Flare in tall rows of torches bold,
   Spire beyond kindling spire.
Then raining gold round silver stem
Soft birches gleam. Outflaming them
   My oaks take ruddier fire.

And with my flowers about her spread
(None brighter than her shining head),
   The lady of my close,
My daughter, walks in girlhood fair.
Friend, could I rear in England's air
   A sweeter English rose?

                1925

The Passing of the Forest

All cannot fade that glorifies the hills,
  Their strength remains, their aspect of command,
Their flush of colour when calm evening stills
  Day's clamour, and the sea-breeze cools the land.
With shout of thunder and with voice of rills,
  Ancient of days in green old age they stand
In grandeur that can never know decay,
Though from their flanks men strip the woods away.

But thin their vesture now — the restless grass,
  Bending and dancing as the breeze goes by,
Catching quick gleams and cloudy shades that pass,
  As shallow seas reflect a wind-stirred sky.
Ah! nobler far their forest raiment was
  From crown to feet that clothed them royally,
Shielding their mysteries from the glare of day,
Ere the dark woods were reft and torn away.

Well may these plundered and insulted kings,
  Stripped of their robes, despoiled, uncloaked, discrowned,
Draw down the clouds with white enfolding wings,
  And soft aërial fleece to wrap them round,
To hide the scars that every season brings,
  The fire's black smirch, the landslip's gaping wound;
Well may they shroud their heads in mantle gray,
Since from their brows the leaves were plucked away!

Gone is the forest world, its wealth of life,
  Its jostling, crowding, thrusting, struggling race,
Creeper with creeper, bush with bush at strife,
  Warring and wrestling for a breathing space;
Below, a realm with tangled rankness rife,
  Aloft, tree columns, shafts of stateliest grace.
Gone is the forest nation. None might stay;
Giant and dwarf alike have passed away.

Gone are the forest birds, arboreal things,
  Eaters of honey, honey-sweet of song,
The tui, and the bell-bird — he who sings
  That brief, rich music we would fain prolong.
Gone the wood-pigeon's sudden whirr of wings;
  The daring robin, all unused to wrong.
Wild, harmless, hamadryad creatures, they
Lived with their trees, and died, and passed away.

And with the birds the flowers, too, are gone
  That bloomed aloft, ethereal, stars of light,
The clematis, the kowhai like ripe corn,
  Russet, though all the hills in green were dight;
The rata, draining from its tree forlorn
  Rich life-blood for its crimson blossoms bright,
Red glory of the gorges — well-a-day!
Fled is that splendour, dead and passed away.

Gone are the forest tracks, where oft we rode
    Under the silver fern-fronds climbing slow,
In cool, green tunnels, though fierce noontide glowed
    And glittered on the tree-tops far below.
There, mid the stillness of the mountain road,
    We just could hear the valley river flow,
Whose voice through many a windless summer day
Haunted the silent woods, now passed away.

Drinking fresh odours, spicy wafts that blew,
    We watched the glassy, quivering air asleep,
Midway between tall cliffs that taller grew
    Above the unseen torrent calling deep;
Till, like a sword, cleaving the foliage through,
    The waterfall flashed foaming down the steep:
White, living water, cooling with its spray
Dense plumes of fragile fern, now scorched away.

Keen is the axe, the rushing fire streams bright,
    Clear, beautiful, and fierce it speeds for Man,
The Master, set to change and stern to smite,
    Bronzed pioneer of nations. Ay, but scan
The ruined beauty wasted in a night,
    The blackened wonder God alone could plan,
And builds not twice! A bitter price to pay
Is this for progress — beauty swept away.

                                        1925

THOMAS BRACKEN

Born in Ireland, Thomas Bracken (1843–1898) arrived in New Zealand in 1869. He worked as a storekeeper, miner and journalist as well as representing Dunedin in Parliament 1881–1884. He was probably New Zealand's most popular poet of the late nineteenth century.

The New Zealand Hymn

God of nations! at Thy feet
In the bonds of love we meet,
Hear our voices, we entreat,
    God defend our Free Land.
Guard Pacific's triple star
From the shafts of strife and war,
Make her praises heard afar,
    God defend New Zealand.

Men of every creed and race
Gather here before Thy face,
Asking Thee to bless this place,
    God defend our Free Land.
From dissension, envy, hate

And corruption guard our State,
Make our country good and great,
    God defend New Zealand.

Peace, not war, shall be our boast,
But, should foes assail our coast,
Make us then a mighty host,
    God defend our Free Land.
Lord of battles, in Thy might,
Put our enemies to flight,
Let our cause be just and right,
    God defend New Zealand.

Let our love for Thee increase,
May Thy blessings never cease,
Give us plenty, give us peace,
    God defend our Free Land.
From dishonour and from shame
Guard our country's spotless name,
Crown her with immortal fame,
    God defend New Zealand.

May our mountains ever be
Freedom's ramparts on the sea,
Make us faithful unto Thee,
    God defend our Free Land.
Guide her in the nations' van,
Preaching love and truth to man,
Working out Thy glorious plan,
    God defend New Zealand.

                    1890

Not Understood

Not understood. We move along asunder,
    Our paths grow wider as the seasons creep
Along the years; we marvel and we wonder
    Why life is life? and then we fall asleep,
        Not undersood.

Not understood. We gather false impressions,
    And hug them closer as the years go by,
Till virtues often seem to us transgressions;
    And thus men rise and fall, and live and die,
        Not understood.

Not understood. Poor souls with stunted vision
    Oft measure giants by their narrow gauge:
The poisoned shafts of falsehood and derision
    Are oft impelled 'gainst those who mould the age,
        Not understood.

Not understood. The secret springs of action,
    Which lie beneath the surface and the show,
Are disregarded; with self-satisfaction

We judge our neighbours, and they often go,
　　Not understood.

Not understood. How trifles often change us!
　　The thoughtless sentence or the fancied slight
Destroy long years of friendship and estrange us,
　　And on our souls there falls a freezing blight;
　　　Not understood.

Not understood. How many breasts are aching
　　For lack of sympathy! Ah! day by day,
How many cheerless, lonely hearts are breaking!
　　How many noble spirits pass away
　　　Not understood!

Oh, God! that men would see a little clearer,
　　Or judge less harshly where they cannot see;
Oh, God! that men would draw a little nearer
　　To one another, they'd be nearer Thee,
　　　And understood.

　　　　　　　　　　　　　　　　(1890)

from The March of Te Rauparaha

Rauparaha's war chant,
Rauparaha's fame song,
Rauparaha's story
Told on the harp strings,
Pakeha harp cords
Tuned by the stranger.
　. . . .
Moan the waves,
Moan the waves,
Moan the waves as they wash Tainui,
Moan the waters of dark Kawhia,
Moan the waves as they sweep the gorges,
Wafting the sad laments and wailings
Of the spirits that haunt the mountains —
Warrior souls, whose skeletons slumber
Down in the caverns, lonely and dreary,
Under the feet of the fierce volcano,
Under the slopes of the Awaroa!
　Moan the winds,
　Moan the winds,
Moan the winds, and waves, and waters,
Moan they over the ages vanished,
Moan they over the tombs of heroes,
Moan they over the mighty chieftains
Sprung from giants of far Hawaiki!
Moan they over the bones of Raka,
Moan they over the Rangatira
Toa, who founded the Ngatitoa!
Moan they over Wera Wera,
　Sire of him,

Sire of him,
Sire of him they called Te Rauparaha!

Echoes of the craggy reeks,
Echoes of the rocky peaks,
  Echoes of the gloomy caves,
  Echoes of the moaning waves,
Echoes of the gorges deep,
Echoes of the winds that sweep
O'er Pirongia's summit steep,
  Chant the Rangatira's praise,
  Chant it in a thousand lays,
Chant the Rangatira's fame,
Chant the Rangatira's name,
  Te Rauparaha, Te Rauparaha!

Sound his praises far and near,
For his spirit still is here
  Flying through the gusty shocks,
  When the sea-ghosts climb the rocks
Clad in foam shrouds, thick and pale,
Woven by the howling gale
  In the ocean's monster loom!
  Warp of green and weft of gloom
Woven into sheets of white
By the wizards of the night;
Chant his name each ocean sprite,
  Te Rauparaha, Te Rauparaha!
  . . . .

'The sea rushed up with plunging shocks,
  Kapai! Rauparaha!
To claim the land and beat the rocks,
  Kapai! Rauparaha!
The rocks stood firm and broke the waves;
So stood the Ngatitoa braves —
Ngatitoa's foes are slaves,
  Kapai! Rauparaha!

'The stars came out to match the sun,
  Kapai! Rauparaha!
To claim the crown that he had won,
  Kapai! Rauparaha!
The sun shot forth its brightest rays,
And quenched the stars in fiery blaze;
Then chant the Ngatitoa's praise,
  Kapai! Rauparaha!

'The Tuis came the Hawk to kill,
  Kapai! Rauparaha!
And yet the Hawk is living still,
  Kapai! Rauparaha!
The Hawk can soar, the Hawk can fight —
The Tuis tried to stay his flight —
The Hawk shall have a feast to-night

Kapai! Rauparaha!
. . . .

'Slaves should have but little words,
   Kapai! Rauparaha!
Little songs for little birds,
   Kapai! Rauparaha!
Little Tuis should not try
With their little wings to fly
Where the Hawk is perched on high,
   Kapai! Rauparaha! . . .'

(1890)

EDWARD TREGEAR

Born in Southampton, Edward Tregear (1846–1931) emigrated in 1863 and worked as a surveyor before becoming the first Secretary of the New Zealand Labour Department in 1892. His first collection of verse, Shadows and Other Verses, *appeared in 1919.*

Te Whetu Plains

A lonely rock above a midnight plain,
   A sky across whose moonlit darkness flies
No shadow from the 'Children of the Rain,'
   A stream whose double crescent far-off lies,
   And seems to glitter back the silver of the skies.

The table-lands stretch step by step below
   In giant terraces, their deeper ledges
Banded by blackened swamps (that, near, I know
   Convolvulus-entwined) whose whitened edges
   Are ghostly silken flags of seeding water-sedges.

All still, all silent, 'tis a songless land,
   That hears no music of the nightingale,
No sound of waters falling lone and grand
   Through sighing forests to the lower vale,
   No whisper in the grass, so wan, and grey, and pale.

When Earth was tottering in its infancy,
   This rock, a drop of molten stone, was hurled
And tost on waves of flames like those we see
   (Distinctly though afar) evolved and whirled
   A photosphere of fire around the Solar World.

Swift from the central deeps the lightning flew
   Piercing the heart of Darkness like a spear,
Hot blasts of steam and vapour thunder'd through
   The lurid blackness of the atmosphere.
   A million years have passed, and left strange quiet here.

Peace, the deep peace of universal death
   Enshrouds the kindly mother-earth of old,
The air is dead, and stirs no living breath
   To break these awful Silences that hold
     The heart within their clutch, and numb the veins with cold.

My soul hath wept for Rest with longing tears,
   Called it 'the perfect crown of human life' —
But now I shudder lest the coming years
   Should be with these most gloomy terrors rife;
     When palsied arms drop down outwearied with the strife

May Age conduct me by a gentle hand
   Beneath the shadows ever brooding o'er
The solemn twilight of the Evening Land,
   Where man's discordant voices pierce no more,
     But sleeping waters dream along a sleeping shore.

Where I, when Youth has spent its fiery strength
   And flickers low, may rest in quietness
Till on my waiting brow there falls at length
   The deeper calm of the Death-Angel's kiss —
     But not, oh God, such peace, such ghastly peace as this.

1919

ARTHUR H. ADAMS

Arthur Henry Adams (1872–1936) was born in Otago. A graduate of Otago University, he became an established literary figure in both Australia and New Zealand. He edited the Red Page *for the Australian paper, the* Bulletin, *and published much New Zealand writing in that capacity.*

The Dwellings of Our Dead

They lie unwatched, in waste and vacant places,
In sombre bush or wind-swept tussock spaces,
   Where seldom human tread
And never human trace is —
   The dwellings of our dead!

No insolence of stone is o'er them builded;
By mockery of monuments unshielded,
   Far on the unfenced plain
Forgotten graves have yielded
   Earth to free earth again.

Above their crypts no air with incense reeling,
No chant of choir or sob of organ pealing;
   But ever over them
The evening breezes kneeling
   Whisper a requiem.

For some the margeless plain where no one passes.
Save when at morning far in misty masses
   The drifting flock appears.

Lo, here the greener grasses
   Glint like a stain of tears!

For some the quiet bush, shade-strewn and saddened,
Whereo'er the herald tui, morning-gladdened,
   Lone on his chosen tree,
With his new rapture maddened,
   Shouts incoherently.

For some the gully where, in whispers tender,
The flax-blades mourn and murmur, and the slender
   White ranks of toi go,
With dropping plumes of splendour,
   In pageantry of woe.

For some the common trench where, not all fameless,
They fighting fell who thought to tame the tameless,
   And won their barren crown;
Where one grave holds them nameless —
   Brave white and braver brown.

But in their sleep, like troubled children turning,
A dream of mother-country in them burning,
   They whisper their despair,
And one vague, voiceless yearning
   Burdens the pausing air . . .

'Unchanging here the drab year onward presses;
No Spring comes trysting here with new-loosed tresses,
   And never may the years
Win Autumn's sweet caresses —
   Her leaves that fall like tears.

And we would lie 'neath old-remembered beeches,
Where we could hear the voice of him who preaches
   And the deep organ's call,
While close about us reaches
   The cool, grey, lichened wall.'

But they are ours, and jealously we hold them;
Within our children's ranks we have enrolled them,
   And till all Time shall cease
Our brooding bush shall fold them
   In her broad-bosomed peace.

They came as lovers come, all else forsaking,
The bonds of home and kindred proudly breaking;
   They lie in splendour lone —
The nation of their making
   Their everlasting throne!

               1899

Written in Australia

The wide sun stares without a cloud:
   Whipped by his glances truculent
The earth lies quivering and cowed!

My heart is hot with discontent —
I hate this haggard continent.

But over the loping leagues of sea
A lone land calls to her children free ;
My own land holding her arms to me
Over the loping leagues of sea.

The old grey city is dumb with heat;
   No breeze comes leaping, naked, rude,
Adown the narrow, high-walled street;
   Upon the night thick perfumes brood:
   The evening oozes lassitude.

But o'er the edges of my town,
   Swept in a tide that ne'er abates,
The riotous breezes tumble down;
   My heart looks home, looks home, where waits
   The Windy City of the Straits!

The land lies desolate and stripped;
   Across its waste has thinly strayed
A tattered host of eucalypt,
   From whose gaunt uniform is made
   A ragged penury of shade.

But o'er my isles the forest drew
   A mantle thick — save where a peak
Shows his grim teeth a-snarl — and through
   The filtered coolness creek and creek
   Tangled in ferns, in whispers speak.

And there the placid great lakes are,
   And brimming rivers proudly force
Their ice-cold tides. Here, like a scar,
   Dry-lipped, a withered watercourse
   Crawls from a long-forgotten source.

My glance, home-gazing, scarce discerns
   This listless girl, in whose dark hair
A starry-red hibiscus burns;
   Her pallid cheeks are like a pair
   Of nuns — they are so fragile-fair;

And like a sin her warm lips flame
   In her wan face; swift passions brim
In her brown eyes, and ebb with shame;
   Her form is sinuous and slim —
   That lyric line of breast and limb!

But one there waits whose brown face glows,
   Whose cheeks with Winter's kisses smart —
The flushing petals of a rose!
   Of earth and sun she is a part;
   Her brow is Greek and Greek her heart.

At love she laughs a faint disdain;
    Her heart no weakly one to charm;
Robust and fragrant as the rain,
    The dark bush soothed her with his balm,
    The mountains gave her of their calm.

Her fresh young figure, lithe and tall,
    Her twilight eyes, her brow benign,
She is the peerless queen of all —
    The maid, the country, that I shrine
    In this far banished heart of mine!

    But over the loping leagues of green
    A lone land waits with a hope serene —
    My own land calls like a prisoner queen —
    But oh! the long loping leagues between!

1899

JOHN BARR OF CRAIGILEE

A Scottish emigrant, John Barr (1809–1889) farmed at a property he christened Craigilee before moving to Dunedin where he was a founder of the Burns Society and became renowned for his poetry reading.

Rise Oot Your Bed

Rise oot your bed, ye worthless wretch,
    The sun's far in the lift,
I never kent a drunken man
    That e'er cam muckle thrift;
See, I've been up since morning grey
    Amang the dirt and weet,
It taks it a', I weel I wat,
    To gar the twa ends meet.

O, woman, will ye haud your tongue,
    My throat is like to crack,
Fling here my breeks, they're at the fire,
    Hung ower the auld chair back.
What time did I come hame yestreen?
    It was a fearfu' nicht;
For Guidsake gie's a nobbler,
    'Twill maybe put me richt.

O weary on your nobblers,
    Your drinking, and your splores,
And weary on your toun exploits,
    Amang your drunken cores.
Ye'll sure be in the newspapers,
    And that ye'll see ere lang,
They needna say Tam Maut is dead
    As lang's ye're fit to gang.

Noo steek your gab, ye've said eneugh,
    And what ye've said's no true,
A pretty pickel ye'd be in
    But for mysel' and pleugh.
Let's see a glass, or haud your tongue,
    I want nane o' your strife,
'Tis pity ye've got sic a man,
    And I've got sic a wife.

And wha's the warst ane o' the twa,
    Ye'll maybe tell me that?
It sets ye weel to lie up there,
    And see me dreepin' wat,
Wi' fechting 'mang the sharney kye,
    'Mang glaur up to the kuits,
Wi' scarce a sark upon my back,
    My taes clean oot my buits.

O swear awa, just swear awa,
    Ye canna bear the truth;
Ye'll what? ye'll rise and tak your nieve
    And gie me ower the mouth:
But, Guidsake, here comes Craigielee,
    Let's a' oor fauts conceal; —
'O come awa, ye're welcome here,
    Our Johnnie's no that weel.'

1861

There's Nae Place Like Otago Yet

There's nae place like Otago yet,
    There's nae wee beggar weans,
Or auld men shivering at our doors,
    To beg for scraps or banes.
We never see puir working folk
    Wi' bauchles on their feet,
Like perfect icicles wi' cauld,
    Gaun starving through the street.

We never hear o' breaking stanes
    A shilling by the yard;
Or poor folk roupit to the door
    To pay the needfu' laird;
Nae purse-proud, upstart, mushroom lord
    To scowl at honest toil,
Or break it down that he, the wretch,
    May feast on roast and boil.

My curse upon them, root and branch,
    A tyrant I abhor;
May despotism's iron foot
    Ne'er mark Otago's shore:

May wealth and labour hand in hand
   Work out our glorious plan,
But never let it be allowed
   That money makes the man.

1861

Grub Away, Tug Away

The birds gang to rest when tir'd wi' their warblin',
   But rest I get nane frae the mornin' sae early;
For either I'm mawin', or thrashin', or sawin',
   Or grubbin' the hills wi' the ferns covered fairly.
     Grub away, tug away, toil till you're weary,
       Haul oot the toot roots and everything near ye;
     Grub away, tug away, toil till you're weary,
       Then take a bit dram, it will help for to cheer ye.

It's no very pleasant this rough way o' livin',
   Sic tuggin', sic ruggin', it makes me banes crazy;
And aye when I rest me the wife's tongue besets me,
   Wi' 'Gang to your wark, man, and dinna turn lazy.'
     Grub away, etc.

Bricht was my brow in life's early dawnin',
   Licht was my heart as the blush of the mornin';
Noo I am dull and wae, like a dark winter's day,
   Deep in some glen where nae sun is adornin',
     Grub away, etc.

O for the wings o' the swift flyin' eaglet,
   Quick ower the sea I would hurry me early,
To the land o' the heather bell, mountain, and foggy dell,
   Land of the brave that my heart lo'es so dearly,
     Grub away, etc.

Haste away, fly away, home to my fatherland,
   Land of the thistle, and mountain, and river,
Haste away, fly away, home to my fatherland,
   There on her bosom, I'd rest me forever.
     Grub away, etc.

1861

JAMES EDWARD FITZGERALD

Born in England in 1818, of Irish descent, educated at Christ's College, Cambridge, James Edward Fitzgerald came to Canterbury on the Charlotte Jane *in 1850. He founded* The Press *in Christchurch, before entering politics. He died in Wellington in 1896.*

The Night-Watch Song of the 'Charlotte Jane'

'Tis the first watch of the night, brothers,
   And the strong wind rides the deep;

And the cold stars shining bright, brothers,
 Their mystic courses keep.
Whilst our ship her path is cleaving
 The flashing waters through,
Here's a health to the land we are leaving,
 And the land we are going to!

First sadly bow the head, brothers,
 In silence o'er the wine,
To the memory of the dead, brothers,
 The fathers of our line.
Though their tombs may not receive us,
 Far o'er the ocean blue,
Their spirits ne'er shall leave us,
 In the land we are going to.

Whilst yet sad memories move us,
 A second cup we'll drain
To the manly hearts that love us
 In our old homes o'er the main —
Fond arms that used to caress us,
 Sweet smiles from eyes of blue,
Lips that no more may bless us,
 In the land we are going to.

But away with sorrow now, brothers,
 Fill the winecup to the brim!
Here's to all who'll swear the vow, brothers,
 Of this our midnight hymn: —
That each man shall be a brother,
 Who has joined our gallant crew:
That we'll stand by one another
 In the world we are going to!

Fill again, before we part, brothers,
 Fill the deepest draught of all,
To the loved ones of our hearts, brothers,
 Who reward and share our toil —
From husbands and from brothers,
 All honour be their due, —
The noble maids and mothers
 Of the land we are going to! —

The wine is at the end, brothers;
 But ere we close our eyes,
Let a silent prayer ascend, brothers,
 For our gallant enterprise —
Should our toil be all unblest, brothers,
 Should ill winds of fortune blow,
May we find God's haven of rest, brothers,
 In the land we are going to.

1900

ANONYMOUS

David Lowston

(c. 1810–1815)

My name is David Lowston, I did seal, I did seal,
My name is David Lowston, I did seal.
Though my men and I were lost,
Though our very lives 'twould cost,
We did seal, we did seal, we did seal.

'Twas in eighteen hundred and ten we set sail, we set sail,
'Twas in eighteen hundred and ten, we set sail.
We were left, we gallant men,
Never more to sail again,
For to seal, for to seal, for to seal.

We were set down in Open Bay, were set down, were set down,
We were set down in Open Bay, were set down.
Upon the sixteenth day,
Of Februar-aye-ay,
For to seal, for to seal, for to seal.

Our Captain, John Bedar, he set sail, he set sail,
Yes, for Port Jackson he set sail.
'I'll return, men, without fail,'
But she foundered in a gale,
And went down, and went down, and went down.

We cured ten thousand skins for the fur, for the fur,
Yes we cured ten thousand skins for the fur.
Brackish water, putrid seal,
We did all of us fall ill,
For to die, for to die, for to die.

Come all you lads who sail the sea, sail the sea,
Come all you jacks who sail upon the sea.
Though the schooner, *Governor Bligh*,
Took on some who did not die,
Never seal, never seal, never seal.

ANONYMOUS

Come All You Tonguers

(c. 1830)

Come all you tonguers and land-loving lubbers,
Here's a job cutting in and boiling down blubbers,
A job for the youngster, or old and ailing,
The Agent will take any man for shore whaling.

I am paid in soap, and sugar, and rum,
For cutting in whale and boiling down tongue.
The Agent's fee makes my blood so t'boil,
I'll push him in a hot pot of oil!

Go hang the Agent, the Company too!
They are making a fortune off me and you.
No chance of a passage from out of this place,
And the price of living's a blooming disgrace!

I am paid in soap, and sugar, and rum,
For cutting in whale and boiling down tongue.
The Agent's fee makes my blood so t'boil,
I'll push him in a hot pot of oil!

A N O N Y M O U S

When We're at the Mataura

The folks are a' gaun mad outricht,
The yellow fever's at its height,
And naething's heard baith day and nicht
    But gold at the Mataura.

There'll be some pretty rows we know,
When ladies drive the bullocks O,
And many a loud 'Come ither, wo!'
    When we're at the Mataura.

They'll make the laws themselves to please,
And set to making Road Trustees,
And nominating M.P.C's.,
    When we're at the Mataura.

Our Tibbies, Bettys, Nellys, Molls,
Will rectify electoral rolls,
And check the bribery at polls,
    When we're at the Mataura.

The land that's waste they'll parcel oot,
In quantities they think will suit,
And sell't to all that's goot the hoot,[1]
    When we're at the Mataura.

---

[1] Utu: Maori word for money.

SELECT BIBLIOGRAPHY

ARTHUR H. ADAMS, *1872–1936*
Maoriland and Other Verses, Sydney, Bulletin Newspaper Co., 1899
The Nazarene: A Study of a Man, London, Philip Wellby, 1902
Collected Verses, Melbourne, Whitcombe & Tombs, 1913

FLEUR ADCOCK, B. *1934*
The Eye of the Hurricane, Wellington, A. H. & A. W. Reed, 1964
Tigers, London, Oxford University Press, 1967
High Tide in the Garden, London, Oxford University Press, 1971
The Scenic Route, London, Oxford University Press, 1974
Below Loughrigg, Newcastle upon Tyne, Bloodaxe Books, 1979
The Inner Harbour, Oxford, Oxford University Press, 1979
Selected Poems, Oxford, Oxford University Press, 1983
The Incident Book, Oxford, Oxford University Press, 1986
Meeting the Comet, Newcastle upon Tyne, Bloodaxe Books, 1988
Time Zones, Oxford, Oxford University Press, 1991

ROB ALLAN, B. *1957*
Karitane Postcards, Christchurch, Hazard Press, 1991

K. O. ARVIDSON, B. *1938*
Riding the Pendulum: Poems 1961–69, Wellington, Oxford University Press, 1973

JOHN BARR OF CRAIGILEE, *1809–1889*
Poems and Songs, Descriptive and Satirical, Edinburgh, John Greig, 1861
Poems, Dunedin, F. Humffray, 1874

BLANCHE BAUGHAN, *1870–1958*
Verses, Westminster, Archibald Constable, 1898
Reuben and other Poems, Westminster, Archibald Constable, 1903
Shingle-Short and Other Verses, Christchurch, Whitcombe & Tombs, 1908
Poems from the Port Hills, Auckland, Whitcombe & Tombs, 1923

JAMES K. BAXTER, *1926–1972*
Beyond the Palisade, Christchurch, Caxton Press, 1944
Blow, Wind of Fruitfulness, Christchurch, Caxton Press, 1948
The Fallen House, Christchurch, Caxton Press, 1953
In Fires of No Return, London, Oxford University Press, 1958
Howrah Bridge and Other Poems, London, Oxford University Press, 1961
Pig Island Letters, London, Oxford University Press, 1966
The Lion Skin, Dunedin, The Bibliography Room, University of Otago, 1967
The Rock Woman: Selected Poems, London, Oxford University Press, 1969
Jerusalem Sonnets, Dunedin, The Bibliography Room, University of Otago, 1970
Autumn Testament, Wellington, Price Milburn, 1972
Runes, London, Oxford University Press, 1973
The Labyrinth: Some Uncollected Poems 1944–72, Wellington, Oxford University Press, 1974

The Holy Life and Death of Concrete Grady, chosen and arranged by J. E. Weir, Wellington, Oxford University Press, 1976
Collected Poems, edited by J. E. Weir, Wellington, Oxford University Press, 1980
Selected Poems, edited by J. E. Weir, Auckland, Oxford University Press, 1982

MARY URSULA BETHELL, *1874–1945*
From a Garden in the Antipodes, by 'Evelyn Hayes' [pseud.], London, Sidgwick and Jackson, 1929
Time and Place, Christchurch, Caxton Press, 1936
Day and Night: Poems 1924–1935, Christchurch, Caxton Press, 1939
Collected Poems, Christchurch, Caxton Press, 1950
Collected Poems, edited by Vincent O'Sullivan, Auckland, Oxford University Press, 1985

TONY BEYER, B. *1948*
Jesus Hobo, Dunedin, Caveman Press, 1971
The Meat and other Poems, Dunedin, Caveman Press, 1974
Dancing Bear, Canberra, Melaleuca Press, 1981
Brute Music, Auckland, Hard Echo Press, 1984
The Singing Ground: Poems, Christchurch, Caxton Press, 1986

PETER BLAND, B. *1934*
Domestic Interiors, Wellington, Wai-te-ata Press, 1964
My Side of the Story: Poems 1960–1964, Auckland, Mate Books, 1964
The Man with the Carpet-Bag, Christchurch, Caxton Press, 1972
Mr Maui, London: London Magazine Editions, 1976
Primitives, Wellington, Wai-te-ata Press, 1979
Stone Tents, London, London Magazine Editions, 1981
The Crusoe Factor, London, London Magazine Editions, 1985
Selected Poems, Dunedin, McIndoe, 1987
Paper Boats, Dunedin, McIndoe, 1991

JENNY BORNHOLDT, B. *1960*
This Big Face, Wellington, Victoria University Press, 1988
Moving House, Wellington, Victoria University Press, 1989
Waiting Shelter, Wellington, Victoria University Press, 1991
How We Met, Wellington, Victoria University Press, 1995

THOMAS BRACKEN, *1843–1898*
The Haunted Vale: A Legend of the Murray, and Other Poems and Legends, Sandhurst, J. K. Robshaw, 1867
Behind the Tomb and Other Poems, Melbourne, Clarson, Massina & Co., 1871
Flowers of the Free Lands, Dunedin, Mills, Dick & Co., 1877
Lays of the Land of the Maori and Moa, London, Sampson, Low, Martin, Searle & Rivington, 1884
Paddy Murphy's Annual, Dunedin, Fergusson & Mitchell, 1886
Musings in Maoriland, Dunedin, Arthur T. Keirle, 1890
Lays and Lyrics, Wellington, Brown, Thomson & Co., 1893
Tom Bracken's Annual, Wellington, 1896

Tom Bracken's Annual No 2, Dunedin, 1897
Not Understood and Other Poems, Wellington, Gordon and Gotch, 1905
Ballads, Palmerston North, Dunmore, 1975

CHARLES BRASCH, *1909–1973*
The Land and the People and Other Poems, Christchurch, Caxton Press, 1939
Disputed Ground: Poems 1939–1945, Christchurch, Caxton Press, 1948
The Estate and Other Poems, Christchurch, Caxton Press, 1957
Ambulando, Christchurch, Caxton Press, 1964
Not Far Off, Christchurch, Caxton Press, 1969
Home Ground, edited by Alan Roddick, Christchurch, Caxton Press, 1974
Collected Poems, edited by Alan Roddick, Auckland, Oxford University Press, 1984

ALAN BRUNTON, B. *1946*
Messengers in Blackface, London, Amphedesma Press, 1973
Black and White Anthology, Taylor's Mistake, Hawk Press, 1976
O Ravachol, Auckland, Red Mole Publications, 1978
And She Said, New York, Alexandra Fisher for Red Mole Enterprises, 1984
New Order, New York, Alexandra Fisher for Red Mole Enterprises, 1986
Day for a Daughter, Wellington. Untold Books, 1989
Slow Passes, 1978–1988, Auckland, Auckland University Press, 1991
Ephphatha, Auckland, Workshop Press, 1994

ALISTAIR CAMPBELL, B. *1925*
Mine Eyes Dazzle: Poems 1947–1949, Christchurch, Pegasus Press, 1950; revised editions 1951 and 1956
Sanctuary of Spirits: Poems, Wellington, Wai-te-ata Press, 1963
Wild Honey, London, Oxford University Press, 1964
Blue Rain: Poems, Wellington, Wai-te-ata Press, 1967
Kapiti: Selected Poems 1947–1971, Christchurch, Pegasus Press, 1972
Dreams, Yellow Lions, Martinborough, Alister Taylor, 1975
The Dark Lord of Savaiki, Pukerua Bay, Te Kotare Press, 1981
Collected Poems 1947–1981, Martinborough, Alister Taylor, 1982
Soul Traps: A Lyric Sequence, Pukerua Bay, Te Kotare Press, 1985
Stone Rain: The Polynesian Strain, Christchurch, Hazard Press, 1992

MEG CAMPBELL, B. *1937*
The Way Back, Pukerua Bay, Te Kotare Press, 1981
A Durable Fire, Pukerua Bay, Te Kotare Press, 1982
Orpheus and Other Poems, Pukerua Bay, Te Kotare Press, 1990

GORDON CHALLIS, B. *1932*
Building, Christchurch, Caxton Press, 1963

JANET CHARMAN, B. *1956*
2 Deaths in 1 Night, Auckland, New Womens Press, 1987
Red Letter, Auckland, Auckland University Press, 1992
End of the Dry, Auckland, Auckland University Press, 1995

GEOFF COCHRANE, B. *1951*
Images of Midnight City, Karori, Hauraki Press, 1976

Solstice, Wellington, Voice Press, 1979
The Sea the Landsman Knows, Wellington, Voice Press, 1980
Taming the Smoke, Wellington, Grape Press, 1983
Kandinsky's Mirror, Wellington, Rat Island Press, 1989
Aztec Noon: Poems, 1976–1992, Wellington, Victoria University Press,
    1992

ALLEN CURNOW, B. *1911*
Valley of Decision, Auckland, Auckland University College Students'
    Association Press, 1933
Enemies: Poems 1934–1936, Christchurch, Caxton Press, 1937
Not in Narrow Seas: Poems with Prose, Christchurch, Caxton Press, 1939
Island and Time, Christchurch, Caxton Press, 1941
Sailing or Drowning, Wellington, Progressive Publishing Society, 1943
Jack Without Magic, Christchurch, Caxton Press, 1946
At Dead Low Water and Sonnets, Christchurch, Caxton Press, 1949
Poems 1949–1957, Wellington, Mermaid Press, 1957
A Small Room With Large Windows: Selected Poems, London, Oxford
    University Press, 1962
Trees, Effigies, Moving Objects: A Sequence of Poems, Wellington, Catspaw
    Press, 1972
An Abominable Temper and Other Poems, Wellington, Catspaw Press, 1973
Collected Poems 1933–1973, Wellington, A. H. & A. W. Reed, 1974
An Incorrigible Music, Auckland, Auckland University Press/Oxford
    University Press, 1979
You Will Know When You Get There: Poems 1979–1981, Auckland,
    Auckland University Press/Oxford University Press, 1982
Selected Poems, Auckland, Penguin Books, 1982
The Loop in Lone Kauri Road: Poems 1983–1985, Auckland, Auckland
    University Press/Oxford University Press, 1986
Continuum: New and Later Poems 1972–1988, Auckland, Auckland
    University Press, 1988
Selected Poems 1940–1989, London, Viking, 1990

WYSTAN CURNOW, B. *1939*
Back in the USA: Poems 1980–82, Auckland, Blacklight Press, 1989
Cancer Daybook, Auckland, Van Guard Xpress, 1989

RUTH DALLAS, B. *1919*
Country Road and Other Poems, 1947–1952, Christchurch, Caxton Press,
    1953
The Turning Wheel, Christchurch, Caxton Press, 1961
Day Book, Christchurch, Caxton Press, 1966
Shadow Show: Poems, Christchurch, Caxton Press, 1968
Song for a Guitar and Other Songs, edited by Charles Brasch, Dunedin,
    University of Otago Press, 1976
Walking on the Snow: Poems, Christchurch, Caxton Press, 1976
Steps of the Sun, Poems, Christchurch, Caxton Press, 1979
Collected Poems, Dunedin, University of Otago Press, 1987

LEIGH DAVIS, B. *1955*
Willy's Gazette, Wellington, Jack Books, 1983

JOHN DICKSON, B. *1944*
What Happened on the Way to Oamaru, Christchurch, Untold, 1986

EILEEN DUGGAN, *1894–1972*
Poems, Dunedin, The New Zealand Tablet, 1921
New Zealand Bird Songs, Wellington, Harry H. Tombs, 1929
Poems, London, Allen and Unwin, 1937
New Zealand Poems, London, Allen and Unwin, 1940
More Poems, London, Allen and Unwin, 1951
Selected Poems, edited by Peter Whiteford, Wellington, Victoria University
    Press, 1994

LAURIS EDMOND, B. *1924*
In Middle Air, Christchurch, Pegasus Press, 1975
The Pear Tree, Christchurch, Pegasus Press, 1977
Salt from the North, Wellington, Oxford University Press, 1980
Seven: Poems, Wellington, Wayzgoose Press, 1980
Wellington Letter: A Sequence of Poems, Wellington, Mallinson Rendel,
    1980
Catching It, Auckland, Oxford University Press, 1983
Selected Poems, Auckland, Oxford University Press, 1984
Seasons and Creatures, Auckland, Oxford University Press, 1986
Summer near the Arctic Circle, Auckland, Oxford University Press, 1988
New and Selected Poems, Auckland, Oxford University Press, 1991
Selected Poems, 1975–1994, Wellington, Bridget Williams Books, 1994
Scenes from a Small City, Wellington, Daphne Brasell Associates, 1994

MURRAY EDMOND, B. *1949*
Entering the Eye, Dunedin, Caveman Press, 1973
Patchwork, Day's Bay, Hawk Press, 1978
End Wall, Auckland, Oxford University Press, 1981
Letters and Paragraphs, Christchurch, Caxton Press, 1987
From the Word Go, Auckland, Auckland University Press, 1992
The Switch, Auckland, Auckland University Press, 1994

KIM EGGLESTON, B. *1960*
From the Face to the Bin: Poems 1978–1984, Greymouth, Strong John Press,
    1984
25 Poems: The Mist Will Rise and the World Will Drip with Gold, Greymouth,
    Strong John Press, 1985

DAVID EGGLETON, B. *1953*
South Pacific Sunrise, Auckland, Penguin Books, 1986
People of the Land, Auckland, Penguin Books, 1988
Empty Orchestra, Auckland, Auckland University Press, 1995

RIEMKE ENSING, B. *1939*
Making Inroads, Wellington, Coal-Black Press, 1980
Letters — Selected Poems, Auckland, The Lowry Press, 1982
Topographies, Auckland, Prometheus Press, 1984
Spells from Chagall, Auckland, The Griffin Press, 1987

The 'KM' File and Other Poems with Katherine Mansfield, Christchurch, Hazard Press, 1993

Dear Mr Sargeson . . ., Whatamango Bay, Cape Catley, 1995

Like I Have Seen the Dark Green Ladder Climbing, Auckland, Pear Tree Press, 1995

A. R. D. FAIRBURN, 1904–1957

He Shall Not Rise, London, Columbia Press, 1930

Dominion, Christchurch, Caxton Press, 1938

Poems, 1929–1941, Christchurch, Caxton Press, 1943

How to Ride a Bicycle in Seventeen Lovely Colours, Auckland, Pelorus Press, 1946

The Rakehelly Man & Other Verses, Christchurch, Caxton Press, 1946

Strange Rendezvous: Poems 1929–1941, With Additions, Christchurch, Caxton Press, 1952

Three Poems: Dominion, The Voyage, & To a Friend in the Wilderness, Wellington, New Zealand University Press, 1952

The Disadvantages of Being Dead and Other Sharp Verses, Wellington, Mermaid Press, 1958

Collected Poems, edited by Denis Glover, Christchurch, Pegasus Press, 1966

Selected Poems, edited by Mac Jackson, Wellington, Victoria University Press, 1995

FIONA FARRELL, B. 1947

Cutting Out, Auckland, Auckland University Press, 1987

JANET FRAME, B. 1924

The Pocket Mirror, New York, Braziller; London, W. H. Allen, 1967; Christchurch, Pegasus Press, 1968

ANNE FRENCH, B. 1956

All Cretans Are Liars, Auckland, Auckland University Press, 1987

The Male As Evader, Auckland, Auckland University Press, 1988

Cabin Fever, Auckland, Auckland University Press, 1990

Seven Days on Mykonos, Auckland, Auckland University Press, 1993

RUTH GILBERT, B. 1917

Lazarus and Other Poems, Wellington, A. H. & A. W. Reed, 1949

The Sunlit Hour, London, Allen and Unwin, 1955

The Luthier, Wellington, A. H. & A. W. Reed, 1966

Collected Poems, Wellington, Black Robin, 1984

DENIS GLOVER, 1912–1980

Thistledown, Christchurch, Caxton Club Press, 1935

Six Easy Ways of Dodging Debt Collectors, Christchurch, Caxton Press, 1936

Thirteen Poems, Christchurch, Caxton Press, 1939

Cold Tongue, Christchurch, Caxton Press, 1940

D Day, Christchurch, Caxton Press, 1944

The Wind and the Sand: Poems 1934–1944, Christchurch, Caxton Press, 1945

Summer Flowers, Christchurch, Caxton Press, 1946

Sings Harry and Other Poems, Christchurch, Caxton Press, 1951

Arawata Bill: A Sequence of Poems, Christchurch, Pegasus Press, 1953
Since Then, Wellington, Mermaid Press, 1957
Enter Without Knocking: Selected Poems, Christchurch, Pegasus Press, 1964, enlarged edition, 1972
Sharp Edge Up: Verses and Satires, Auckland, Blackwood and Janet Paul, 1968
Myself When Young, Christchurch, Nag's Head Press, 1970
To a Particular Woman, Christchurch, Nag's Head Press, 1970
Diary to a Woman, Wellington, Catspaw Press, 1971
Dancing to My Tune, edited by Lauris Edmond, Wellington, Catspaw Press, 1974
Wellington Harbour, Wellington, Catspaw Press, 1974
Clutha: River Poems, Dunedin, McIndoe, 1977
Come High Water, Palmerston North, Dunmore Press, 1977
For Whom the Cock Crows, Dunedin, McIndoe, 1978
Or Hawk or Basilisk, Wellington, Catspaw Press, 1978
To Friends in Russia, Christchurch, Nag's Head Press, 1979
Towards Banks Peninsula, Christchurch, Pegasus Press, 1979
Selected Poems, edited by Allen Curnow, Auckland, Penguin Books, 1981
Selected Poems, edited by Bill Manhire, Wellington, Victoria University Press, 1995

BERNADETTE HALL, B. *1945*
Heartwood, Christchurch, Caxton Press, 1989
Of Elephants, etc, Wellington, Untold Books, 1990
The Persistent Levitator, Wellington, Victoria University Press, 1994

MICHAEL HARLOW, B. *1937*
Edges, Athens, Lycabethis Press, 1974
Nothing But Switzerland and Lemonade, Eastbourne, Hawk Press, 1980
Today Is the Piano's Birthday: Poems, Auckland, Auckland University Press, 1981
Vlaminck's Tie, Auckland, Auckland University Press/Oxford University Press, 1985
Giotto's Elephant: Poems, Dunedin, McIndoe, 1991

DINAH HAWKEN, B. *1943*
It Has No Sound and Is Blue, Wellington, Victoria University Press, 1987
Small Stories of Devotion, Wellington, Victoria University Press, 1991
Water, Leaves, Stones, Wellington, Victoria University Press, 1995

PAUL HENDERSON [RUTH FRANCE] *1913–1967*
Unwilling Pilgrim, Christchurch, Caxton Press, 1955
The Halting Place, Christchurch, Caxton Press, 1961

KERI HULME, B. *1947*
The Silences Between (Moeraki Conversations), Auckland, Auckland University Press/Oxford University Press, 1982
Strands, Auckland, Auckland University Press, 1992

SAM HUNT, B. *1946*
Bracken Country, Wellington, Glenbervie Press, 1971
Bottle Creek Blues, Wellington, Bottle Press, 1972
From Bottle Creek, Wellington, Alister Taylor, 1972

South into Winter, Wellington, Alister Taylor, 1973
Time to Ride, Martinborough, Alister Taylor, 1975
Drunkard's Garden, Wellington, Hampson Hunt, 1977
Collected Poems 1963–1980, Harmondsworth, Penguin Books, 1980
Running Scared, Christchurch, Whitcoulls, 1982
Approaches to Paremata, Auckland, Penguin Books, 1985
Selected Poems, Auckland, Penguin Books, 1987
Making Tracks: A Selected 50 Poems, Christchurch, Hazard Press, 1991
Down the Backbone, Auckland, Hodder Moa Beckett, 1995

ROBIN HYDE [IRIS WILKINSON], *1906–1939*
The Desolate Star and Other Poems, Christchurch, Whitcombe & Tombs,
    1929
The Conquerors and Other Poems, London, Macmillan, 1935
Persephone in Winter, London, Hurst & Blackett, 1937
Houses by the Sea and the Later Poems of Robin Hyde, edited by Gloria
    Rawlinson, Christchurch, Caxton Press, 1952
Selected Poems, edited by Lydia Wevers, Auckland, Oxford University Press,
    1984

KEVIN IRELAND, B. *1933*
Face to Face, Christchurch, Pegasus Press, 1963
Educating the Body, Christchurch, Caxton Press, 1967
A Letter from Amsterdam, London, Amphedesma Press, 1972
Orchids, Hummingbirds, and Other Poems, Auckland, Auckland University
    Press/Oxford University Press, 1974
A Grammar of Dreams, Wellington, Wai-te-ata Press, 1975
Literary Cartoons, Auckland, Islands/Hurricane, 1977
The Dangers of Art, Poems 1975–1980, Auckland, Cicada Press, 1980
Practice Night in the Drill Hall, Auckland, Oxford University Press, 1984
The Year of the Comet: Twenty-six 1986 Sonnets, Auckland, Islands, 1986
Selected Poems, Auckland, Oxford University Press, 1987
Tiberius at the Beehive, Auckland, Auckland University Press, 1990
Skinning a Fish, Christchurch, Hazard Press, 1994

MICHAEL JACKSON, B. *1940*
Latitudes of Exile, Dunedin, McIndoe, 1976
Wall, Dunedin, McIndoe, 1980
Going On, Dunedin, McIndoe, 1985
Duty-Free: Selected Poems, 1965–1988, Dunedin, McIndoe, 1989

LOUIS JOHNSON, *1924–1988*
Stanza and Scene, Wellington, Handcraft Press, 1945
Roughshod Among the Lilies, Christchurch, Pegasus Press, 1951
The Sun Among the Ruins, Christchurch, Pegasus Press, 1951
The Dark Glass, Wellington, Handcraft Press, 1955
*News of Molly Bloom: The Passionate Man and the Casual Man: Two
    Poems*, Christchurch, Pegasus Press, 1955
New Worlds for Old: Poems, Wellington, Capricorn Press, 1957
The Night Shift: Poems on the Aspects of Love, Wellington, Capricorn Press,
    1957
Bread and a Pension, Christchurch, Pegasus Press, 1964
Land Like a Lizard, Brisbane, Jacaranda Press, 1970

Selected Poems, Bathurst, NSW, Mitchell College of Advanced Education, 1972
Fires and Patterns, Brisbane, Jacaranda Press, 1975
Coming and Going, Wellington, Mallinson Rendel, 1982
Winter Apples, Wellington, Mallinson Rendel, 1984
True Confessions of the Last Cannibal: New Poems, Plimmerton, Antipodes Press, 1986
Last Poems, Plimmerton, Antipodes Press, 1990

ANDREW JOHNSTON, B. 1963
How to Talk, Wellington, Victoria University Press, 1993

M. K. JOSEPH, 1914–1981
Imaginary Islands, Auckland, Whitcombe and Tombs, 1950
The Living Countries, Hamilton, Paul's Book Arcade, 1959
Inscription on a Paper Dart: Selected Poems 1945–1972, Auckland, Auckland University Press/Oxford University Press, 1974

JAN KEMP, B. 1949
Against the Softness of Woman, Dunedin, Caveman Press, 1976
Diamonds and Gravel, Wellington, Hampson Hunt, 1979
Ice-breaker Poems, Auckland, Coal-Black Press, 1980
Five Poems, Singapore, Arte & Materia, 1988
The Other Hemisphere, Washington D.C., Three Continents Press, 1991

FIONA KIDMAN, B. 1940
Honey and Bitters, Dunedin, Caveman Press, 1975
On the Tightrope, Christchurch, Pegasus, 1978
Going to the Chathams: Poems 1977–1984, Auckland, Heinemann, 1985
Wakeful Nights: Poems, Selected and New, Auckland, Vintage, 1991

HILAIRE KIRKLAND, *1941–1975*
Blood Clear & Apple Red, Wellington, Wai-te-ata Press, 1981

MICHELE LEGGOTT, B. *1956*
Like This?, Christchurch, Caxton Press, 1988
Swimmers, Dancers, Auckland, Auckland University Press, 1991
DIA, Auckland, Auckland University Press, 1994

GRAHAM LINDSAY, B. *1952*
Thousand-Eyed Eel: A Sequence of Poems from the Maori Land March, Taylor's Mistake, Hawk Press, 1976
Public, Dunedin, Ridge Pole, 1980
Big Boy, Auckland, Auckland University Press, 1986
Return to Earth, Christchurch, Hazard Press, 1991
The Subject, Auckland, Auckland University Press, 1994

IAIN LONIE, *1932–1988*
Recreations, Poems, Wellington, Wai-te-ata Press, 1967
Letters from Ephesus, Dunedin, Bibliography Room, University of Otago, 1970
Courting Death, Wellington, Wai-te-ata Press, 1984
The Entrance to Purgatory, Dunedin, McIndoe, 1986
Winter Walk at Morning, Wellington, Victoria University Press, 1991

LEN LYE, *1901–1982*
Figures of Motion: Selected Writings, edited by Wystan Curnow and Roger Horrocks, Auckland, Auckland University Press, 1984

RACHEL MCALPINE, B. *1940*
Lament for Ariadne, Dunedin, Caveman Press, 1975
Stay at the Dinner Party, Dunedin, Caveman Press, 1977
Fancy Dress, Auckland, Cicada Press, 1979
House Poems, Wellington, Nutshell Books, 1980
Recording Angel, Wellington, Mallinson Rendel, 1983
Thirteen Waves, Feilding, Homeprint, 1986
Selected Poems, Wellington, Mallinson Rendel, 1988
Tourist in Kyoto, Wellington, Nutshell Books, 1993

JESSIE MACKAY, *1864–1938*
The Spirit of the Rangatira & Other Ballads, Melbourne, Robinson, 1889
The Sitter on the Rail and Other Poems, Christchurch, Simpson & Williams, 1891
From the Maori Sea, Christchurch, Whitcombe & Tombs, 1908
Land of the Morning, Christchurch, Whitcombe & Tombs, 1909
The Bride of the Rivers & Other Verses, Christchurch, Simpson & Williams, 1926

CILLA MCQUEEN, B. *1949*
Homing In, Dunedin, McIndoe, 1982
Anti-Gravity, Dunedin, McIndoe, 1984
Wild Sweets, Dunedin, McIndoe, 1986
Benzina, Dunedin, McIndoe, 1988
Berlin Diary, Dunedin, McIndoe, 1990
Crik'ey: New and Selected Poems 1978–1994, Dunedin, McIndoe, 1994

JOHN MALE, B. *1910*
Poems from a War, Wellington, Black Light Press, 1989

BILL MANHIRE, B. *1946*
The Elaboration, Wellington, Square and Circle, 1972
How to Take Off Your Clothes at the Picnic, Wellington, Wai-te-ata Press, 1977
Good Looks, Auckland, Auckland University Press/Oxford University Press, 1982
Zoetropes: Poems 1972–1982, Sydney, Allen & Unwin/Wellington, Port Nicholson Press, 1984
Milky Way Bar, Wellington, Victoria University Press, 1991
The Old Man's Example, Wellington, Wrist & Anchor Press, 1990

KATHERINE MANSFIELD, *1888–1923*
Poems, London, Constable, 1923
Poems of Katherine Mansfield, edited by Vincent O'Sullivan, Auckland, Oxford University Press, 1988

R. A. K. MASON, *1905–1971*
The Beggar, Auckland, Privately printed, 1929
No New Things — Poems 1924–1929, Auckland, Spearhead, 1934

End of Day, Christchurch, Caxton Press, 1936
This Dark Will Lighten: Selected Poems 1923–1941, Christchurch, Caxton
   Press, 1941
Collected Poems, edited by Allen Curnow, Christchurch, Pegasus Press, 1962

DAVID MITCHELL, B. *1940*
Pipe Dreams in Ponsonby, Auckland, Stephen Chan, 1972; Dunedin,
   Caveman Press, 1975

ELEANOR ELIZABETH MONTGOMERY
Songs of the Singing Shepherd, Wanganui, A. D. Willis, 1885
Hinemoa, Wanganui, A. D. Willis, 1887
The Land of the Moa, Wanganui, A. D. Willis, 1890
The Tohunga and Incidents of Maori Life, Wanganui, A. D. Willis, 1896

ELIZABETH NANNESTAD, B. *1956*
Jump, Auckland, Auckland University Press, 1986

JOHN NEWTON, B. *1959*
Tales from the Angler's Eldorado, Christchurch, Untold, 1985

JAMES NORCLIFFE, B. *1946*
The Sportsman and Other Poems, Auckland, Hard Echo, 1987
Letters to Dr Dee, Christchurch, Hazard, 1993

GREGORY O'BRIEN, B. *1961*
Location of the Least Person, Auckland, Auckland University Press, 1987
Dunes & Barns, Auckland, Modern House, 1988
Man with a Child's Violin, Christchurch, Caxton Press, 1990
Great Lake, Sydney, Local Consumption Publications, 1991
Malachi, Adelaide, Little Esther, 1993
Days Beside Water, Auckland, Auckland University Press, 1993

PETER OLDS, B. *1944*
Lady Moss Revived, Dunedin, Caveman Press, 1972
Freeway, Dunedin, Caveman Press, 1974
Doctor's Rock, Dunedin, Caveman Press, 1976
Beethoven's Guitar, Dunedin, Caveman Press, 1980
After Looking for Broadway, Auckland, One Eyed Press, 1985

W. H. OLIVER, B. *1925*
Fire Without Phoenix: Poems 1946–1954, Christchurch, Caxton Press, 1957
Out of Season, Wellington, Oxford University Press, 1980
Poor Richard, Wellington, Port Nicholson Press, 1982

BOB ORR, B. *1949*
Blue Footpaths, London, Amphedesma Press, 1971
Poems for Moira, Eastbourne, Hawk Press, 1979
Cargo, Wellington, Voice Press, 1983
Red Trees, Auckland, Auckland University Press/Oxford University
   Press/Silverfish, 1985
Breeze, Auckland, Auckland University Press, 1991

CHRIS ORSMAN, B. *1955*
Ornamental Gorse, Wellington, Victoria University Press, 1994

VINCENT O'SULLIVAN, B. *1937*
Our Burning Time, Wellington, Prometheus Books, 1965
Revenants, Wellington, Prometheus Books, 1969
Bearings, Wellington, Oxford University Press, 1973
From the Indian Funeral, Dunedin, McIndoe, 1976
Butcher & Co, Wellington, Oxford University Press, 1977
Brother Jonathan, Brother Kafka, Wellington, Oxford University Press, 1980
The Rose Ballroom and Other Poems, Dunedin, McIndoe, 1982
The Butcher Papers, Auckland, Oxford University Press, 1982
The Pilate Tapes, Auckland, Oxford University Press, 1986
Selected Poems, Auckland, Oxford University Press, 1992

ALISTAIR PATERSON, B. *1929*
Caves in the Hills, Christchurch, Pegasus, 1965
Birds Flying, Christchurch, Pegasus, 1973
Cities and Strangers, Dunedin, Caveman Press, 1976
The Toledo Room: A Poem for Voices, Dunedin, Pilgrims South Press, 1978
Qu'appelle, Dunedin, Pilgrims South Press, 1982
Odysseus Rex, Auckland, Auckland University Press, 1986
Incantations for Warriors, Auckland, Earl of Seacliff Art Workshop, 1987

JOANNA PAUL, B. *1945*
Imogen, Eastbourne, Hawk Press, 1978

ROMA POTIKI, B. *1958*
Stones in her Mouth: Poems, Auckland, IWA Associates, 1992

GLORIA RAWLINSON, *1918–1995*
Gloria's Book, Wellington, printed by Whitcombe and Tombs, 1933
The Perfume Vendor, London, Hutchinson, 1935
Verses, Auckland, Unicorn Press, 1935
Music in the Listening Place, London, Cassell, 1938
The Islands Where I Was Born, Wellington, Handcraft Press, 1955
Of Clouds and Pebbles, Hamilton, Paul's Book Arcade, 1963
Gloria in Excelsis, Auckland, The Pear Tree Press, 1995

WILLIAM PEMBER REEVES, *1857–1932*
New Zealand and Other Poems, London, Grant Richards, 1898

ALAN RIACH, B. *1957*
For What It Is (with Peter McCarey), Christchurch, Untold Books, 1986
This Folding Map, Auckland, Auckland University Press, 1990
An Open Return, Wellington, Untold Books, 1991
First and Last Songs, Auckland, Auckland University Press, 1995

IAIN SHARP, B. *1953*
Why Mammals Shiver, Auckland, One Eyed Press, 1981
She Is Trying to Kidnap the Blind Person, Auckland, Hard Echo Press, 1985
The Pierrot Variations, Auckland, Hard Echo Press, 1985

KEITH SINCLAIR, *1922–1993*
Songs for a Summer, Christchurch, Pegasus Press, 1952
Strangers or Beasts, Christchurch, Caxton Press, 1954

A Time to Embrace, Auckland, Paul's Book Arcade, 1963
The Firewheel Tree, Auckland, Auckland University Press/Oxford University Press, 1973
Moontalk: Poems New & Selected, Auckland, Auckland University Press, 1993

ELIZABETH SMITHER, B. *1941*
Here Come the Clouds, Martinborough, Alister Taylor, 1975
You're Very Seductive William Carlos Williams, Dunedin, McIndoe, 1978
The Sarah Train, Eastbourne, Hawk Press, 1980
Casanova's Ankle, Auckland, Oxford University Press, 1981
The Legend of Marcello Mastroianni's Wife, Auckland, Auckland University Press/Oxford University Press, 1981
Shakespeare's Virgins, Auckland, Auckland University Press/Oxford University Press, 1983
Professor Musgrove's Canary, Auckland, Auckland University Press, 1986
A Pattern of Marching, Auckland, Auckland University Press, 1989
A Cortège of Daughters, Newcastle upon Tyne, Cloud, 1993
The Tudor Style: Poems New and Selected, Auckland, Auckland University Press, 1993

KENDRICK SMITHYMAN, *1922–1995*
Seven Sonnets, Auckland, Pelorus Press, 1946
The Blind Mountain and Other Poems, Christchurch, Caxton Press, 1950
The Gay Trapeze, Wellington, Handcraft Press, 1955
Inheritance, Hamilton, Paul's Book Arcade, 1962
Flying to Palmerston, Wellington, Oxford University Press for the University of Auckland, 1968
Earthquake Weather, Auckland, Auckland University Press/Oxford University Press, 1972
The Seal in the Dolphin Pool, Auckland, Auckland University Press/Oxford University Press, 1974
Dwarf with a Billiard Cue, Auckland, Auckland University Press/Oxford University Press, 1979
Stories about Wooden Keyboards, Auckland, Auckland University Press/Oxford University Press, 1985
Are You Going to the Pictures?, Auckland, Auckland University Press, 1987
Selected Poems, Auckland, Auckland University Press, 1989
Auto/Biographies: Poems, 1987, 1988, 1989, Auckland, Auckland University Press, 1992

MARY STANLEY, *1919–1980*
Starveling Year, Christchurch, Pegasus Press, 1953; rev. ed., Auckland, Auckland University Press, 1994

C. K. STEAD, B. *1932*
Whether the Will Is Free: Poems 1954–1962, Auckland, Paul's Book Arcade, 1964
Crossing the Bar, Auckland, Auckland University Press/Oxford University Press, 1972
Quesada, Auckland, The Shed, 1975
Walking Westward, Auckland, The Shed, 1979

Geographies, Auckland, Auckland University Press/Oxford University Press, 1982
Poems of a Decade, Dunedin, Pilgrims South Press, 1983
Paris: A Poem, Auckland, Auckland University Press/Oxford University Press, 1984
Between, Auckland, Auckland University Press, 1988
Voices, Welington, GP Books, 1990

ROBERT SULLIVAN, B. *1967*
Jazz Waiata, Auckland, Auckland University Press, 1990
Piki Ake! Poems 1990–92, Auckland, Auckland University Press, 1993

APIRANA TAYLOR, B. *1955*
Eyes of the Ruru, Wellington, Voice Press, 1979

EDWARD TREGEAR, *1846–1931*
Shadows and Other Verses, Wellington, Whitcombe & Tombs, 1919
The Verse of Edward Tregear, edited by K. R. Howe, Palmerston North, Nagare Press, 1989

BRIAN TURNER, B. *1944*
Ladders of Rain, Dunedin, McIndoe, 1978
Ancestors, Dunedin, McIndoe, 1981
Listening to the River, Dunedin, McIndoe, 1983
Bones, Dunedin, McIndoe, 1985
All That Blue Can Be, Dunedin, McIndoe, 1989
Beyond, Dunedin, McIndoe, 1992

HONE TUWHARE, B. *1922*
No Ordinary Sun, Auckland, Blackwood and Janet Paul, 1964; reprinted, Dunedin, McIndoe, 1977
Come Rain Hail, Dunedin, The Bibliography Room, University of Otago, 1970
Sap-Wood & Milk, Dunedin, Caveman Press, 1972
Something Nothing, Dunedin, Caveman Press, 1974
Making a Fist of It, Dunedin, Jackstraw Press, 1978
Selected Poems, Dunedin, McIndoe, 1980
Year of the Dog: Poems New and Selected, Dunedin, McIndoe , 1982
Mihi: Collected Poems, Auckland, Penguin Books, 1987
Short Back & Sideways: Poems and Prose, Auckland, Godwit Press, 1992
Deep River Talk: Collected Poems, Auckland, Godwit Press, 1993

RICHARD VON STURMER, B. *1957*
We Xerox Your Zebras, Auckland, Modern House, 1988
A Network of Dissolving Threads, Auckland, Auckland University Press, 1991

ARNOLD WALL, *1869–1966*
Blank Verse Lyrics and Other Poems, London, David Nutt, 1900
London Lost and Other Poems, Auckland, Whitcombe and Tombs, 1922
The Pioneer and Other Poems, Wellington, A. H. & A. W. Reed, 1948

Ian Wedde, b. *1946*
Homage to Matisse, London, Amphedesma Press, 1971
Made Over, Auckland, Stephen Chan, 1974
Earthly: Sonnets for Carlos, Akaroa, Amphedesma Press, 1975
Spells for Coming Out, Auckland, Auckland University Press/Oxford University Press, 1977
Castaly, Poems 1973–1977, Auckland, Auckland University Press/Oxford University Press, 1980
Georgicon, Wellington, Victoria University Press, 1984
Tales of Gotham City, Auckland, Auckland University Press/Oxford University Press, 1984
Driving into the Storm: Selected Poems, Auckland, Oxford University Press, 1987
Tendering, Auckland, Auckland University Press, 1988
The Drummer, Auckland, Auckland University Press, 1993

Albert Wendt, b. *1939*
Inside Us the Dead: Poems 1961–1974, Auckland, Longman Paul, 1976
Shaman of Visions, Auckland, Auckland University Press, 1984
Photographs, Auckland, Auckland University Press, 1995

Virginia Were, b. *1960*
Juliet Bravo Juliet, Wellington, Victoria University Press, 1989

Damien Wilkins, b. *1963*
The Idles, Wellington, Victoria University Press, 1993

David McKee Wright, *1869–1928*
Aorangi and Other Verse, Dunedin, Mills, Dick & Co., 1896
Station Ballads and Other Verses, Dunedin, J. G. Sawell (Wise's), 1897
Wisps of Tussock: New Zealand Rhymes, Oamaru, Andrew Fraser, 1900
New Zealand Chimes, Wellington, W. J. Lankshear, 1900

ACKNOWLEDGEMENTS

Fleur Adcock: 'Wife to Husband', reprinted by permission of the author, 'Notes on Propertius', 'Unexpected Visit', 'Incident', 'For a Five Year Old', 'Advice to a Discarded Lover', 'A Surprise in the Peninsula', 'Against Coupling', 'Kilpeck', 'The Soho Hospital for Women', 'Below Loughrigg', 'Crab', 'Icon' and 'Excavations' from *Selected Poems*, reprinted by permission of Oxford University Press, UK and the author; **Rob Allen:** from 'Karitane Postcards', reprinted by permission of Hazard Press; **K. O. Arvidson:** 'The Tall Wind', 'Fish and Chips on the Merry-Go-Round' and 'The Four Last Songs of Richard Strauss', reprinted by permission of the author; **James K. Baxter:** 'High Country Weather', 'The Bay', 'Blow, wind of fruitfulness', 'The Cave', 'Wild Bees', 'Poem in Matukituki Valley', 'Lament for Barney Flanagan', 'Crossing Cook Strait', 'My love late walking', 'Ballad of Calvary Street', 'On the Death of her Body', 'At Taiere Mouth', 'A Takapuna Business Man Considers his Son's Death in Korea', 'Pig Island Letters', 'A Small Ode on Mixed Flatting', 'Jerusalem Sonnets', 'The Ikons', 'He Waiata mo Te Kare' and 'Autumn Testament', reprinted with permission of Mrs J. Baxter; **Tony Beyer:** 'Cut Lilac', 'Working Loose', 'Changing Ground', 'Lord Cobham Avenue', 'Sanctuary' and 'Early Weather', reprinted by permission of the author; **Peter Bland:** 'Kumara God', 'The Happy Army', 'Letters Home — New Zealand 1885' and 'A Last Note from Menton', reprinted by permission of the author; **Jenny Bornholdt:** 'Reading the body', 'The Bathers', 'Make Sure', 'Estonian Songs', 'The Man Dean Went to Photograph', 'The Boyfriends' and 'Instructions for How to Get Ahead of Yourself While the Light Still Shines', reprinted by permission of Victoria University Press; **Charles Brasch:** 'Forerunners', 'A View of Rangitoto', 'Great Sea', from 'The Islands', 'Oreti Beach', from 'The Estate', from 'In Your Presence', 'Signals', 'Down Ferry Road', 'Shoriken' and from 'Home Ground', reprinted by permission of Alan Roddick for the estate of Charles Brasch; **Alan Brunton:** 'It Was Night In the Lonesome October', reprinted by permission of Auckland University Press and Alan Brunton; **Alistair Te Ariki Campbell:** 'At a Fishing Settlement', from 'Elegy', 'The Return', 'Bitter Harvest', 'Bon Voyage', from 'Sanctuary of Spirits', 'Green', from 'The Dark Lord of Savaiki' and 'Soul Traps', reprinted by permission of the author; **Meg Campbell:** 'The Ancestors', 'Calvary Hospital', 'Concession', 'Tess', 'After Loving' and 'Aftermath', reprinted by permission of the author; **Gordon Challis:** 'The Postman', 'The Thermostatic Man', 'After Shock Treatment', 'The Asbestos-Suited Man In Hell', 'Thin Partition' and 'The Iceman', reprinted by permission of the author; **Janet Charman:** 'two deaths in one night', 'the smell of her hair' and 'not so fast', reprinted by permission of Auckland University Press and the author; **Geoff Cochrane:** 'Aztec Noon', 'Suicide Abroad', 'An Ambulance' and 'The Maritime Cook', reprinted with permission of Victoria University Press, 'A Lyric' and 'Polygon Wood', reprinted by permission of the author; **Allen Curnow:** 'Wild Iron', 'House and Land', 'The Unhistoric Story', 'The Skeleton of the Great Moa in the Canterbury Musuem, Christchurch', 'Landfall in Unknown Seas', 'Spectacular Blossom', 'He Cracked a Word', 'A Small Room with Large Windows', from 'Trees, Effigies, Moving Objects', 'Moror Assassinato', 'An Incorrigible Music', 'You Will Know When You Get There', 'A Passion for Travel', 'The Parakeets at Karekare', 'Canto of Signs Without Wonders' and 'The Loop in the Lone Kauri Road', reprinted by permission of the author and Auckland University Press; **Wystan Curnow:** 'Cancer Daybook', 'Now That I Have It', 'Now to Face the Known Facts', 'For the Present', 'Leap for Sue', 'Get Me For Not' and 'Chemotherapy is Not Taking Life Lightly', reprinted by permission of the author; **Ruth Dallas:** 'Deep in the Hills', 'Wild Plum', 'Rainy Sunday', 'Shadow Show (1968)', 'A Girl's Song', 'In Central Otago', 'Kyeburn Diggings', 'Pickers Wanted', 'Living with a Cabbage-tree', 'The Lamp', 'The Weather Clock', 'On Reading Love Poems', 'Photographs of Pioneer Women', 'Pioneer Woman with Ferrets', 'The Falling House', 'A New Dress', 'The Leopard', 'Girl with Pitcher' and 'Jenny's Song', reprinted by permission of the author; **Leigh Davis:** from 'Willy's Gazette', reprinted by permission of the author; **John Dickson:** from 'Jonah', reprinted by permission of the author and Untold Books; **Eileen Duggan:** 'Rosa Luxembourg', 'Tua Marina', 'And at the End', 'Had It Been You', 'The Tides Run up the Wairau', 'Twilight', 'The Bushfeller', 'Cloudy Bay', 'The Country', 'Brooding', 'The Bushwoman', 'Night', 'The Answer', 'Truth', 'Two Towns', 'Tide' and 'The Dead Queen', reprinted by permission of the author; **Maurice Duggan:** 'Ponsonby Circa 1930', 'Take a Peck at Papa Pupa', 'Winter Solstice' and 'In the Territory', reprinted by permission of the Estate of Maurice Duggan; **Lauris Edmond:** 'Before the Funeral', 'Ohakune Fires', 'The Pear Tree', 'Wellington Letter', 'Going to Moscow', 'The Distaff Line', 'The Names', 'Camping', 'Things' and 'The Ghost Moth', from *Selected Poems, 1975–1994*, Bridget Williams Books, 1994, reprinted by permission of Bridget Williams Books; **Murray Edmond:** 'Shack', 'Poems of the End Wall', 'About Wasps', 'The Blue Boy' and 'A Letter about Cars', reprinted by permission of the author; **Kim Eggleston:** 'This Heart of Mine' and 'Invisible', reprinted by permission of the author; **David Eggleton:** 'Painting Mount Taranaki' and 'God Defend New Zealand', reprinted by permission of the author; **Riemke Ensing:** from 'Topographics' and 'Naming', reprinted by permission of the author; **A. R. D. Fairburn:** 'Rhyme of the Dead Self', from 'Dominion', 'Elements', 'Full Fathom Five', 'Tapu', 'The Cave', 'A Farewell', 'Winter Night', 'The Estuary' and 'I'm Older Than You, Please Listen', reprinted by permission of the Estate of A. R. D. Fairburn and Richards Literary Agency; **Fiona Farrell:** 'Charlotte O'Neill's Song' and 'Reading about the Kendalls, Cambridge 1983', reprinted by permission of Auckland University Press and the author; **Janet Frame:** 'The Dead', 'O Lung Flowering Like A Tree', 'Yet Another Poem About a Dying Child', 'Wyndham', 'The Dreams', 'Impard A Willow-Cell in Sordure', 'Instructions For Bombing with Napalm', 'At Evans Street', 'The Place' and 'The Clown, from *The Pocket Mirror*, Vintage NZ, reprinted by permission of Random House; **Anne French:** 'Eucalypts Greenlane', 'All Cretans are Liars', 'The Lady Fishermen', 'Cabin Fever', 'Simultaneous Equations', 'A Summer Storm' and 'All You May Depend On', reprinted by permission of Anne French; **Ruth Gilbert:** 'Betrothed to Lazarus', 'The Sisters of Lazarus', 'Lazarus

Speaks' and 'Jacob', published by A.H. & A.W. Reed, reprinted by permission of the author; **Denis Glover**: 'The Road Builders', 'Threnody', 'The Magpies', 'Centennial', 'Sings Harry', 'Home Thoughts', from 'Arawata Bill', 'Brightness' and 'Here Is the News', reprinted by permission of the Estate of Denis Glover and Richards Literary Agency; **Bernadette Hall**: 'Amica', reprinted by permission of Caxton Press, 'Miriama', 'Drawing A Conclusion On A Paper Dart', 'Anorexia' and 'Cancer Ward', reprinted by permission of the author and Victoria University Press, 'Bowl', reprinted by permission of the author and Untold Books; **Michael Harlow**: 'Today is the Piano's Birthday', 'Poem Then, for Love' and 'Vlaminck's Tie / the persistent imaginal', reprinted by permission of the author and Auckland University Press; **Dinah Hawken**: 'Writing Home', from 'Small Stories of Devotion', 'A New Word' and 'Quiet Hills', reprinted by permission of Victoria University Press; **Paul Henderson (Ruth France)**: 'Return Journey' and 'Elegy', reprinted by permission of the Estate of Ruth France; **Keri Hulme**: from 'Fishing the Olearia Tree' and 'He Hōhā ', reprinted by permission of the author and Auckland University Press; **Sam Hunt**: 'Stabat Mater', 'My Father Scything', 'A Valley Called Moonshine', 'School Policy on Stickmen', 'You House the Moon', 'My Father Today', 'Birth of a Son', 'Requiem' and 'Harold Saunders, Boatbuilder, Tory Channel', reprinted by permission of the author; **Robin Hyde**: 'The Beaches', 'The Houses', 'Pihsien Road', 'What is it makes the Stranger?' and 'The Deserted Village', reprinted by permission of Derek Challis for the Estate of Robin Hyde; **Kevin Ireland**: 'Thorn and Wind', 'Striking A Pose', 'A Kuala Lumpur Notebook', 'Expedition to a Mountain Lake', 'Intimations of Mortality', from 'The Year of the Comet' and 'Pinnacle Ridge, Mt Ruapehu', reprinted by permission of the author; **Michael Jackson**: 'Pioneers', 'The Moths', 'Nightmare of Mushrooms', 'Seven Mysteries' and 'Stone', reprinted by permission of the author; **Louis Johnson**: 'Song in the Hutt Valley', 'Magpie and Pines', 'Here Together Met', 'Bread and a Pension', 'Death of the Bosun's Mate', 'The Seventies', 'The Perfect Symbol' and 'Uneasy Resident', reprinted by permission of Cecilia Johnson; **Andrew Johnston**: 'How to Talk', 'The Picture' and 'Fool Heart', reprinted by permission of the author and Victoria University Press, 'The Sounds', reprinted by permission of the author; **M. K. Joseph**: 'Off Cape Leeuwin', 'Secular Litany', 'Mercury Bay Eclogue' and 'The Nurses' Song of the Earth', reprinted by permission of the Estate of M. K. Joseph; **Jan Kemp**: 'Poem' and 'Paperboygirl', reprinted by permission of the author; **Fiona Kidman**: 'Makara Beach, Spring' and 'Earthquake Weather', from *Wakeful Nights*, published by Vintage NZ, 1991, reprinted by permission of Random House; **Michele Leggott**: 'Tigers' and 'Blue Irises', reprinted by permission of the author; **Graham Lindsay**: 'Seeing As How', from *Return to Earth*, Hazard, 1991, reprinted by permission of Hazard Press, 'Big Boy', Playground', 'Context of Words', 'White Cherry', 'Actually', 'Zero' and 'Gull's Eye', reprinted by permission of the author and Auckland University Press; **Iain Lonie**: 'By Foreign Hands', 'Point of No Return', 'The Winter Walk at Morning', 'Lines on a Photograph', 'Proposal at Allans Beach' and 'Exile', reprinted by permission of Victoria University Press; **Len Lye**: 'Dazing Sunlight', 'Chair in your Hair', 'The Beautiful Weather A Lovely Moll' and from 'Passing the Buck to the Brontës', reprinted by permission of Len Lye Foundation; **John Male**: 'Political Footnote', from 'Four Italian Seasons', 'Girl with her Hair Cut

Short' and 'Not All of Us', reprinted by permission of John Male; **Bill Manhire:** 'The Old Man's Example', 'Children', 'A Scottish Bride', 'What it Means to be Naked', 'Declining the Naked Horse', 'The Prayer', 'Out West', 'Jalopy: The End of Love', 'Our Father', 'Wingatui', 'How to Take Off Your Clothes at the Picnic', 'A Death in the Family', 'Magasin', 'Hirohito', 'Phar Lap', 'My Sunshine', 'The Selenolgist', 'Milky Way Bar', 'On Originality', 'The Pickpocket', 'The Elaboration' and 'Zoetropes', reprinted by permission of the author; **Rachel McAlpine:** Zig-Zag Up A Thistle' and 'Before the Fall', reprinted by permission of the author and Mallinson Rendel Publishers; **Cilla McQueen:** 'Homing In', 'Matinal', 'To Ben, at the Lake', 'Living Here', 'Vegetable Garden Poem I', 'Vegetable Garden Poem IV', 'Dogwobble', 'The Mess We Made at Port Chambers' and 'Recipe for One', reprinted by permission of the author; **R. A. K. Mason:** 'Old Memories of Earth', 'The Vigil', 'Body of John', 'Sonnet of Brotherhood', 'Wayfarers', 'The Spark's Farewell to Its Clay', 'Latter-Day Geography Lesson', 'Song of Allegiance', 'A Fragment', 'On the Swag', 'Judas Iscariot', 'Footnote to John ii4', 'Ecce homunculus', 'The Young Man Thinks of Sons', 'Be Swift O Sun' and 'Our love was a grim citadel', reprinted by permission of the Estate of R. A. K. Mason and Richards Literary Agency; **David Mitchell:** 'my lai/remuear/ponsonby' and 'Olive Grove / Noon', reprinted by permission of the author; **Elizabeth Nannestad:** 'Black Dress', 'Queen of the River', 'The Kiss', 'La Strada', 'Ramos', 'Immediately After —' and 'Rooster', reprinted by permission of the author; **John Newton:** 'Opening the Book' and 'Blood Poisoning', reprinted by permission of the author; 'Lunch' and 'Ferret Trap', reprinted by permission of the author and Untold Books; **James Norcliffe:** 'The True Story of Soap', reprinted by permission of the author; **Gregory O'Brien:** 'Carnival', 'Verandah on Kauri Point Road', from 'Sea Wall and Egg' and 'The Camera is a Small Room', reprinted by permission of the author, 'A Visiting Card' and 'The Ten Most Beautiful Women In the World', reprinted by permission of the author and Auckland University Press; **Vincent O'Sullivan:** 'Dognotting in Quezaltenango', 'New Delhi — January', from 'Butcher and Co.', from 'The Butcher Papers', 'Elegy', from 'Brother Johnathan, Brother Kafka', 'Waikato-Taniwha-Rau', 'Don't Knock the Rawleigh's Man', 'liberal', 'Corner', 'Freudiana', 'Late Romantic', 'Surfacing', 'Note from the Gardener', 'As We Say of Love, Sometimes', 'Hiroshima', 'Matinée' and 'Excellent People', reprinted by permission of the author; **Peter Olds:** 'My Mother Spinning' and 'Thoughts of Jack Kerouac — & Other Things', reprinted by permission of the author; **W. H. Oliver:** 'Silent Revolution', 'Counter-revolution' and 'Parihaka', from *Out of Season*, Oxford University Press, 1980, reprinted by permission of the author; Bob Orr: 'Love Poem', 'Container Terminal', 'My Grandmother's Funeral' and 'My Father's Bomber Jacket', reprinted by permission of the author; **Chris Orsman:** 'Ornamental Grose', 'Ancestral' and 'Death by Drowning', reprinted by permission of Victoria University Press; Alistair Paterson: from 'Odysseus Rex', reprinted by permission of the author and Auckland University Press; **Joanna Margaret Paul:** from 'Imogen', reprinted by permission of Joanna Margaret Paul/Hawke Press; **Roma Potiki:** 'The Flax', 'Compulsory class visits', 'For a Father in Hiding', 'Palazzi', 'And My Heart Goes Swimming' and 'Bound To', reprinted by permission of the author; **Gloria Rawlinson:** 'The Islands Where I Was

Born', 'The Hare in the Snow' and 'Ms and the Cat-Child', reprinted by permission of the author; **Alan Riach:** from 'An Open Return', reprinted by permission of the author and Untold Books; **Iain Sharp:** 'Air', 'A Game for Children', 'The Sanctuary' and 'The Iain Sharp Poem', reprinted by permission of the author; **Keith Sinclair:** 'Memorial to a Missionary', 'The Bomb is Made' and from 'Te Kaminara', reprinted with permission of the author and Auckland University Press; **Elizabeth Smither:** 'Casanova's Ankle', 'Here Come the Clouds', 'Swimming', ' A Cortège of Daughters', 'The O in Shakespeare Explained', 'Fr Anselm Williams...', 'Finger to Finger', 'The Veronica's Veil Technique', 'I Think Joan Didion Has Died', 'Temptations of St Anthony by His Housekeeper', 'Visiting Juliet Street', 'Error on a Quiz Programme', 'The Sea Question' and 'The Legend of Marcello Mastroianni's Wife', reprinted by permission of the author; **Kendrick Smithyman:** 'Hint for the Incomplete Angler', 'Blackleg', 'An Ordinary Day Beyond Kaitaia', 'Colville', 'Waitomo', from 'Reading the Maps An Academic Exercise', 'Stories About Wooden Keyboards', 'Deconstructing' and 'Carp', reprinted by permission of M. A. Edgcumbe; **Mary Stanley:** 'Love by Candlelight', 'Sestina', 'Per Diem et per Noctem', 'Night Piece', 'Morepork', 'The Wife Speaks', 'To B' and 'Question without Answer', reprinted by permission of A. I. Smithyman; **C. K. Stead:** from 'Pictures in a Gallery Undersea', from 'Walking Westward', from 'Twenty-two Sonnets', 'At the Grave of Governor Hobson', from 'The Clodian Songbook' and 'After The Wedding', reprinted by permission of the author; **J. C. Sturm:** 'Maori to Pakeha' and 'Splitting the Stone', reprinted by permission of Mrs Jacqueline Baxter; **Robert Sullivan:** 'I Walked Over the Hill', 'Sitting in Front of Karetu Marae', 'Doing It', 'Southerly', 'Christmas Day' and 'On Display', reprinted by permission of the author; Apirana Taylor: 'Sad Joke on a Marae', 'Te Kooti', 'A Departure', 'Taiaha Haka Poem' and 'The Womb', reprinted by permission of the author; **Brian Turner:** 'Wilson Boy's Boat', 'The Initiation', 'Chevy', 'Drain' and 'Fish', reprinted by permission of the author; **Hone Tuwhare:** 'The River is an Island', 'I Talk with my Cousin' and 'Monologue', reprinted with permission of the author; **Richard Von Sturmer:** from 'Expresso Love Letters' and from 'Dreams', reprinted by permission of the author; **Ian Wedde:** 'Mahia April 1978', 'Barbary Coast', 'Ruth', from 'Earthly: Sonnets for Carlos' and 'Pathway to the Sea', reprinted by permission of the author; **Albert Wendt:** 'The Mountains of Ta'ū', reprinted by permission of the author and Auckland University Press, 'I, God Uphere', 'Town and Village', from 'Short Songs', 'Colonialism: Independence', 'No Return' and 'My Mother Dances', reprinted by permission of the author; **Virginia Were:** 'We Listen for You on the Radio', reprinted by permission of the author and Victoria University Press; **Damien Wilkins:** 'My Father's Stutter' and 'The Prodigals', reprinted by permission of the author and Victoria University Press.

Details for the acknowledgements are as supplied by copyright holders. Every effort has been made to trace the original source of all material contained in this book. Where the attempt has been unsuccessful, the editor and publisher would be pleased to hear from the author/publisher concerned to rectify any omission.

INDEX